Celebrate

PAUL HOLLYWOOD

Celebrate

Joyful Baking All Year Round

Photography by Haarala Hamilton

BLOOMSBURY PUBLISHING
NEW YORK · LONDON · OXFORD · NEW DELHI · SYDNEY

To my wife, Melissa

14 **Cakes**

52 **Spring**

88 **Summer**

132 **Fall**

174 **Winter**

222 **Party**

Celebrate

For me, a good celebration is, first of all, about the company – if you have great company coming round, it inspires you to bake something really special. The chapters in this book take you through my favorite seasonal bakes, as well as cakes and party food for all year round. They are the recipes I've picked up from my travels abroad, ideas inspired by my time inside the *Baking Show* tent and meals-to-remember shared with friends.

Baking is like a hug, it's a joy, it's a little bit indulgent. It's also a getaway, where you can spend time making something for someone else to show them that you care. I think we should all be looking for an excuse to celebrate as often as we can. So, these are the bakes to make throughout the seasons, to celebrate the important events and people in your life, whatever the time of year.

Celebrate the Seasons

When I'm baking for celebrations, I like to work with what's in season. Of course, you can buy almost anything in the supermarket all year round now, but traditionally people baked with whatever was available. I love it when people bake particular things at certain times of the year, so that each event becomes associated with those ingredients, and so we don't just make the same things all the time. What we feel like baking is very seasonal too. It's a mood, and we tend to alter what we want to bake as the seasons change.

In spring, when those long, dark, winter months finally give way to brighter days, we start to crave lighter bakes and fresh flavors. You can't beat a lemon drizzle at this time of year, and I've shared my luxury version, layered with lemon buttercream and homemade lemon curd, on page 73. Around Easter, we also start to see the first crops of fruit and vegetables appear, and my asparagus tart on page 56 is perfect for a springtime celebration – or just to celebrate the arrival of spring itself.

In summer, I love to sit outside as much as I can, enjoying the warmer weather – often at a barbecue with friends and family. That's when I make a lot of flatbreads, like the Mexican gorditas on page 259, finishing them off on the grill. It may come as a surprise, but my favorite place to be is actually in my garden, not the kitchen. I think it comes from my Cyprus days. It's amazing to see how the colors change throughout the year, and it's reflected in the baking I do too.

There's an abundance of seasonal ingredients in the summer months and our cooking becomes so much more colorful and varied. Soft fruits – strawberries, raspberries, red currants – are the epitome of summer for me and I like to celebrate them in a classic Summer pudding (page 94) or Eton mess (page 92). I've also included my recipe for Mojito cupcakes (page 106); serve them at your next summer party and no one will be able to resist.

As we head into fall, stone fruits, apples and pears are ripe for the picking, and we begin to crave more comforting treats. I find people are drawn to the kitchen when someone is cooking and it becomes the glue that holds everyone together in a warm hug. It's the season I start throwing all those warming spices into my baking – cinnamon, cloves, allspice; think Apple doughnuts (page 146), Blueberry lattice pie (page 140) and Spiced loaf cake (page 145). Harvest festival is also celebrated in the UK around this time of year, and I often make a Wheatsheaf (page 168) for our local village church. It's a real investment of time, but it looks absolutely incredible when it starts to take shape, and it is a fantastic skill to master.

But it's in winter, when it's cold and dark outside, that baking feels the most seasonal. Traditional British favorites, such as Christmas pudding (page 185), Mince pies (page 182) and the Spanish Roscón de Reyes (page 194), with rich dried fruits and deep spiced flavors, are the perfect way to mark the end of the year and to welcome in a new one. At this festive time, people once again find themselves gathering in the kitchen, maybe helping to prepare the appetizers… or just with a glass of wine in their hand! I'm here for it all.

Celebrate other Cultures

As you look through the recipes, you'll see that I've also included lots of international bakes, reflecting all the travel I've been lucky enough to do. Wherever I am, people often bring me food to try and it's definitely one of the perks of my job! We have some fantastic classic bakes here in Britain and I'm very proud of our baking heritage, but there's a whole world of incredible baking out there for us to try.

In each of the places all over the world that I've visited I have learned something new. Across Europe, and especially around the Mediterranean, I love how they really go to town on their food. The whole family gets together to celebrate whatever is going on in their lives – birthdays, Christenings, promotions, as well as national and local festivals – there might be forty people. And food is right at the center, with the whole table laden with a huge variety of dishes. Easter is especially important in Europe, and I've included two of my favorite Easter recipes: Crostata pasquale (page 64), a sweet Sardinian tart from my good friend Nino, and the Greek spiced Easter bread, Tsoureki (page 80) from my time spent in Cyprus.

Elsewhere, in Norway, I was introduced to the famous 'sun bun' – Solboller (page 115), which is baked to celebrate the return of lighter, warmer days after the darkness of winter. In Japan, I was shown how to make Shokupan, the lightest, softest bread I've ever eaten – you really can teach an old dog new tricks! It's like a puffy cloud – try it yourself on page 218. While in Miami, I made Key lime pie in the place it was invented and, with its intense lime flavor and crunchy base, I think it might be the perfect dessert for your summer celebration (see page 102).

That's what I love most about visiting other countries: seeing how baking is so universal and the way it brings people together. We can learn from each other, experience other cultures and try new things. It's how we get to widen our taste palate and broaden our horizons.

Celebrate Each Other

Throughout the year there are, of course, lots of festivals and events with classic bakes associated with them, but I'd love us to find even more occasions to celebrate with the people we care about, and to connect baking with our own special moments. Let's go big on all the traditional celebrations, but why not make more of the smaller events too? The start of the school summer vacation, Halloween or a regular reunion with old friends. It doesn't need to be complicated. Start with cake bars like the Cherry marble cake bars (page 26) or for something a bit indulgent, the Brownie bars on page 74. Cake bars are such a great way in to baking: they're hard to get wrong, easy to transport and always a crowd pleaser.

For a more sophisticated occasion, the Hazelnut and orange cake on page 33 looks incredible, and is flavored with orange in four different ways, including a secret surprise in the middle. And then there's a cake that's been a big feature of my life for the past 10 years: the chocolate cake on page 44 (pictured opposite). It's the one that you see in the opening credits to *The Great British Baking Show*, and it's still one of the best chocolate cakes you'll ever taste.

Baking isn't all about sweet things – although let's be honest, most of the time that's what we crave – and there are plenty of savory recipes to try too. From the Zucchini, feta and fava bean quiche (page 118), which showcases beautiful seasonal summer vegetables, to my Savory fall roulade (page 160) or my brand-new twist on a classic hot dog (page 162). Anyone who knows me, knows how much I love hot dogs and this recipe takes your classic sausage, onions and ketchup or mustard and wraps them up in bread dough, which you then bake all together. It's so good, and hopefully you'll be more likely to keep the front of your shirt clean while you eat it!

Whatever the season and whatever the occasion, let's find the bakes that mean something to us. Feel free to make these recipes your own: personalize them, include your favorite ingredients and decorate them so they have even more meaning to the people in your life. Let's make more time to be with each other, to celebrate good food and great company, all year round.

Cakes

A celebration isn't a proper celebration without a cake, either as part of an afternoon tea or maybe with a glass of something bubbly. And of all the types of baking, I think cakes probably evoke the most memories, bringing us right back to those first childhood birthday parties. There are cakes in this chapter for every occasion and in every style. From showstoppers guaranteed to impress, like the Rainbow cake (page 36) with its multi-colored layers and frosting stripes, to the individual Elderflower cupcakes (page 42), you'll find the ideal choice for your next party.

If you're not sure where to start, cake bars are the perfect entry-level baking. Try making the Cherry marble cake bars (page 26), which have cherry compote swirls through an almond sponge, or the Coconut and passion fruit cake bars (page 30) with mascarpone and fresh passion fruit frosting on top. They're simple to make and everyone will love them.

Chocolate cake is an easy win too, and I've included two of them in this chapter for you to choose from. The Chocolate fudge cake on page 18 is so versatile you can serve it up for a low-key get-together or a more sophisticated party. Decorate it however you like, depending on who you're making it for. If you want to keep things simple, just cover it with buttercream, then stick as many candles as possible on the top. Or, straight from the *Baking Show* tent, is my chocolate cake on page 44. If you don't already know the story, there's a raspberry missing from the decoration – I don't know how it happened but it winds me up even today! So if you want to be authentic to that version, decorate it with perfect raspberry spirals – and then deliberately take one out.

Baking is such a simple way to make any occasion feel extra special, so let's start baking more cakes to create even more of those happy memories.

Chocolate Fudge Cake

I'm a big fan of chocolate cake, and this one is simple and elegant – perfect for every day but special enough for a birthday too. Change up the decorations to turn it into a showstopper – it looks great drizzled with melted white chocolate.

10 slices

1½ sticks (175g) unsalted butter, softened, plus extra to grease

1 cup plus 2 tbsp (225g) light brown sugar

1 cup (200g) superfine sugar

3 large eggs, at room temperature

1 tsp vanilla extract

2 cups (250g) all-purpose flour

1¼ cups (125g) unsweetened cocoa powder

2½ tsp baking powder

½ tsp fine salt

1½ cups plus 1 tbsp (375g) sour cream

2 tbsp milk

Chocolate frosting

7 oz (200g) bittersweet chocolate, broken into small pieces

⅔ cup (65g) unsweetened cocoa powder

½ cup (120g) boiling water

2½ sticks (300g) unsalted butter, softened

1¼ cups (120g) confectioners' sugar

To finish

3 packages assorted coated chocolate balls, such as Sixlets (including gold, bronze effect), in different sizes

1. Heat your oven to 350°F. Grease 3 × 8-inch round cake pans and line the bases with parchment paper.

2. Using a stand mixer fitted with the whisk attachment, beat the butter and both sugars together until the mixture is pale and fluffy. Scrape down the sides of the bowl with a spatula and whisk again.

3. In a separate bowl, beat the eggs with the vanilla extract. With the mixer still running on a low speed, slowly pour in the beaten egg mix.

4. Sift the flour with the cocoa powder, baking powder and salt. Add a large spoonful to the whisked mixture and stir in, then mix in a large spoonful of the sour cream. Repeat until all the flour and sour cream are incorporated, adding the milk with the final addition. Beat until you have a smooth batter.

5. Divide the mixture equally between the prepared pans. Bake in the oven for 20–25 minutes until the cakes are risen and slightly shrunk away from the sides of the pans.

6. Leave the cakes to cool in the pans for 5 minutes before removing and transferring to wire racks to cool completely.

7. To make the chocolate frosting, melt the chocolate in a heatproof bowl set over a saucepan of simmering water. Stir until smooth and set aside to cool. In another bowl, mix the cocoa powder with the boiling water to make a smooth, thick paste. In a large bowl, beat the butter until soft then add the confectioners' sugar and whisk until pale and fluffy. Add the melted chocolate and cocoa paste and beat until smooth.

8. To assemble, place one cake layer on your serving plate or cake stand and spread with one-quarter of the frosting. Place a second cake layer on top and spread with another quarter of the frosting. Sit the final cake layer on top and cover the top and sides with the remaining frosting.

9. Use a serrated-edge cake decorating comb around the side of the cake to create a decorative effect. Arrange the assorted chocolate balls on top of the cake to finish.

Drip Cake

The 'drip' decorating technique is now really popular and I think it looks incredible. You can use it with ganache, frosting or melted chocolate, on all kinds of cakes. The trick is to get the consistency just right.

10–12 slices

Madeira cake
2¾ cups (340g) all-purpose flour
2¾ tsp baking powder
1 cup plus 2 tbsp (230g) superfine sugar
2 sticks (230g) unsalted butter, softened, plus extra to grease
4 large eggs, at room temperature
2 tbsp milk

Vanilla buttercream
1¾ sticks (200g) unsalted butter, softened
4 cups (400g) confectioners' sugar, sifted
1 tsp vanilla extract

To assemble
½ cup raspberry preserves

To decorate
5 oz (125g) white chocolate, broken into small pieces
½ tsp vegetable oil
Red food gel coloring
Red summer fruits (raspberries, red currants, cherries etc)

---

1. Heat your oven to 300°F. Grease 2 deep 7-inch round cake pans and line with parchment paper.

2. To make the cake, put all the cake ingredients into a stand mixer fitted with the paddle attachment. Mix on low speed until smoothly combined then increase the speed to medium and beat for 1 minute.

3. Divide the mixture evenly between the prepared cake pans and gently smooth the tops to level. Place on the middle shelf of the oven and bake for 1–1¼ hours until the cakes are golden brown and a cake tester inserted into the middle comes out clean.

4. Leave the cakes to cool in the pans for 10 minutes, then remove and transfer to a wire rack. Leave to cool completely.

5. To make the vanilla buttercream, in a bowl using a hand mixer, beat the butter until very soft. Add the confectioners' sugar a heaping spoonful at a time, whisking until fully incorporated after each addition. Continue to beat until the buttercream is light and fluffy. Finally, beat in the vanilla extract.

6. To assemble, trim a thin slice off the top of each cake to level if necessary. Slice each cake in half horizontally so you have 4 layers in total. Place one base layer in the center of a thin cake board.

7. Spread half of the raspberry preserves on the bottom layer, being careful not to go right to the edge, then cover with another cake layer. Spread with about a third of the vanilla buttercream and place another cake layer on top. Spread with the remaining preserves and cover with the final cake layer. Trim the outside edge of the cakes so they are level.

8. Transfer the cake to a cake decorating turntable. Spread a thin layer of vanilla buttercream around the side of the cake, then hold a plain cake scraper against the side of the cake and revolve the turntable with the other hand to create an even finish. Spread a thin layer of buttercream on top of the cake and level it, using an offset spatula.

9. Place the cake in the fridge to leave the buttercream covering to firm up for at least 30 minutes.

Continued overleaf

Continued from page 20

10 For the drip topping, put the white chocolate and vegetable oil into a small heatproof bowl and melt over a saucepan of simmering water (or carefully in short bursts in the microwave, stirring well in between). Remove from the heat and stir until smooth then stir through a little red gel coloring to achieve the desired color.

11 Leave the red drip topping to cool slightly and thicken to the required consistency: it needs to have some substance so it cools and sets as it drips down the side of your cake. If too thin it will run straight down.

12 Transfer the cake to a cake stand or flat serving plate. Spoon a third of the red drip topping into a paper piping bag and snip off the tip. Pipe around the edge of the cake and let slowly trickle over the side to create a drip pattern. Carefully spread the rest of the red topping on top of the cake.

13 Place the cake in the fridge for another 30 minutes to let the drip topping set.

14 Decorate the top of the cake with fresh red fruits just before serving.

Decorating tip
To get a really smooth finish to the buttercream around the side of the cake, you need to use a cake decorating turntable (easily obtainable and inexpensive). I suggest you leave the cake on the cake board when you transfer it to your serving plate or cake stand, unless you have a cake lifter to help you move it to and from the turntable.

Japanese Cheesecake

Also known as 'cotton cheesecake', this is much softer and lighter than a traditional New York-style cheesecake. It is so airy and fluffy, it's almost soufflé-like. I first ate it when I was in Japan and was blown away.

6–8 slices

---

4 tbsp (55g) unsalted butter, plus extra to grease

¼ cup (50g) superfine sugar, plus 3 tbsp

¾ cup plus 1 tbsp (210g) cream cheese

1½ tbsp yuzu juice

½ cup (120g) whole milk

5 large eggs, separated

3 tbsp (35g) all-purpose flour, sifted

2 tbsp (20g) cornstarch, sifted

¼ tsp cream of tartar

1. Grease an 8-inch springform pan and line with parchment paper, making sure the paper comes at least 2 inches above the rim of the pan. Wrap foil around the outside of the pan.

2. Put the butter, 3 tbsp superfine sugar, the cream cheese, yuzu juice and milk into a saucepan over a low heat and stir until the sugar is dissolved and the mixture is completely smooth. Transfer to a large bowl and leave to cool.

3. Heat your oven to 325°F (don't use the convection function if your oven has this).

4. Add the egg yolks to the cooled mixture, one at a time, mixing well after each addition. Sift the flour and cornstarch together over the mixture, then fold in using a large metal spoon, until well combined and smooth.

5. In another large, very clean bowl, using a hand mixer, beat the egg whites with the cream of tartar until soft peaks form. Add the ¼ cup superfine sugar, a heaping tablespoonful at a time, whisking well after each addition. Once all the sugar is incorporated you should have a silky meringue.

6. Using a large metal spoon, stir a spoonful of meringue into the cake batter. Now gently fold in the rest of the meringue, a spoonful at a time. When it is all incorporated, the mixture should still be fluffy. Pour the cake batter into the prepared pan.

7. Pour enough boiling water into a roasting pan to come halfway up the sides. Sit the springform pan in the water bath and carefully transfer to the middle shelf of the oven. Bake in the oven for 25 minutes.

8. Lower the oven setting to 250°F and bake for a further hour. Now turn the oven off and leave the cheesecake inside with the door slightly open to cool for an hour.

9. Lift the springform pan out of the water bath. Carefully remove the cheesecake from the pan and transfer to a serving plate.

Cherry Marble Cake Bars

Cherries work really well in baked sponges as they bring a bit of sharpness, and their intense color is perfect for marbling. The secret to successful marbling is less is more. Work slowly in a spiral and don't overdo it – you're not mixing them together.

12 slices

2 sticks (225g) unsalted butter, softened, plus extra to grease

1 cup plus 2 tbsp (225g) superfine sugar

1¾ cups plus 1 tbsp (225g) all-purpose flour

2¾ tsp baking powder

1 cup (100g) almond flour

5 large eggs, at room temperature, beaten

scant 2 cups (about 400g) cherry preserves

1 Heat your oven to 350°F. Grease a 9 × 13-inch baking pan, 2 inches deep, and line with baking paper.

2 Put the butter, sugar, flour, baking powder, almond flour and eggs into a bowl and beat together with a hand mixer for 2–3 minutes, until the mixture is light and fluffy.

3 Spoon half the cake mixture into the prepared pan and dollop half of the cherry preserves over the surface. Cover with the remaining cake mixture and dollop the remaining preserves on top. Using a skewer or cake tester, lightly swirl the cherry preserves through the mixture. Gently level the surface with the back of a spoon.

4 Bake in the oven for 40 minutes or until risen, golden and firm to the touch. Leave the cake to cool in the pan before cutting into slices to serve.

Also pictured overleaf

Coconut and Passion Fruit Cake Bars

Cake bars remind me of bake sales as a kid. I remember making them when I was a boy scout! They're a great way to get into baking, and you can play around with different flavors and toppings. One thing to remember is to leave them to cool before you slice up – don't rush it.

12 squares

1¾ sticks (200g) unsalted butter, softened, plus extra to grease

1 cup (200g) superfine sugar

Finely grated zest of 2 limes

3 large eggs, at room temperature, beaten

1⅔ cups (200g) all-purpose flour

1 tsp vanilla extract

1¼ cups (100g) unsweetened shredded coconut

3 tbsp milk

Topping

1 cup (9 oz/250g) mascarpone

1 tbsp confectioners' sugar

Finely grated zest and juice of 2 limes

3 passion fruit

⅓ cup (25g) toasted coconut chips

1. Heat your oven to 350°F. Grease a 9 × 13-inch baking pan, 2 inches deep, and line with parchment paper.

2. In a large bowl, beat the butter, sugar and lime zest together, using a hand mixer, until light and fluffy. Gradually add the beaten eggs, beating well after each addition and adding a spoonful of flour halfway through. Add the vanilla extract and stir in.

3. Whisk the remaining flour and the baking powder together in a separate bowl. Using a spatula or large metal spoon, carefully fold in the rest of the flour and the shredded coconut. Finally, incorporate the milk until smoothly combined.

4. Transfer the mixture to the prepared pan and gently smooth the surface to level. Bake in the oven for 25–30 minutes until risen and springy to the touch.

5. Leave the sponge to cool in the pan for 10 minutes then carefully turn out onto a wire rack and leave to cool completely.

6. For the topping, in a bowl, mix the mascarpone with the confectioners' sugar and lime juice. Cut each passion fruit in half and scoop out the seeds and juice into a small bowl. Add half of the passion fruit pulp to the mascarpone and stir to mix; save the rest for decoration.

7. Spread the mascarpone over the top of the cooled sponge, using an offset spatula. Trickle over the remaining passion fruit pulp and sprinkle with the toasted coconut chips and grated lime zest to finish. Cut into squares to serve.

Hazelnut and Orange Cake

Hazelnut and orange is one of my favorite flavor combinations. I've introduced orange four ways into this cake: zest and juice in the mixture, a surprise center of marmalade, a Swiss meringue orange buttercream and beautiful dried oranges on top.

15–20 slices

Dehydrated orange slices
2–3 oranges (ideally including blood oranges and clementines)

Cake layers
2 sticks plus 5 tbsp (300g) salted butter, softened, plus extra to grease

1½ cups (300g) light brown sugar

Finely grated zest and juice of 1 large orange

6 large eggs, at room temperature, beaten

1¾ cups plus 1 tbsp (225g) all-purpose flour

1½ cups (150g) hazelnut flour (or almond flour)

2¾ tsp baking powder

Orange buttercream
¾ cup (170g) egg whites (about 4 large eggs)

1½ cups (300g) granulated sugar

A pinch of fine salt

2 sticks plus 1 tbsp (250g) unsalted butter, in pieces, softened

Finely grated zest and juice of 1 large orange

To assemble
1 heaping cup (about 340g) good-quality thin-cut orange marmalade

¼ heaping cup (50g) roasted hazelnuts

1. First prepare the dehydrated orange slices for the decoration. Heat your oven to 250°F. Line 2 or 3 baking sheets with parchment paper. Thinly slice the oranges into 1/16-inch thick slices and lay on the prepared baking sheets. Place in the oven for 45 minutes–1 hour until the orange slices are completely dried out. Transfer them to wire racks to cool.

2. Heat your oven to 350°F. Grease 4 × 6-inch round cake pans and line with parchment paper (or you can use 2 pans and bake in batches, re-greasing and lining the pans between bakes).

3. Using a stand mixer fitted with a paddle attachment, beat the butter and sugar together on medium speed for 5–7 minutes until pale and fluffy. Add the orange zest and juice and mix until incorporated. Slowly add the beaten eggs, mixing well between each addition and adding a spoonful of the flour halfway through.

4. In a separate bowl, mix the rest of the flour, hazelnut flour and baking powder together. Carefully fold into the whisked mixture using a spatula or large metal spoon until just incorporated; do not over-mix.

5. Divide the mixture evenly between the prepared pans and gently spread to level. Bake in the oven for 20–25 minutes until risen and golden brown.

6. When you remove the sponges from the oven, leave them to cool in the pans for 5 minutes and then turn them out onto wire racks and leave to cool completely.

7. To make the orange buttercream, put the egg whites, sugar and salt into the bowl of a stand mixer and mix to combine, then sit the bowl over a saucepan of simmering water, making sure the base of the bowl is not in direct contact with the water. Heat, stirring occasionally, until the mixture is at 159–160°F (check with an instant-read thermometer). Then place the bowl on your stand mixer, fit the whisk attachment and whisk the meringue as it cools down until it forms stiff peaks; this will take at least 10 minutes.

Continued overleaf

Continued from page 33

8   Now, with the mixer on a low speed, slowly add the soft butter, 1–2 tbsp at a time. Don't worry if the mixture starts to split; once all the butter is incorporated it will suddenly come together to form a thick, silky buttercream. Finally add the orange zest and juice and mix to combine.

9   To assemble the cake, place one cake layer on a thin cake board. Spread about one-fifth of the buttercream on top and work it out towards the edges to leave a crater in the center. Fill this crater with one third of the marmalade. Position a second cake layer on top and then repeat the orange buttercream/marmalade layer. Repeat these layers once more and then place the final cake layer on top.

10 Transfer the cake to a cake decorating turntable. Put a third of the remaining buttercream into a piping bag fitted with a ¾-inch plain piping tip; set aside.

11 Spread a thin layer of buttercream around the side of the cake, then hold a plain cake scraper against the side of the cake and revolve the turntable with the other hand to create an even finish. Now spread a thin layer of buttercream on top of the cake and level using an offset spatula as neatly as you can. Carefully transfer the cake to a cake stand or flat serving plate (see decorating tip on page 23).

12 Blitz ¼ cup of the roasted hazelnuts in a blender to chop roughly and press around the base of the cake. Pipe a buttercream border around the top of the cake and decorate with the dried orange slices and remaining roasted hazelnuts.

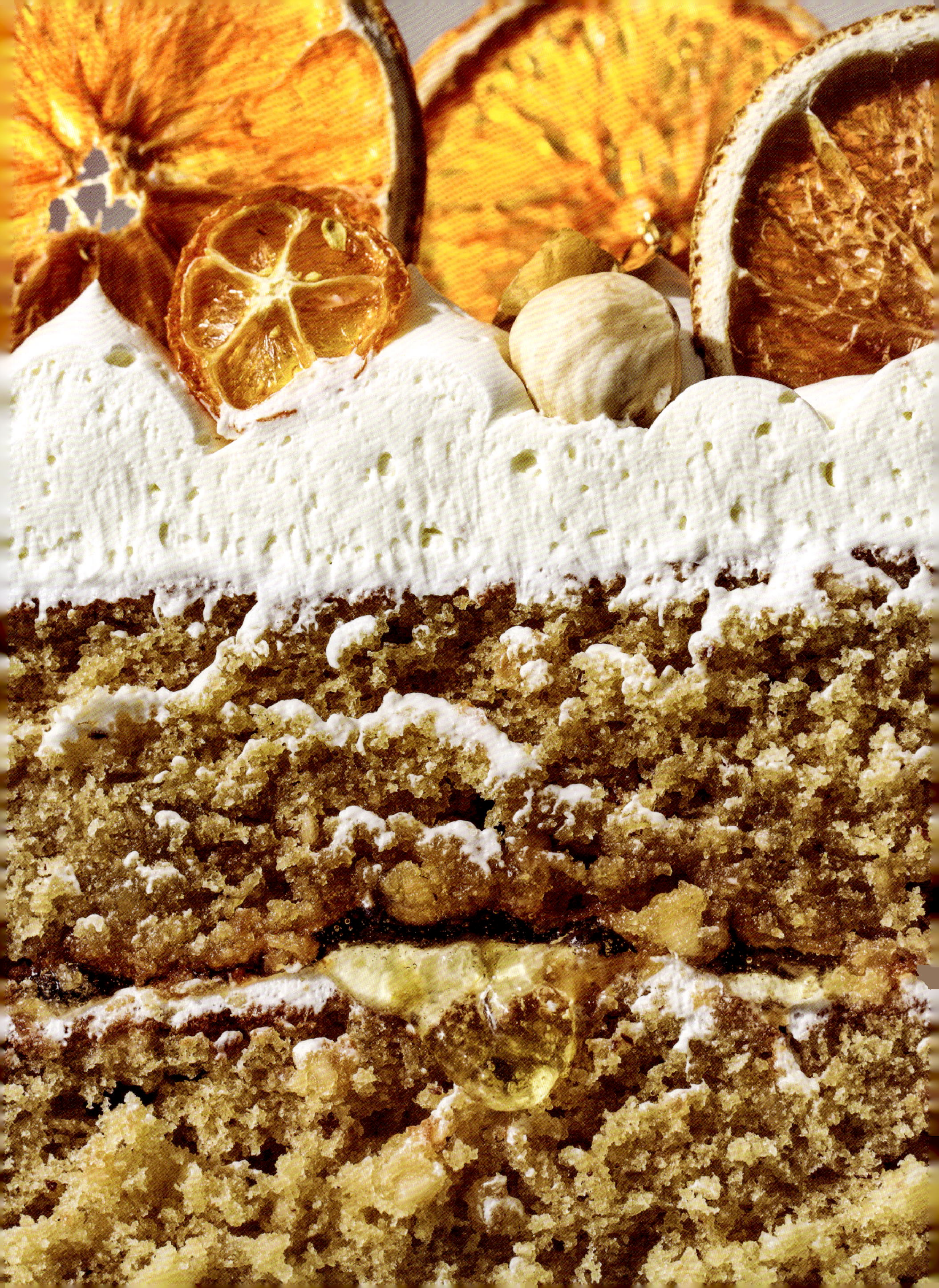

Rainbow Cake

If you're looking to make an impact, this is the cake for you! The vibrant frosting is already very impressive, and then you slice the cake open to reveal all the different colored layers inside. It's a great one to practice your piping and spatula skills too.

About 24 slices

4 sticks (450g) unsalted butter, softened, plus extra to grease

2¼ cups (450g) superfine sugar

8 large eggs, at room temperature

3⅔ cups (450g) all-purpose flour

5½ tsp baking power

2 tsp vanilla extract

3 tbsp whole milk

5 different food gel colorings (purple, green, orange, yellow and pink)

Buttercream

5 sticks (570g) unsalted butter, softened

2¼ lbs (1kg) plus 1½ cups (150g) confectioners' sugar

½ cup whole milk

To finish

2 tbsp rainbow sprinkles

1. Heat your oven to 350°F. Grease 5 × 8-inch round cake pans and line the bases with parchment paper (or you can use 2 or 3 pans and bake in batches, re-greasing and lining the pans between bakes).

2. Using a stand mixer fitted with the paddle attachment, beat the butter and sugar together on medium speed until light and fluffy. Add the eggs, one at a time, mixing until just incorporated and adding a spoonful of flour with each egg.

3. Sift the remaining flour and baking powder together over the mixture and then mix in on a low speed. Finally, add the vanilla extract and milk and mix for 2 minutes.

4. Divide the cake mixture evenly between 5 bowls – to ensure they are equal you can measure or weigh the mixture into the bowls (if doing by weight, simply weigh the mixture and divide the quantity by 5, then weigh out each portion). Color each portion a different hue of the rainbow, adding a small amount of coloring on the end of a toothpick (once baked the color will become more intense).

5. Spoon the cake mixture into the prepared pans and gently level the surface. Bake in the oven for 20–25 minutes until risen and golden. Leave in the pans to cool for 10 minutes then transfer to a wire rack to cool completely.

6. Meanwhile, make the buttercream. Using a stand mixer fitted with the whisk attachment, beat the butter until very soft, then add the confectioners' sugar a little at a time until it is all incorporated. Add the milk and mix for a couple of minutes until light and fluffy.

7. If necessary, trim a thin slice off the top of the each cake to level it, and trim the sides so there are no crisp edges. Place the first layer (ideally purple) on a 10-inch round cake board. Spread a thin layer of buttercream on top, keeping it level. Repeat to sandwich all the cake layers together with a thin layer of buttercream in between. Carefully transfer the cake to a turntable.

Continued overleaf

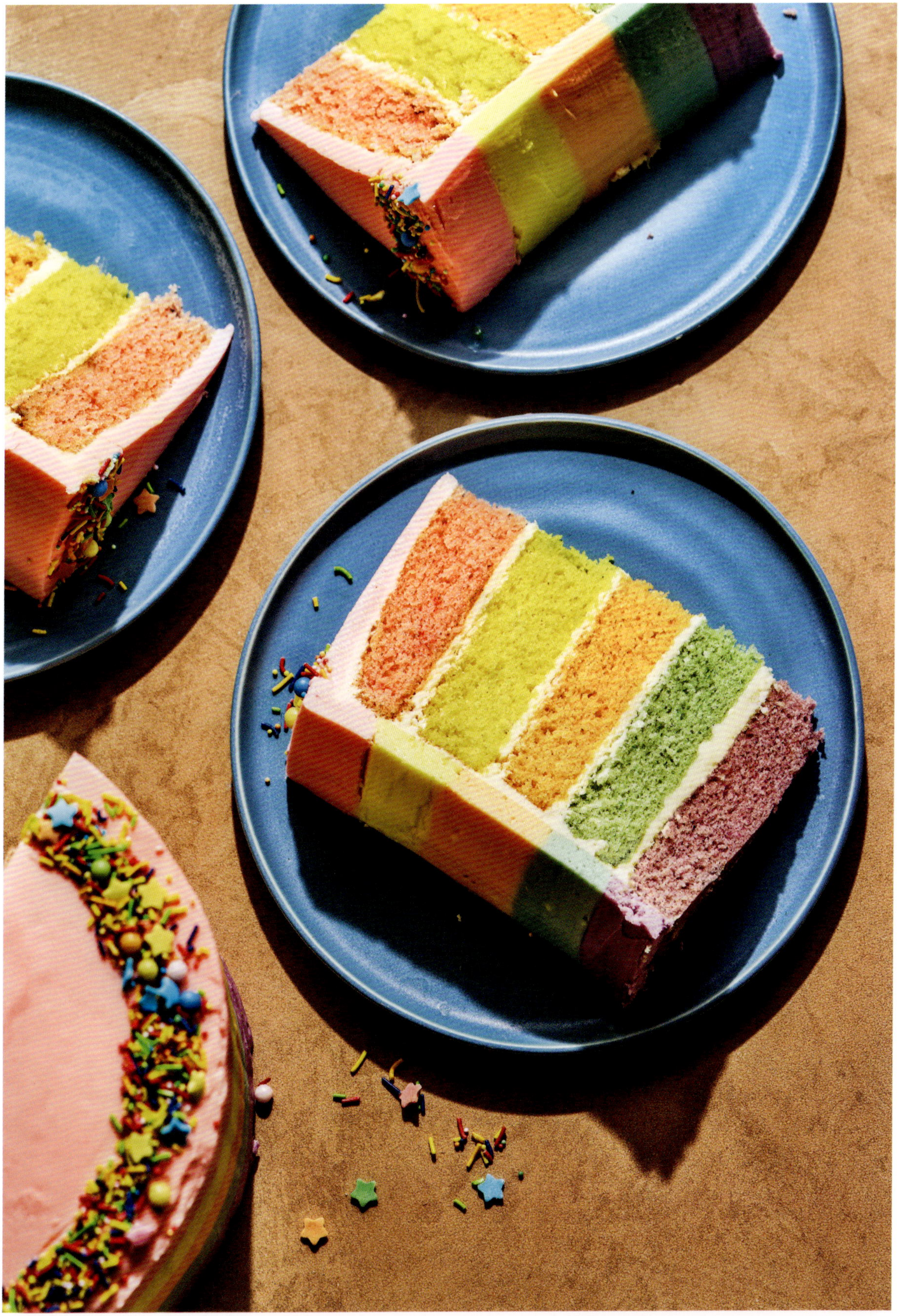

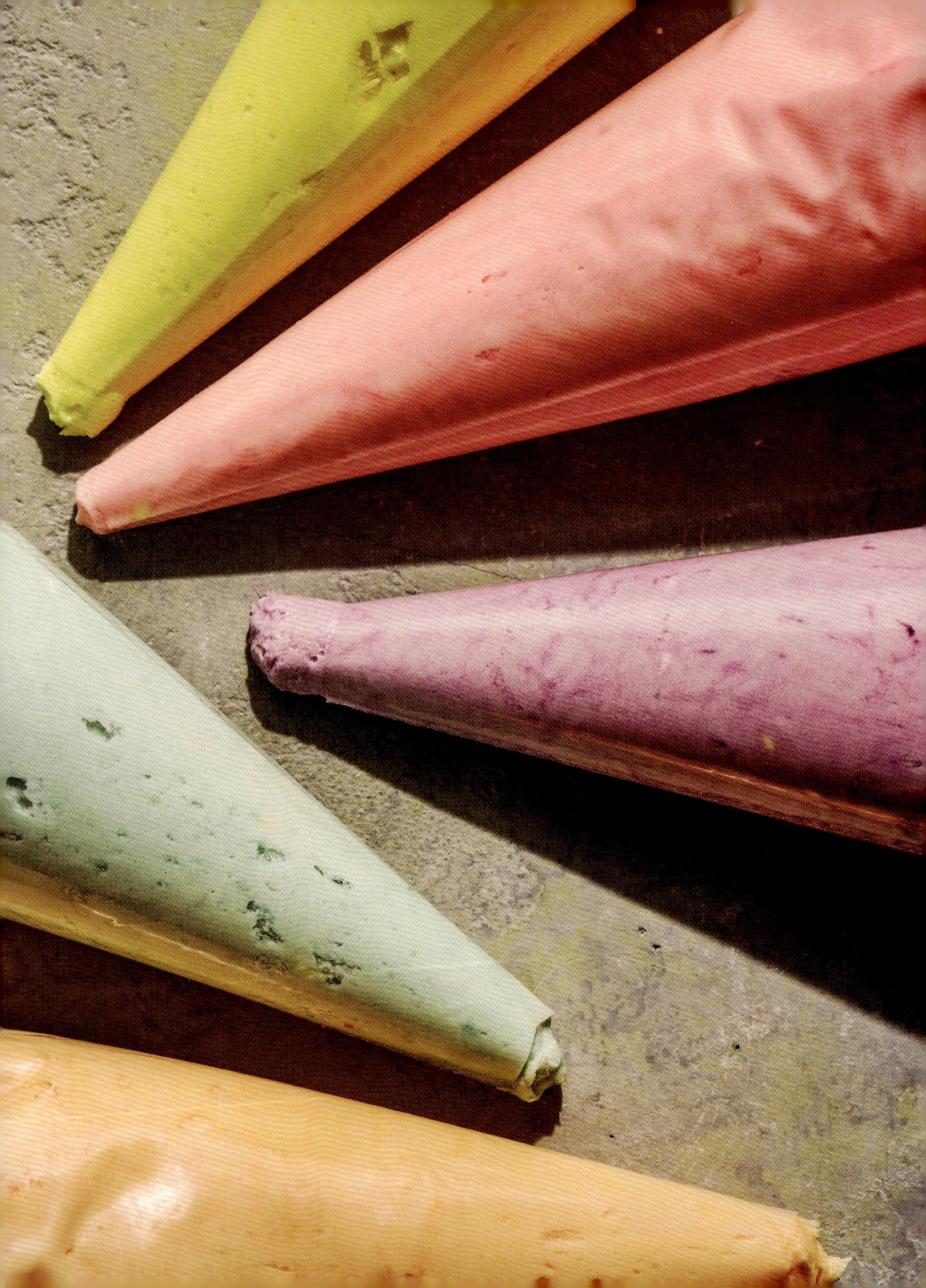

Continued from page 36

8   Spread a thin layer of buttercream around the sides, using a plain cake scraper to smooth it and remove any excess. Spread a thin layer of buttercream on top of the cake and smooth out evenly with a wet offset spatula. Now, keeping the scraper vertical against the side of the cake, revolve the turntable with the other hand to even the thin buttercream layer. Place the cake in the fridge for at least 10 minutes.

9   Divide the remaining buttercream between 5 bowls. Using a toothpick, add a gel coloring sparingly to each bowl to achieve the desired shade and beat well until evenly incorporated.

10 Put the colored buttercream into 5 separate paper piping bags. Snip the end off each bag so that when you come to pipe the opening is almost half the depth of each cake layer. Pipe 2 bands of the base layer color (I used purple) around the bottom layer. Repeat around the other layers using the corresponding colored buttercream, working from bottom to top.

11 Hold the cleaned scraper vertically against the side and turn the turntable with the other hand to neaten the sides. Repeat until smooth. On the final turn, dampen the scraper with water to achieve a very smooth finish. Carefully transfer the cake to a cake stand or flat serving plate (see decorating tip on page 23). Decorate the top edge of the cake with a border of rainbow sprinkles.

Also pictured overleaf

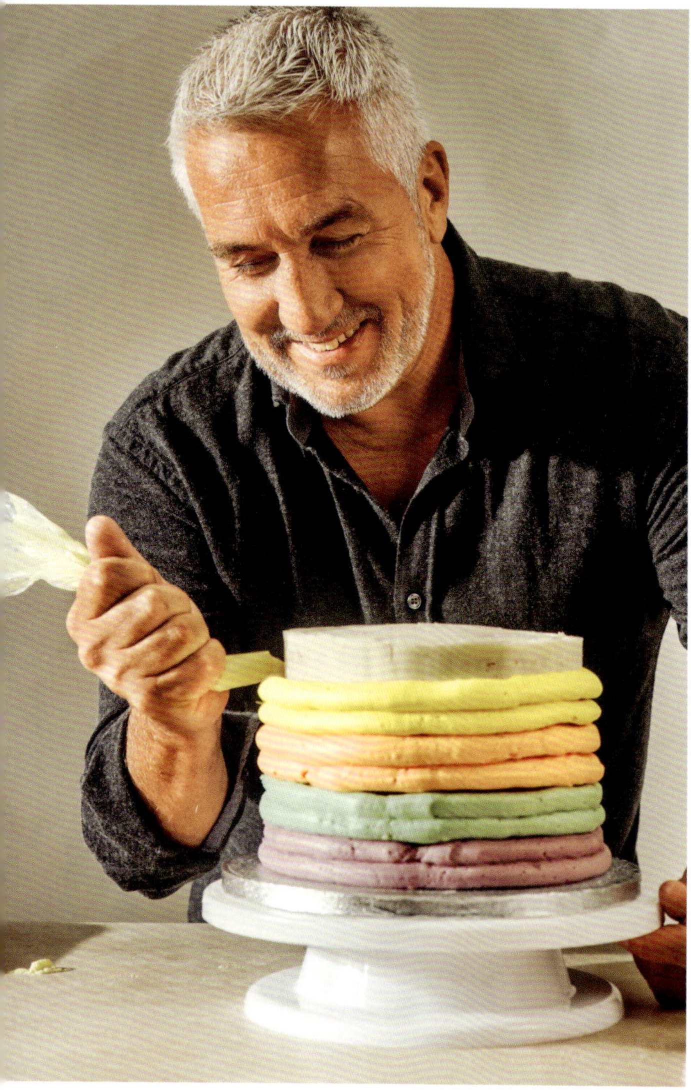
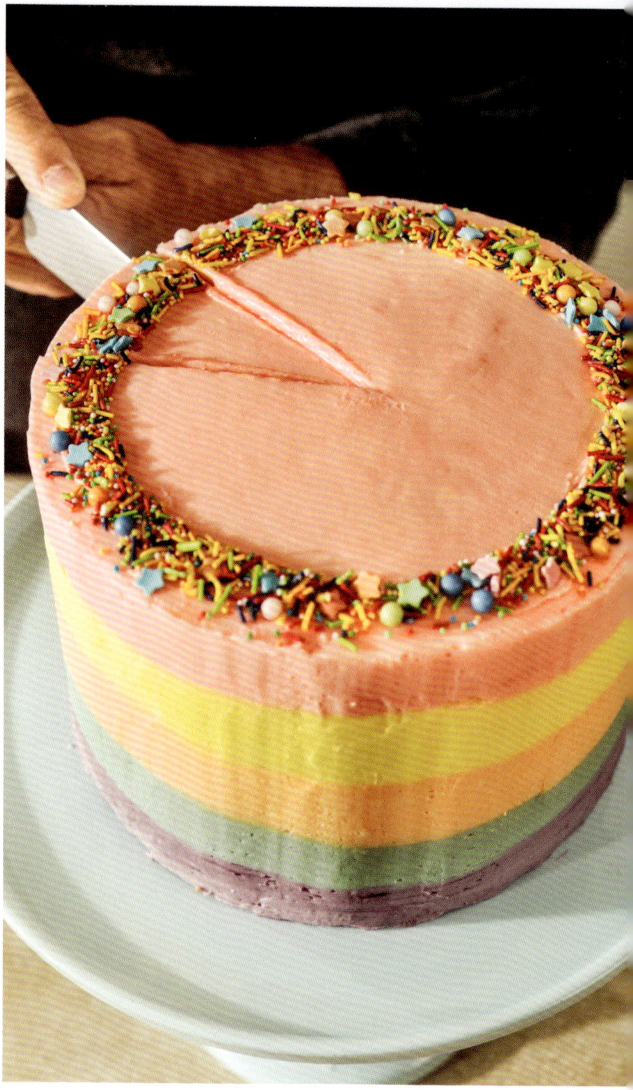

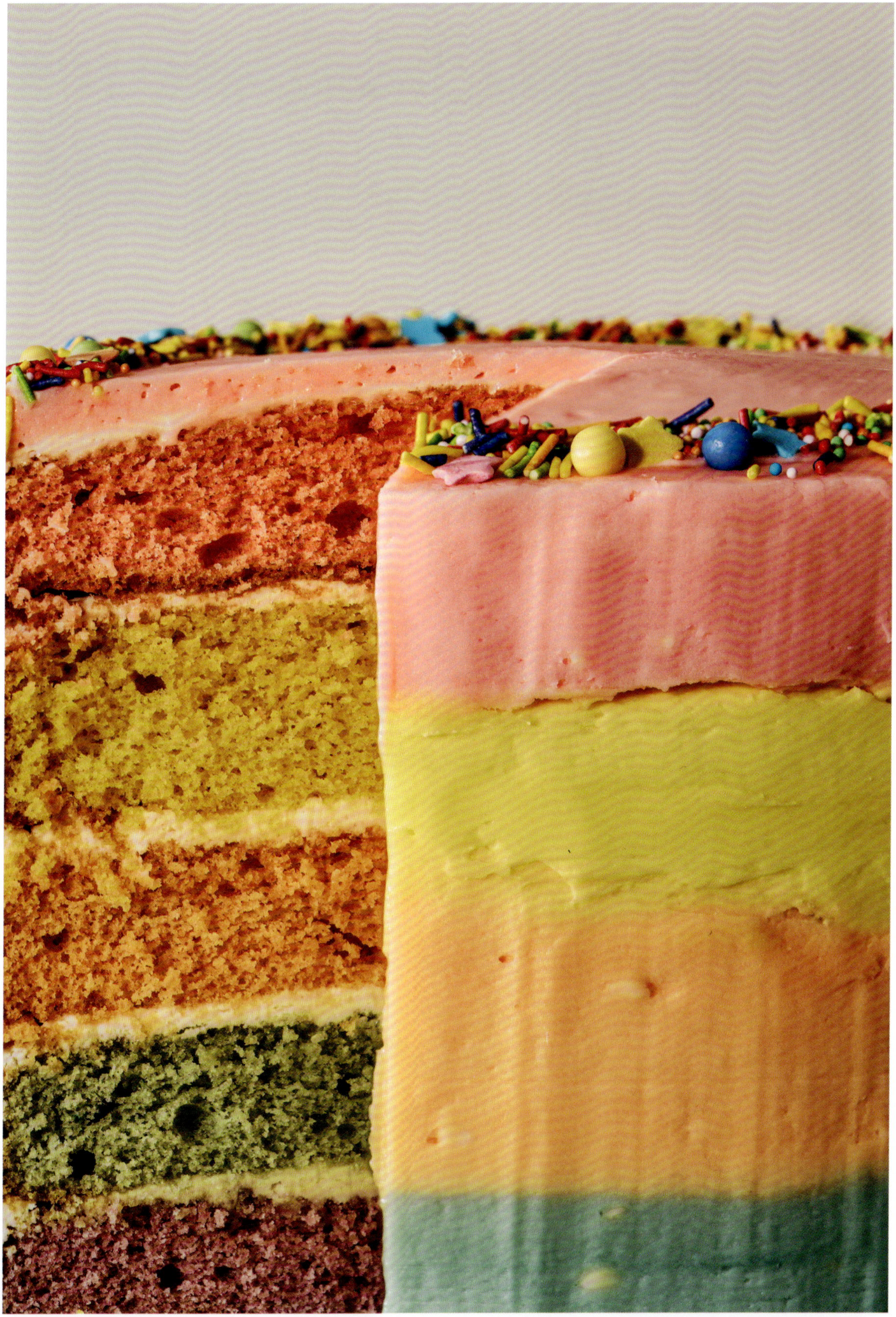

Elderflower Cupcakes

You don't need a lot of syrup to give these stunning cupcakes a delicious taste of elderflower. It adds a delicate back note to the sponge, while the lime elderflower frosting on top is a big flavor hit.

Makes 12

1¾ sticks (200g) unsalted butter, softened
1 cup (200g) superfine sugar
Finely grated zest of 1 lime
3 large eggs, at room temperature
5 tbsp elderflower syrup
1⅔ cups (200g) all-purpose flour
1¾ tsp baking powder

Frosting
1 stick plus 1 tbsp (125g) unsalted butter, softened
2½ cups (250g) confectioners' sugar, sifted
Finely grated zest of 1 lime
1 tbsp elderflower syrup

To decorate
Edible flowers (such as pansies or marigolds)

1. Heat your oven to 350°F. Line a 12-cup muffin pan with paper cups.

2. Using a stand mixer fitted with the paddle attachment, beat the butter, superfine sugar and lime zest together until the mixture is pale and fluffy. Scrape down the sides of the bowl with a spatula and mix again.

3. In a separate bowl, beat the eggs with the elderflower syrup. With the mixer running on a low speed, gradually pour in the beaten egg mix. Stop the mixer as soon as the mixture is smoothly combined.

4. Sift the flour and baking powder over the mixture and fold in, using a large spatula or metal spoon, until thoroughly combined.

5. Divide the mixture evenly between the paper muffin cups. Bake in the oven for 20–25 minutes until the cupcakes are risen and golden, and spring back when lightly touched. Transfer to a wire rack to cool.

6. To make the frosting, put the butter and half the confectioners' sugar into a bowl with the lime zest and beat using a hand mixer until light and fluffy. Add the remaining confectioners' sugar and beat until smoothly combined. Mix in the elderflower syrup to make a smooth frosting.

7. Spread or pipe the frosting on top of the cupcakes and decorate with edible flowers.

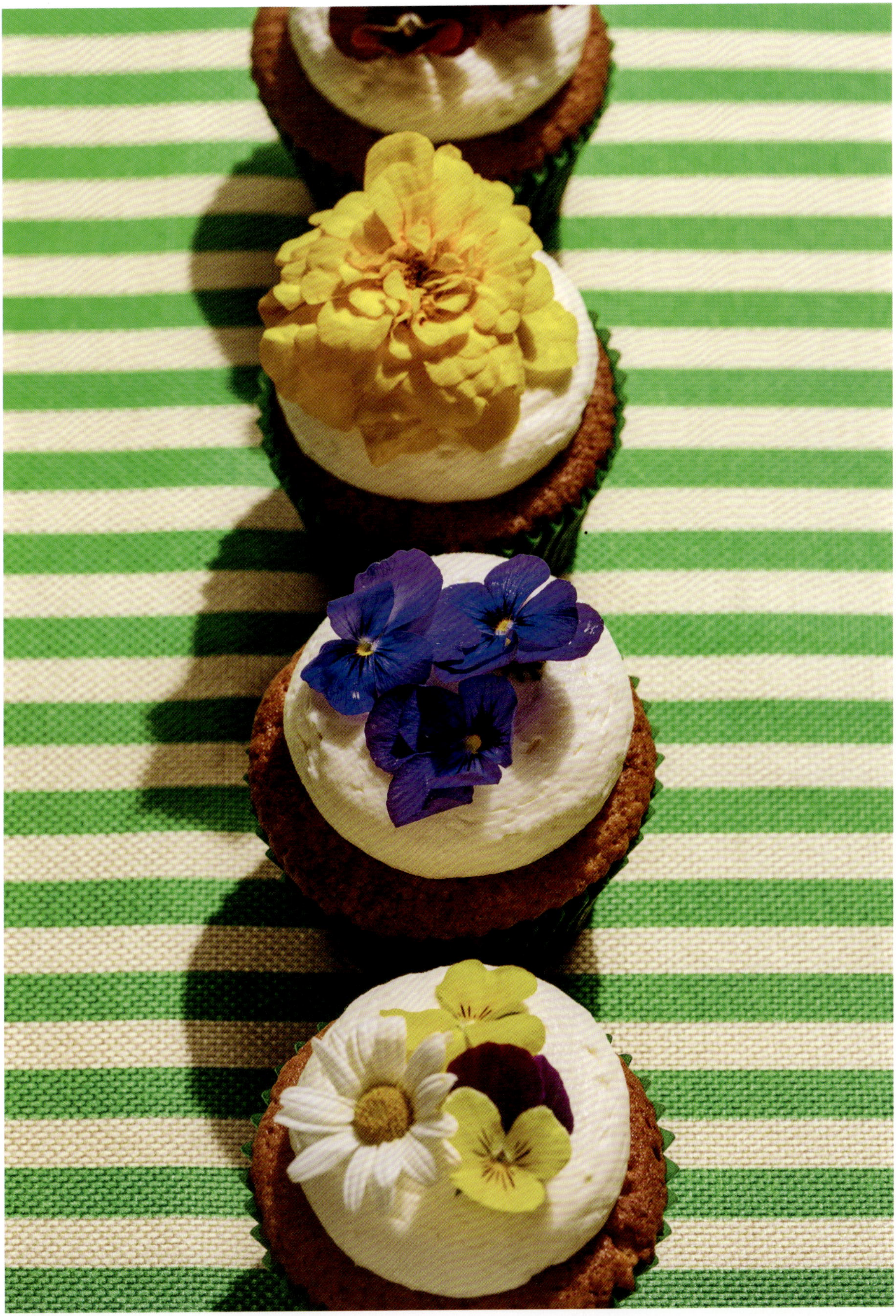

Paul's Chocolate Cake

Most of you will recognize this iconic chocolate cake – it might even be the most famous cake in the world! To recreate the version featured on *Baking Show*, arrange the raspberries neatly on top, starting in the middle and working outwards in a spiral.

12 slices

1½ sticks (170g) unsalted butter, softened, plus extra to grease

1 cup plus 2 tbsp (225g) light brown sugar

1 cup (200g) superfine sugar

3 large eggs, at room temperature, beaten

1 tsp vanilla extract

1½ cups plus 1 tbsp (375g) sour cream

2 cups (250g) all-purpose flour

1¼ cups (125g) unsweetened cocoa powder

1½ tsp baking powder

½ tsp fine salt

1½ cups (150g) frozen raspberries

Chocolate frosting

4 oz (110g) bittersweet chocolate, broken into small pieces

¾ cup (75g) cocoa powder

5 tbsp (75g) boiling water

1½ sticks (180g) unsalted butter, softened

scant ¾ cup (70g) confectioners' sugar

Ganache

7 oz (200g) bittersweet chocolate, broken into small pieces

¾ cup plus 1 tbsp (200g) heavy cream

2 tbsp (30g) unsalted butter, in pieces, softened

To decorate

9 oz (250g) fresh raspberries

1. Heat your oven to 350°F. Grease 3 × 8-inch round cake pans and line the bases with parchment paper.

2. Using a stand mixer fitted with the whisk attachment, beat the butter and both sugars together until light and fluffy. Scrape down the sides of the bowl with a spatula and whisk again. With the mixer on a low speed, slowly pour in the beaten eggs, then incorporate the vanilla extract and sour cream.

3. Sift the flour with the cocoa, baking powder and salt. Add a large spoonful to the whisked mixture and mix in on a low speed, then repeat to incorporate the rest and make a smooth batter. Finally, using a spatula, fold through the frozen raspberries.

4. Divide the mixture evenly between the prepared pans and bake in the oven for 25 minutes until the cakes are risen and slightly shrunk from the side of the pan. Leave the cakes in the pans for 5 minutes then remove and transfer to wire racks to cool completely.

5. For the frosting, melt the chocolate in a heatproof bowl over a saucepan of simmering water; set aside to cool slightly. In another bowl, mix the cocoa and boiling water to a thick paste. In a large bowl, beat the butter until very soft then whisk in the confectioners' sugar until pale and fluffy. Add the melted chocolate and cocoa paste and beat until smooth.

6. To assemble, place one cake layer on a stand, spread with a third of the chocolate frosting and cover with a second cake layer. Spread with half of the remaining frosting and top with the final cake layer. Spread the rest of the frosting over the top and around the side of the cake in an even, thin layer. Leave to set for about 1 hour.

7. For the ganache, melt the chocolate in a heatproof bowl over a saucepan of simmering water. Remove from the heat, add the heavy cream and mix until evenly combined. Add the softened butter and beat until smooth.

8. Pour the ganache over the top of the cake and encourage it to run down the sides. Leave to cool slightly and then clean the cake stand. Arrange the fresh raspberries around the top of the cake to serve.

Also pictured overleaf

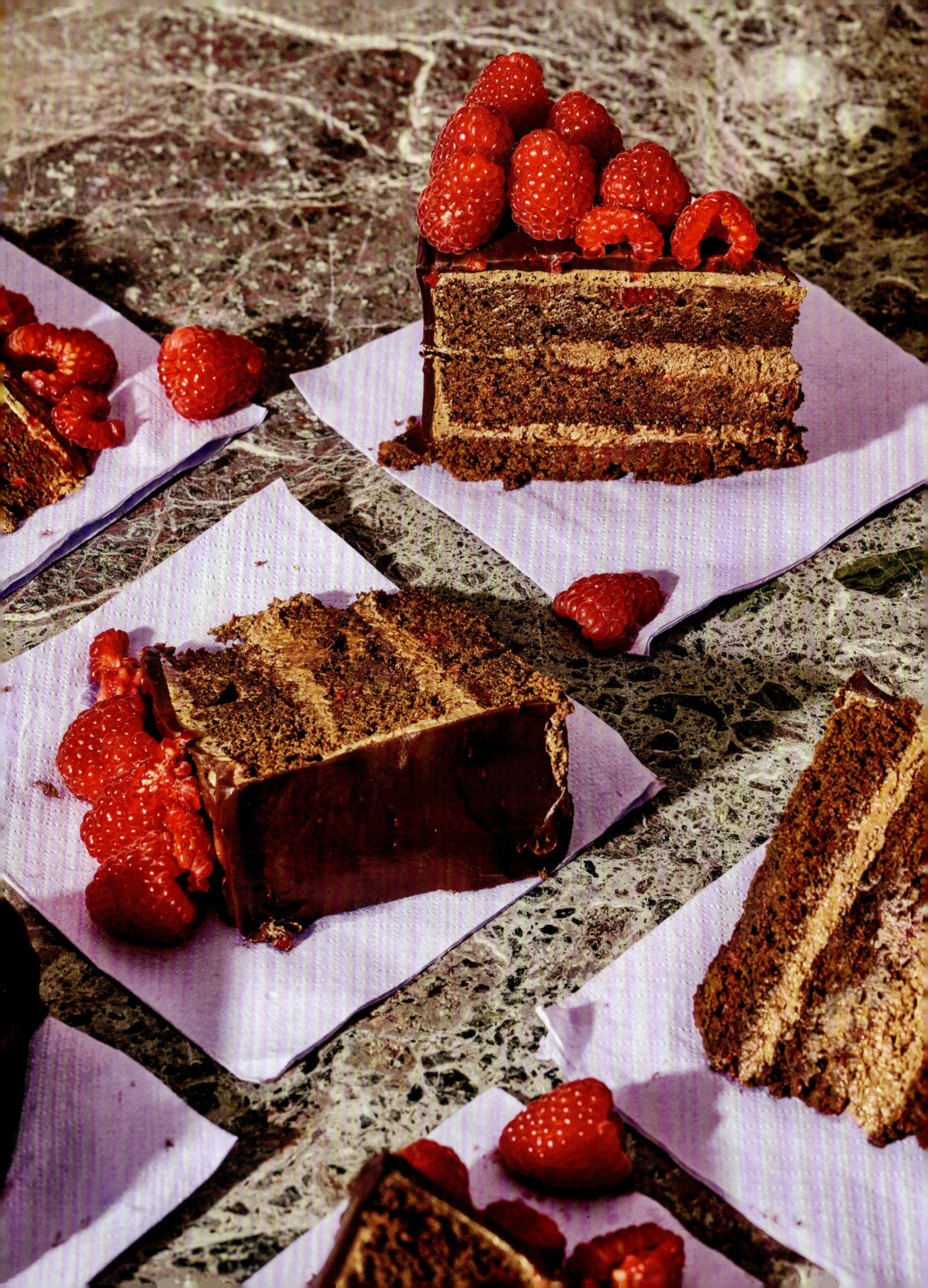

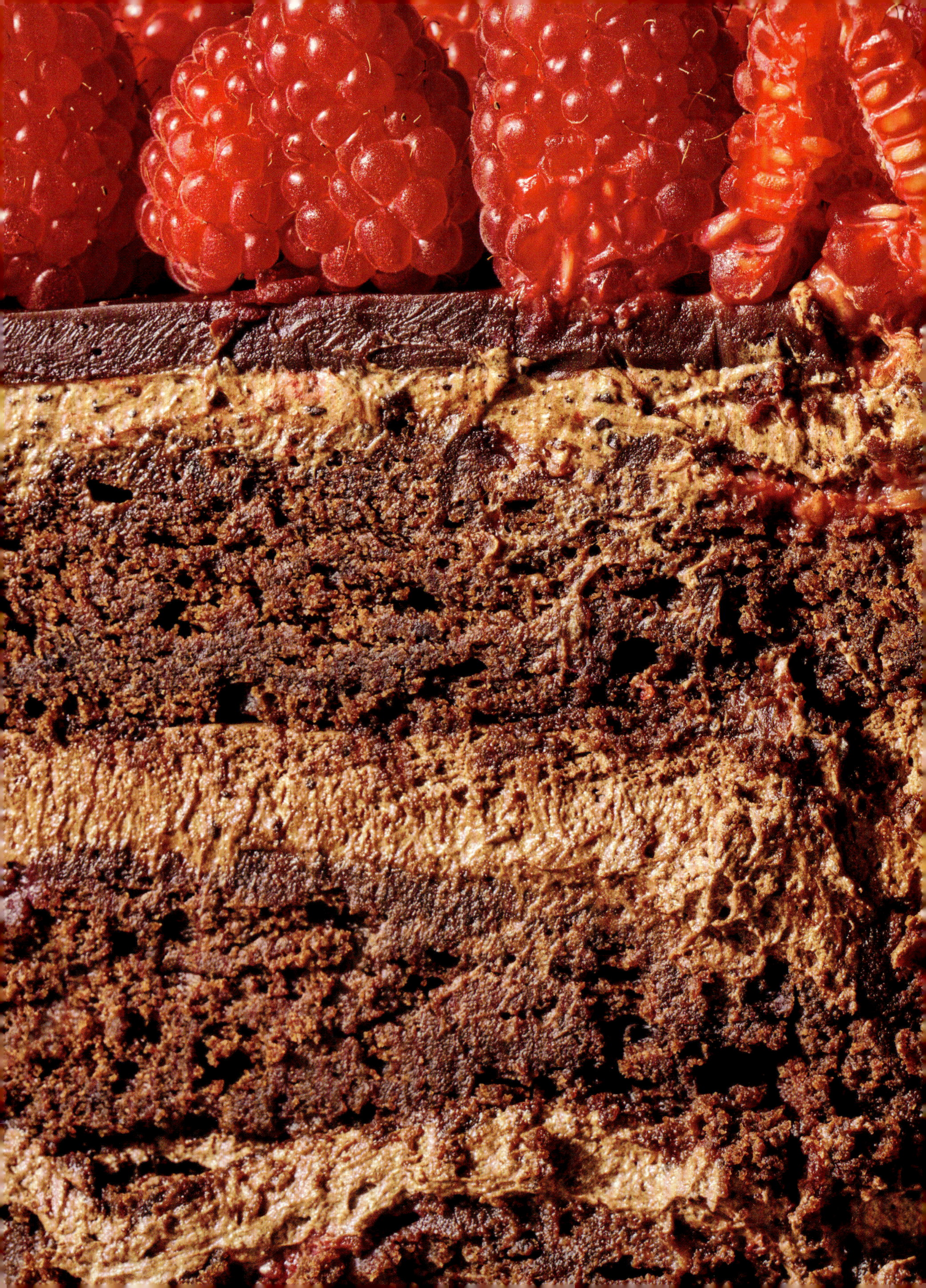

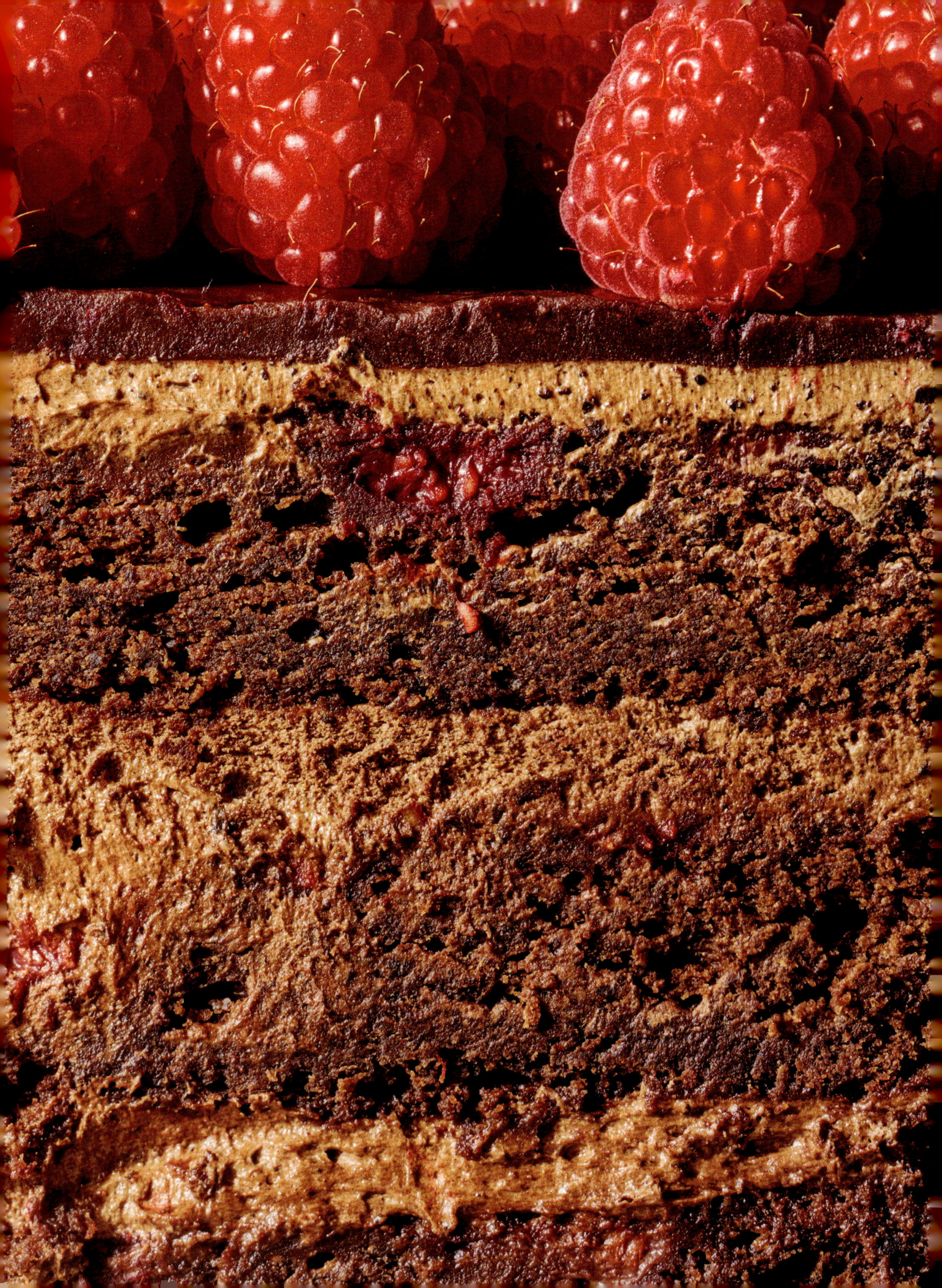

Spiced Maple Bundt Cake

I think everyone should have a bundt pan in their kitchen! It's a ring-shaped pan, with a hole in the middle, designed to ensure a deep cake cooks more evenly. Most bundt pans are fluted or have a swirl pattern to give the cake a lovely decorative effect.

10–12 slices

3¼ sticks (370g) unsalted butter, softened, plus extra to grease
1 cup plus 2 tbsp (220g) light brown sugar
Finely grated zest of 1 orange
6 large eggs, at room temperature
3 cups (370g) all-purpose flour
3 tsp baking powder
1 tsp ground cinnamon
1 tsp ground ginger
½ cup (140g) maple syrup
⅔ cup (150g) plain whole milk yogurt

Maple glacé icing
1⅓ cups (130g) confectioners' sugar
¼ tsp ground cinnamon
1 tbsp maple syrup, plus a little more if needed

Popcorn crunch
7 cups (about 100g) sweet and salty popcorn, roughly crushed

1 Heat your oven to 350°F. Grease a 12-cup bundt pan with butter (or spray it with non-stick baking spray).

2 Using a stand mixer fitted with the paddle attachment, beat the butter, sugar and orange zest together on medium speed for 3–5 minutes until light and fluffy, stopping to scrape down the sides of the bowl a couple of times. Add the eggs, one at a time, beating well between each addition and adding a spoonful of flour with the last two.

3 Sift the flour, baking powder, cinnamon and ginger together over the mixture and beat on a medium-low speed until combined. Add the maple syrup and yogurt and mix to a thick dropping consistency.

4 Spoon the mixture into the prepared pan and, using a spatula, push it slightly up the sides of the pan – this helps the sponge to rise evenly. Tap the pan on the work surface a few times, to release any air bubbles.

5 Bake in the oven for 50–60 minutes, until a cake tester inserted deep into the cake comes out clean. Leave it to cool in the pan for 10 minutes then turn out and place on a wire rack. Leave to cool completely.

6 To make the maple glacé icing, mix the ingredients together in a bowl until smooth, adding a little more maple syrup if necessary to achieve a thick pouring consistency.

7 Spoon the maple icing on top of the cake, letting it drip slightly down the sides, then sprinkle the crushed popcorn on top. Leave the glacé icing to set for around 15 minutes before slicing the cake to serve.

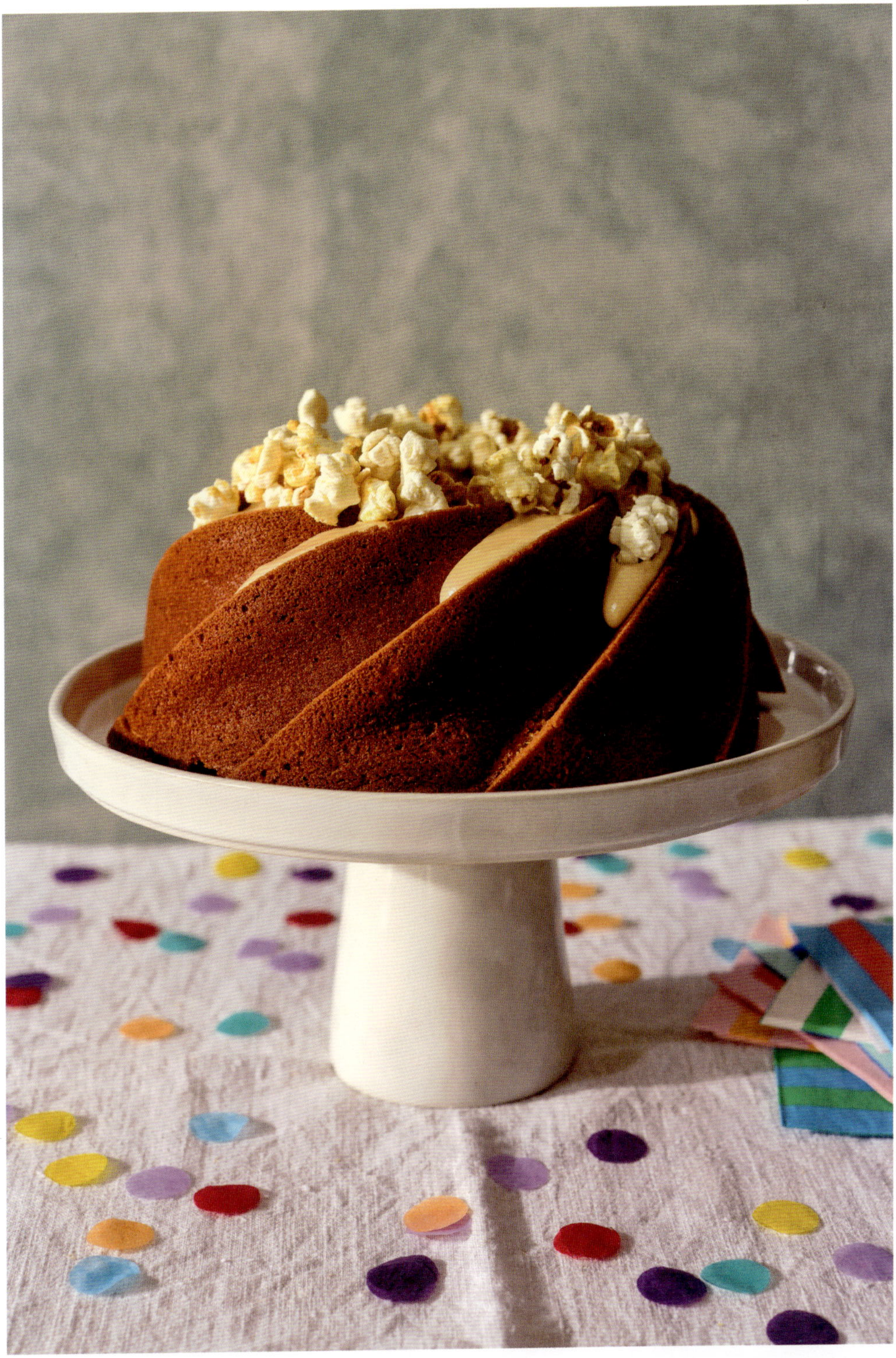

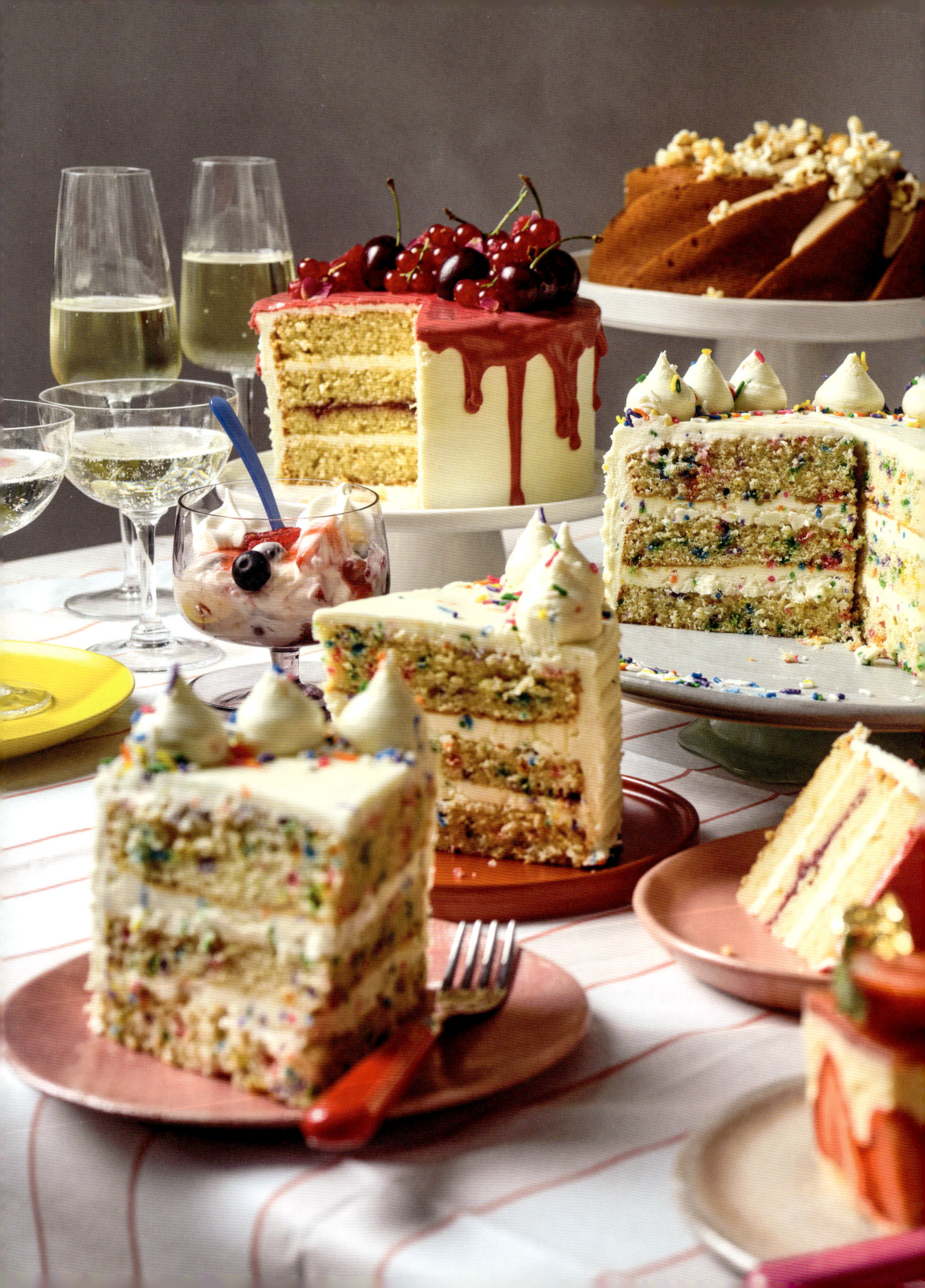

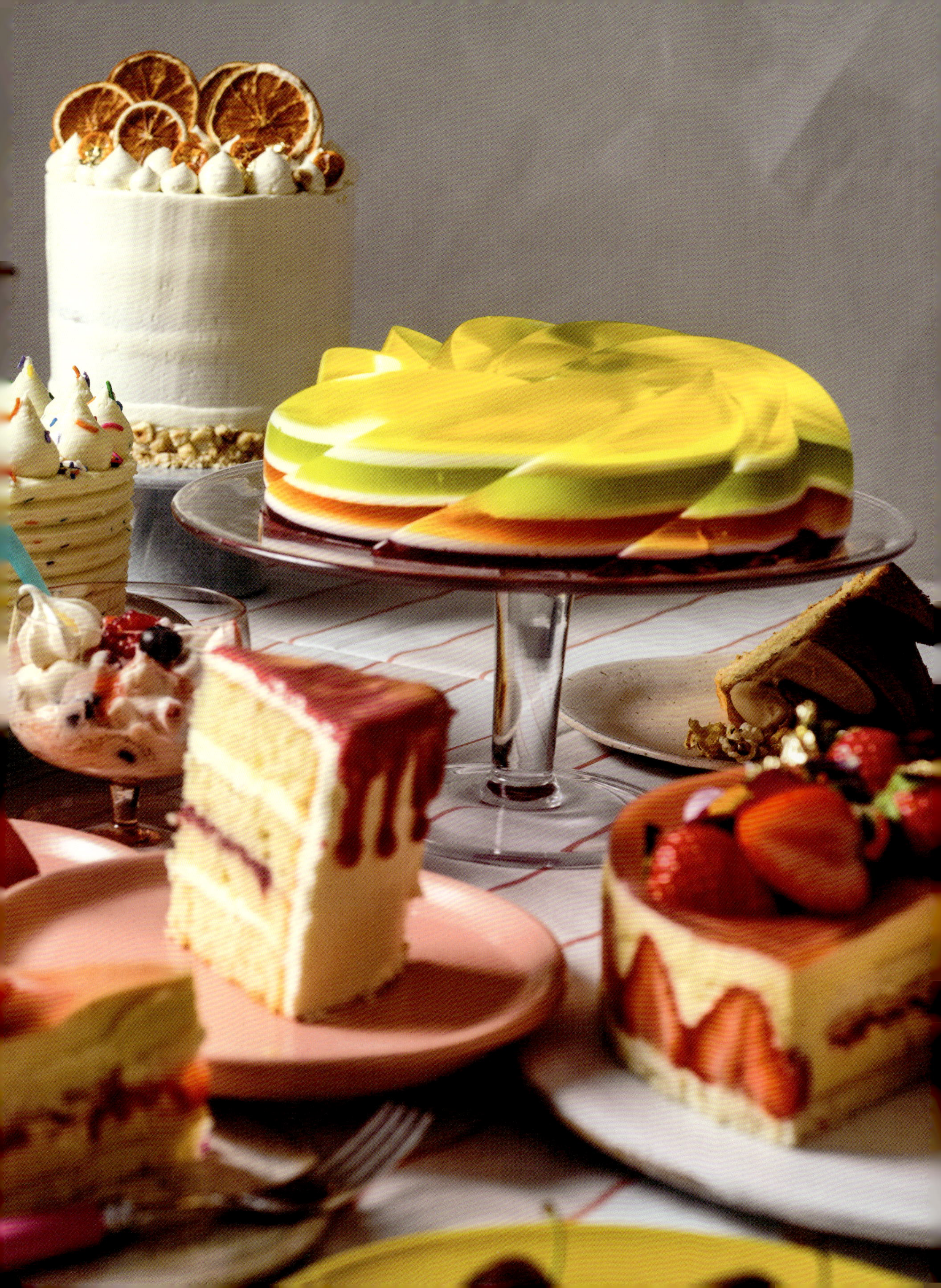

Spring

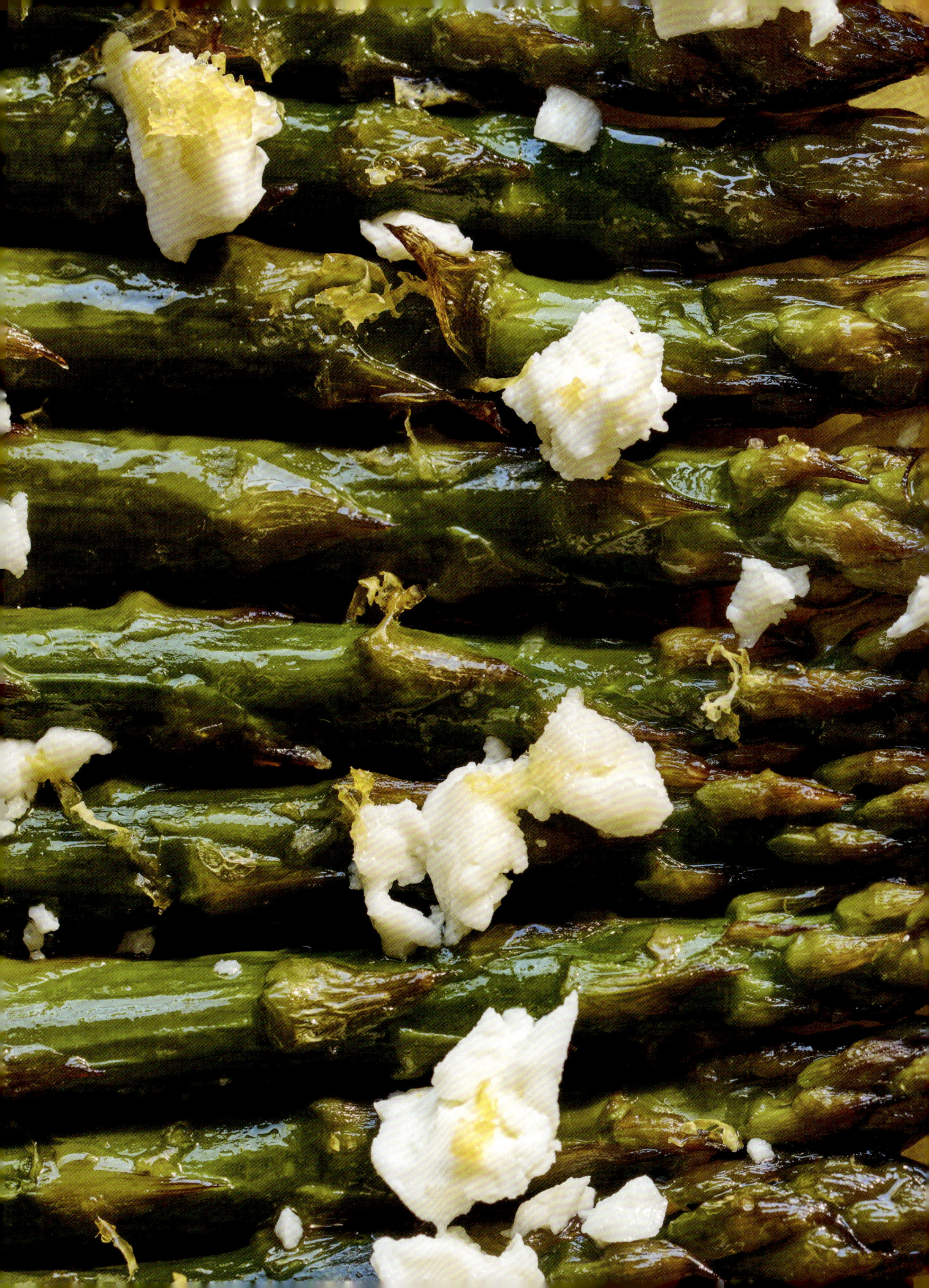

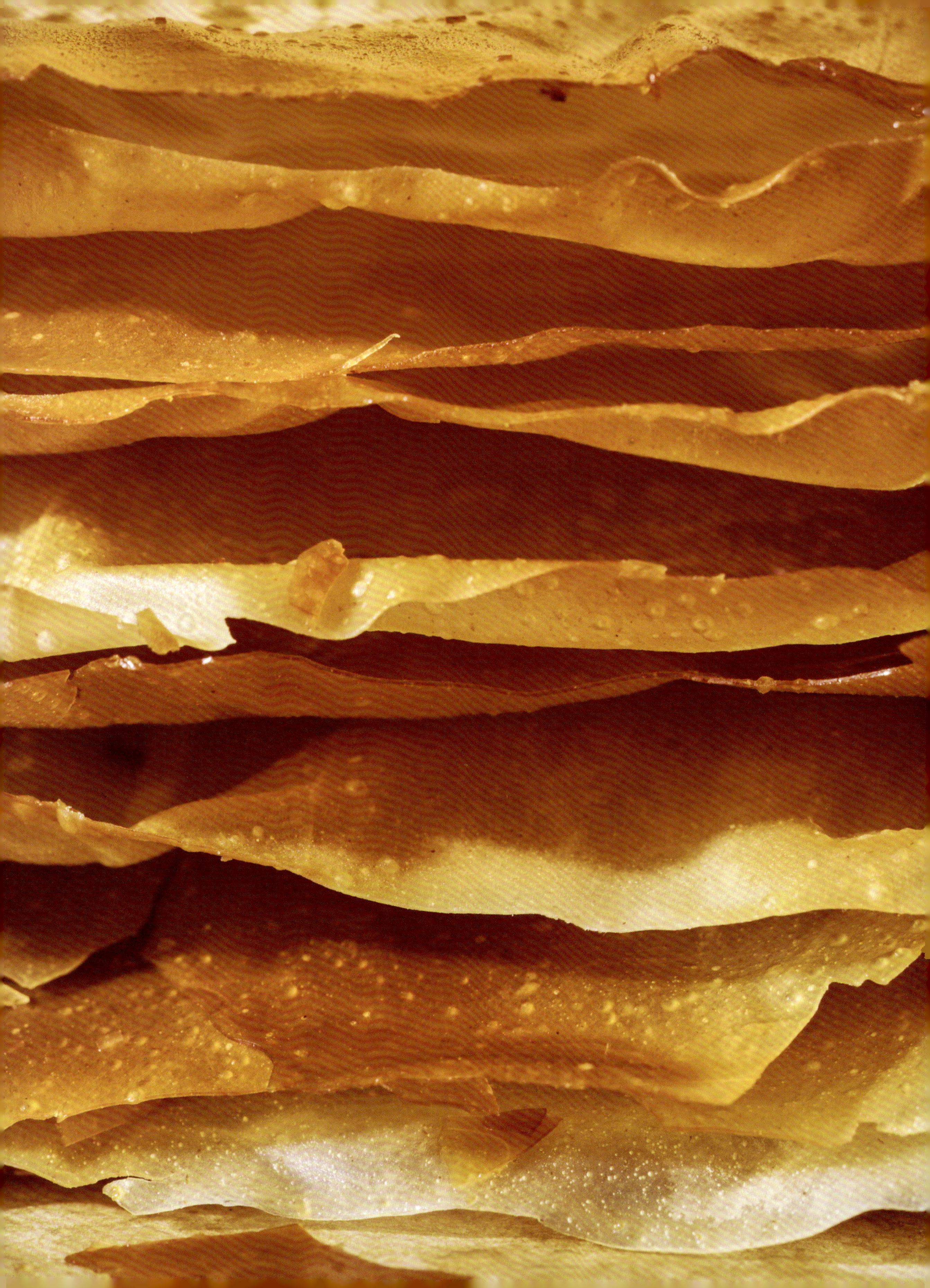

Spring is a very optimistic time of year. Those never-ending winter days have finally come to an end, the weather is getting warmer and the colors outside are starting to change. Everything feels brighter and lighter, and we begin to reflect this in our baking. I find myself using lots of citrus flavors at this time of year, as they are so fresh and uplifting. I love lemon in baking, and the Lemon Easter bread on page 60 combines lemon with bread – my other passion – so you're definitely on to a winner!

Spring is also the season to enjoy local asparagus. It is such a fantastic vegetable but it is only around for about six weeks, so I think we should all be eating lots of it while it's available. It's perfect in the Asparagus, feta and phyllo tart on page 56.

Pink, hothouse rhubarb is also only in season for a few weeks, so grab it while you can – it's brilliant in the oaty Rhubarb and apple crumble on page 70. Being Northern, I love anything with custard and this reminds me so much of going round to my grandmother's house. In fact, one of the first things I learned to bake at my dad's bakery were the Custard tarts on page 68. I remember dropping a whole pan of about sixty tarts when I was loading them into the oven one day – my dad docked it off my wages! So, take your time and don't make the same mistake I did.

Easter is a great opportunity to get people together, and my individual Tsoureki loaves on page 80 offer up something a bit different. They are decorated with hard-boiled eggs dyed red to represent the blood of Christ. These eggs are traditionally used to play a game called *tsougrisma*, where the eggs are tapped together until they crack – whoever wins will have good luck for the rest of the year.

Asparagus, Feta and Phyllo Tart

I'm a big fan of asparagus and it works beautifully with creamy, salty feta, crumbly phyllo pastry, and a little honey drizzled on top. With my favorite Greek flavors, this tart reminds me of my time working as a chef in Cyprus.

Serves 4

---

8 oz (225g) asparagus spears
2 tbsp (35g) unsalted butter
2 sheets of phyllo pastry (each approximately 18 × 14 inches), thawed if frozen
¼ cup (25g) crumbled feta
½ tsp honey
Finely grated zest of ½ lemon
Salt and black pepper

1. Heat your oven to 400°F.

2. Trim the woody ends off the asparagus so the spears will fit into an 8-inch ovenproof frying pan or skillet. Melt 2 teaspoons of the butter in the frying pan and season with salt and pepper then lay the asparagus in the pan so the spears sit tightly together (they will shrink on cooking).

3. Cut 4 circles of phyllo, 8 inches in diameter (the same size as the pan). Melt the remaining butter in a small saucepan.

4. Brush the surface of one phyllo round with butter then sit another round on top. Repeat to layer the other phyllo rounds on top, brushing each with butter. Sit the sandwiched phyllo on top of the asparagus and push the edges down the side of the pan. Bake in the oven for 35–40 minutes until the pastry is crisp and a rich golden-brown color.

5. Invert a serving plate or board over the pan, then holding the plate/board and pan tightly together, turn them upside down to unmold the tart onto the plate. Scatter over the feta, drizzle with honey and grate over some lemon zest to serve.

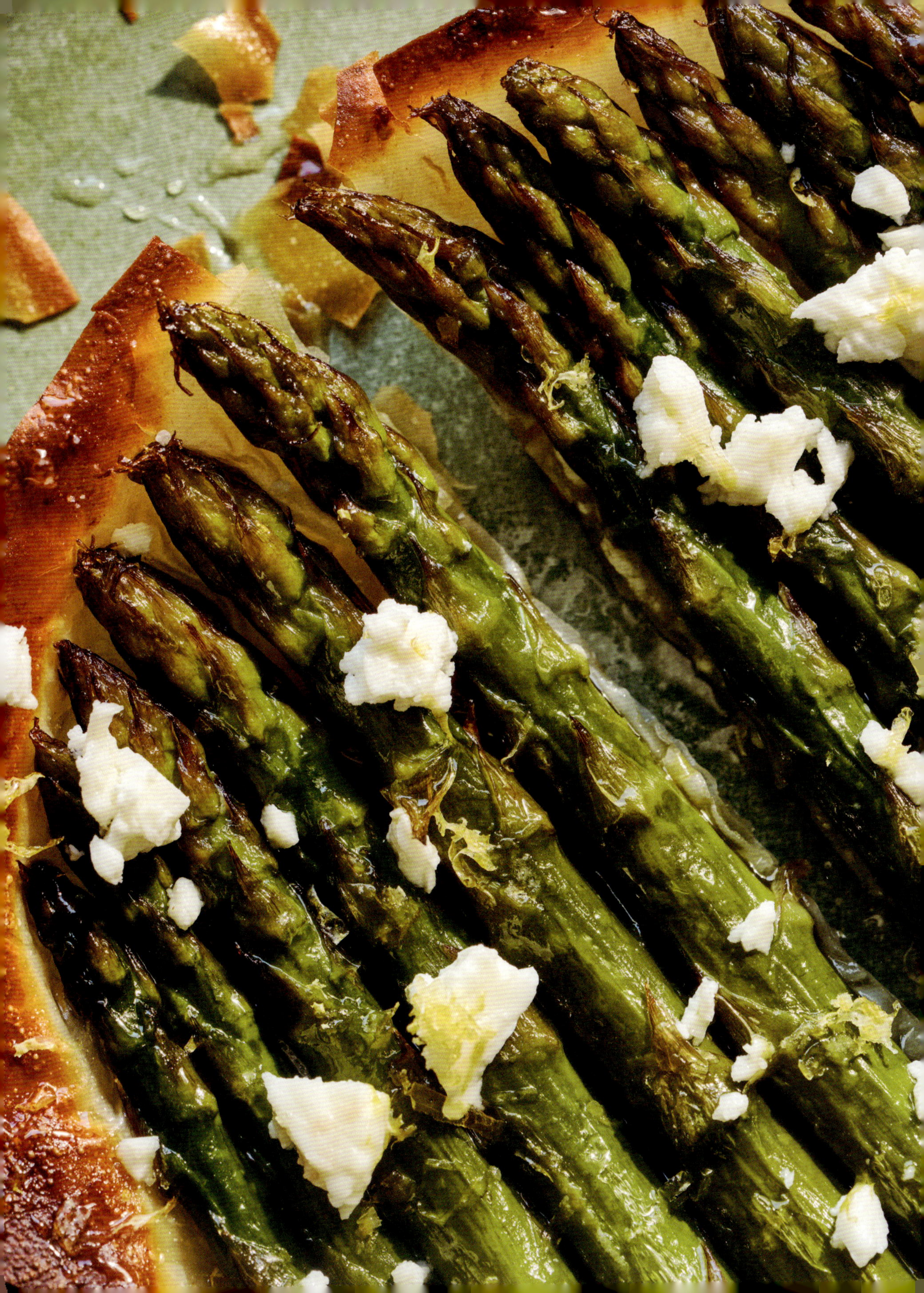

Polish Easter Babka

Babka is the perfect hybrid between a bread and a cake. I first saw this version when I was in Warsaw. It's eaten year round in Poland but with its citrusy Easter flavors, it has a fresh springtime feel. It's lovely to make and is topped with a sweet rum glacé.

12-16 slices

¾ cup (80g) mixed dried fruit (raisins, golden raisins, zante currants)

3 tbsp dark rum

2⅓ cups plus 1 tbsp (300g) bread flour, plus extra to dust

1 × ¼-oz (7g) packet instant yeast

½ tsp fine salt

¼ cup (50g) superfine sugar

4 tbsp (60g) unsalted butter, diced and softened, plus extra to grease

Finely grated zest of 1 orange

2 large eggs, at room temperature, beaten

About ½ cup (115g) warm whole milk

Rum syrup

½ cup (100g) granulated sugar

¼ cup (60ml) water

2 tbsp rum

Rum icing

1 cup (100g) confectioners' sugar, sifted

2 tbsp rum

1. Put the dried fruit into a bowl, pour on the rum and set aside to soak.

2. Put the flour into a stand mixer fitted with the dough hook. Add the yeast, salt, sugar, butter, orange zest, eggs and two-thirds of the milk and mix on a low speed to form a dough. Add as much of the remaining milk as needed to bring the dough together. Increase the mixer speed to high and work for 2 minutes.

3. Cover the bowl and leave the dough to rise for 1 hour or until doubled in size; it will be soft and a little sticky.

4. Drain the soaked dried fruit, then add to the dough and mix on a low speed until evenly combined. Cover the bowl and leave the dough to rise for a further 1 hour or until doubled in size again.

5. Heat your oven to 350°F. Lightly grease a 10-cup bundt pan with butter.

6. Tip the risen dough onto a lightly floured surface and punch down by folding the dough inwards repeatedly to knock out the air. Transfer to the prepared bundt pan, distributing the dough evenly. Cover and leave to proof until doubled in size.

7. Once proofed, bake the babka in the oven for 35–40 minutes, until risen and firm to the touch.

8. Meanwhile, prepare the rum syrup. Put the sugar and water into a small saucepan over a medium heat to dissolve the sugar then bring to a boil. Remove from the heat and add the rum.

9. As you take the babka from the oven, gently poke the surface all over with a toothpick, then slowly pour on the rum syrup. Leave for about 20 minutes until the syrup is absorbed, then loosen the edges and turn the babka out of the pan. Place on a wire rack; leave to cool completely.

10. For the rum icing, mix the confectioners' sugar and rum together until smoothly combined. Drizzle decoratively over the cooled babka and leave to set before slicing to serve.

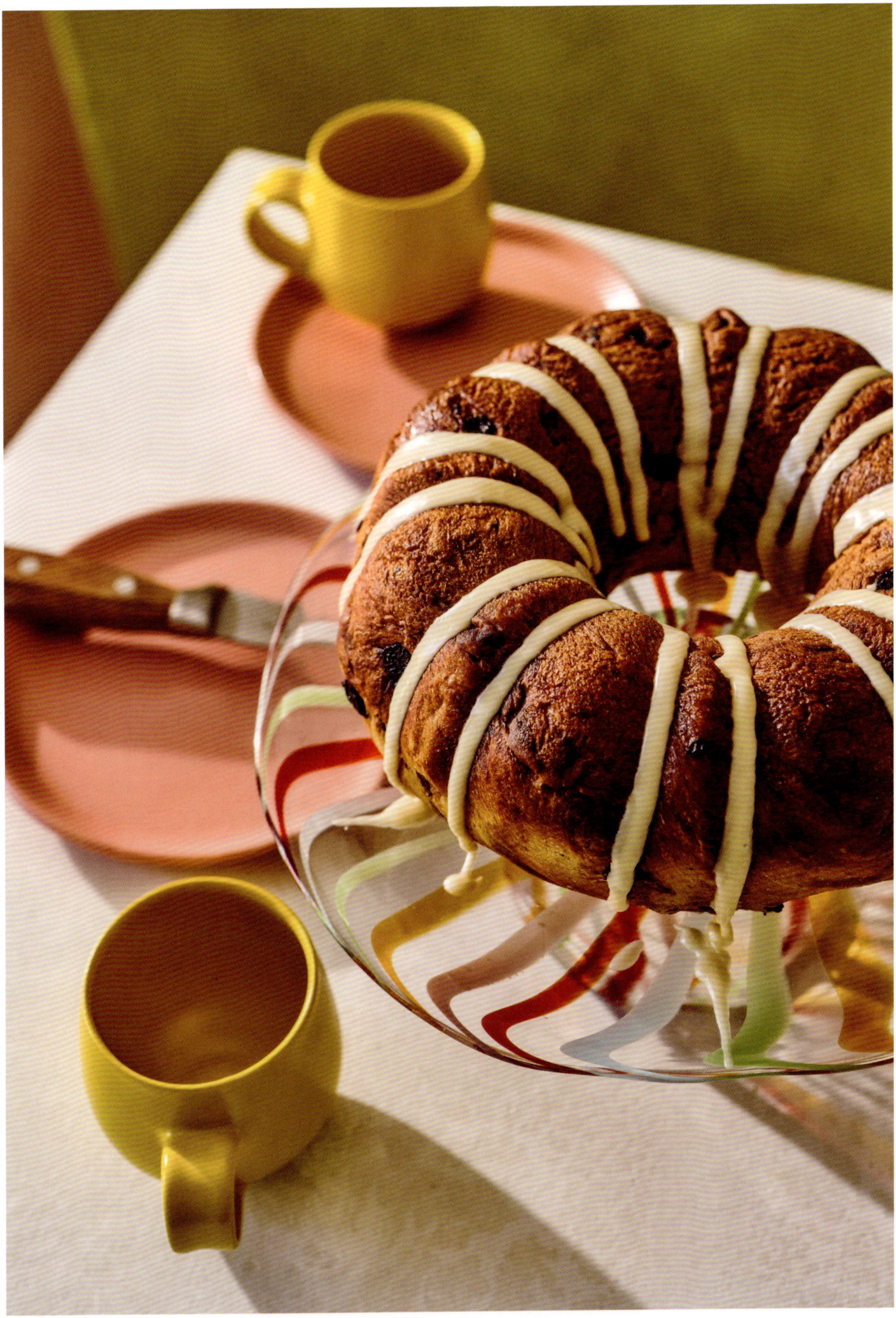

Lemon Easter Bread

A sweet, enriched bread that takes a bit of time to rise and proof, but stick with it and don't be tempted to rush these stages. It has a beautiful lemon curd swirled through the dough, so you get that lovely tang of lemon with every bite.

12 slices

Dough
4 cups (500g) bread flour, plus extra to dust
1¼ tsp (7g) fine salt
¼ cup (50g) superfine sugar
1 × ¼-oz (7g) packet instant yeast
Finely grated zest of 2 lemons
3 large eggs, at room temperature, beaten
½ cup plus 1 tbsp (140g) warm milk
1½ sticks (180g) unsalted butter, diced and softened

Lemon curd filling
Finely grated zest and juice of 4 lemons
scant 1 cup (190g) superfine sugar
7 tbsp (100g) unsalted butter
3 large eggs, plus an extra yolk, beaten

To glaze and finish
1 large egg, beaten
7 tbsp (100g) apricot preserves
4 tsp (20ml) water
scant 1 cup (100g) sliced almonds, toasted

1. Place the flour, salt, sugar, yeast, lemon zest, eggs and warm milk in a stand mixer fitted with the dough hook and mix slowly for 5 minutes. Increase the speed to medium and mix for a further 10 minutes.

2. With the mixer on medium speed, gradually add the softened butter and mix for 4 minutes until incorporated. The dough should be quite soft and elastic to the touch. Transfer to a large bowl, cover and place in the fridge to rise slowly for 2 hours.

3. In the meantime, make the lemon curd. Put the lemon zest and juice, sugar and butter into a heatproof bowl over a saucepan of simmering water. Stir until the butter is melted then take the pan off the heat. Whisk in the beaten eggs and extra yolk then place the bowl back over the simmering water. Stir for 10–15 minutes until the mixture thickens enough to coat the back of the spoon; don't let it boil or it will split. Remove from the heat and leave to cool.

4. Line a baking sheet with parchment paper. Tip the risen dough out onto a lightly floured surface and punch down by folding the dough inwards repeatedly to knock out the air. Now roll the dough out to a rectangle, 16 × 8 inches, with a long side facing you. Spread the lemon curd evenly all over the surface. Starting at a long side, roll the dough up to enclose the filling and press the edges to seal. Roll slightly to even out.

5. Cut the dough roll into 12 even slices. Lay these, cut side up, on the lined baking sheet in neat rows, about ¼ inch apart (i.e. close enough so that when they rise and bake, their sides will be touching). Cover and leave to proof for 2 hours.

6. Heat your oven to 350°F.

7. Brush the dough spirals with beaten egg and bake for 20–25 minutes until golden brown. Meanwhile, in a small saucepan, warm the apricot preserves with the water to make a glaze, then pass through a strainer into a bowl.

8. As you take the baking sheet out of the oven, brush the buns with the apricot glaze and top with the toasted almonds. Transfer to a wire rack to cool.

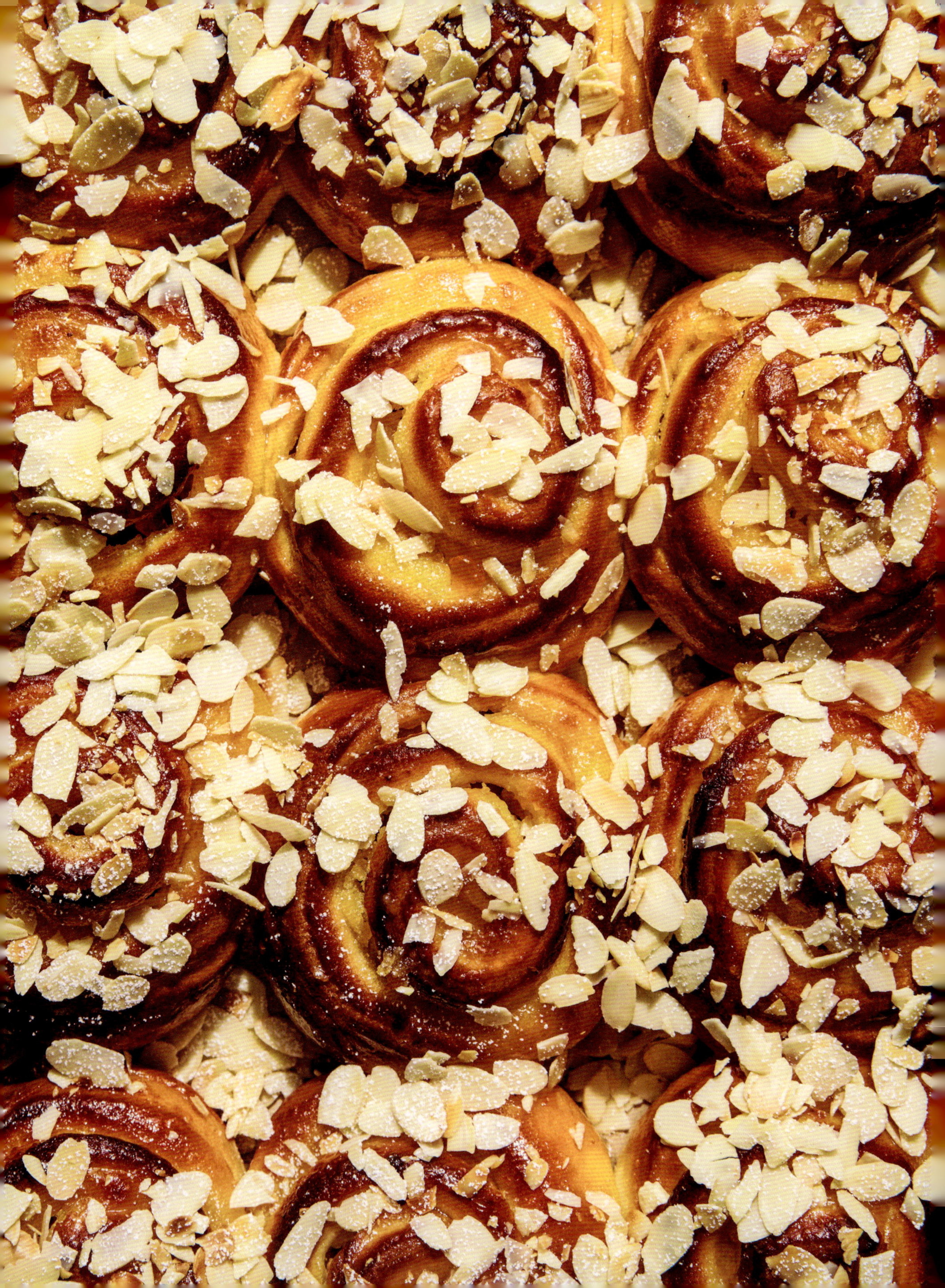

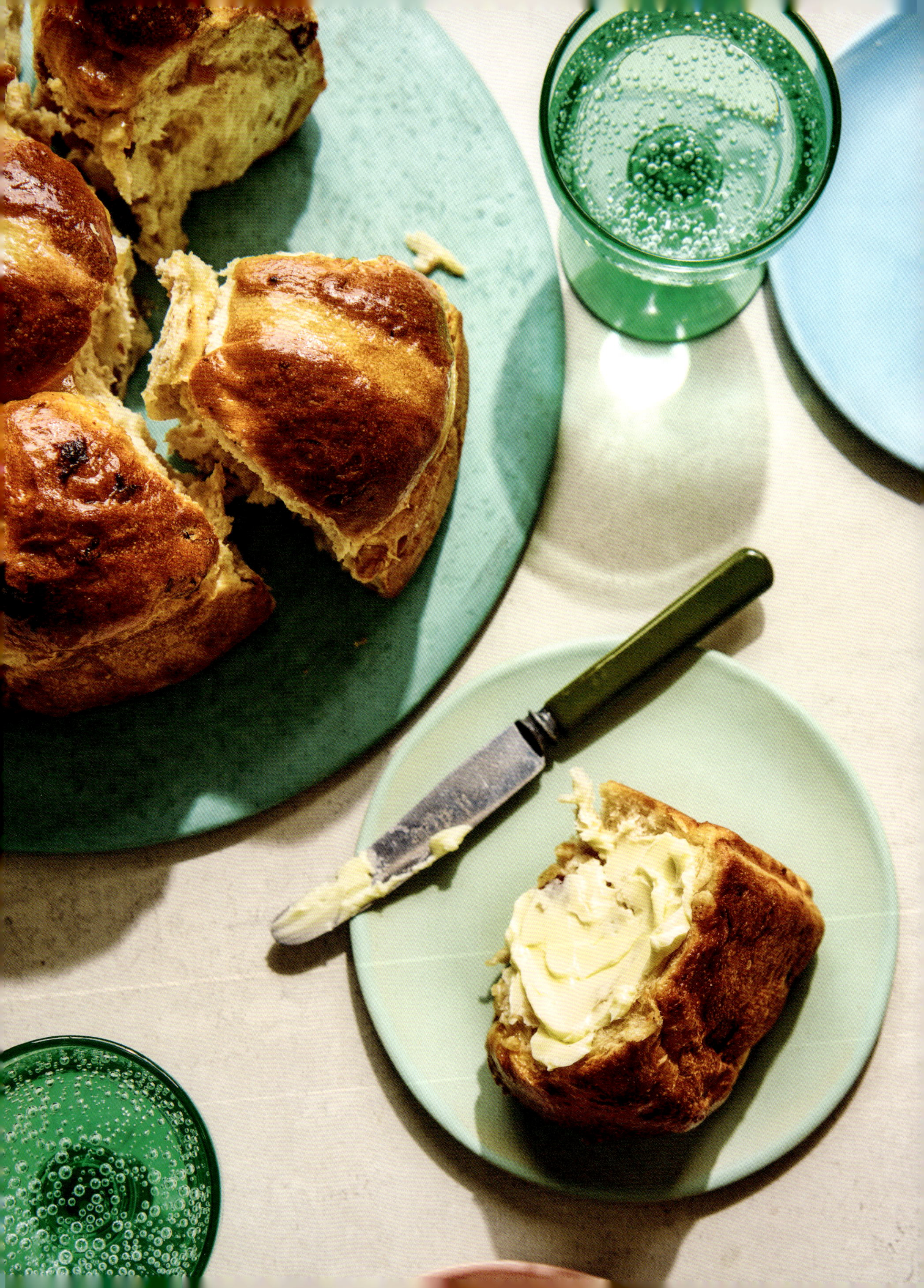

Hot Cross Bun Loaf

I'll let you into a secret: I actually make hot cross buns all year round. I love them! These apple, orange and dried fruit buns have been made into a large loaf, almost like a pull-apart bread. I like to toast thick slices and spread them generously with butter.

10 slices

Dough
4 cups (500g) bread flour, plus extra to dust
1¼ tsp (7g) fine salt
¼ cup (50g) superfine sugar
1 × ¼-oz (7g) packet instant yeast
1¼ cups plus 1 tbsp (310g) warm whole milk
3 tbsp (40g) unsalted butter, diced and softened

Filling
1 orange
1 Granny Smith apple
1¼ cups (150g) raisins
scant ¼ cup (80g) diced candied peel (preferably a mixture of lemon and orange)
2 tsp ground cinnamon

Cross
¾ cup plus 1 tbsp (100g) all-purpose flour
⅓ cup (80g) water

Sugar syrup
½ cup (100g) superfine sugar
7 tbsp (100g) boiling water

To serve
Butter, for spreading

1. Put the flour, salt, sugar, yeast and warm milk into a stand mixer fitted with the dough hook and mix on a low speed for 5 minutes. Increase the speed to medium, add the butter and mix for a further 10 minutes until you have a soft, elastic dough. Cover the bowl and leave the dough to rise for 2 hours.

2. Meanwhile, finely grate the zest from the orange and set aside. Slice off all the peel and pith from the orange then cut between the membranes to release the segments; roughly chop these. Peel and grate the apple, avoiding the core.

3. Add the orange zest and chopped segments, grated apple, raisins, diced peel and ground cinnamon to the dough and mix on a low speed for 3 minutes. Re-cover and leave to rise for another 2 hours.

4. Line a baking sheet with parchment paper. Tip the risen dough out onto a lightly floured surface and punch out by folding the dough inwards repeatedly to knock out the air. Divide into 10 even-sized pieces and shape into balls.

5. Place one of the dough balls in the middle of the lined baking sheet and arrange the remaining balls around it, to create a circle of rolls. Cover and leave to proof for 2 hours until doubled in size and when lightly pressed with your finger the dough springs back.

6. Heat your oven to 400°F.

7. Meanwhile, for the cross, mix the flour and water together to form a smooth paste and place in a piping bag fitted with a plain piping tip (or snip the tip off the bag if using a paper one).

8. Once the hot cross bun round is risen, pipe one big cross, in confident solid lines, over the top. Bake in the oven for 20 minutes until golden brown. In the meantime, to make the sugar syrup, dissolve the sugar in the boiling water then leave to cool.

9. As you take the hot cross bun loaf out of the oven, brush the surface with the sugar syrup to glaze. Transfer to a wire rack and leave to cool completely before serving, with butter for spreading.

Celebrate

Crostata Pasquale

My Sardinian friend, Nino, gave me this family recipe. It's made with a classic Sardinian pastry, sweetened with condensed milk and flavored with vanilla. The rich ricotta filling is dotted with chocolate chips and orange zest, and it's topped with a beautiful lattice.

Serves 10

Pie dough

2¾ cups plus 2 tbsp (360g) '00' extra-fine plain flour, plus extra to dust

A pinch of fine salt

1½ sticks (180g) chilled unsalted butter, diced, plus a little extra, softened, to grease

½ cup (140g) sweetened condensed milk

½ tsp vanilla bean paste

Filling

2½ cups (22 oz/600g) good-quality whole milk ricotta

½ cup (150g) sweetened condensed milk

½ tsp vanilla bean paste

½ cup (100g) good-quality bittersweet chocolate baking chips

Finely grated zest of 1 orange

To glaze and finish

1 large egg, beaten

Confectioners' sugar, to dust

1. To make the pie dough, combine the flour and salt in a large bowl, then add the diced butter and rub in with your fingers until the mixture is a sandy texture. Add the sweetened condensed milk and vanilla paste and mix to combine and form a smooth dough. Wrap in plastic wrap and place in the fridge to rest for 30 minutes.

2. To make the filling, pass the ricotta through a fine strainer into a bowl. Add the sweetened condensed milk, vanilla paste, chocolate chips and orange zest and stir until evenly combined.

3. Heat your oven to 350°F. Grease a shallow 8-inch springform pan with butter and line the base with parchment paper.

4. Take the dough out of the fridge and divide in half. Roll out one half on a lightly floured surface to a 12-inch round and use to line the base and sides of the prepared springform pan, forming a pie crust.

5. Roll out the other half of the dough to an ⅛ inch thick and cut strips, 9 inches long and ½ inch wide, to decorate the top of the tart.

6. Transfer the filling to the pie crust and spread evenly. Arrange the strips of pie dough over the surface in a lattice pattern, brushing them with the beaten egg to glaze and trimming off the excess. Bake in the oven for 50 minutes until the filling is set and the pastry is golden.

7. Leave the tart in the pan for 5 minutes, then carefully release from the pan and place on a wire rack to cool.

8. Before serving, sift a little confectioners' sugar over the surface of the tart to finish. This rich tart is absolutely delicious but it's quite sweet so you'll only need a small slice.

Also pictured overleaf

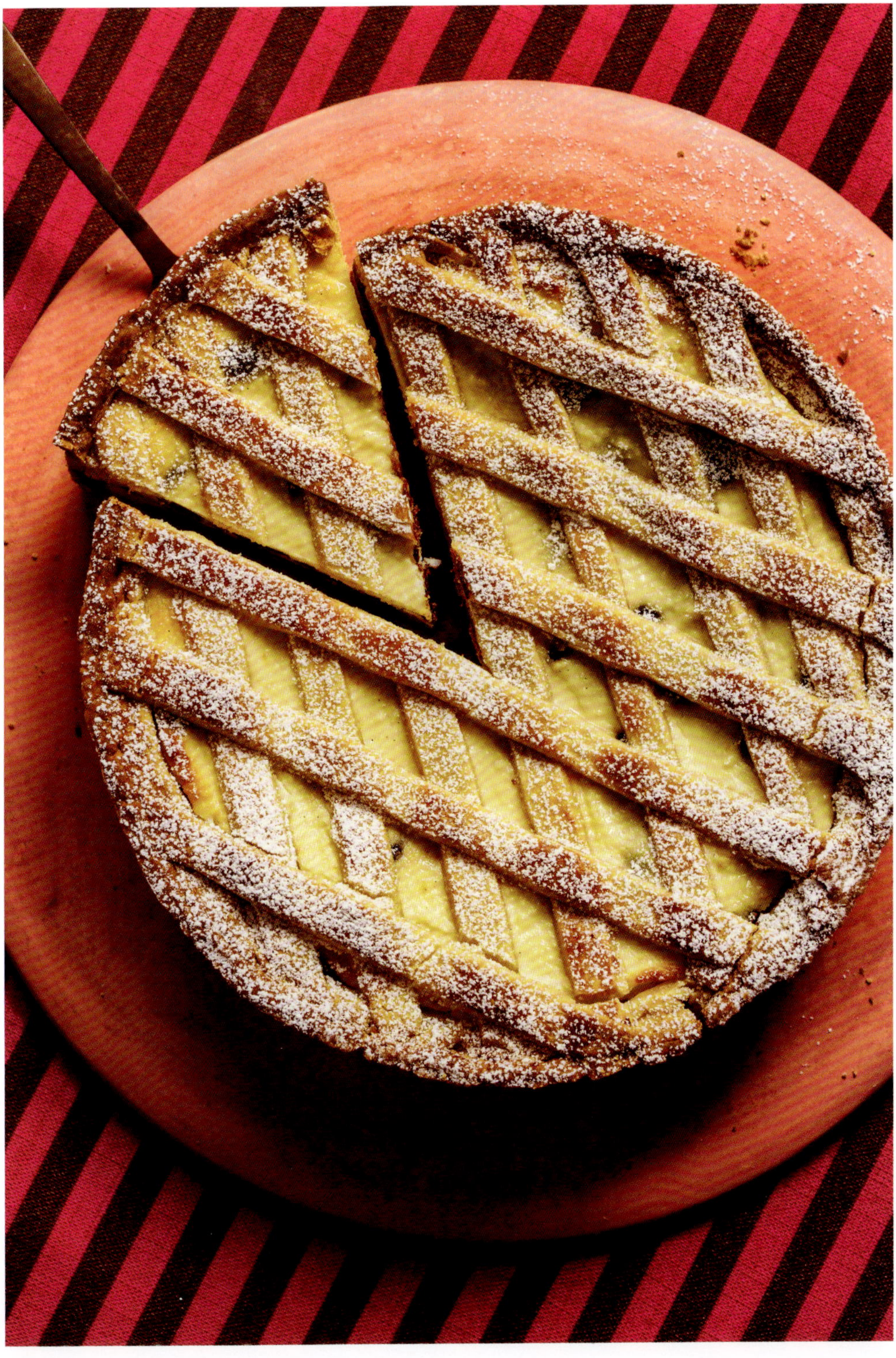

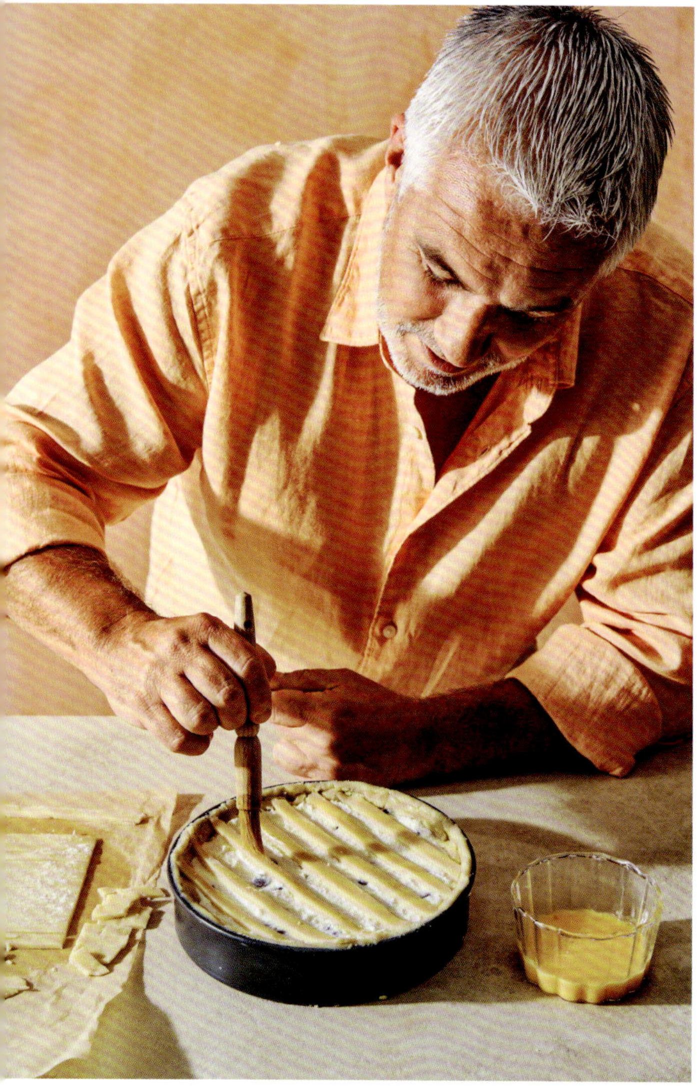
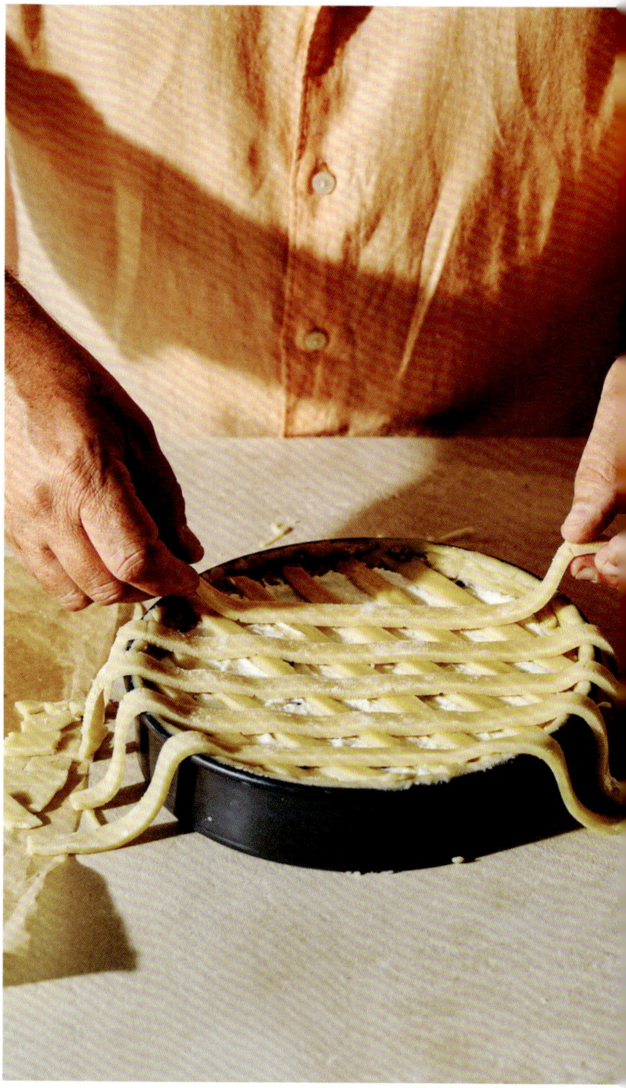

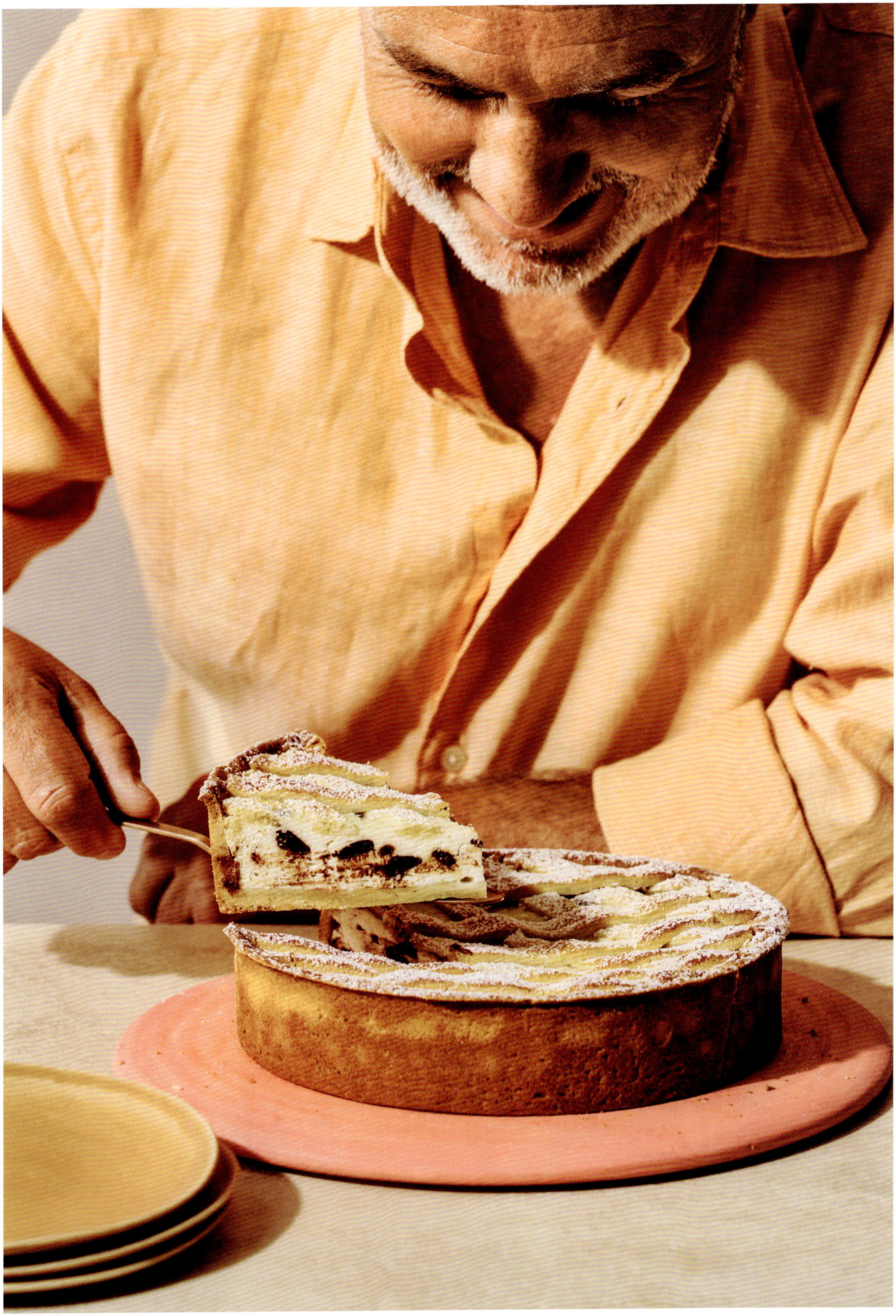

Custard Tarts

We used to make pans and pans of these in my dad's bakery. With their sweet pastry and rich custard filling, they were always very popular.
Be careful getting them into the oven as they can be quite wobbly.

Makes 12

Pie dough
1¾ cup plus 1 tbsp (225g) all-purpose flour, plus extra to dust
3 tbsp confectioners' sugar
1 stick plus 1 tbsp (125g) chilled unsalted butter, diced, plus extra to grease
1 large egg
½ tsp lemon juice
1–2 tbsp ice-cold water

Custard filling
¾ cup (175g) whole milk
¾ cup plus 3 tbsp (225g) heavy cream
1 cinnamon stick
7 large egg yolks
⅓ cup (70g) superfine sugar
½ tsp ground cinnamon

1. To make the pie dough, mix the flour and confectioners' sugar together in a large bowl. Add the butter and rub in using your fingers until the mixture resembles fine breadcrumbs. Make a well in the center. In a small bowl, beat the egg with the lemon juice and 1 tbsp cold water then pour into the well and mix into the flour, using a dinner knife.

2. Bring the pie dough together using one hand, adding a little more cold water if needed to do so. Gently knead the pie dough into a ball and flatten to a disc. Wrap in plastic wrap and refrigerate for at least 20 minutes.

3. Heat your oven to 350°F and place a large baking sheet inside to heat up. Lightly grease a 12-cup muffin pan with butter.

4. On a lightly floured surface, roll out the pie dough to an ⅛ inch thick. Using a 4-inch biscuit cutter, cut out circles and use to line the muffin pan. Re-roll the pastry trimmings to cut more circles as needed. Place in the fridge to rest while you prepare the filling.

5. To make the custard filling, pour the milk and cream into a saucepan, add the cinnamon stick and slowly bring to a boil. Meanwhile, whisk the egg yolks and sugar together in a bowl until well blended. Pour the creamy milk onto the whisked mixture, stirring as you do so. Strain the mixture through a fine strainer into a pitcher and let settle for a few minutes.

6. Take the muffin pan from the fridge and carefully pour the custard mixture into the tart crusts to fill them almost to the brim. Sprinkle a little ground cinnamon over each tart. Carefully transfer to the oven and place on the hot baking sheet. Bake for 25–30 minutes until the pastry is golden and the custard is just set and caramelized in places.

7. Remove from the oven and leave the tarts in the muffin pan for at least 15 minutes before carefully removing and transferring them to a wire rack to cool. Enjoy warm or cold.

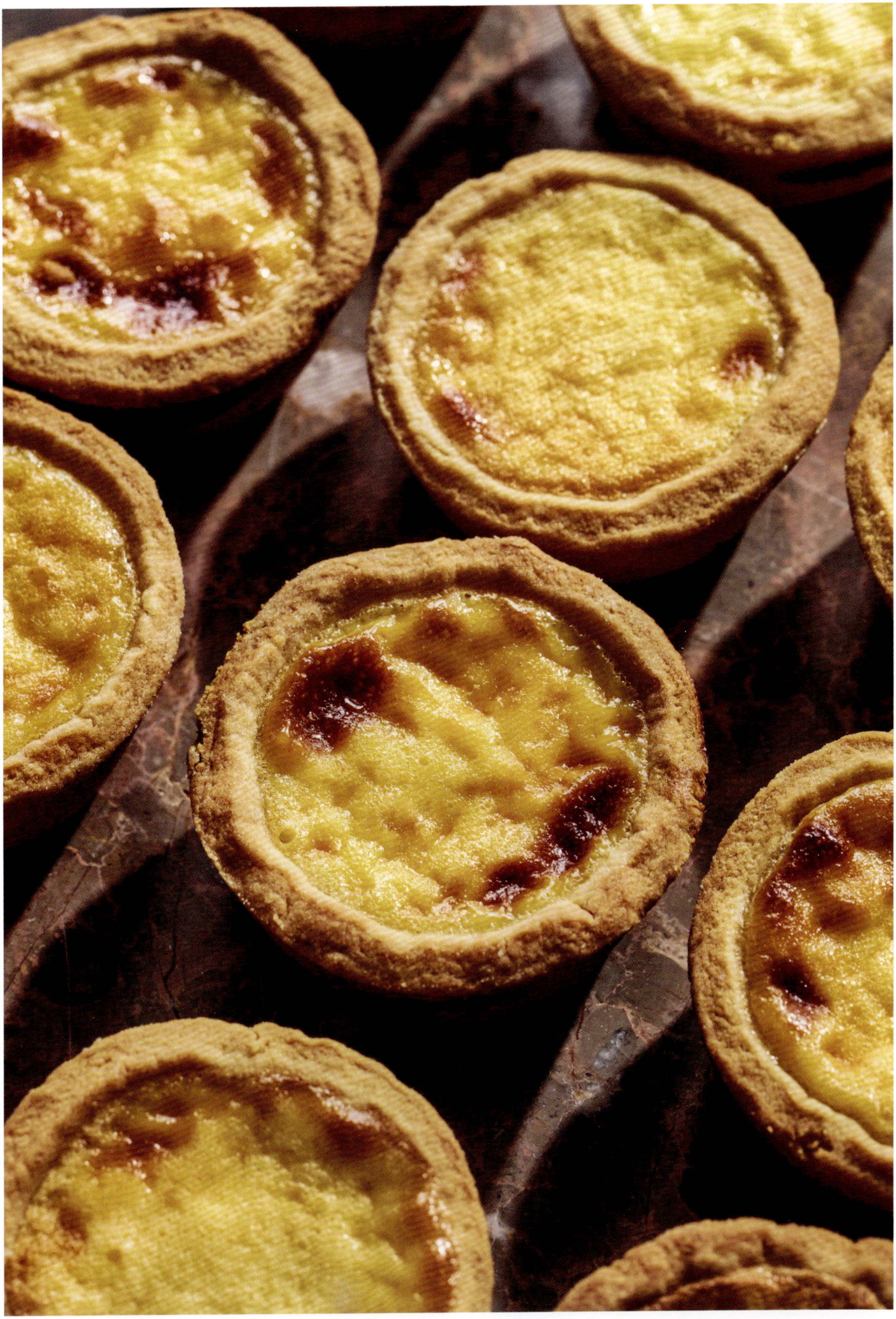

Rhubarb and Apple Crumble

This is a great comforting dessert for colder, early spring days, when tender, pink, hothouse rhubarb is around. I love to have it with loads of custard or crème anglaise but it's also delicious with ice cream.

Serves 4

Crumble topping

¾ cup plus 1 tbsp (100g) all-purpose flour

heaping ½ cup (50g) quick-cooking oats

1 stick plus 1 tbsp (125g) chilled unsalted butter, cut into cubes, plus extra, softened, to grease

3 tbsp (35g) turbinado sugar

3 tbsp (35g) superfine sugar

Fruit

1 lb (450g) Granny Smith apples

2 tbsp water

3 tbsp superfine sugar

1 lb (450g) rhubarb, trimmed

To serve

Vanilla ice cream, heavy cream, crème anglaise or custard

1. Heat your oven to 400°F and grease a shallow ovenproof dish, about 7 × 11 inches.

2. To make the crumble topping, combine the flour and oats in a large bowl, add the butter and rub in with your fingers until the mixture resembles coarse breadcrumbs. Add both sugars and stir through. Sprinkle with a little cold water and rub through until you have a lumpy, crumbly mixture. Place in the freezer to chill for 10 minutes, or in the fridge until you're ready to bake.

3. For the filling, peel, quarter and core the apples and then cut into chunks. Place in a saucepan with the water and 2 tbsp of the sugar. Cook over a medium heat until the apples begin to soften but retain their shape, adding a little extra water if needed. Meanwhile, cut the rhubarb into ¾-inch lengths.

4. Spoon the cooked apple into the prepared ovenproof dish, distribute the rhubarb over the top and sprinkle with the remaining 1 tbsp sugar. Scatter the crumble over the top of the fruit but don't press it down. Bake in the oven for about 30 minutes until the crumble topping is golden brown and the fruit is bubbling up around it.

5. Remove from the oven and leave to stand for 10 minutes to let the crumble settle. Serve with ice cream, heavy cream, crème anglaise or custard.

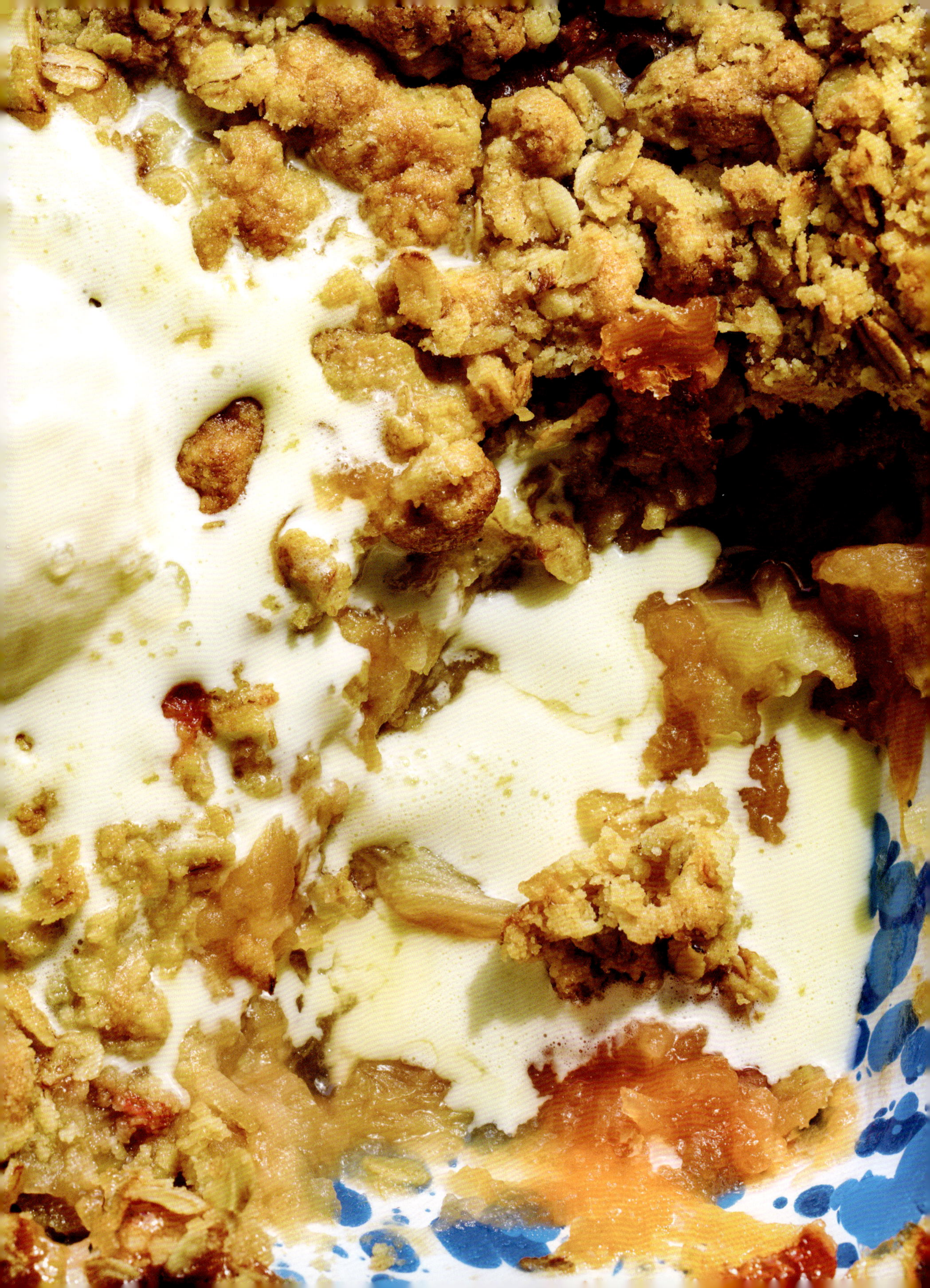

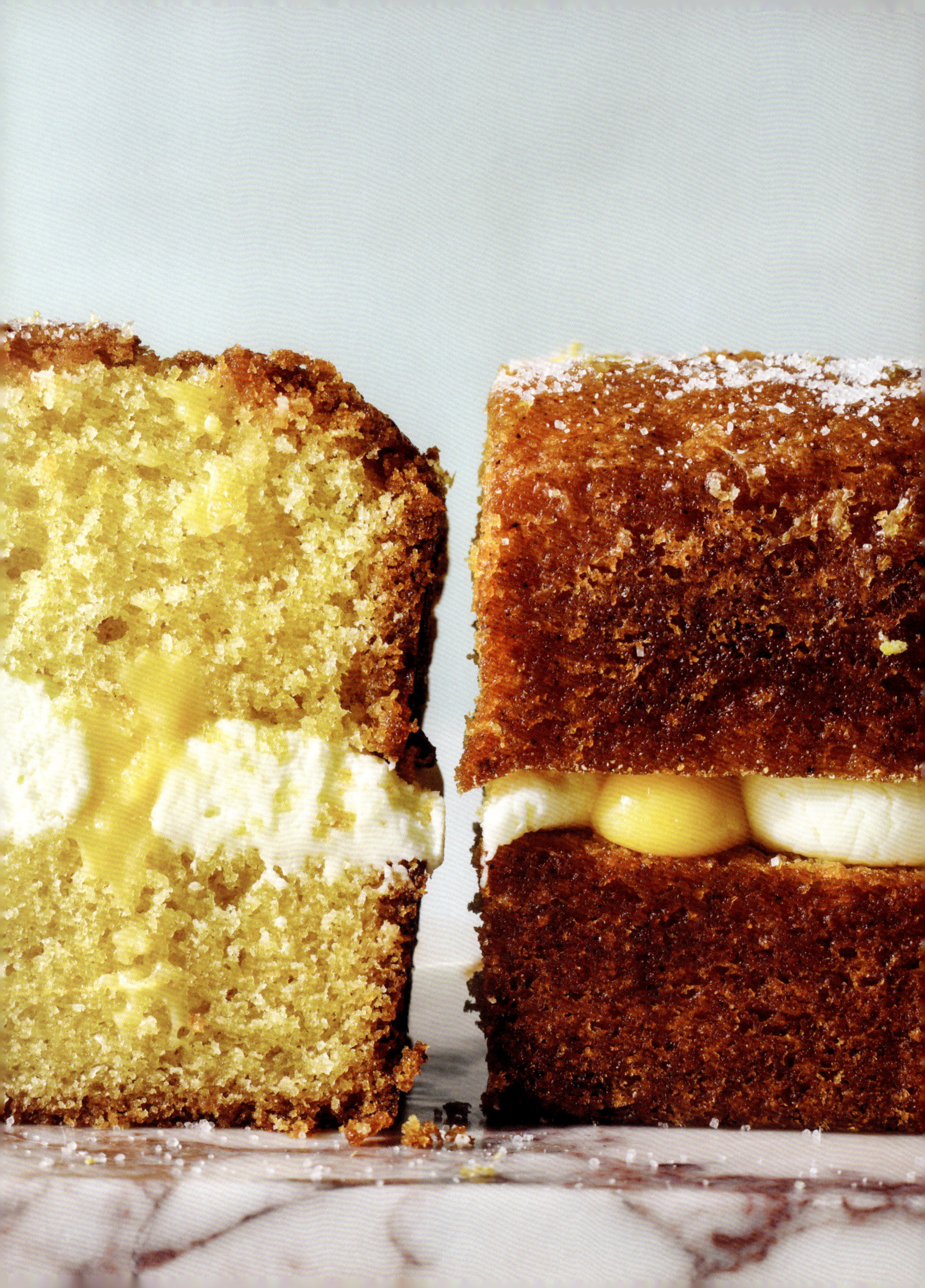

Lemon Drizzle Loaf Cake

I love a good lemon drizzle! For an extra-indulgent spin on the classic cake, this one is layered with lemon curd and a lemon buttercream filling. The lemon drizzle infuses the delicate sponge with its intense flavor and makes it deliciously moist. You can use orange instead, or any other citrus fruit.

8–10 slices

1½ sticks (175g) unsalted butter, softened, plus extra to grease

¾ cup plus 2 tbsp (175g) superfine sugar

Finely grated zest and juice of 2 lemons

3 large eggs, at room temperature

1⅓ cups plus 1 tbsp (175g) all-purpose flour

1¾ tsp baking powder

A pinch of fine salt

About 2 tbsp milk

½ cup (100g) granulated sugar

Lemon curd filling

Finely grated zest and juice of 2 large lemons

½ cup (100g) superfine sugar

3 tbsp (50g) unsalted butter, diced

3 large eggs, plus 1 extra yolk, beaten

Lemon buttercream

5 tbsp (80g) unsalted butter, softened

Finely grated zest of ½ lemon

2½ cups (250g) confectioners' sugar, sifted

2 tbsp milk

1. Heat your oven to 350°F. Grease and line a 2-lb (or 2-pound) loaf pan with parchment paper.

2. In a large bowl, beat the butter, superfine sugar and half the lemon zest together using a hand mixer until light and fluffy. Add the eggs, one at a time, beating until well combined before adding the next.

3. Sift the flour, baking powder and salt together over the mixture. Fold in carefully, using a spatula or large metal spoon, then add enough milk to achieve a dropping consistency (i.e. the mixture just falls off the spoon).

4. Spoon the mixture into the prepared pan and gently level the surface. Bake in the oven for 45–55 minutes until the loaf cake is risen and a cake tester inserted into the center comes out clean.

5. To make the lemon drizzle, in a small pitcher, mix the lemon juice with the remaining grated zest and the granulated sugar. While the cake is still warm, prick holes all over the top using a toothpick and trickle over the lemon drizzle. Let the cake cool before removing from the pan.

6. In the meantime, make the lemon curd. Put the lemon zest and juice, sugar and butter into a heatproof bowl over a saucepan of simmering water. Stir until the butter is melted then take the pan off the heat. Whisk in the beaten eggs and extra yolk then place the bowl back over the simmering water. Stir for 10–15 minutes until the mixture thickens enough to coat the back of the spoon; don't let it boil or it will split. Remove from the heat and leave to cool. Once cooled, spoon into a piping bag fitted with a ½-inch plain piping tip.

7. To make the lemon buttercream, put the butter, lemon zest and confectioners' sugar into a bowl and beat with a hand mixer to combine. Add the milk and beat until smooth. Spoon into a piping bag fitted with a ½-inch plain piping tip.

8. To assemble, slice the cake in half horizontally, Pipe alternate blobs of buttercream and lemon curd on the bottom layer and sandwich together with the top cake layer.

Brownie Bars

Oreos work brilliantly in brownies, adding crunch, flavor and their sweet creamy filling. They look great, too. The little chunks of chocolate in the filling also stay intact, giving extra texture. It's critical to never over-bake a brownie – you want that lovely bit of goo inside.

16 squares

7oz (200g) bittersweet chocolate, broken into chunks

1¾ sticks (200g) unsalted butter, diced, plus extra to grease

½ cup plus 1 tbsp (115g) light brown sugar

¾ cup (150g) superfine sugar

3 large eggs, at room temperature, beaten

1 cup plus 2 tbsp (150g) all-purpose flour

1 tsp salt

¼ cup (50g) good-quality white chocolate baking chips

¼ cup (50g) good-quality dark chocolate baking chips

22 chocolate sandwich cookies (I use Oreos)

1. Heat your oven to 350°F. Grease an 8-inch square cake pan and line with parchment paper.

2. Put the bittersweet chocolate chunks and butter into a saucepan and heat gently until melted. Add both sugars and stir until dissolved. Transfer to a bowl, add the beaten eggs and mix with a balloon whisk until smoothly combined.

3. Sift the flour and salt together over the mixture and then fold through until thoroughly combined.

4. Transfer half the mixture to the prepared pan and smooth it out to the edges and into the corners. Sprinkle over half the white and bittersweet chocolate chips. Arrange 16 cookies in lines across the batter.

5. Pour the remaining brownie mixture evenly over the cookie layer, smoothing it out gently. Sprinkle the rest of the chocolate chips over the surface. Break the remaining 6 cookies into small pieces and scatter over the top.

6. Bake in the oven for 25–30 minutes until the brownie is set at the edges but still slightly wobbly in the middle.

7. Leave to cool completely in the pan, then chill in the fridge overnight for best results. Cut into 16 squares and enjoy! Any brownies that are not eaten straight away can be kept in an airtight container at room temperature for up to 5 days.

Also pictured overleaf

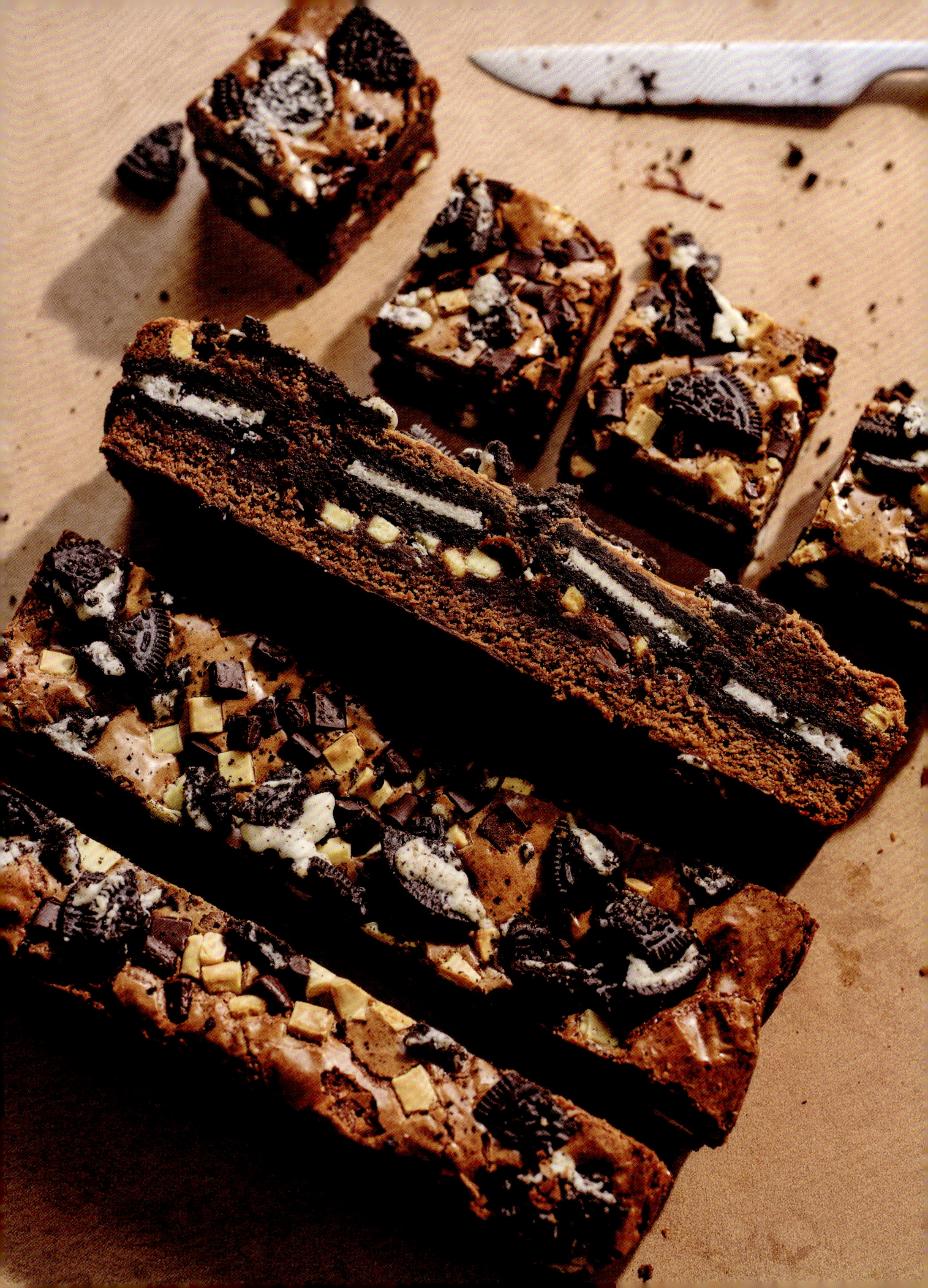

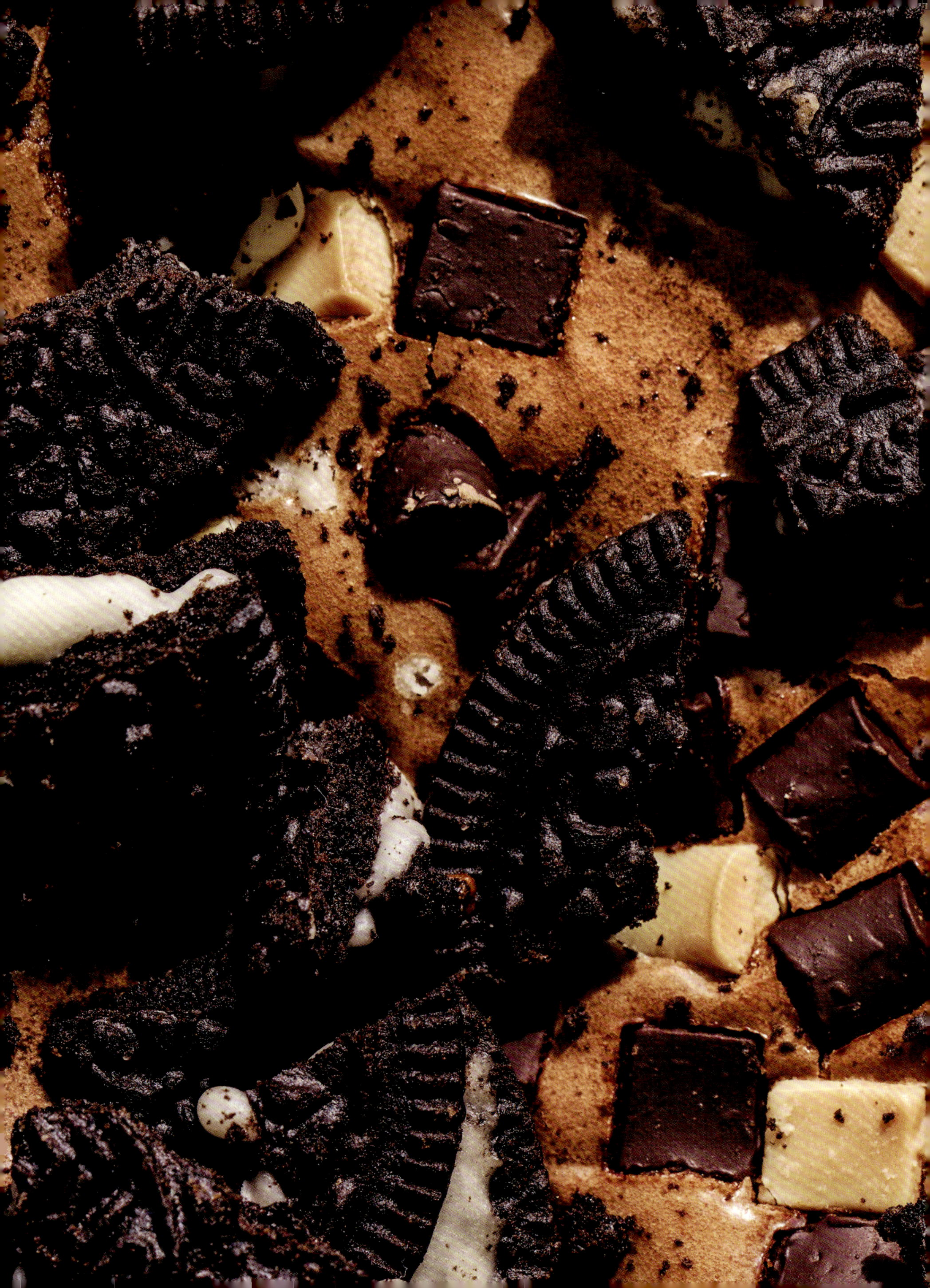

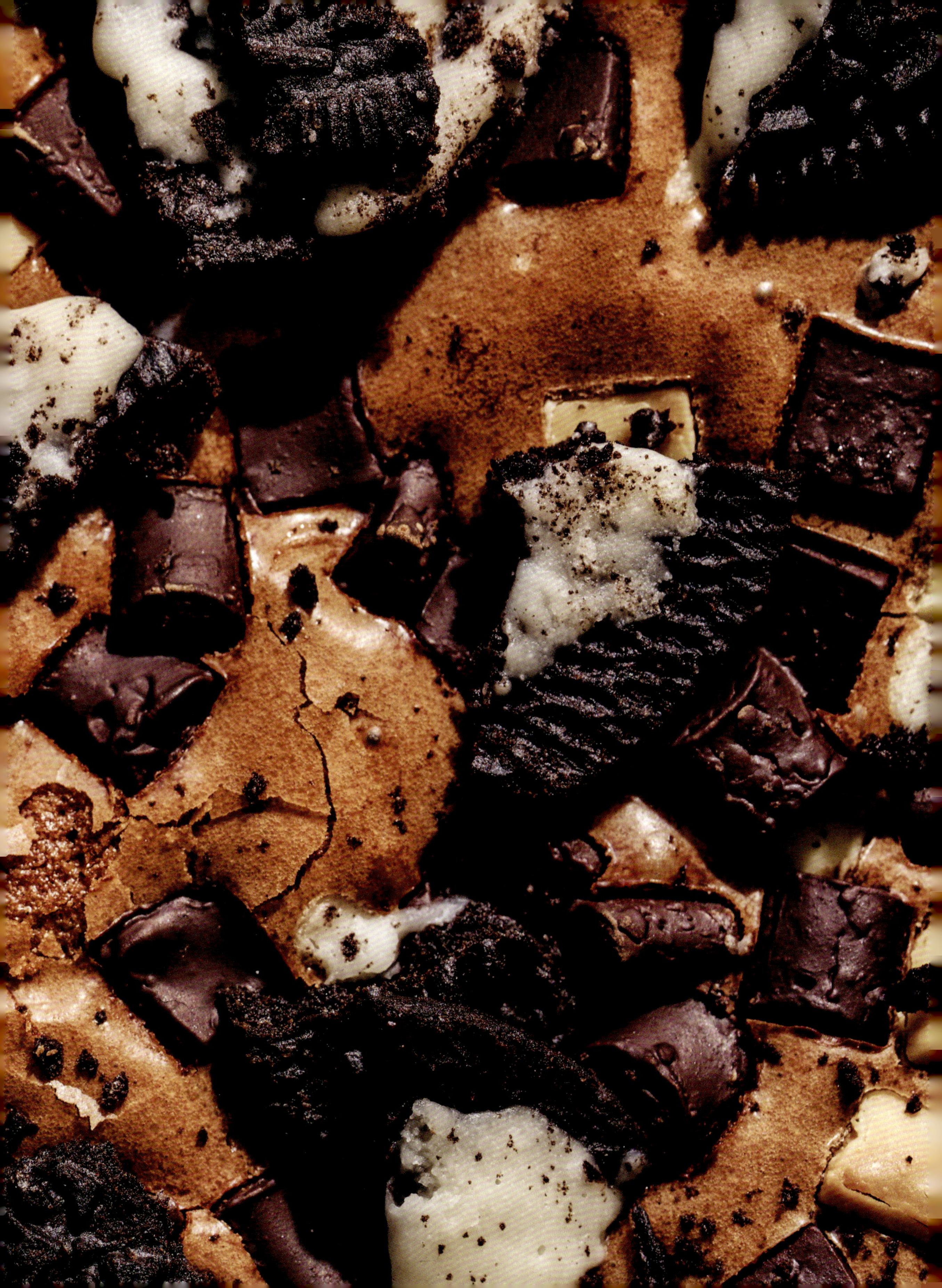

Chocolate Easter Nests

These are probably one of the first things you make when you're four years old – I used to make them with my mother and I'd always get into trouble for eating too many! Sweet and chocolatey, they're perfect for parties and bake sales.

Makes 12

8–10 Shredded Wheat (large biscuits) or 8 cups (200g) Rice Krispies

6 oz (175g) milk chocolate

6 oz (175g) bittersweet chocolate

1 stick plus 5 tbsp (185g) unsalted butter

⅔ cup (185g) Lyle's golden syrup

Topping
5–7 oz (150–200g) candy-coated mini chocolate eggs

1. Line a 12-cup muffin pan with paper muffin cups.

2. Put the cereal into a large bowl and crush the Shredded Wheat, if using. Finely chop all the chocolate.

3. Put the butter and golden syrup into a medium saucepan and heat gently, stirring occasionally, until the butter is melted and the mixture is smoothly combined. Remove from the heat, add the chocolate and stir until it is melted and the mixture is smooth.

4. Pour the chocolate mix over the cereal and stir until well combined. Spoon the mixture into the paper muffin cups, dividing it evenly. Make a slight hollow in the center with the back of a teaspoon.

5. Arrange 3 candy-coated eggs in each chocolate nest hollow. Leave the nests to set firmly before serving.

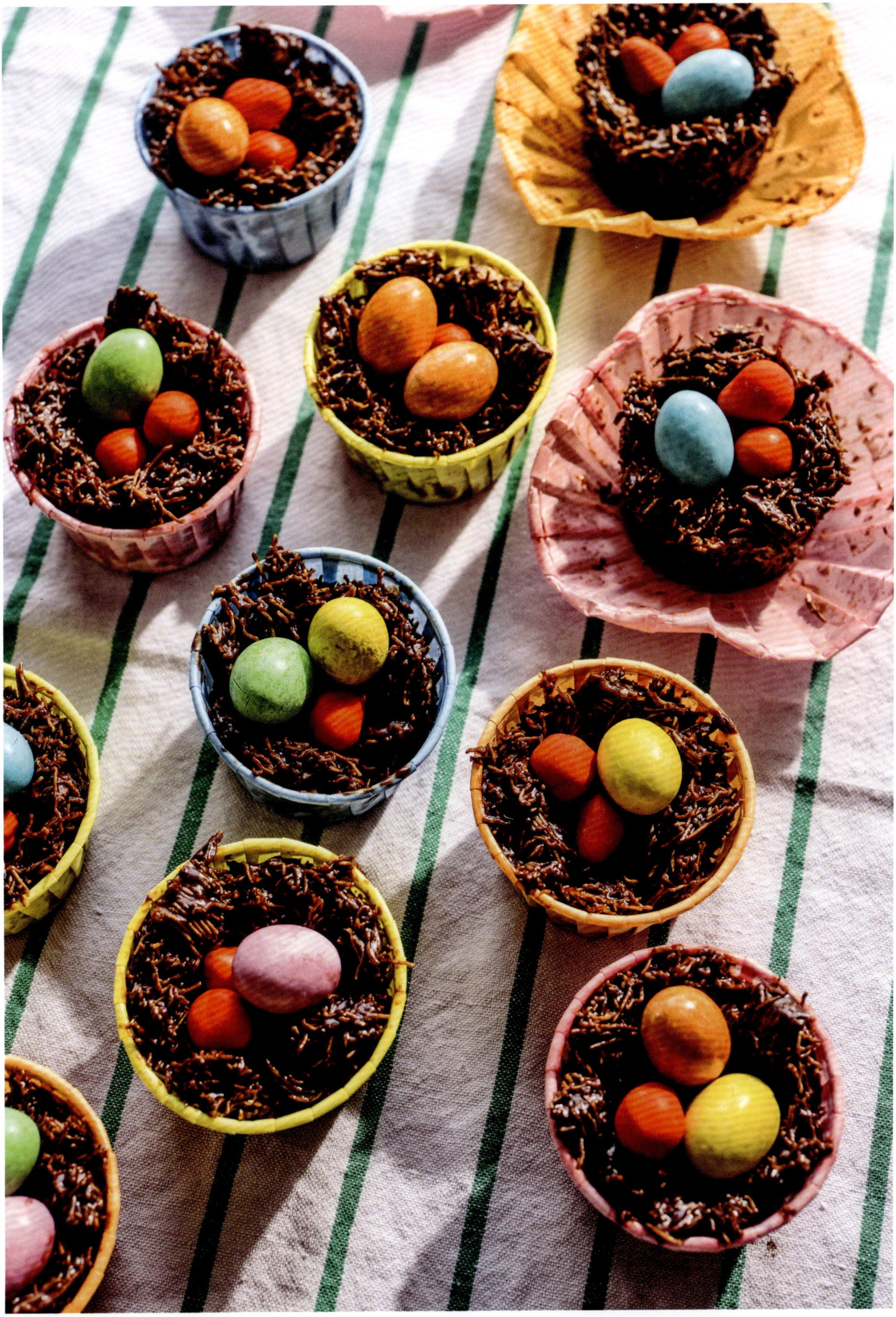

Tsoureki

A Greek Easter bread flavored with two distinctive spices: mahleb, which has an almond-like flavor with a hint of rose; and mastika, which has a strong aniseed taste. Here, I've made individual breads rather than a whole loaf, and topped them with quail rather than hen eggs.

Makes 4

Dough
4 cups (500g) bread flour, plus extra to dust
1¼ tsp (7g) fine salt
3¾ tsp instant yeast
1 tsp mastika
1 tsp mahleb powder
1⅓ cups (320g) warm water
2 tbsp (30g) unsalted butter, diced and softened

To assemble
1 large egg, beaten, to glaze
½ cup (80g) sesame seeds
12 quail eggs
Red food coloring

1. Place the flour, salt, yeast, mastika, mahleb and warm water in a stand mixer fitted with the dough hook and mix slowly for 5 minutes. Increase the speed to medium speed and mix for a further 10 minutes.

2. With the mixer on medium speed, gradually add the softened butter to the dough and mix for 4 minutes until incorporated. The dough should be quite sticky and very elastic to the touch. Transfer the dough to a large bowl, cover and leave to rise for 2 hours.

3. Line a large baking sheet with parchment paper. Tip the risen dough out onto a lightly floured surface and punch down by folding the dough inwards repeatedly to knock out the air. Re-cover and leave to rise for a further 2 hours.

4. Divide the dough into 4 portions. Now divide each portion into 3 equal pieces and roll each of these into a rope, 12 inches in length. Press each trio of ropes together at one end and then braid them together. Press the other ends of the ropes together to seal.

5. Transfer the 4 braid to the baking sheet, spacing them well apart to give room for them to expand. Cover with plastic wrap and leave to proof for 1–2 hours until almost doubled in size.

6. Heat your oven to 400°F.

7. Lower the quail eggs into a saucepan of boiling water and par-boil for 3 minutes. Drain the eggs and pat dry with paper towels. Now paint the shells with red food coloring (to represent the blood of Christ).

8. Brush the loaves with beaten egg and sprinkle with sesame seeds. Place 3 painted quail eggs on each of the 4 loaves and gently press them into the dough. Bake in the oven for 25 minutes until golden brown.

9. Transfer the breads to a wire rack and leave to cool before serving.

Also pictured overleaf

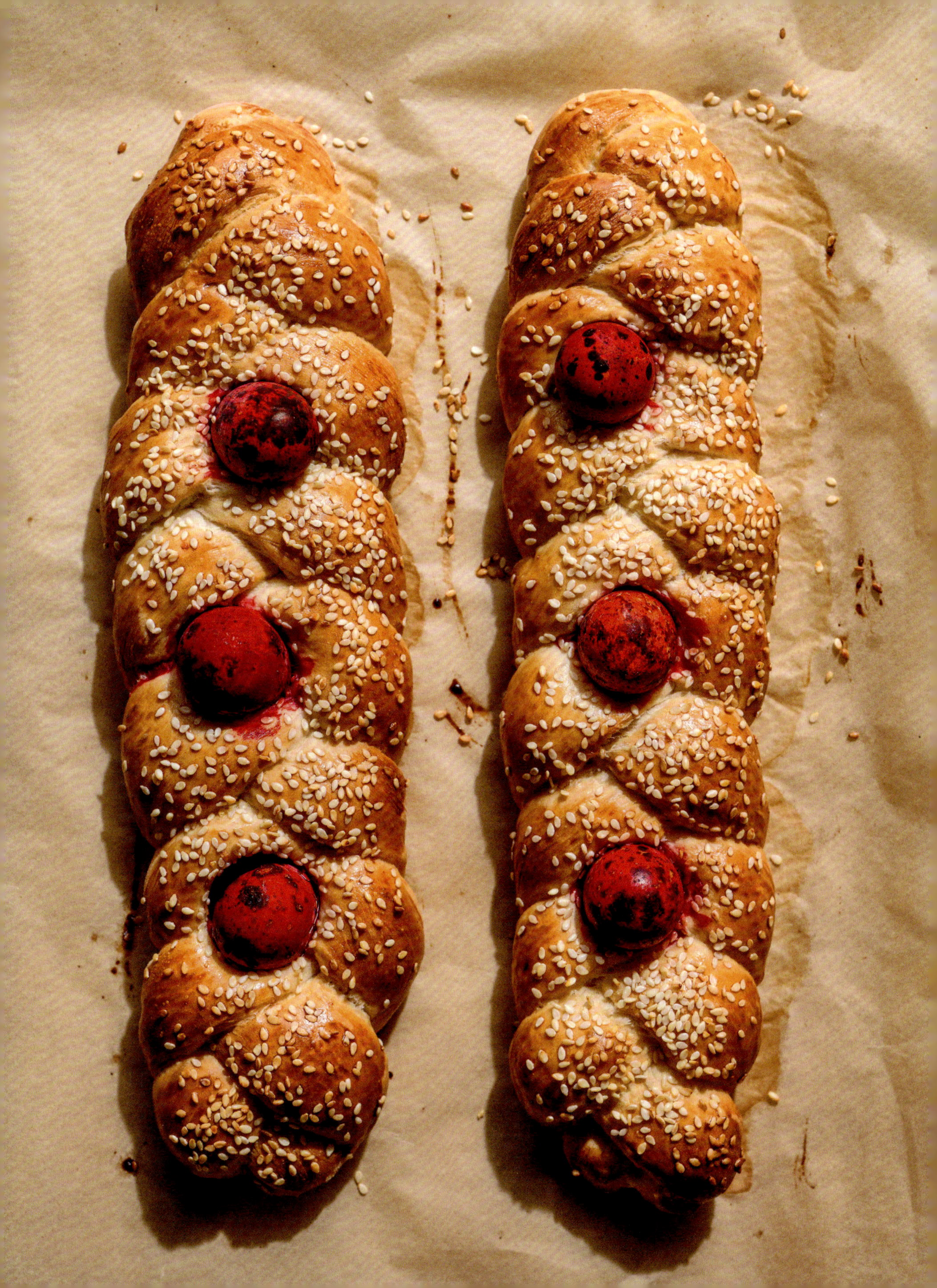

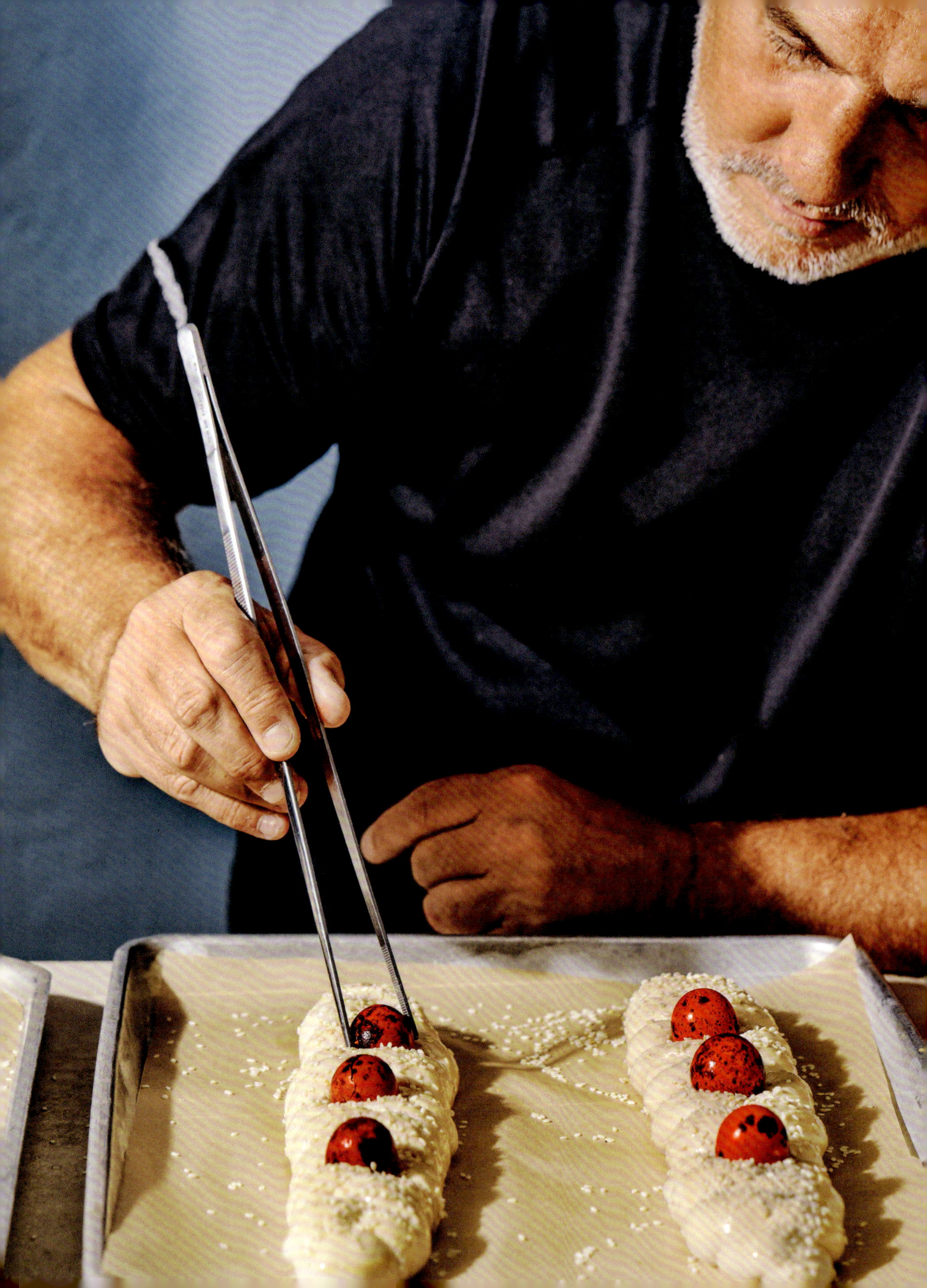

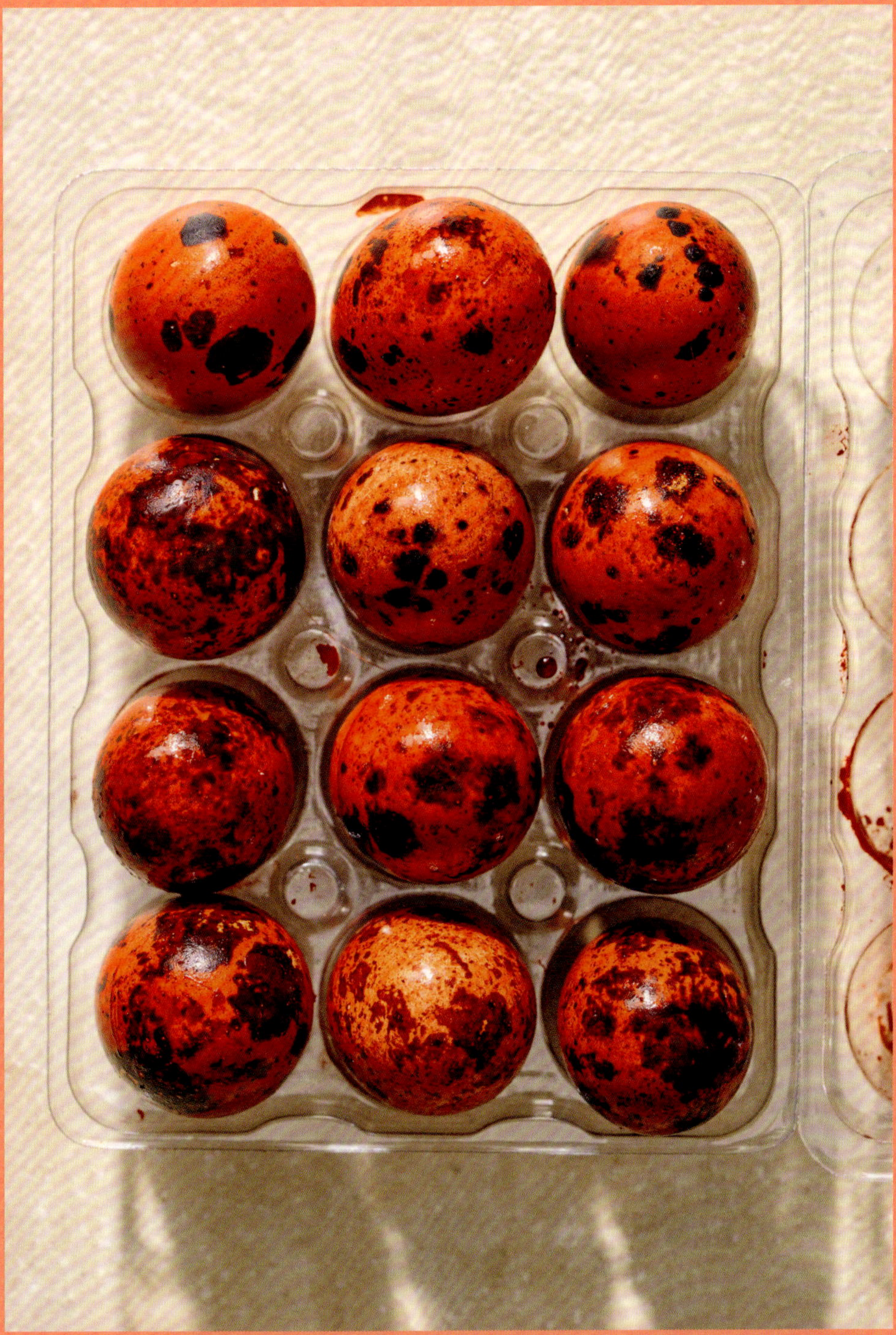

St Patrick's Day Loaf

Soda bread is a great first intro into bread making. It's very easy, and as there's no yeast in the recipe you don't need to proof it. It can be made and on the table within an hour. Made with Guinness, molasses and buttermilk, and rolled in oats, this loaf tastes fantastic and goes really well with cheese.

Makes 1 loaf

⅓ cup plus 1 tbsp (50g) whole wheat pastry flour

3⅔ cups (450g) all-purpose flour, plus extra to dust

1 tsp (5g) fine salt

1 tsp (5g) baking soda

3 tbsp (50g) Guinness

3 tbsp (55g) molasses

1⅓ cups plus 2 tbsp (350g) buttermilk

Topping

1 cup (100g) quick-cooking oats

1 Heat your oven to 400°F and line a baking sheet with parchment paper.

2 Put the flours, salt and baking soda into a large bowl and stir together. Make a well in the center and add the Guinness, molasses and buttermilk. Mix with a dinner knife to combine and then use one hand to bring the dough together.

3 Tip the dough out onto a lightly floured surface and fold at least 6 times. Shape into a ball and roll in the oats to coat, then place on the lined baking sheet.

4 Using a large, sharp knife, cut a deep cross in the dough. Bake in the oven for 30 minutes until golden brown and the loaf sounds hollow when tapped on the base. Transfer to a wire rack to cool.

Also pictured overleaf

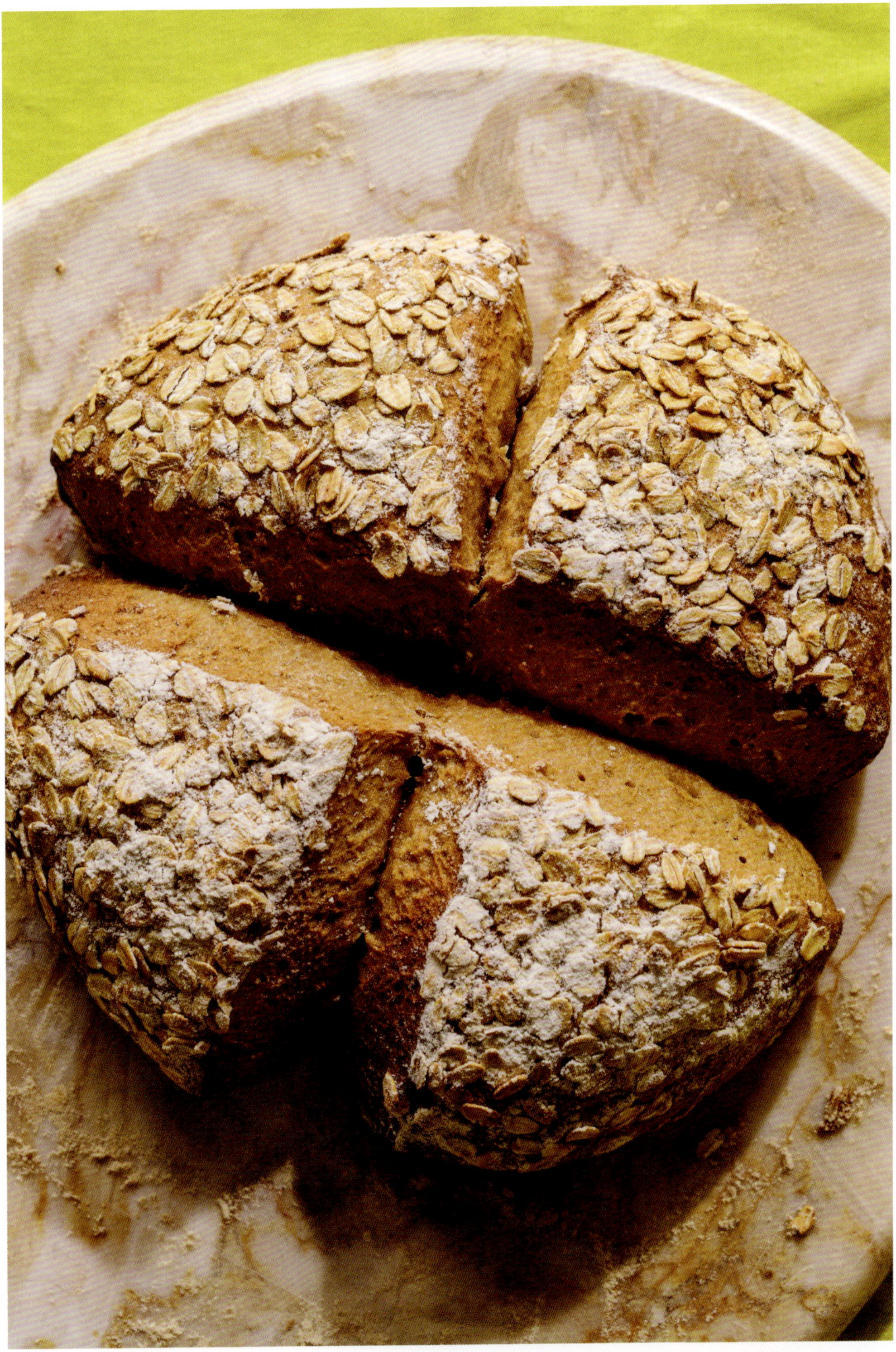

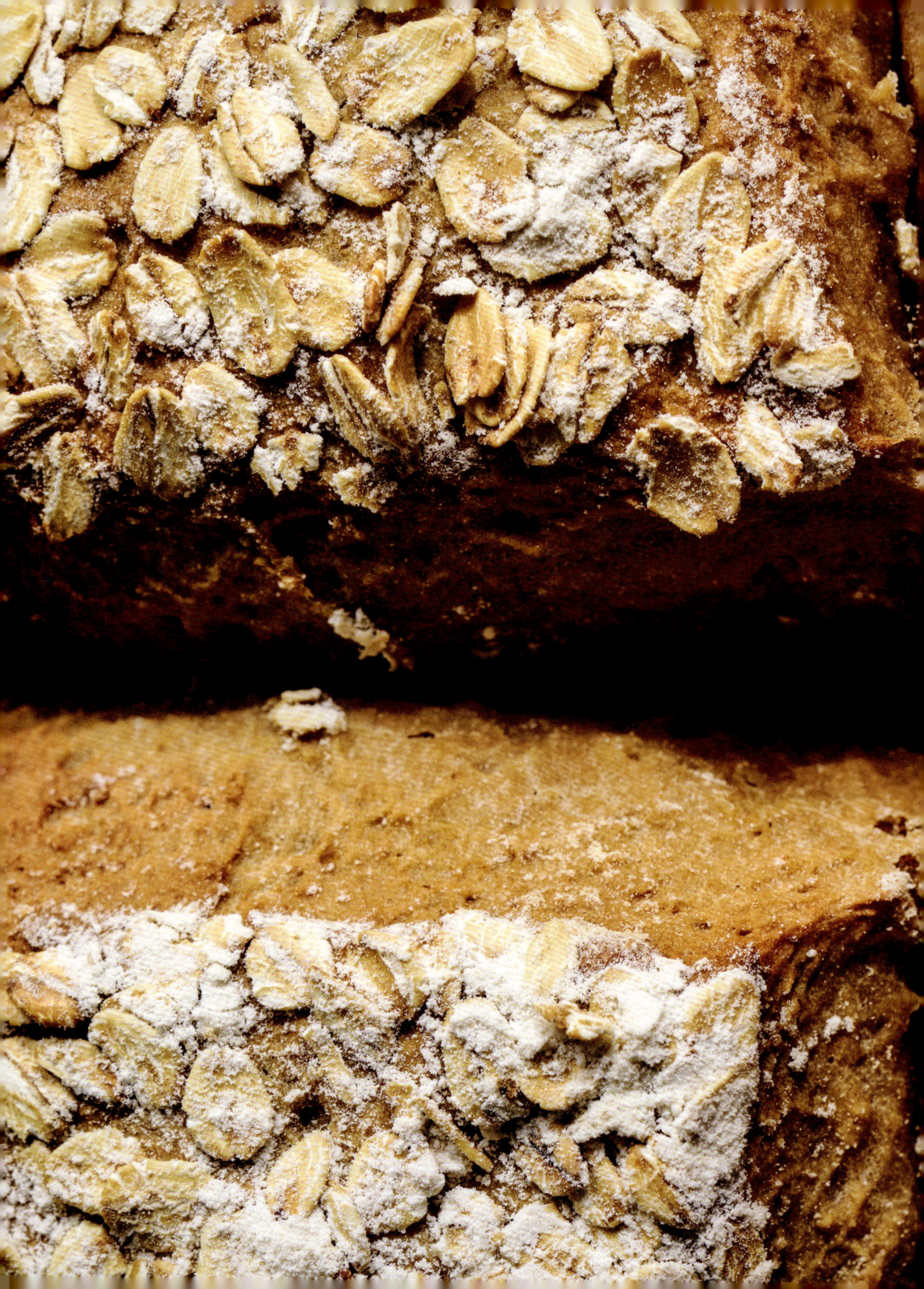

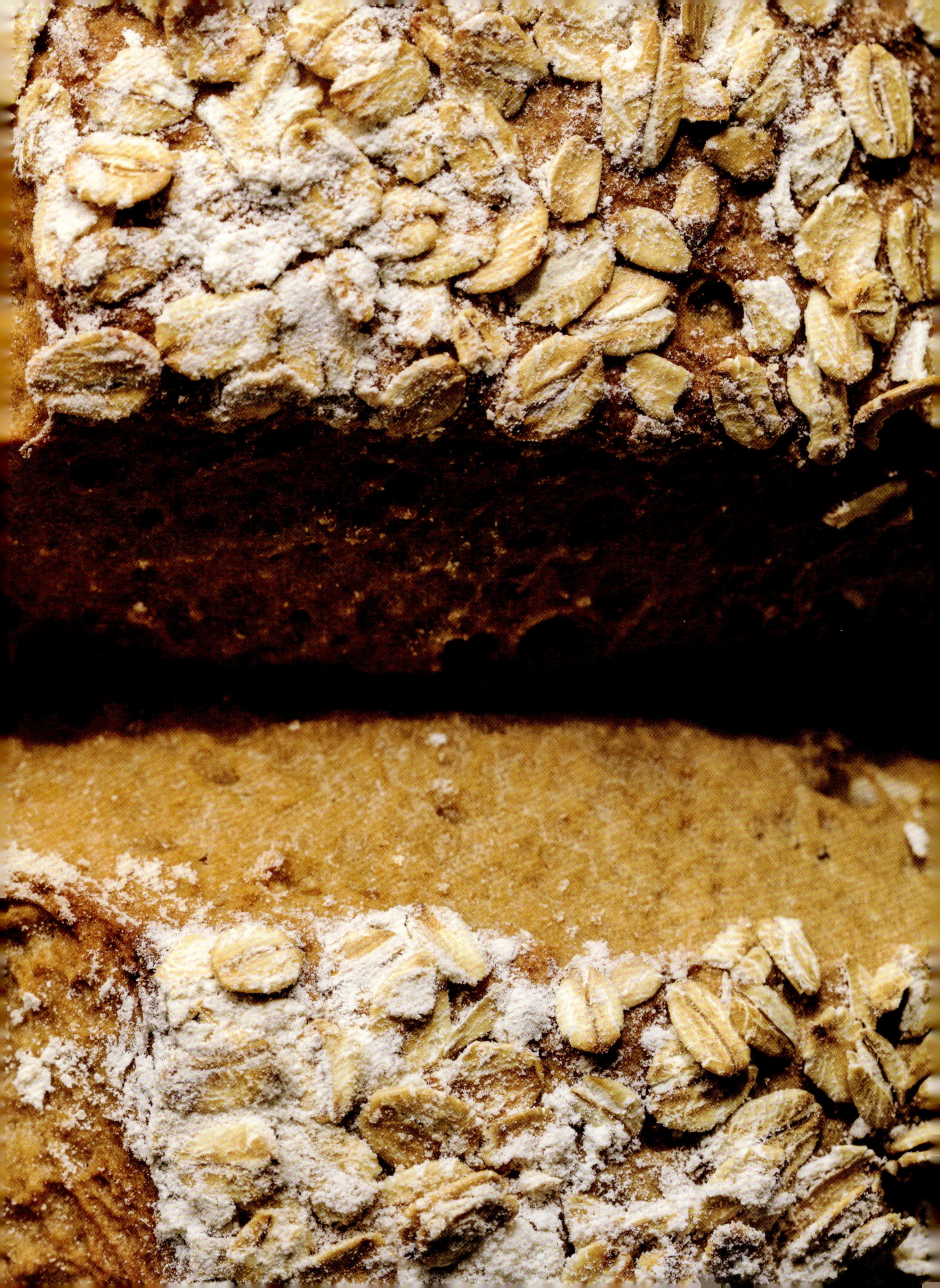

Summer

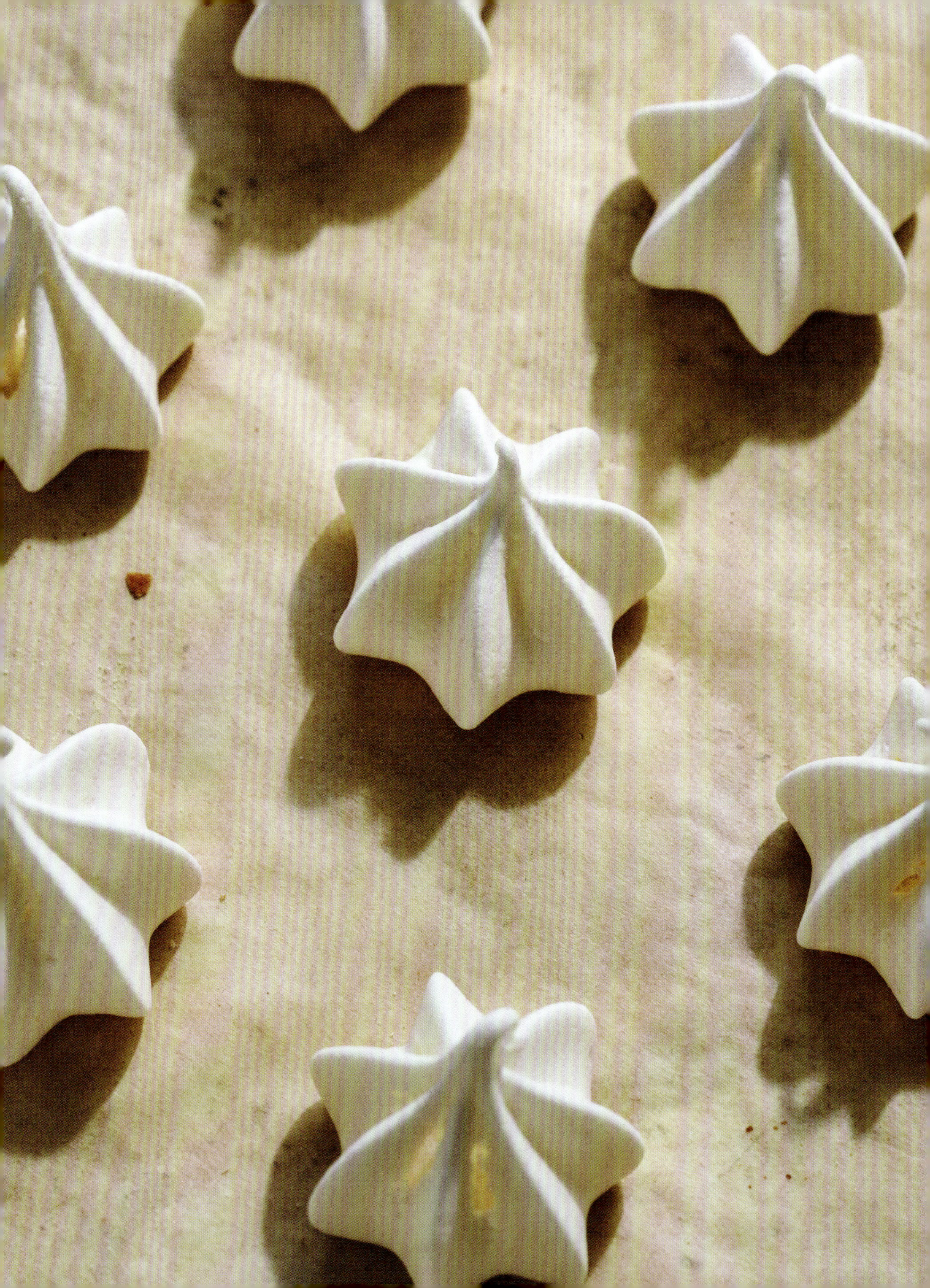

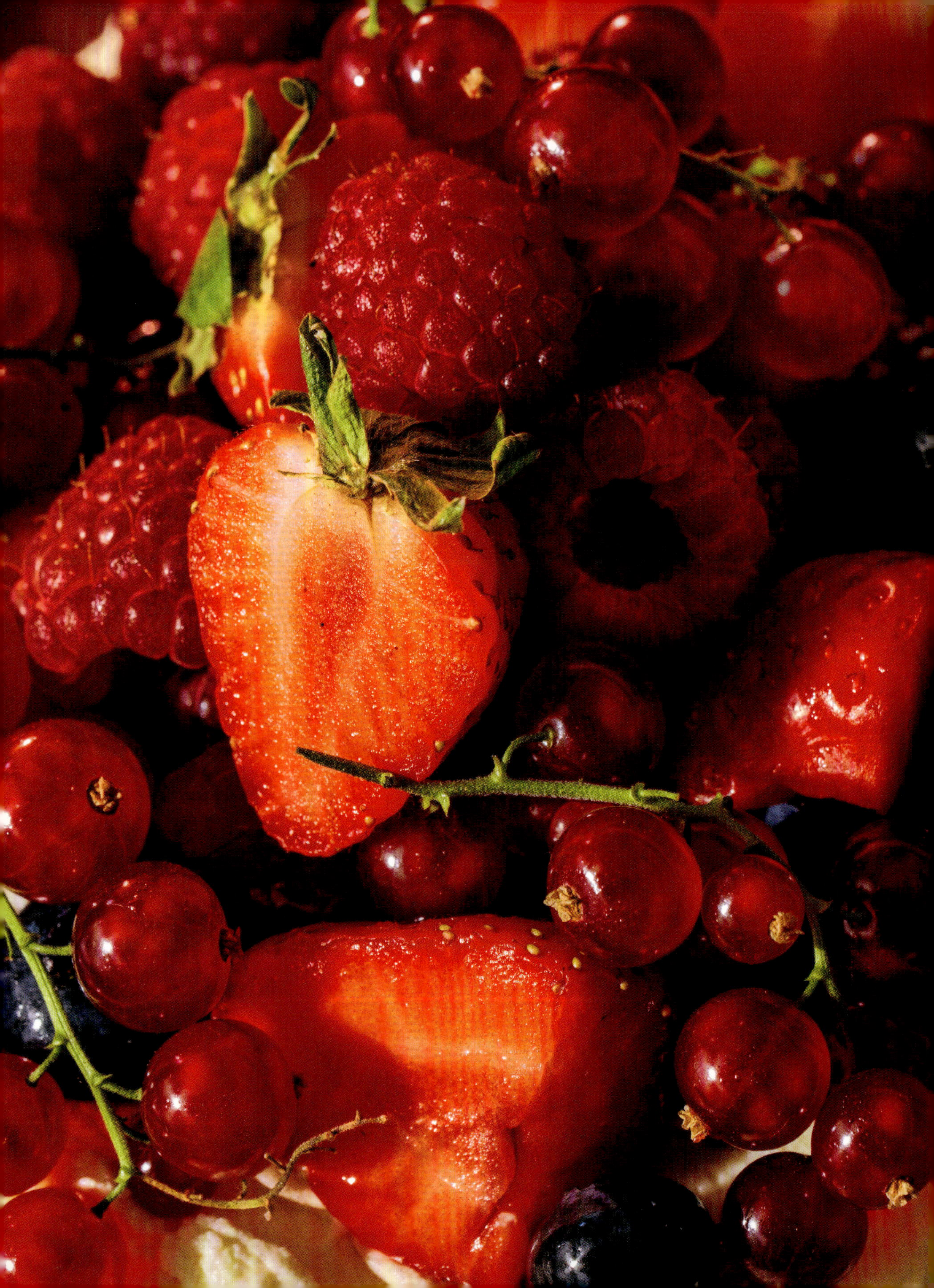

The wonderful thing about baking in summer is that it presents us with a huge amount of choice. There's so much fruit and vegetables going on now so baking is more vibrant and varied than at any other time of year.

Take advantage of all those incredible soft fruits available and make an Eton mess (page 92), Fraisier cake (page 99) or classic British Summer pudding (page 94). Zucchini are in their prime now too, so celebrate them in the Zucchini and lime cake on page 110 or in a gorgeous quiche where they are spiralled out and interlaid with feta and fava beans (see page 118). I think quiche is ready for a comeback in a big way. It's fantastic for showcasing seasonal vegetables and can look stunning as a centerpiece on the table – the key is to keep everything neat and sharp, especially when you're trimming back the edges of the pastry.

Throughout the summer, I try to eat outside as often as I can, soaking up those warm days and long evenings. You don't want to be spending ages in a hot kitchen at this time of year either, so most of these recipes can be made quickly or in advance, to be enjoyed as part of a picnic spread, or barbecue or lunch in the garden, leaving you more time with friends and family. The loaf on page 126 is perfect for sandwiches to take on a picnic, and the Garlic and onion focaccia (page 130) and Taboon breads (page 129) are great served simply with salads, dips or grilled meats.

I'm also excited to share with you the Tiramisu ice cream cake on page 96. I'm actually surprised I haven't included this recipe anywhere before as it combines two of my all-time favorite things: the delicate crispy sponge in tiramisu with the indulgence of ice cream. It's a perfect summer dessert. In winter, you'd be forever trying to get it to warm up so it softens enough to serve – but in the summer, it's spot on.

Eton Mess

This is ideal for a summer gathering, and it's easy to double up the quantities. Every element is delicious and the meringue kisses on top make it feel extra special. Traditionally, Eton mess is made only with strawberries, but it's a fantastic way to showcase any summer soft fruits.

Serves 6

Meringues
2 large egg whites

½ cup plus 2 tbsp (120g) superfine sugar

Mess
1¼ lbs (600g) strawberries, hulled

2 tbsp confectioners' sugar

1⅔ cups (400g) heavy cream

¾ cup plus 1 tbsp (200g) whole milk Greek yogurt

7 oz (200g) other summer berries (such as halved raspberries, red currants, blueberries)

1. Begin by making the meringues. Heat your oven to 230°F and line a large baking sheet with parchment paper.

2. Put the egg whites into a large, clean bowl and beat with a hand mixer to stiff peaks. Gradually whisk in the superfine sugar a little at a time, beating well after each addition. When all the sugar is incorporated the meringue should be shiny and thick enough to hold a stiff peak.

3. Place 4 large dollops of meringue on the lined baking sheet, leaving space in between. Put the remaining meringue into a piping bag fitted with a ½-inch star piping tip and pipe into tiny stars on the paper.

4. Slide the baking sheet onto the bottom shelf of your oven and bake for 1 hour, or until the meringues peel away from the paper easily. Leave to cool on the baking sheet placed on a wire rack.

5. For the mess, put one third of the strawberries into a food processor with ½ tbsp confectioners' sugar and pulse to a smooth purée. Halve or quarter the remaining strawberries into bite-sized pieces.

6. In a large bowl, whip the cream with the remaining 1½ tbsp confectioners' sugar until the mixture forms soft peaks. Fold in the Greek yogurt.

7. To assemble, crumble the large meringues and add them to the cream with the remaining strawberries and your other chosen berries, saving a few to finish. Gently fold the crushed meringues and fruit through the cream, then add the strawberry purée and swirl through.

8. Divide the Eton mess between 6 serving glasses and top with the tiny meringue stars and a few berries to serve.

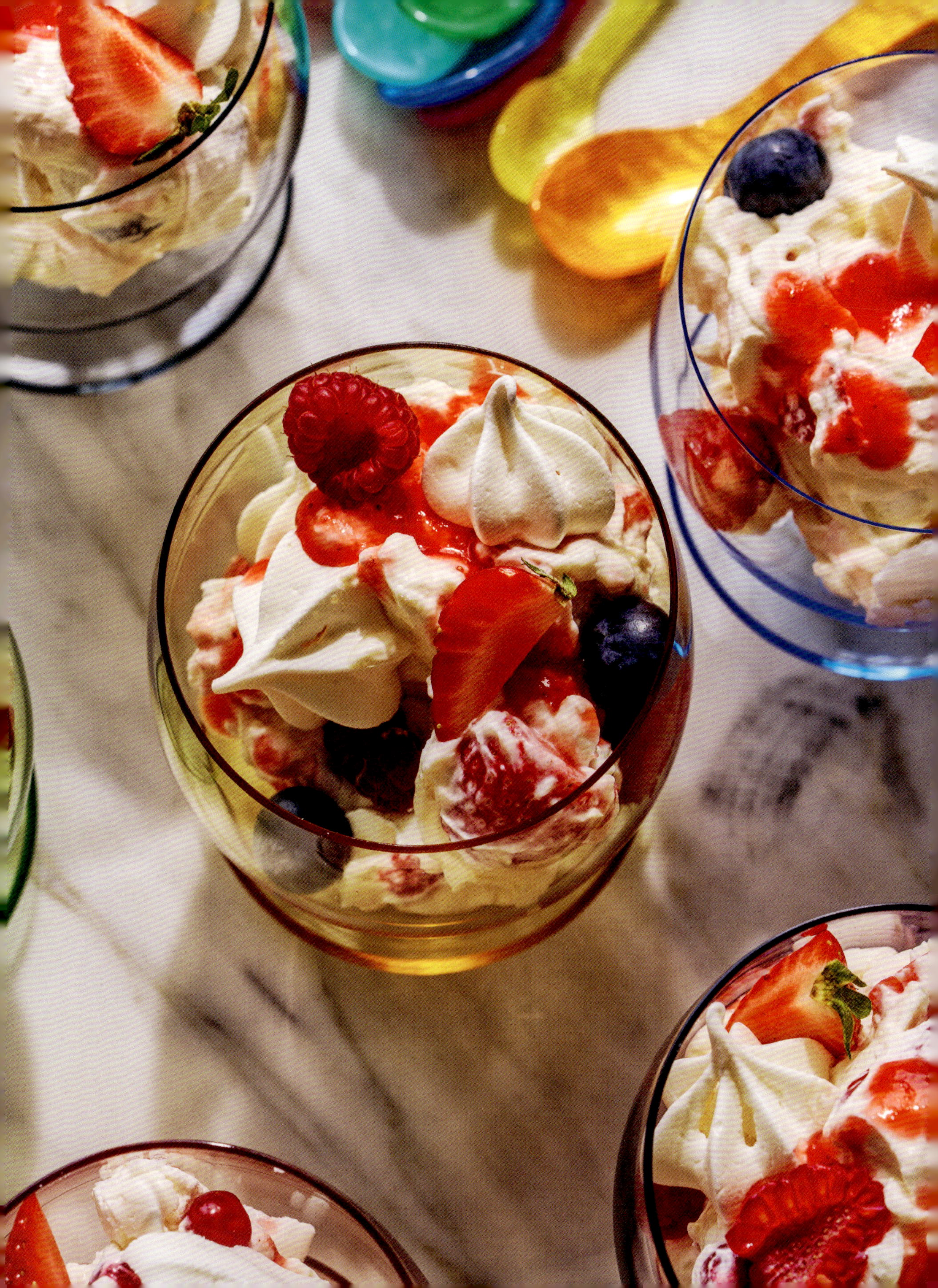

Summer Pudding

Nothing says midsummer more than a vibrant, juicy summer pudding. The key is to leave the pudding in the fridge for a long time, so all the juices soak into the bread – giving it that fantastic color. It works best with sliced white bread, preferably from a loaf you've made yourself (see my recipe on page 126).

Serves 6

8 slices of slightly stale white bread, crusts removed

2 lbs (900g) mixed soft fruits (raspberries, red currants etc)

2 tbsp water

2–3 tbsp superfine sugar

To finish and serve

Extra raspberries and red currants

A little edible gold leaf (optional)

Vanilla ice cream or heavy cream

1. Line a 1-quart pudding basin or mixing bowl with plastic wrap, leaving enough overhanging the rim of the bowl to cover the top of the pudding. Cut a circle of bread to line the bottom of the bowl and position it. Cut a large circle, the diameter of the top, and set aside. Line the side of the bowl with bread slices, cutting them to fit together snugly, with no gaps.

2. Place the fruit in a small saucepan with the water and 2 tbsp sugar. Bring to a simmer over a low heat then taste to check the sweetness and add a little more sugar if needed.

3. Fill the bread-lined bowl with the hot fruit and most of its syrup; save the rest of the syrup for serving. Cover with the large bread round and fold the excess plastic wrap over the top. Sit a small plate on top (that just fits inside the rim of the bowl) and weigh it down with a 1-lb weight (or a can of beans). Place in the fridge overnight.

4. To serve, uncover the pudding and invert a serving plate over the top of the bowl. Holding the plate and bowl tightly together, turn them both over, to unmold the pudding onto the plate. Remove the plastic wrap. Spoon the reserved syrup over the top of the pudding, covering any pale patches.

5. Arrange a handful of berries and red currants on top of the pudding and decorate with a little gold leaf if you like. Serve, cut into wedges, with ice cream or heavy cream.

Variations

I've used only red fruits here, but you can introduce blackberries and/or black currants if you have them too – though the bread won't be such a uniform red color.

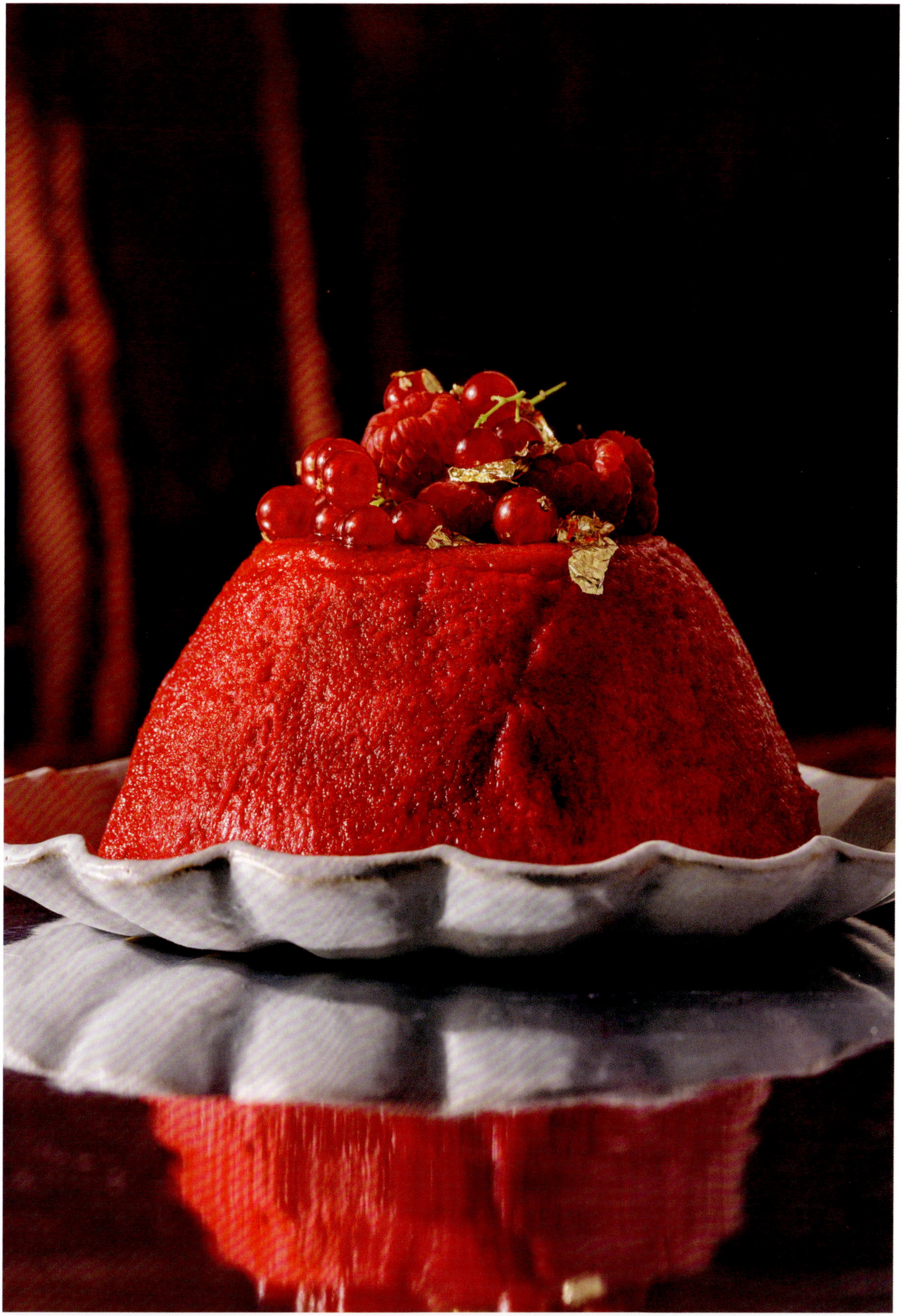

Tiramisu Ice Cream Cake

I'm a big, big fan of both tiramisu and ice cream so, for me, this cake is pure indulgence. It's fairly straightforward to make but looks incredible. Just be sure you cut the savoiardi layers accurately and chill the cake properly, so it all holds together.

Serves 8–10

Savoiardi layer

½ cup plus 1 tbsp (70g) all-purpose flour
2 tbsp (20g) semolina flour
2 large eggs, separated
½ cup (100g) superfine sugar
1 tsp vanilla bean paste
1–2 tbsp confectioners' sugar

Coffee soak

7 tbsp (100g) strong coffee
1 tbsp (15g) superfine sugar
2 tbsp (30g) Marsala wine (optional)

To assemble

2 × 1-pint containers of vanilla ice cream, softened in the fridge for 30 minutes until spreadable
½ cup (120g) mascarpone
½ tsp vanilla extract
3 tbsp (30g) unsweetened cocoa powder

1. For the savoiardi layer, heat your oven to 350°F. Grease a jelly roll pan, about 15 × 10 inches, and line with parchment paper. Sift the flour and semolina together and set aside.

2. Using a stand mixer fitted with the whisk attachment, whisk the egg whites to soft peaks. Add 2 tbsp of the superfine sugar and continue to whisk until you have a thick, glossy meringue.

3. In another bowl, using a hand mixer, beat the egg yolks, remaining superfine sugar and vanilla paste together until pale and thickened. Using a spatula, carefully fold this through the meringue, then add the flour and semolina mix and fold in very gently.

4. Carefully pour the mixture onto the prepared baking sheet and gently spread out evenly. Sift the confectioners' sugar evenly all over the surface and bake in the oven for 18–20 minutes. Leave in the pan for 5 minutes then carefully turn out onto a wire rack and leave to cool.

5. To assemble, line a 2-lb loaf pan with plastic wrap as neatly as you can, leaving enough overhanging the edges to cover the top. For the coffee soak, heat the ingredients together in a saucepan until the sugar is dissolved, then take off the heat and leave to cool.

6. Transfer the savoiardi to a board and cut into 3 rectangles, one to line the base of your pan, one to fit the top and one for the middle; these must fit tightly, so if your pan is wider at the top take this into account.

7. Dip a third of the savoiardi into the coffee soak for 1–2 seconds on each side, then arrange in a layer in the loaf pan. Spoon on half of the ice cream and spread to an even layer. Repeat these layers, then finish with a final layer of soaked savoiardi. Fold the overhanging plastic wrap over the top and place in the freezer for at least an hour.

8. When you are ready to serve, lightly whip the mascarpone with the vanilla extract until soft peaks form. Uncover the loaf pan and invert a serving plate over it. Holding the plate and loaf pan tightly together, turn them upside down to unmold the ice cream cake onto the plate. Remove the plastic wrap. Pipe mascarpone all over the top and finish with a generous dusting of cocoa. Cut into slices and serve straight away.

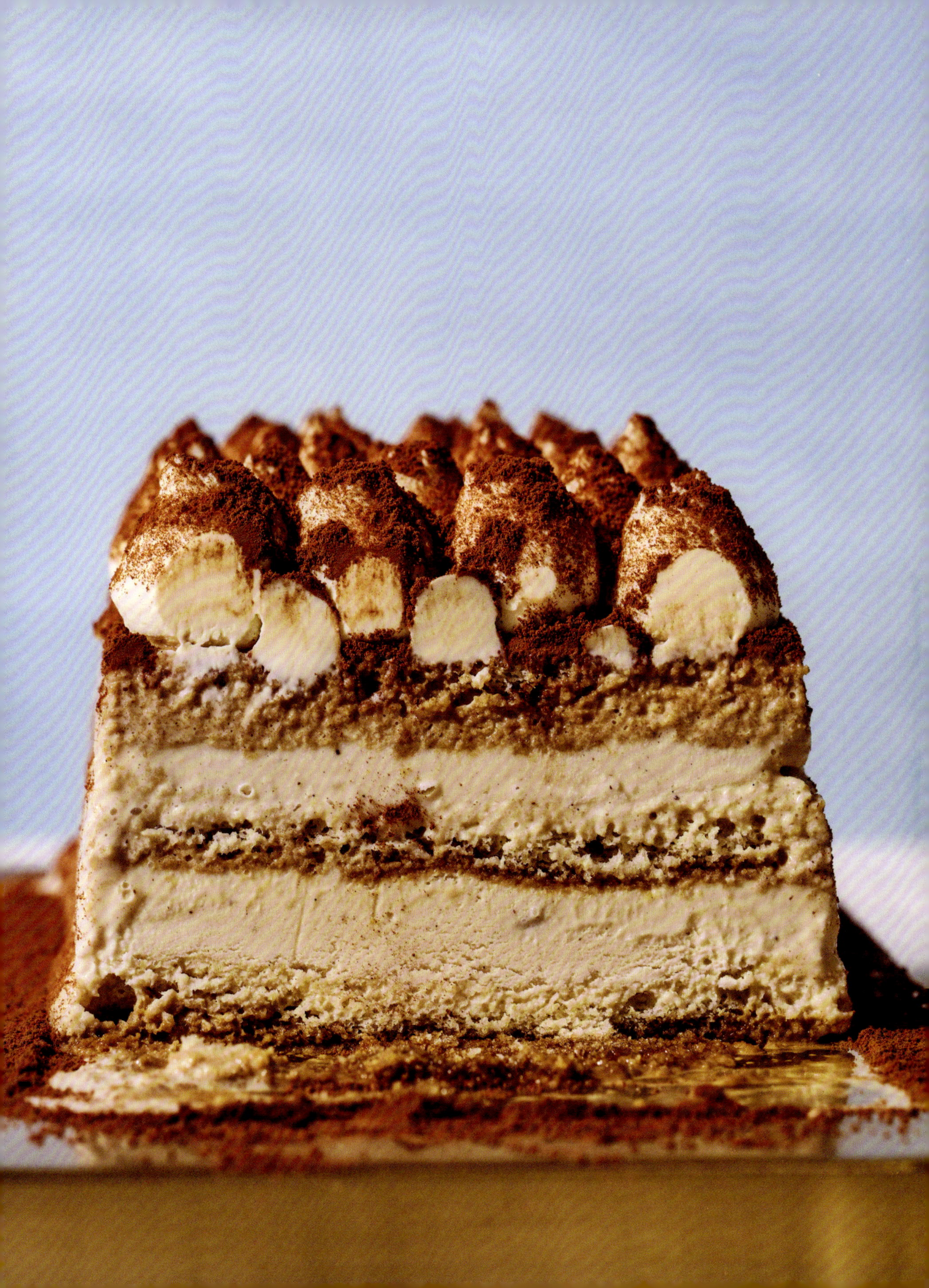

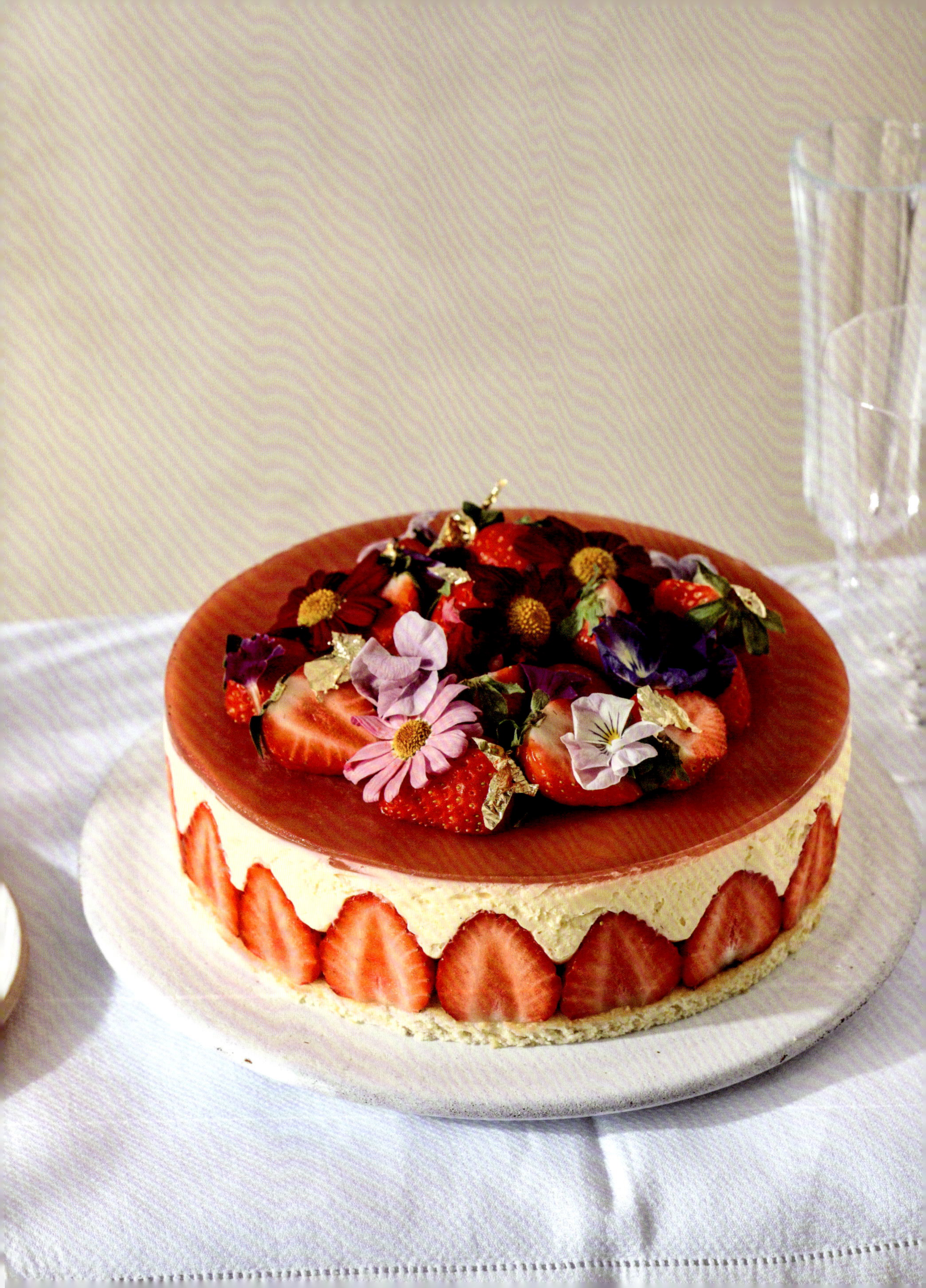

Fraisier Cake

With layers of genoise, crème diplomat and fresh strawberries, this French classic turns inexpensive ingredients into a cake that looks like you've spent a small fortune in a professional bakery. The secret is to arrange the strawberries neatly and use the crème to hold them in place while you fill the middle. The final reveal is incredibly impressive.

Serves 10–12

Genoise sponge

½ cup plus 2 tbsp (125g) superfine sugar

4 large eggs, at room temperature

1 tsp vanilla bean paste

2 tbsp (25g) unsalted butter, melted, plus extra to grease

1 cup (125g) all-purpose flour, sifted

Crème diplomat

2 tsp unflavored gelatin powder

1¾ cups plus 2 tbsp (450g) whole milk

1 tsp vanilla bean paste

6 large egg yolks

½ cup (100g) superfine sugar

⅓ cup (45g) all-purpose flour

¾ cup plus 1 tbsp (200g) heavy cream

Strawberry filling

10 oz (260g) strawberries, hulled and diced

A squeeze of lemon juice

1 tbsp superfine sugar

Decorative edge

7 oz (200g) even-sized strawberries, hulled and halved

Strawberry jelly

¾ tsp unflavored gelatin powder

4 oz (100g) strawberries, hulled

2 tbsp water

1 tbsp superfine sugar

1. For the genoise sponge, heat your oven to 375°F. Grease a jelly roll pan, about 15 × 10 inches, and line with parchment paper.

2. Put the sugar, eggs and vanilla paste into a large heatproof bowl and set over a saucepan of simmering water. Whisk, using a hand mixer, for 8–10 minutes until the mixture is very pale and tripled in volume.

3. Remove from the heat and slowly pour in the melted butter, folding it in as you do so. Now gently fold in the sifted flour until fully incorporated, making sure you don't knock out the air.

4. Pour the mixture on the lined jelly roll pan and spread gently to level. Bake in the oven for 18–22 minutes until golden brown and starting to shrink away from the sides of the pan. A cake tester inserted into the center of the cake should come out clean.

5. Leave the cake to cool in the pan for 5 minutes then turn out onto a wire rack and leave to cool completely.

6. To make the crème diplomat, put 2 tbsp water in a small bowl and sprinkle over the 2 tsp gelatin, then set aside. Put the milk and vanilla paste into a saucepan over a low heat and slowly bring to a boil.

7. Meanwhile, in a small bowl, whisk the egg yolks and sugar together until pale and then whisk in the flour. Gradually pour the hot vanilla milk onto the egg mixture, whisking as you do so. Pour the mixture back into the pan and cook over a low heat, whisking constantly, for 5–6 minutes until the mixture is thickened. Take off the heat.

8. Stir the hydrated gelatin and then stir through the custard until melted and smooth. Pour the mixture into a bowl, press a sheet of plastic wrap onto the surface to prevent a skin forming and place in the fridge to cool for 30 minutes. Once it is cooled, whip the cream in a bowl to soft peaks and then fold through the custard mixture.

Continued overleaf

Continued from page 99

To decorate
6–8 strawberries, hulled
Edible flowers
Edible gold leaf (optional)

9. To assemble the cake, you will need an 8-inch mousse ring mold set on a baking sheet, or a springform cake pan. For the filling, mix the diced strawberries with the lemon juice and sugar; set aside. Cut an 8-inch round of genoise sponge to fit the mold, making sure it will be a tight fit. Cut a second, smaller sponge round, about 6 inches in diameter.

10. Place the larger genoise round in the base of the mold/pan. Carefully position the halved strawberries around the edge of the pan, cut side facing outwards, packing them in as tightly as you can. Pour half of the crème diplomat on top of the sponge and use a small offset spatula or spoon to spread it out, making sure it extends to the strawberries; this will hold them in place.

11. Spoon the diced strawberry filling evenly into the mold/pan and cover with the smaller sponge round. Top with the remaining crème diplomat, spreading it right to the edge of the pan, then level and smooth the surface with an offset spatula. Place in the fridge for 1–2 hours to set.

12. To make the strawberry gelée, put 1 tbsp water in a small bowl, sprinkle over the ¾ tsp gelatin and set aside. Meanwhile, blitz the strawberries, water and sugar together in a blender to make a purée, then pass through a strainer into a small saucepan, bring to a boil and then take off the heat. Stir the hydrated gelatin through the hot strawberry purée until fully melted. Let cool for 5 minutes.

13. Pour the liquid gelée over the set cake and then return it to the fridge for 15 minutes or until the gelée has set.

14. To serve, transfer the cake to a large flat serving plate, then run a warm small knife around the inside of the mousse ring or springform pan to loosen the cake and carefully release it. Decorate with halved strawberries and edible flowers. Finish with a little gold leaf, if you like.

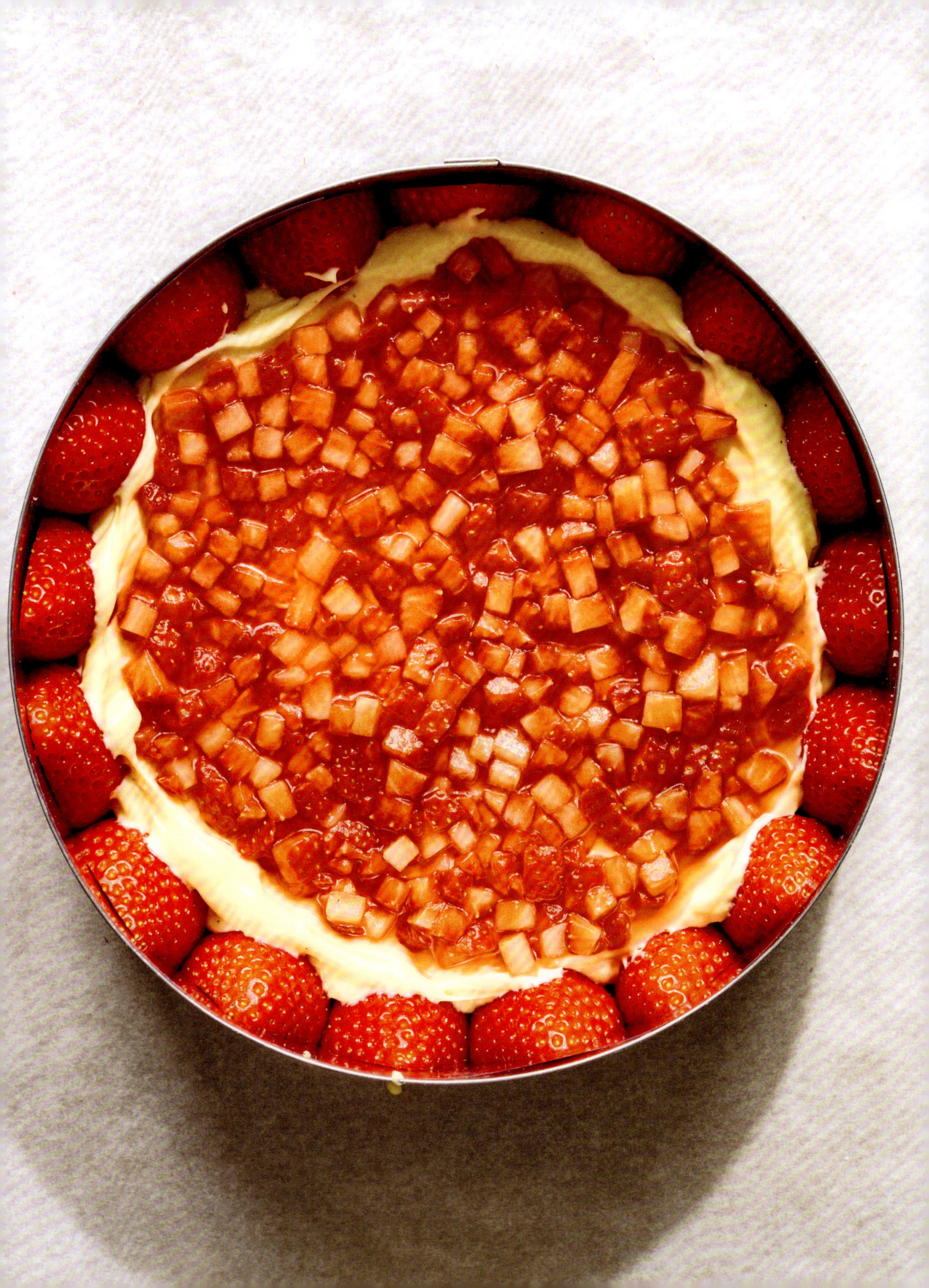

Key Lime Pie

I love strong flavors, especially lime, so if anyone makes me a Key lime pie on the *Baking Show*, they're going to get a handshake! I made it when I was in Miami, where it was invented. With its crunchy crumb base, creamy filling and tangy lime flavor, to me it's just the perfect dessert.

Serves 8–10

Dehydrated lime slices
1 lime

Base
7 oz (200g) digestive biscuits or graham crackers (about 12½ sheets)

1 stick plus 1 tbsp (125g) unsalted butter, melted

Filling
4 large egg yolks

1 × 14-oz (400g) can sweetened condensed milk

Finely grated zest and juice of 5 limes

To decorate
1 cup (250g) heavy cream

Finely grated zest of 1 lime

1. First, prepare the dehydrated lime slices for the decoration. Heat your oven to 230°F. Line a baking sheet with parchment paper. Thinly slice the lime into 1/16-inch thick slices and lay on the prepared baking sheet. Place in the oven for 1½–2 hours until the lime slices are completely dried out. Transfer to a wire rack to cool.

2. For the base, place the digestive biscuits or graham crackers in a food processor and pulse to a crumb-like texture (not too fine). Tip into a bowl, pour over the melted butter and stir to combine.

3. Spoon the crumb mixture into a loose-bottomed rectangular tart pan, approximately 14 × 4 inches, or an 8-inch round tart pan, 1¼ inches deep. Press it evenly onto the base and push the mixture up the sides of the pan to create a crust. Place in the fridge for 30 minutes or so to set.

4. Heat your oven to 300°F.

5. To make the filling, in a large bowl, whisk the egg yolks and sweetened condensed milk together until smoothly combined. Add the lime zest and juice and whisk again until smooth.

6. Pour the lime filling into the prepared crust and bake in the oven for 25–30 minutes until risen and just set. Leave to cool in the pan, then chill in the fridge for 2 hours before serving.

7. To finish, whip the cream in a bowl to firm peaks then put into a piping bag fitted with a ½-inch plain piping tip. Pipe a decorative cream border on the pie, arrange the dried lime slices on top and finish with a sprinkling of lime zest. Serve cut into slices.

Also pictured overleaf

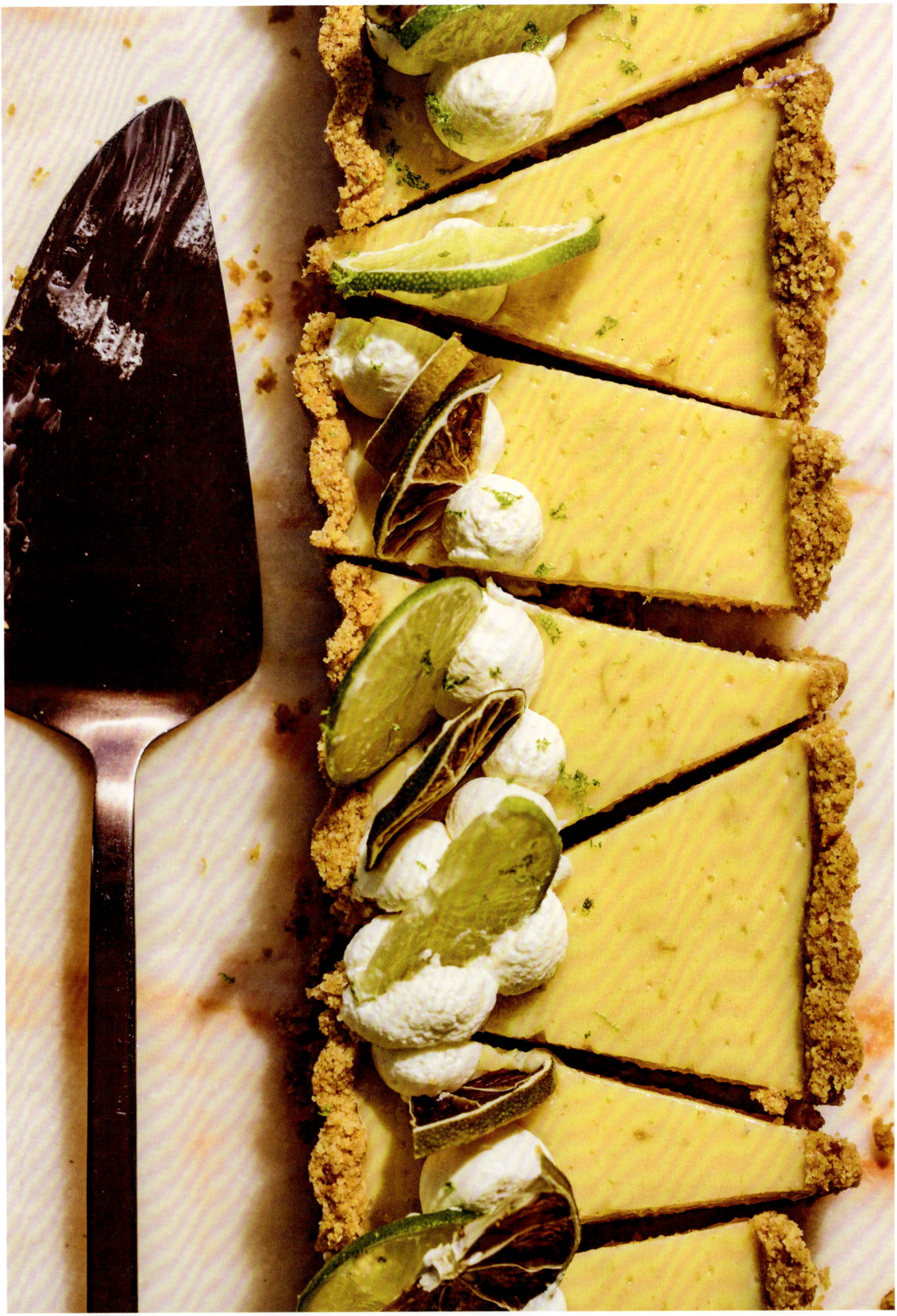

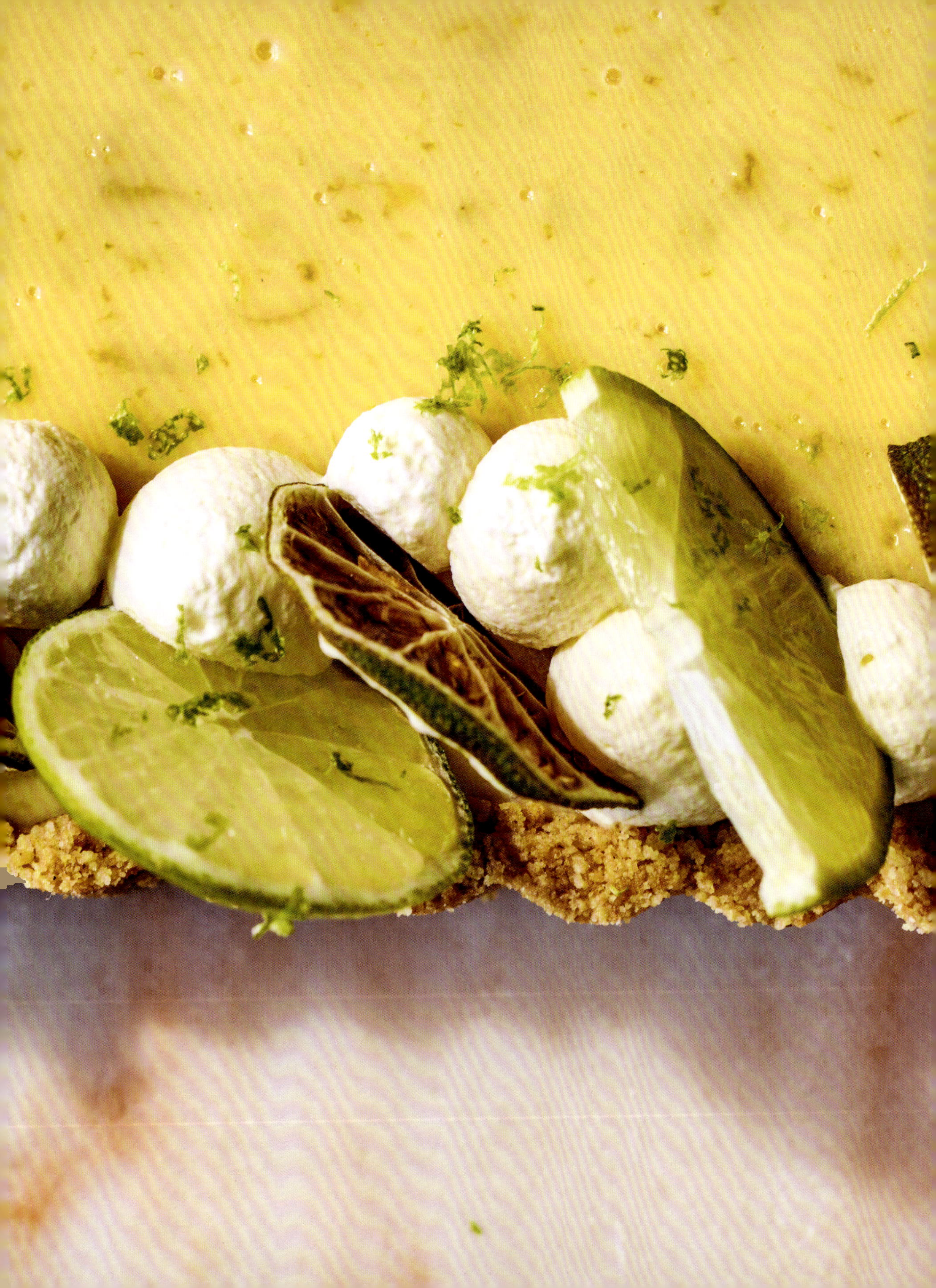

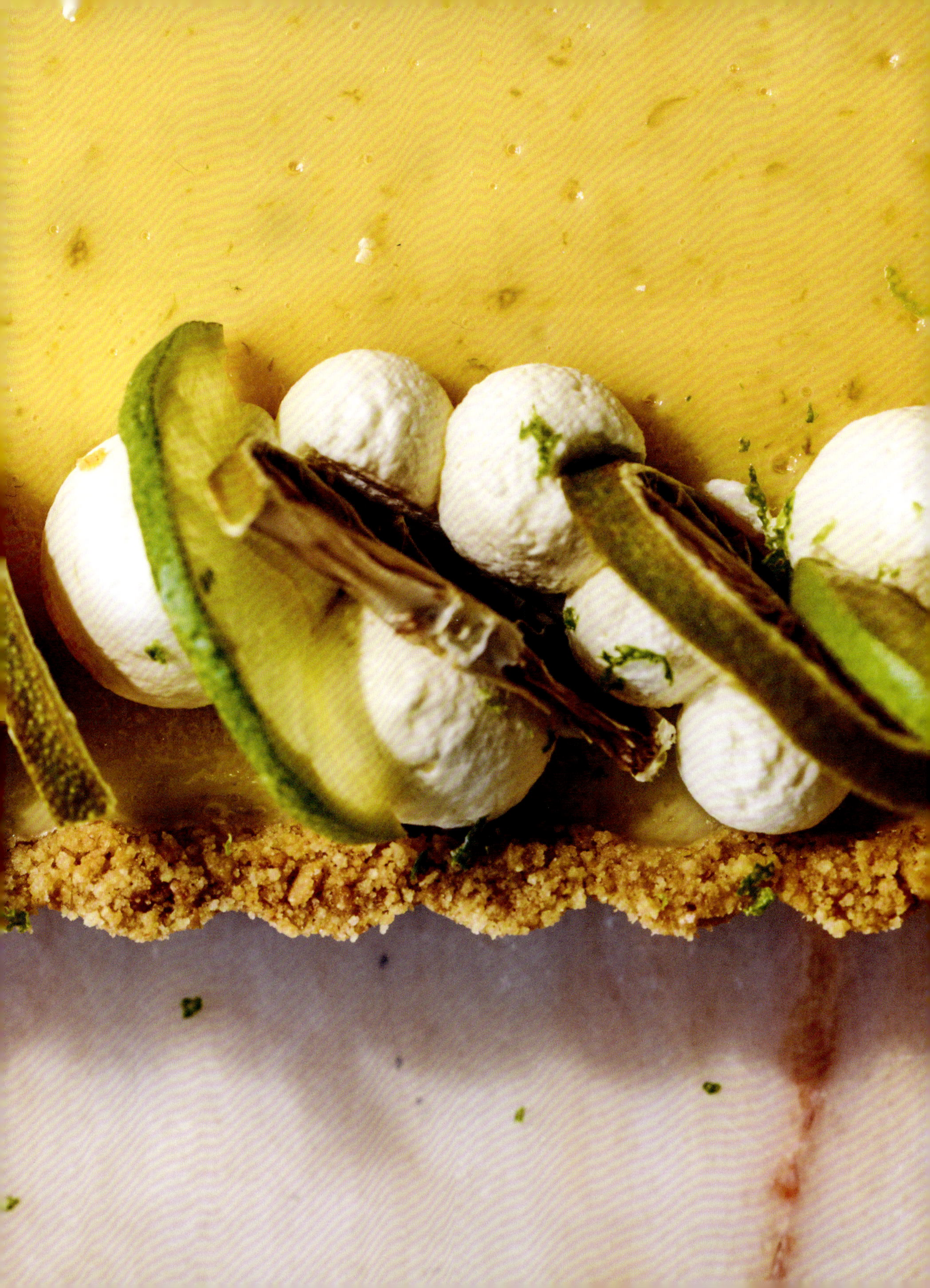

Mojito Cupcakes

A mojito is my go-to cocktail of choice, so I had to come up with a baked version! Drizzled with a rum syrup and topped with lime and mint buttercream, these cupcakes are as good to look at as they are to eat. Omit the rum if you like, they'll still be delicious.

Makes 12

Dehydrated lime slices
1 lime

Cake mixture
1¼ sticks (150g) salted butter, softened
½ cup (100g) light brown sugar
¼ cup (50g) superfine sugar
3 large eggs, at room temperature
1 tsp vanilla bean paste
1 cup plus 2 tbsp (150g) all-purpose flour
2 tsp baking powder
2 tbsp milk

Rum syrup
5 tbsp (75g) rum
⅓ cup plus 1 tbsp (75g) dark brown sugar
Juice of 1 lime

Lime and mint buttercream
1¾ sticks (200g) unsalted butter, softened
Finely grated zest and juice of 1 lime
1 tbsp boiling water
4 cups (400g) confectioners' sugar, sifted
2 sprigs of mint, leaves picked and finely chopped

To decorate
A few lime hard candies, crushed
12 small sprigs of mint
12 colorful paper straws

1. First, prepare the dehydrated lime slices for the decoration. Heat your oven to 230°F. Line a baking sheet with parchment paper. Thinly slice the lime into 1⁄16-inch thick slices and lay on the prepared sheet. Place in the oven for 1½–2 hours until completely dried out. Transfer to a wire rack to cool.

2. Heat your oven to 350°F. Line a 12-cup muffin pan with paper muffin cups.

3. Using a stand mixer fitted with the paddle attachment, beat the butter and both sugars together until light and fluffy. Scrape down the sides of the bowl with a spatula and mix again. In another bowl, beat the eggs with the vanilla paste. Slowly add to the mixer on low speed, stopping the motor as soon as it is combined.

4. Sift the flour and baking powder together. With the mixer running on a low speed, add the flour a third at a time and then incorporate the milk; do not over-mix. Divide the mixture evenly between the paper cups.

5. Bake in the oven for 18–22 minutes until the cakes are risen and golden, and spring back when lightly touched. Meanwhile, for the rum syrup, put the ingredients into a saucepan, heat to dissolve the sugar and simmer for 3–5 minutes until thickened slightly. Take off the heat.

6. As you take the cupcakes from the oven, prick the surface of each one with a toothpick and trickle over 1 tsp rum syrup. Transfer to a wire rack and leave to cool.

7. To make the lime and mint buttercream, using a stand mixer fitted with the whisk attachment, whisk the butter until very light and pale in color. Add the lime zest and juice with the boiling water and mix briefly. Now gradually whisk in the confectioners' sugar, 2–3 tbsp at a time. Finally, add the chopped mint and mix briefly. Put the buttercream into a piping bag fitted with a ¾-inch plain piping tip.

8. To decorate the cupcakes, pipe a dome of buttercream on each one and top with a sprinkling of lime candies, a sprig of mint and a dehydrated lime slice. Add a paper straw for visual effect!

Also pictured overleaf

Celebrate

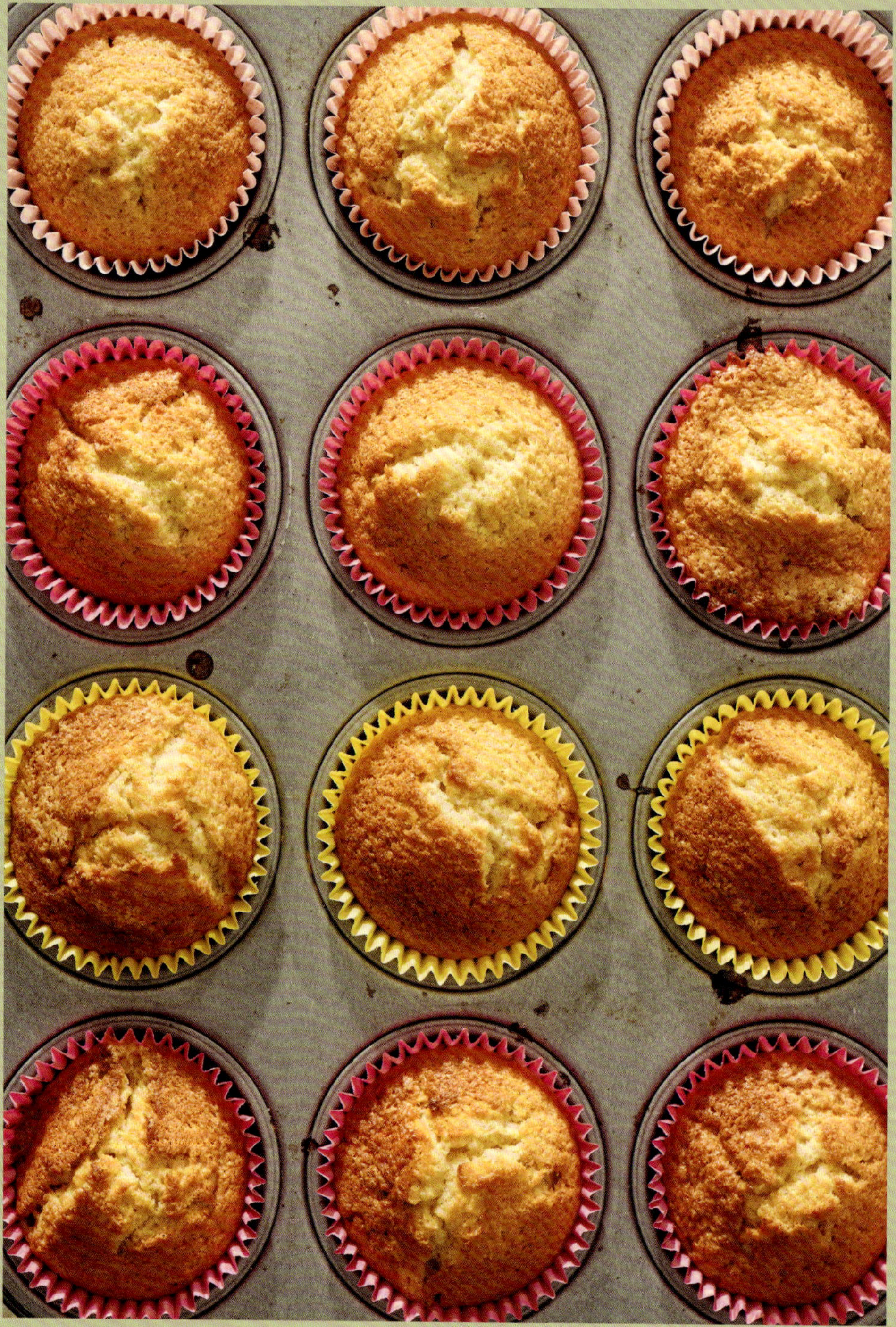

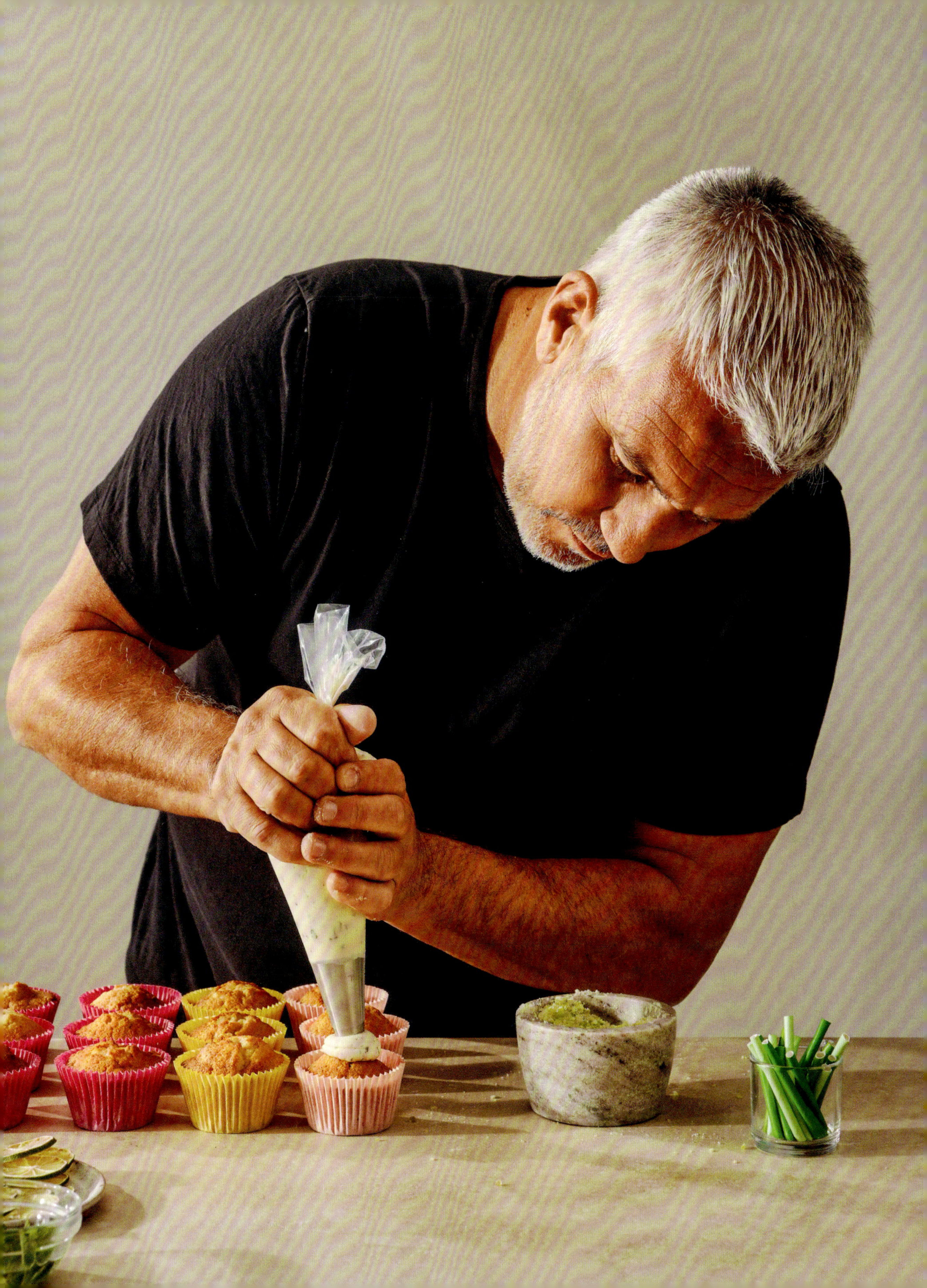

Zucchini and Lime Cake

Zucchini work amazingly well in this cake, keeping it lovely and moist. It's also a great way to sneak a bit of extra vegetables into your kids! Cream cheese frosting is the classic carrot cake topping, but it works brilliantly on this cake too.

10–12 slices

2⅓ cups plus 1 tbsp (300g) all-purpose flour

2 tsp pumpkin pie spice

2¾ tsp baking powder

4 large eggs, at room temperature

1¼ cups (250g) light brown sugar

Finely grated zest and juice of 2 limes

1 cup plus 1 tbsp (250g) vegetable oil, plus extra to grease

10 oz (300g) zucchini (about 1 large or 2 small)

1½ tbsp poppy seeds

Cream cheese frosting

7 tbsp (100g) unsalted butter, softened

2 cups (200g) confectioners' sugar

7 tbsp (100g) full-fat cream cheese

To finish

Finely grated zest of 1 lime

1. Heat your oven to 350°F. Lightly oil a 9-inch round springform pan and line with parchment paper.

2. Sift the flour, pumpkin pie spice and baking powder together into a bowl.

3. In another large bowl, beat the eggs with the sugar and lime zest and juice, then add the vegetable oil and mix well.

4. Coarsely grate the zucchini then tip onto a clean cloth. Gather the edges of the cloth, twist and squeeze out as much liquid as you can from the zucchini.

5. Add the zucchini to the egg mixture, along with the poppy seeds and fold through. Finally, fold in the flour mix until thoroughly combined.

6. Transfer the mixture to the prepared springform pan and smooth the surface. Bake in the oven for 1 hour–1 hour 10 minutes, or until a cake tester inserted into the center comes out clean.

7. Leave the cake to cool in the pan for 20 minutes then release from the pan and transfer to a wire rack. Leave to cool completely.

8. In the meantime, make the cream cheese frosting. Using a hand mixer, beat the butter until very soft. Add the confectioners' sugar, a third at a time, mixing until combined after each addition. Add the cream cheese and fold through to make a smooth frosting.

9. Spread the frosting on top of the cake, using an offset spatula, and sprinkle with the lime zest to decorate.

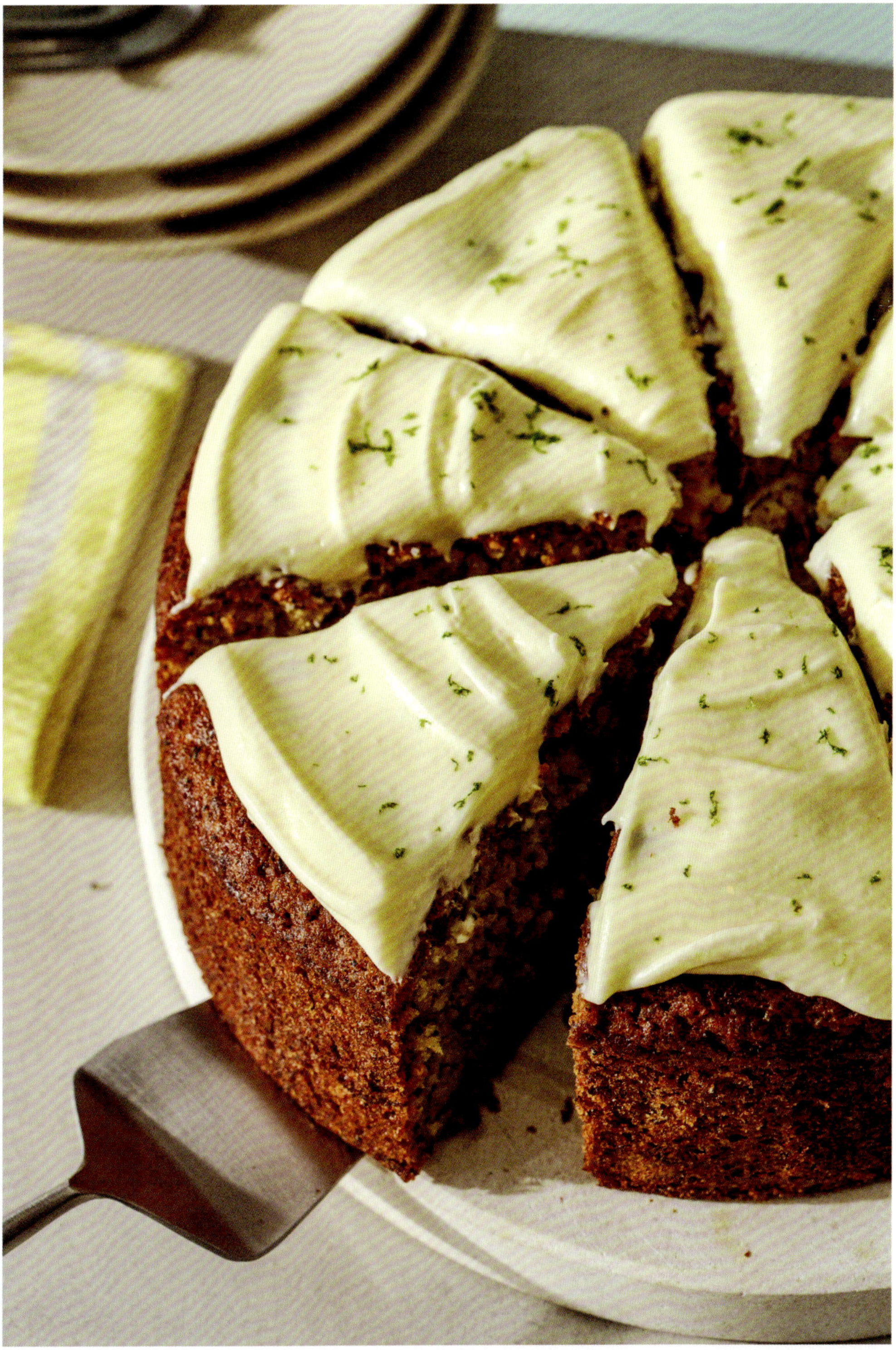

Strawberry Heart Scones

I've been baking scones for over 40 years! The trick is to use bread flour rather than regular flour: the extra protein in bread flour gives scones a great rise. It's also important to not overwork the dough. Served with preserves, fresh strawberries and cream, these scones are a real teatime treat.

Makes 6

2⅓ cups plus 1 tbsp (300g) bread flour
1 tbsp baking powder
3 tbsp (45g) chilled unsalted butter, diced
1 tbsp superfine sugar
⅔ cup (160g) whole milk, plus extra to brush
All-purpose flour, to dust

Filling
¾ cup (175g) heavy cream
4 oz (100g) strawberries, hulled and sliced
⅓ cup (80g) strawberry preserves

To finish
Confectioners' sugar, to dust

1. Heat your oven to 400°F and line a large baking sheet with parchment paper.

2. Sift the flour and baking powder together into a large bowl. Add the butter and rub in, using your fingertips, until the mixture resembles fine breadcrumbs. Stir in the sugar.

3. Make a well in the center and pour in the milk. Mix carefully, using a dinner knife in a cutting and folding motion, until the mixture starts to come together. Now just give the dough a couple of folds, keeping it nice and light.

4. Tip the dough onto a lightly floured surface and gently pat or roll to a ¾-inch thickness. Using a 3-inch heart-shaped cutter dipped in flour, cut out 5 hearts, making sure you don't wiggle the cutter around or they will lose their shape and won't rise nicely in the oven. Place on the lined baking sheet. Gently re-roll the dough trimmings and cut out another heart. Place on the lined baking sheet.

5. Brush the tops of the scones with a little milk and bake in the oven for 12–15 minutes or until risen and golden. Transfer to a wire rack to cool.

6. To serve, whip the cream in a bowl to soft peaks. Cut the scones in half. Arrange a layer of sliced strawberries on the bottom half of each scone, top with cream and then add a generous spoonful of preserves. Sandwich together with the other scone halves and dust with confectioners' sugar to serve.

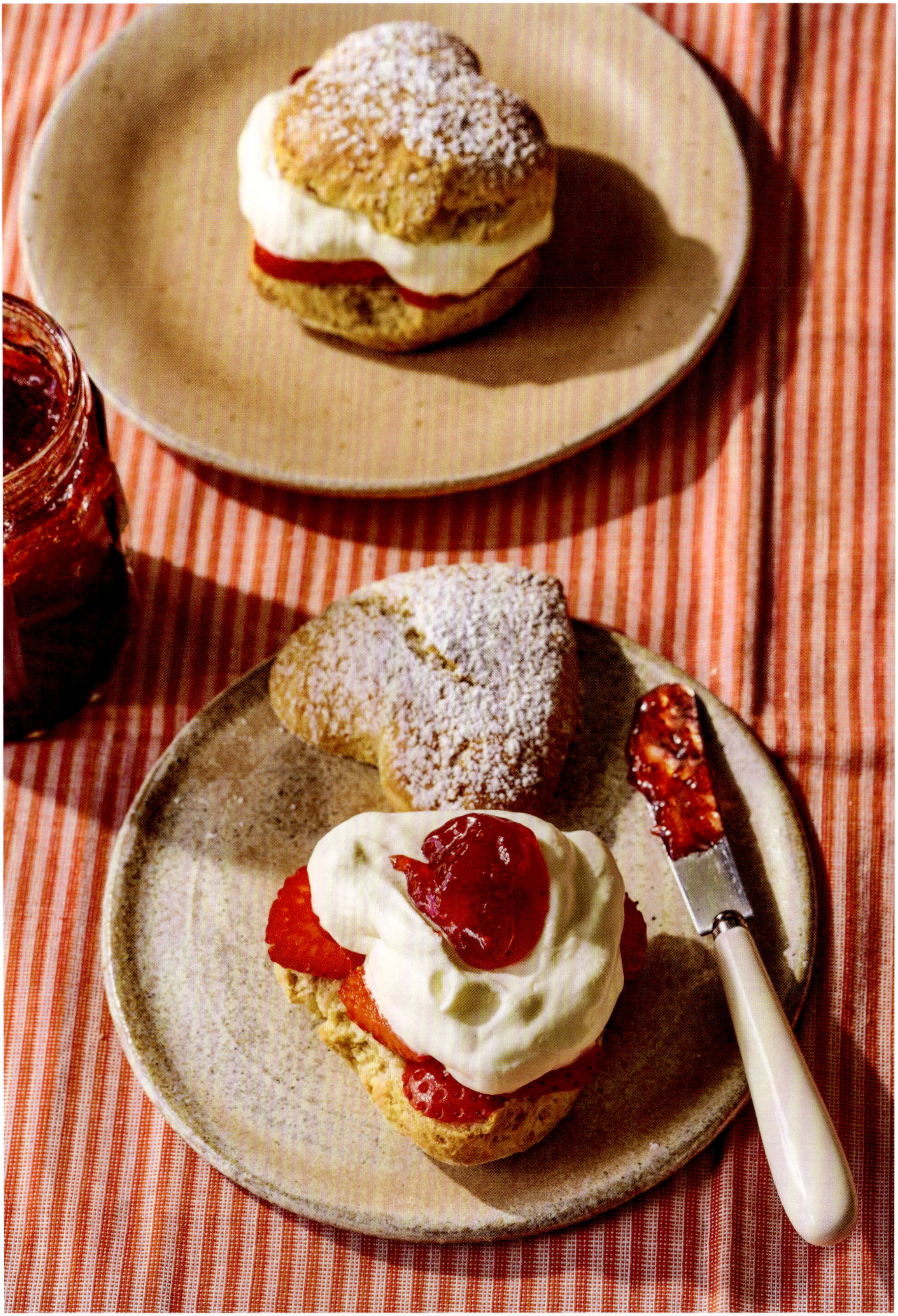

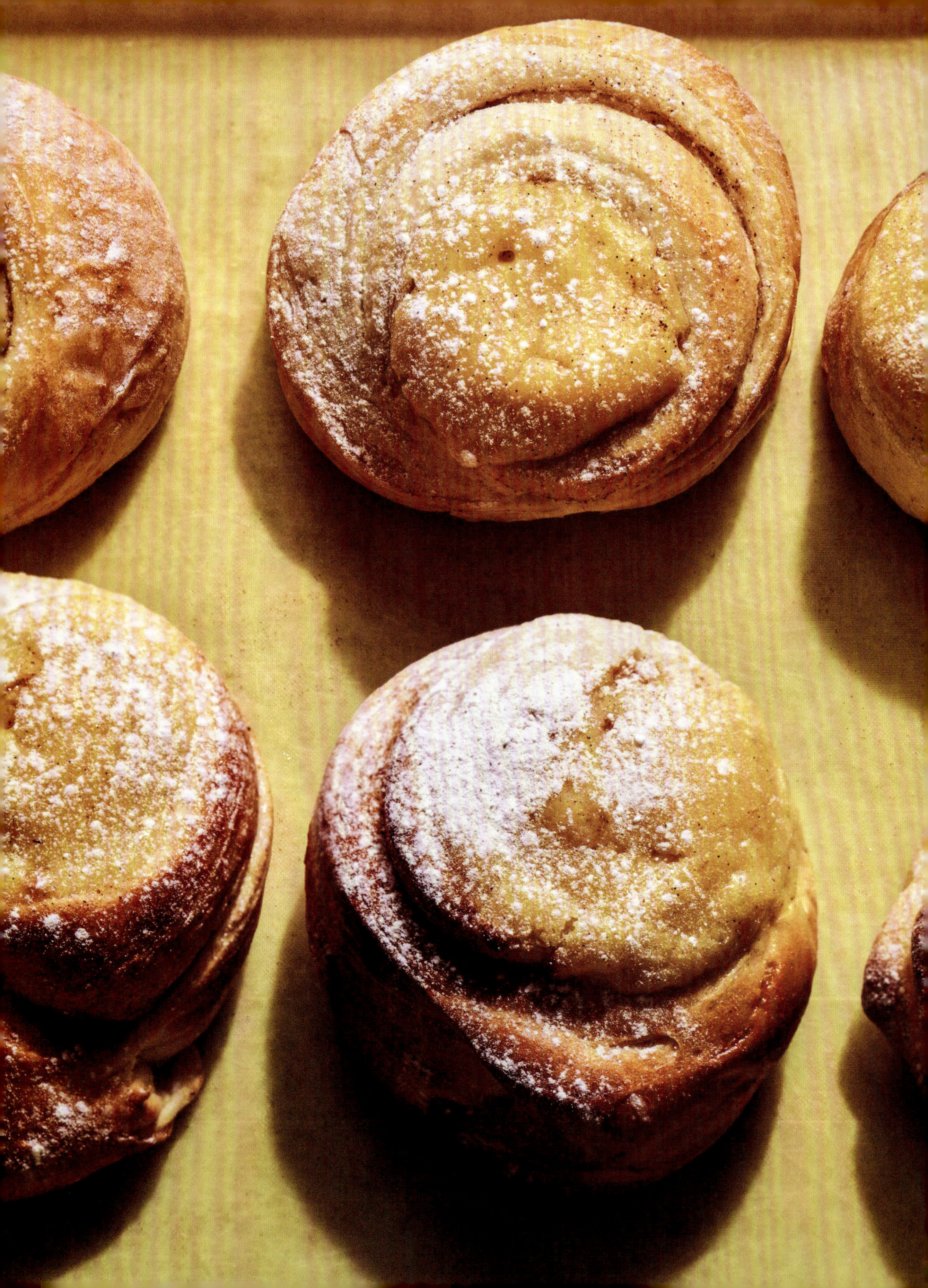

Solboller

I came across this delicious cinnamon pastry with its crème pâtissière filling when I was in Norway. Solboller (or *solskinnsboller*) are popular throughout Scandinavia and their name literally means 'sun bun'. They are eaten in the summer to celebrate the return of the sun after the long winter of dark days.

Makes 10

Dough
4 cups (500g) bread flour, plus extra to dust
1¼ tsp (8g) fine salt
3 tbsp (40g) superfine sugar
2¼ tsp (8g) instant dried yeast
1 tsp ground cardamom
1⅓ cups (320g) whole milk, at room temperature
3 tbsp (50g) unsalted butter, in pieces, softened

Crème pâtissière
¾ cup (180g) whole milk
3 tbsp (50g) heavy cream
2 tsp vanilla bean paste
4 large egg yolks
⅓ cup (70g) superfine sugar
2 tbsp (25g) cornstarch
2½ tbsp (40g) unsalted butter, in pieces, softened

Cinnamon filling
1¼ sticks (150g) unsalted butter, melted
⅓ cup plus 1 tbsp (80g) superfine sugar
2 tsp ground cinnamon

To finish
1 large egg, beaten
Confectioners' sugar, to dust

1. To make the dough, put the flour, salt, sugar, yeast, cardamom and warm milk into a stand mixer fitted with the dough hook. Mix on low speed for 5 minutes. Add the butter, increase the speed to medium and mix for a further 10 minutes until the dough is smooth and elastic.

2. Tip the dough into a bowl, cover and leave to rise for 3 hours.

3. To make the crème pâtissière, put the milk, cream and vanilla paste into a saucepan over a low heat and slowly bring to a simmer. Meanwhile, in a bowl, whisk the egg yolks with the sugar and cornstarch until smoothly combined. Pour on a little of the hot milk mix, stirring well, then pour on the remaining milk, whisking as you do so. Pour back into the pan and cook, stirring continuously, until thickened. Take off the heat and stir through the softened butter. Press a piece of plastic wrap onto the surface to prevent a skin forming and leave to cool.

4. Line a baking sheet with parchment paper. Tip the risen dough out onto a floured surface and roll out to a rectangle 12 × 8 inches, with a long side facing you. For the filling, pour the melted butter evenly over the surface then sprinkle the sugar and ground cinnamon evenly on top.

5. Starting from a long edge, roll up the dough tightly, enclosing the filling, and seal the edges with your fingers. Cut into 1¼-inch slices and lay these, cut side up, on the lined baking sheet, spacing them apart. Cover and leave to proof for 1½ hours.

6. Heat your oven to 400°F.

7. Using your fingers, make an indentation in the middle of each of the risen buns. Put the cooled crème pâtissière into a piping bag fitted with a ½-inch plain piping tip and pipe a good dollop into the middle of each of the buns. Brush the surrounding dough with beaten egg and bake in the oven for 20 minutes until golden brown.

8. Transfer the buns to a wire rack to cool slightly. Serve while still warm from the oven, sprinkled with confectioners' sugar.

Also pictured overleaf

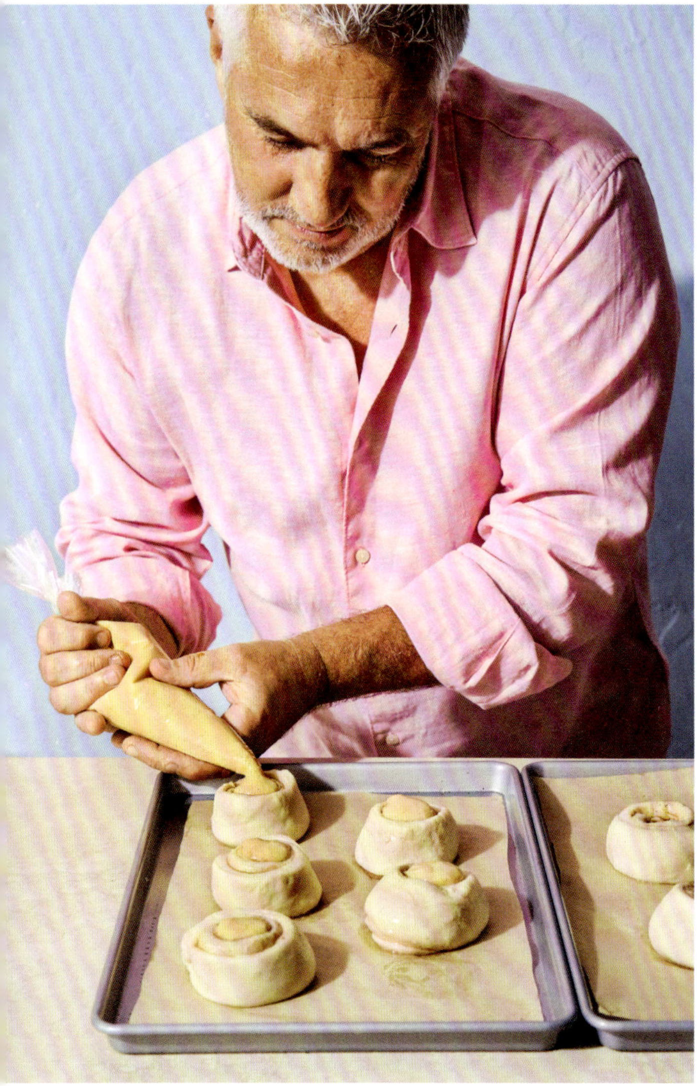
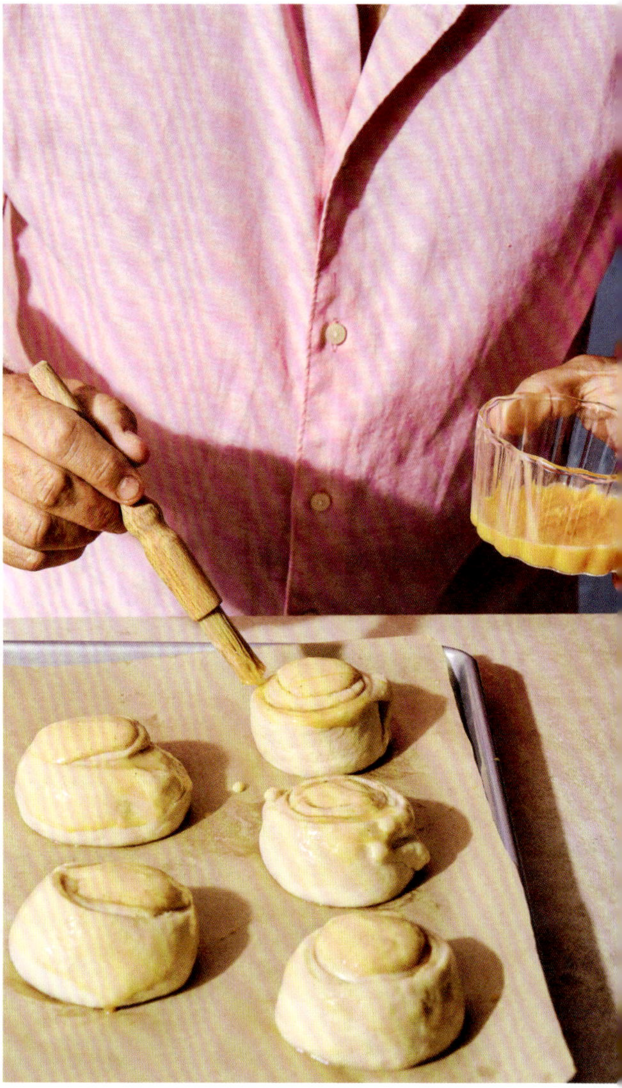

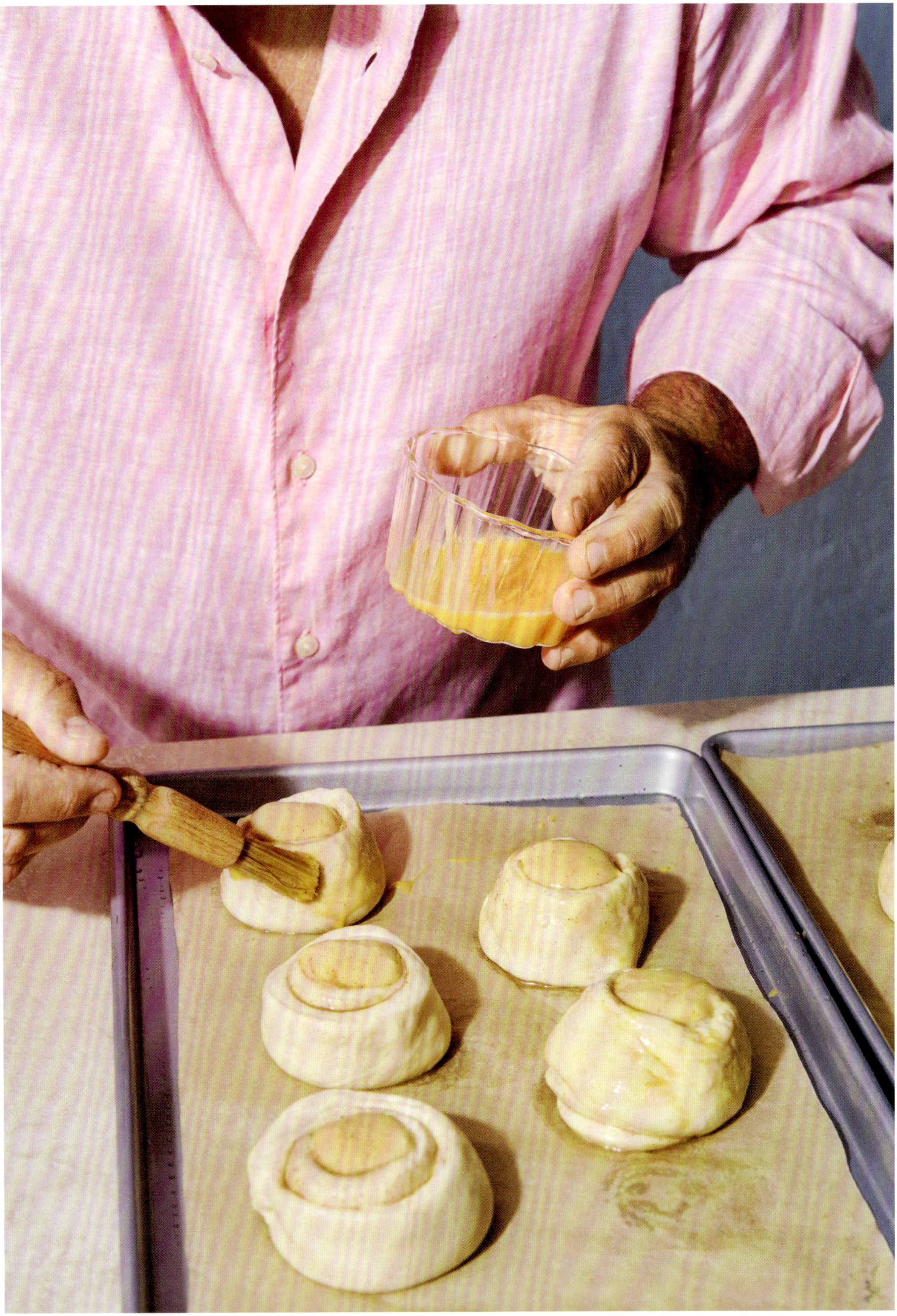

Zucchini, Feta and Fava Bean Quiche

This quiche is a thing of beauty: zucchini ribbons are spiralled in the pastry case and interspersed with fava beans and feta, then baked in a creamy egg custard. You can also throw in some peas or edamame beans if you have any. Please don't over-bake it – you want the filling to still have a slight wobble in the middle.

Serves 6

Pie dough
1¾ cup plus 1 tbsp (225g) all-purpose flour, plus extra to dust
A pinch of fine salt
4 tbsp (60g) chilled unsalted butter, diced
4 tbsp (60g) chilled vegetable shortening, diced
3–5 tbsp water

Filling
2 zucchini, trimmed
1 cup (100g) crumbled feta
⅔ cup (75g) shelled and skinned fava beans
4 large eggs, plus an extra 2 yolks
¾ cup plus 1 tbsp (200g) heavy cream
1½ tbsp grainy mustard
1 tbsp chopped chives
Salt and white pepper

1. For the pie dough, put the flour and salt into a large bowl, add the butter and shortening and rub in using your fingers until the mixture resembles fine breadcrumbs. Add just enough cold water to bring the dough together. Turn out onto a lightly floured surface, knead briefly until smooth then wrap in plastic wrap. Chill in the fridge for 30 minutes.

2. Heat your oven to 400°F and have ready a 9-inch fluted loose-bottomed tart pan, 1½ inches deep.

3. Roll out the pie dough on a lightly floured surface to a ¹⁄₁₆-inch thick and use it to line the tart pan, leaving most of the excess hanging over the edge. (Keep a little raw dough to patch any cracks later.) Line the tart crust with parchment paper and then fill with pie weights (or uncooked rice).

4. Bake 'blind' for 15 minutes, then remove the paper and weights (or rice) and return the tart crust to the oven for 8 minutes or until it looks dry and lightly colored. Use a small, sharp knife to trim away the excess dough from the edge. Patch any cracks with the saved pie dough.

5. To prepare the filling, using a vegetable peeler, shave the zucchini into ribbons. Stack a handful of these on top of each other, then start to roll into a pinwheel, continually adding ribbons. Place this zucchini rosette in the center of the tart crust. Holding it in position with one hand, keep adding zucchini ribbons to the outside until the zucchini slices start to lean on the edge of the crust and hold themselves in.

6. Scatter the feta over the zucchini, letting it drop in the gaps between the zucchini ribbons. Add the fava beans, gently slotting them in among the zucchini.

7. In a bowl, whisk the eggs, extra yolks, cream, mustard and chives together. Season with salt and a pinch of white pepper. Pour the mixture into the tart crust and bake in the oven for 25–30 minutes, until the filling is just set and golden brown.

8. Leave the quiche to cool in the pan on a wire rack for 5 minutes before removing. Serve warm or cold.

Also pictured overleaf

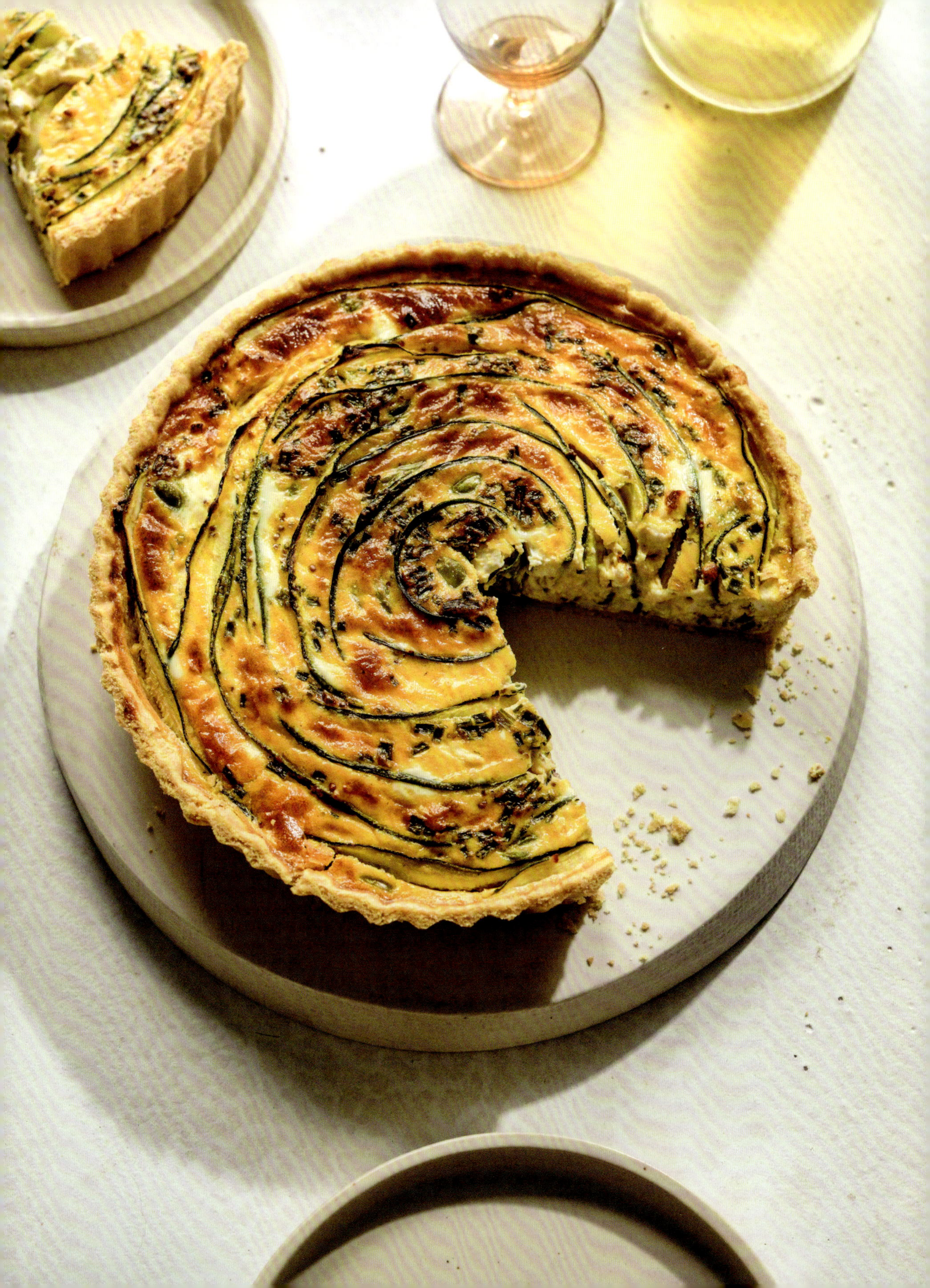

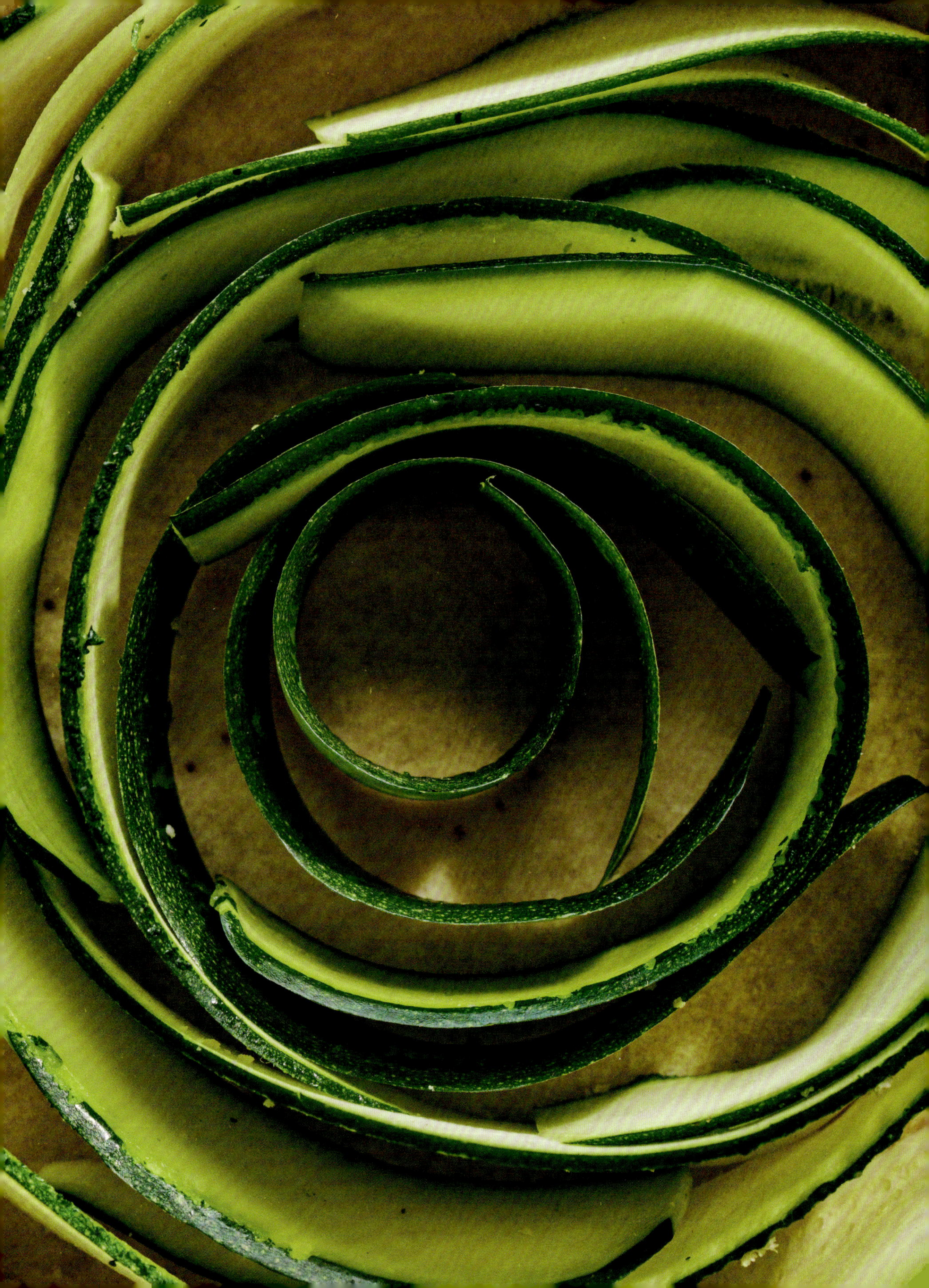

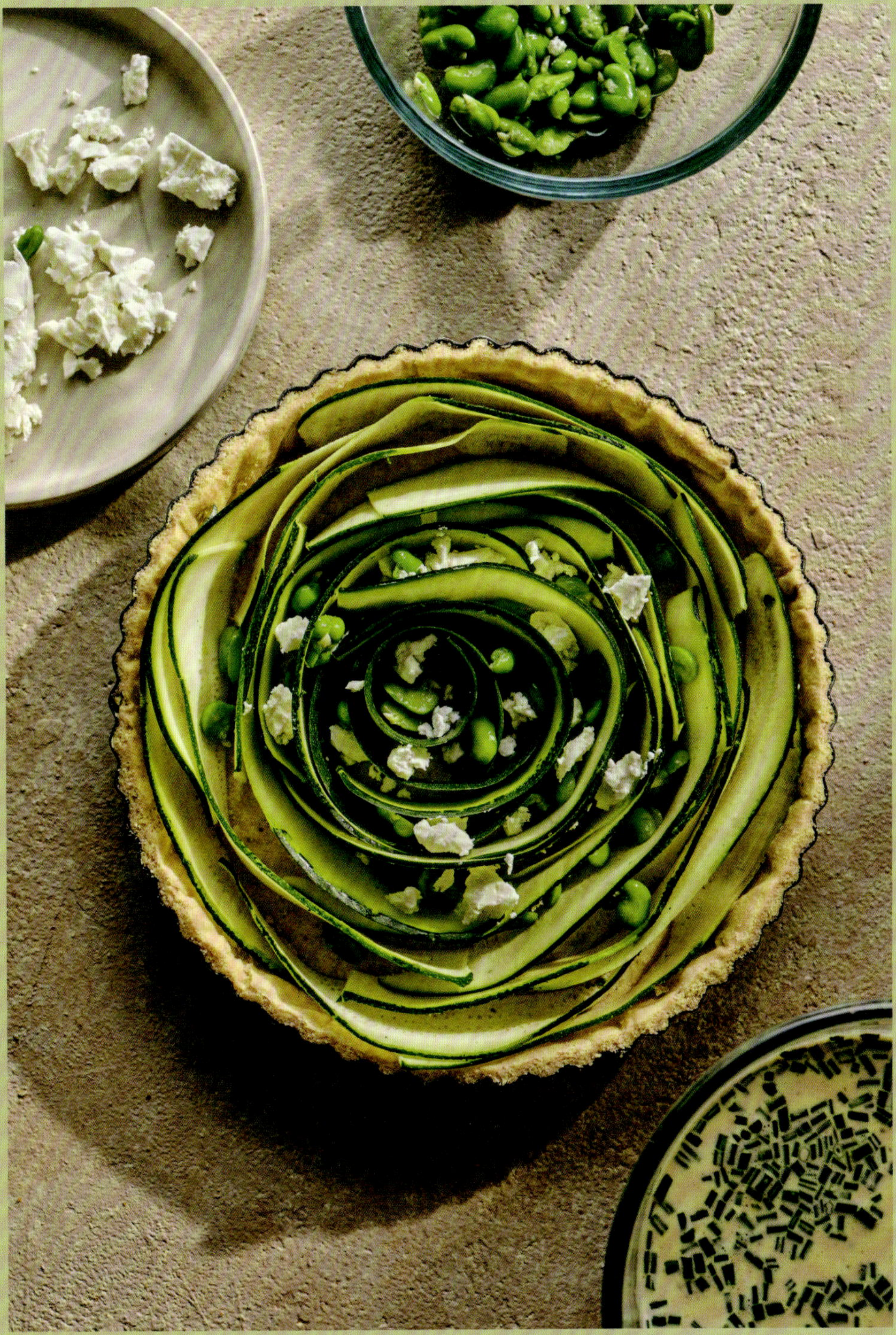

Hand-held Beef Pies

Packed with flavor, these little hot water crust pies are perfect as part of a buffet, to take on a picnic, or to eat at a sports game! Have fun with the lids – you can do lattice, initials or whatever decoration takes your fancy.

Makes 12

Filling
1 tbsp vegetable oil
1 small onion, finely chopped
1 celery stalk, finely chopped
1 small carrot, finely chopped
6 oz (175g) ground beef
½ tbsp all-purpose flour
½ cup (125g) beef broth
A generous dash of Worcestershire sauce
1 tbsp frozen peas
Salt and black pepper

Hot water dough
2 cups (250g) all-purpose flour, plus extra to dust
⅓ cup plus 1 tbsp (50g) bread flour
½ tsp fine salt
2½ tbsp (40g) chilled unsalted butter, cut into small dice
3 tbsp (50g) chilled vegetable shortening, cut into small pieces
7 tbsp (100g) water
1 large egg yolk, beaten, to glaze

1. First, make the filling. Heat the oil in a wide saucepan over a medium-low heat. Add the onion, celery and carrot and fry for about 10 minutes until soft but not colored.

2. Increase the heat to high and add the ground beef to the pan. Cook until browned, stirring and breaking up the beef with a wooden spoon as it cooks. Sprinkle the flour over the beef and stir well, then pour in the broth and add the Worcestershire sauce.

3. Bring to a simmer, stirring, and cook until the liquor is thickened. Taste and season with salt and pepper. Tip the filling into a bowl and stir through the peas. Leave to cool.

4. Heat your oven to 400°F. Lightly grease a 12-cup muffin pan.

5. To make the hot water crust dough, mix the flours and ¼ tsp salt together in a large bowl. Add the butter and rub in with your fingers until the mixture resembles breadcrumbs.

6. Put the shortening, water and ¼ tsp salt into a saucepan and place over a medium heat until the mixture just begins to boil. Immediately pour the hot liquid onto the flour mixture and mix together vigorously with a wooden spoon.

7. As soon as the dough is cool enough to handle, tip it out onto a lightly floured surface and knead to form a smooth ball. Divide the dough into 2 pieces, one larger than the other (roughly two-thirds and one-third).

8. Working as quickly as you can, roll out the larger piece of dough to about a ⅛ inch thick; it should be glossy and still warm enough to touch. Using a 3½-inch biscuit cutter, cut out 12 rounds to line the muffin pan. Gently press into the molds, shaping the dough to fit the sides.

Continued overleaf

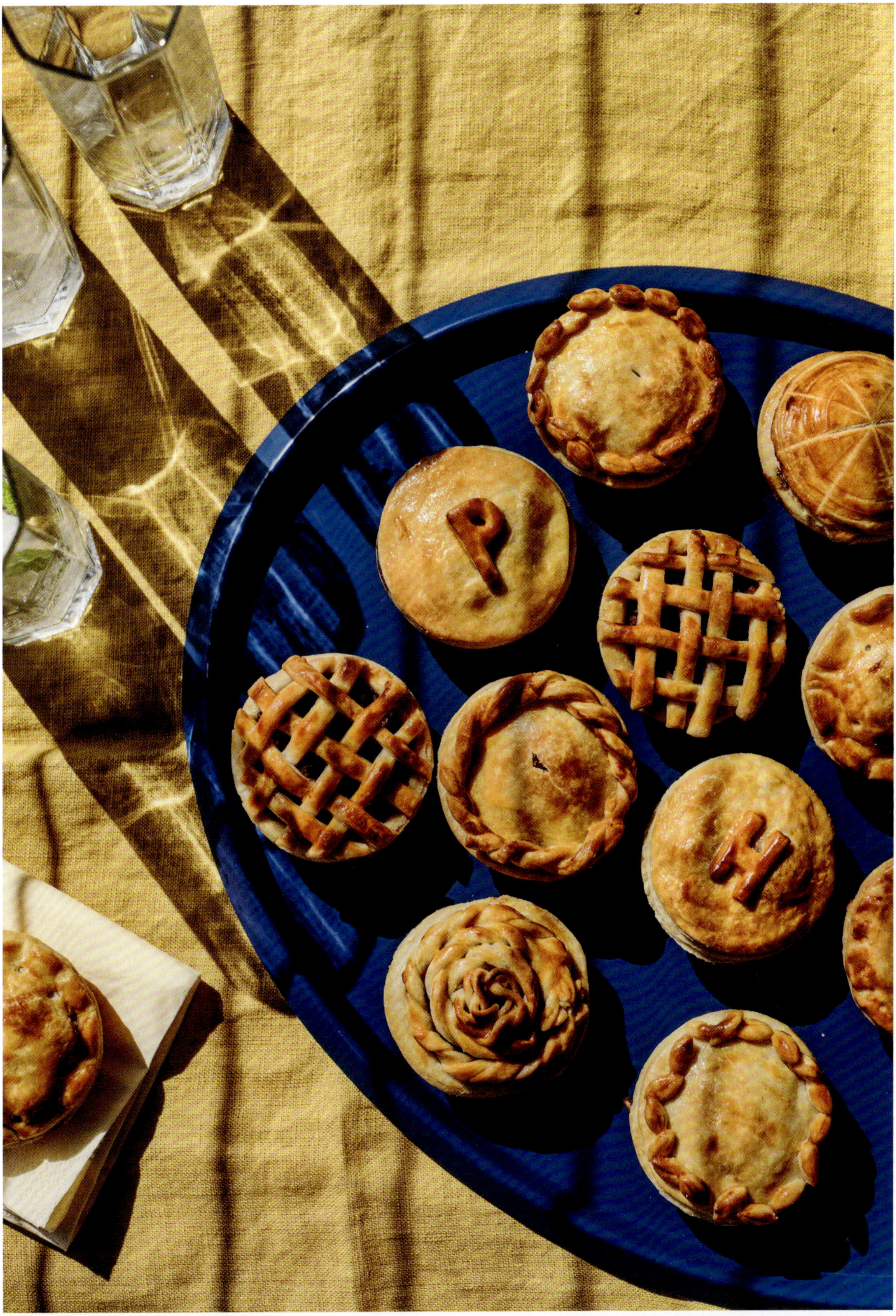

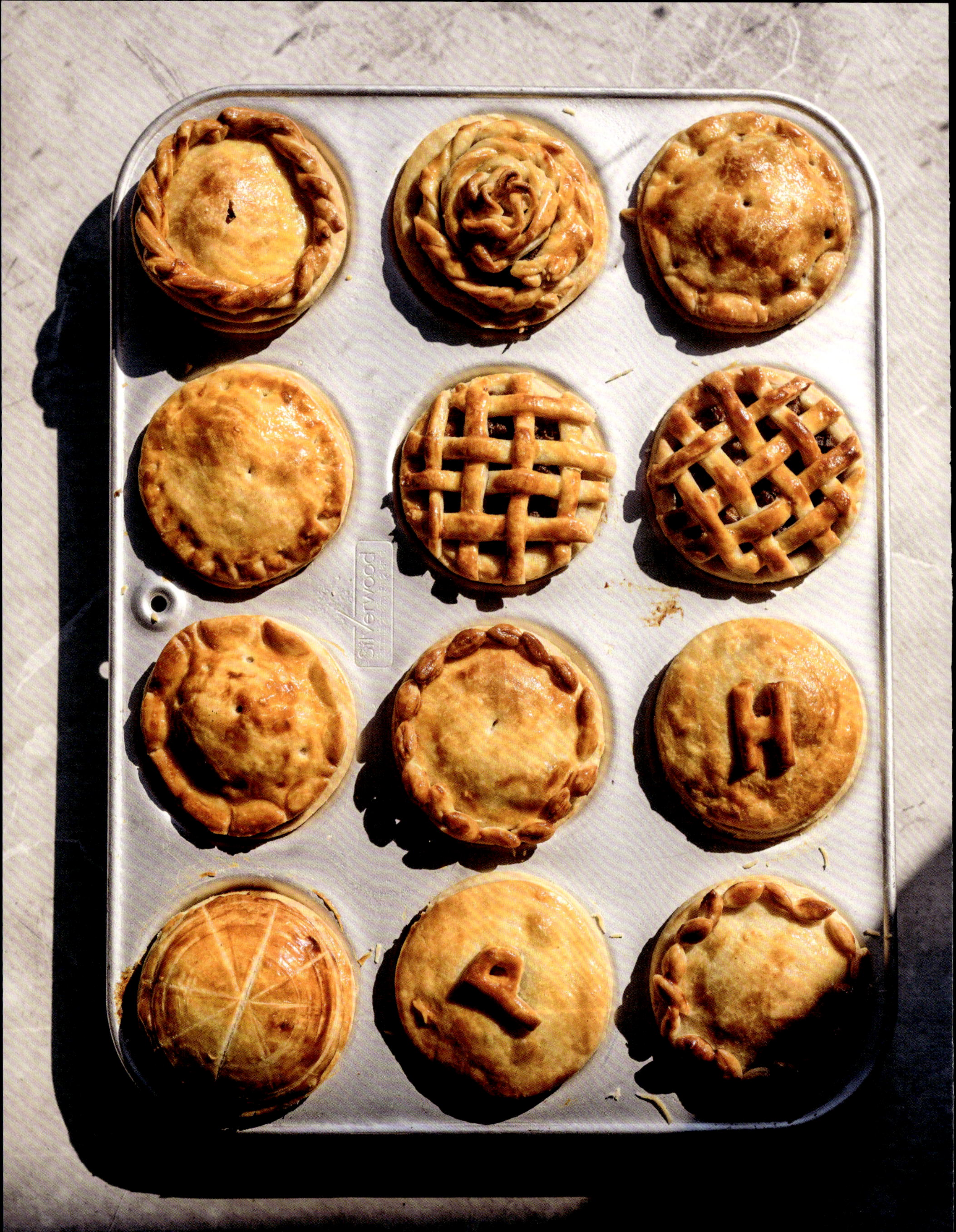
Silverwood

Continued from page 122

9   Immediately roll out the other piece of dough and use a 2½-inch cutter to cut out 12 pie lids. Lift away the trimmings and re-roll them to cut out more lids as necessary; save the final trimmings. As the dough cools, it stiffens and becomes more brittle to handle, so continue to work quickly.

10 Put a heaping soupspoonful of filling into each crust. Wet the rim of the crusts with a little water and position the lids. Gently press the edges together to seal. Use a skewer or cake tester to make a hole in the middle of each pie lid and brush the lids with beaten egg.

11 Cut leaves, initials, lattice strips or other decorations from the rolled-out dough trimmings and position on top of the pies; brush these with egg glaze too. Bake the pies in the oven for 25–30 minutes until the pies are golden brown and crisp.

12 Leave the pies to rest in the pan for 5 minutes then carefully unmold, using a small offset spatula to help remove them from the pan. Serve hot or at room temperature.

Classic Sandwich Bread

This is a great all-rounder loaf, perfect for toast or finger sandwiches for an afternoon tea. And it's an ideal easy recipe to get you into bread making. It's all about the kneading process and fermentation as the dough rises. The more slowly it rises, the more flavor you will get into your loaf.

Makes 1 loaf

Sponge
1⅔ cups (200g) bread flour
¾ cup (180g) water
1 tsp (3g) instant yeast

Dough
2⅓ cups (300g) bread flour, plus extra to dust
⅔ cup plus 1 tbsp (170g) water
1 tsp (4g) instant yeast
1¼ tsp (7g) fine salt
A little oil, to grease the pan

1. To prepare the sponge, put the ingredients into a stand mixer fitted with the dough hook and mix on a low speed for 5 minutes. Cover and leave to rise for 2 hours.

2. Add the dough ingredients to your sponge and mix on low speed for 5 minutes until smoothly combined to form a dough. Increase the speed to medium and mix for a further 10 minutes to knead the dough until it is soft and elastic. Cover and leave to rise for 3 hours.

3. Lightly oil a 1-lb loaf pan. Tip the dough onto a lightly floured surface and punch down by folding the dough inwards repeatedly to knock out the air. Flatten the dough slightly into a rectangle, fold in the edges and roll up into a sausage.

4. Place the dough, seam side down, in the prepared loaf pan. Put the pan into a large plastic bag and leave to proof for about 2 hours until the dough is doubled in size and beautifully domed.

5. Heat your oven to 400°F.

6. Spray plenty of water into your oven as you put the loaf in (this creates steam, which helps to produce the perfect crust). Bake the loaf in the oven for 35 minutes or until golden and cooked through. To check, tip the loaf out of the pan and tap the base – it should sound hollow. Transfer to a wire rack to cool.

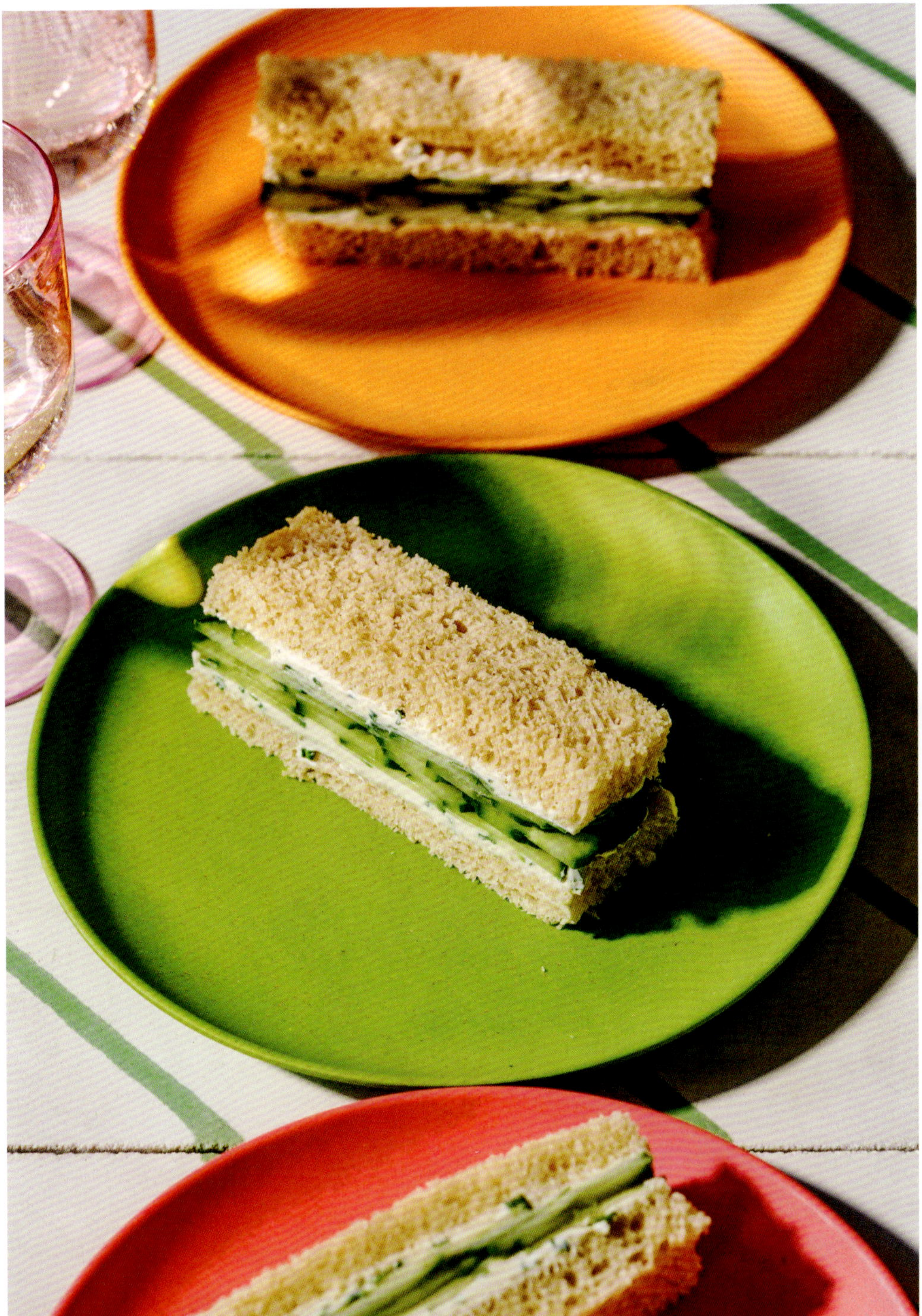

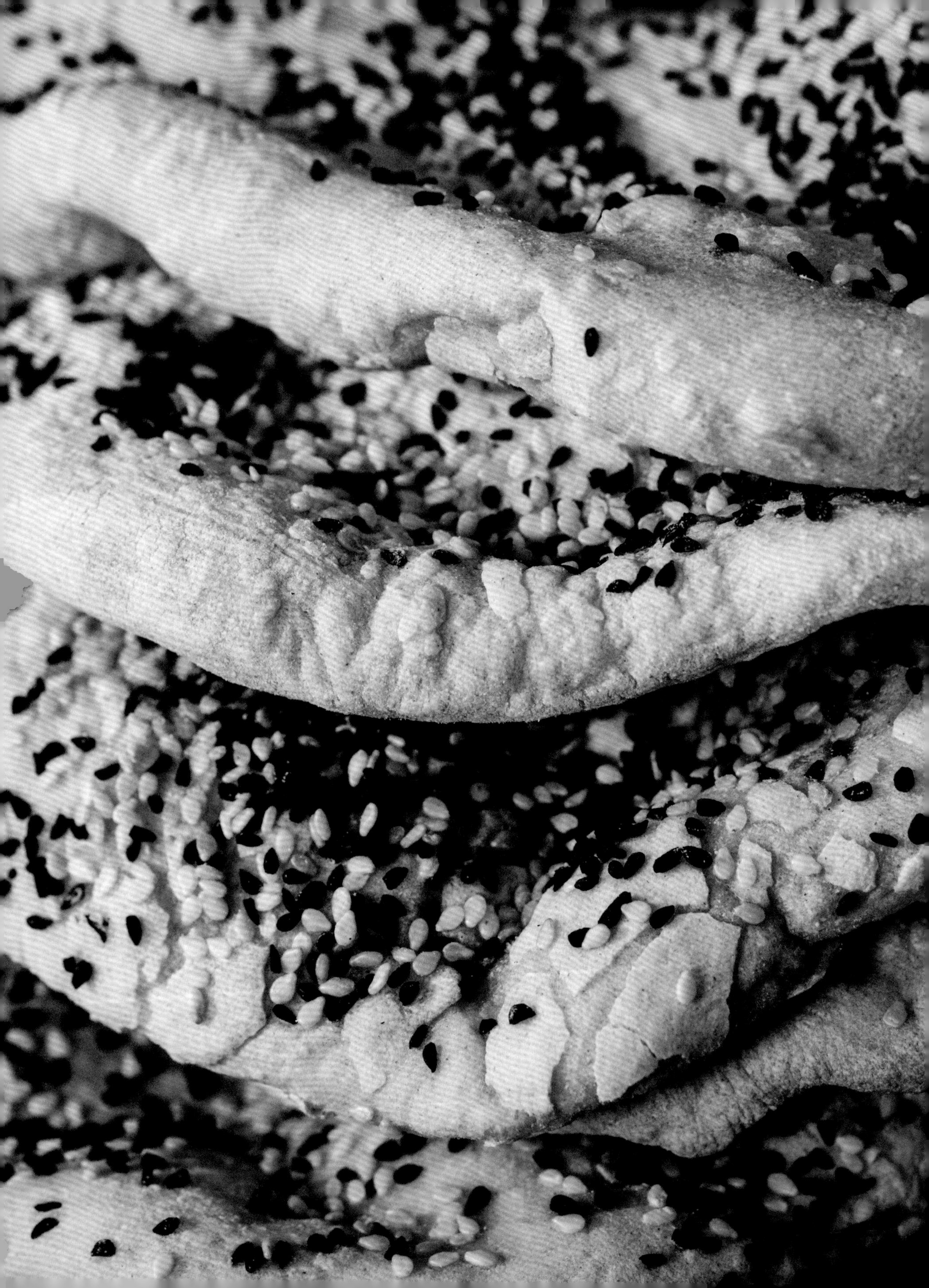

Taboon Bread

Baked over very hot pebbles that give it distinctive indentations, taboon is an ancient Palestinian bread named after the traditional clay oven it is cooked in. The bread puffs up as it cooks. Ideal as part of a mezze or used for wraps, taboon is also great for soaking up the juices from a stew.

Makes 10

4⅓ cups (550g) bread flour, plus extra to dust
1 tsp (5g) fine salt
1¾ tsp (5g) instant yeast
1½ cups (350g) water

Toppings
⅔ cup (100g) sesame seeds
½ cup (80g) nigella seeds

1. To make the dough, stir the flour, salt and yeast together in a large bowl. Make a well in the middle and pour in the water. Mix well to form a smooth dough that comes together in a ball. Turn the dough out onto a lightly floured surface and knead well for at least 10 minutes until smooth and elastic. (Alternatively, use a mixer fitted with the dough hook to mix and knead the dough, mixing on a low speed for a couple of minutes, then kneading on medium speed for 7–8 minutes.)

2. Cover the bowl and leave the dough to rise for 2 hours.

3. Tip the dough onto a lightly floured surface and divide into 10 equal pieces. Shape into balls.

4. Heat your oven to 475°F, i.e. very hot! Cover a sturdy baking sheet with well-washed, medium-sized pebbles and place in the oven to heat up for 1 hour.

5. Roll out one of the dough balls to a 10-inch round, brush lightly with water and sprinkle with sesame and nigella seeds. Place directly on the hot pebbles on the baking sheet in the oven. Cook for 3 minutes then turn the bread over and bake for a further 2–3 minutes.

6. Wrap in a clean kitchen towel to keep warm and soft while you shape and cook the rest of the dough balls in the same way. Serve as soon as they are all cooked.

Garlic and Onion Focaccia

Focaccia looks impressive but it's quite simple to make. It's also versatile: tomatoes, roasted peppers, olives, rosemary and thyme are all great additions; just make sure you use good extra virgin olive oil. You can eat it on its own, as part of a meal, or do what I do and make it into a big sandwich with lots of mustard!

10–12 squares

Dough
4 cups (500g) bread flour
¾ tsp (5g) fine salt
1 × ¼-oz (7g) packet instant yeast
1⅔ cups (400g) water
A little light olive oil, to oil

Topping
⅔ cup (150g) extra virgin olive oil
6 oz (180g) onions, sliced
About 1 tbsp dried oregano
Flaky sea salt

Garlic butter
1¼ sticks (150g) unsalted butter
6 garlic cloves, finely chopped

1. To make the dough, put the flour, salt and yeast into a stand mixer fitted with the dough hook and mix on a low speed for 5 minutes, gradually adding 1¼ cups of the water as you do so. Increase the speed to medium and slowly add the remaining water. Continue to mix for 14 minutes on medium until the dough is smooth and elastic.

2. Transfer the dough to an oiled large bowl, cover and leave to rise for 1 hour.

3. Uncover the dough and gently fold it from the edges into the middle, rotating the bowl as you do so. Re-cover the bowl and leave to rise for a further hour.

4. Repeat the folding process, then cover again and leave the dough to rise for another 2 hours.

5. Liberally oil the base of a 15 × 10-inch jelly roll pan. Gently tip the dough out onto an oiled surface and stretch it out into a rectangle, the size of your pan. Lift the dough into the pan and use your fingertips to spread it to the edges. Drizzle with around 3 tbsp of the extra virgin olive oil, cover and leave to proof for an hour.

6. Heat your oven to 400°F.

7. Using your fingers, push the onions into the focaccia, pressing firmly down to the base to create indentations, without disturbing the surrounding risen focaccia too much. Sprinkle liberally with oregano and flaky sea salt and drizzle generously with the rest of the extra virgin olive oil. Bake in the oven for 25–30 minutes until golden brown.

8. Meanwhile, for the garlic butter, melt the butter in a saucepan, add the chopped garlic and season with a little salt and pepper. When the focaccia comes out of the oven, brush the garlic butter all over the surface and drizzle with more extra virgin olive oil. Transfer to a wire rack to cool.

9. Serve the focaccia cut into squares.

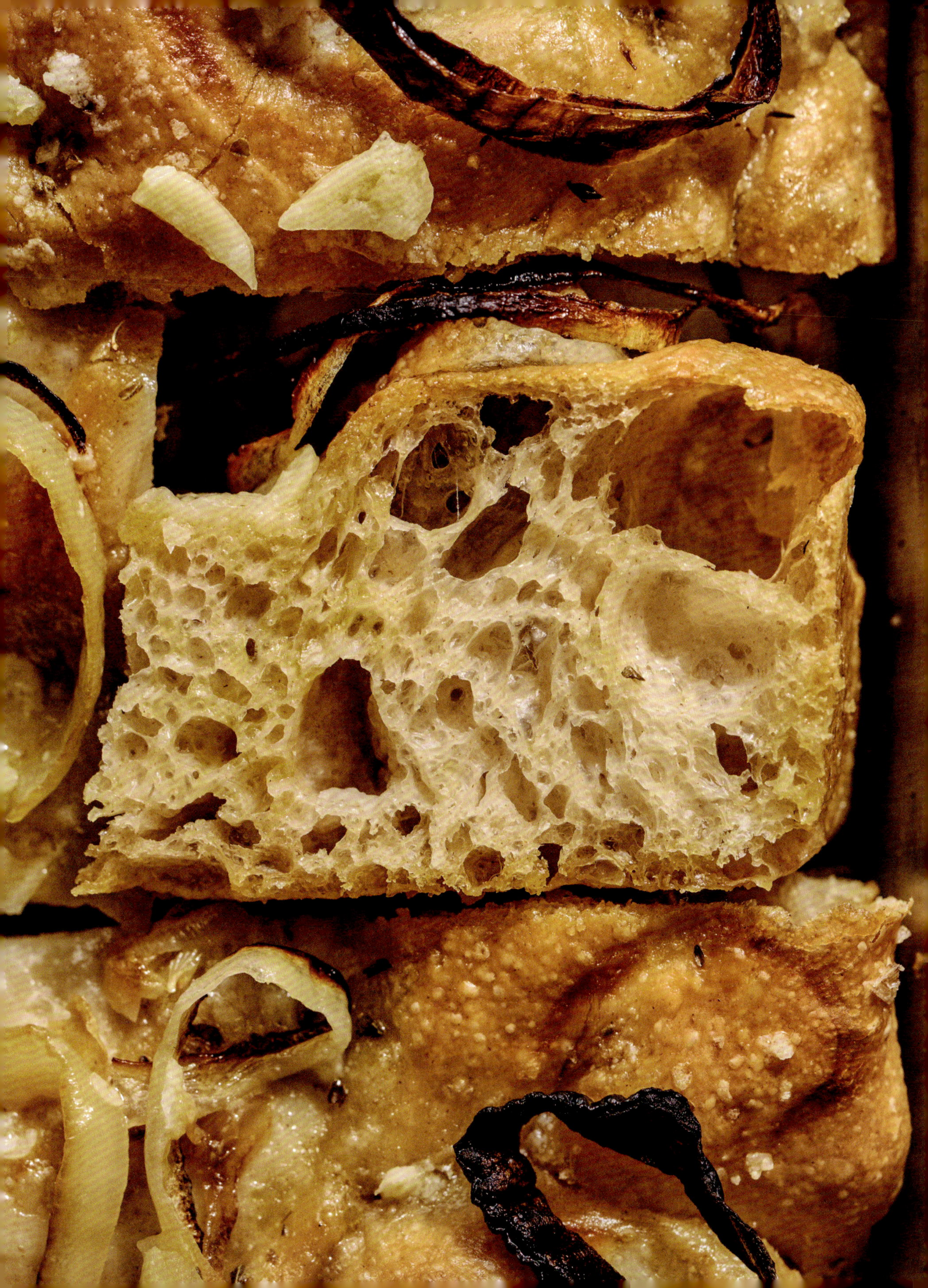

Fall

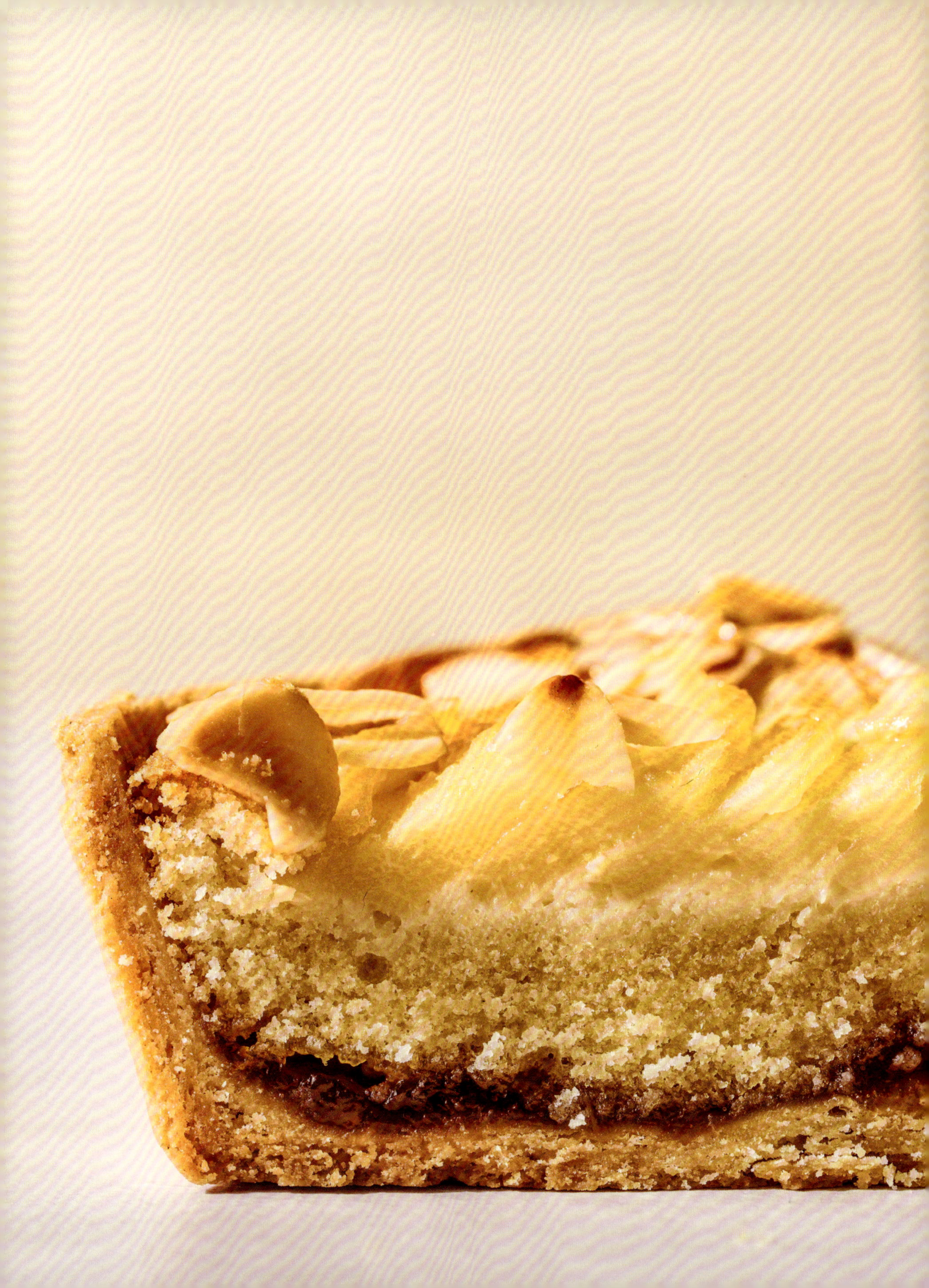

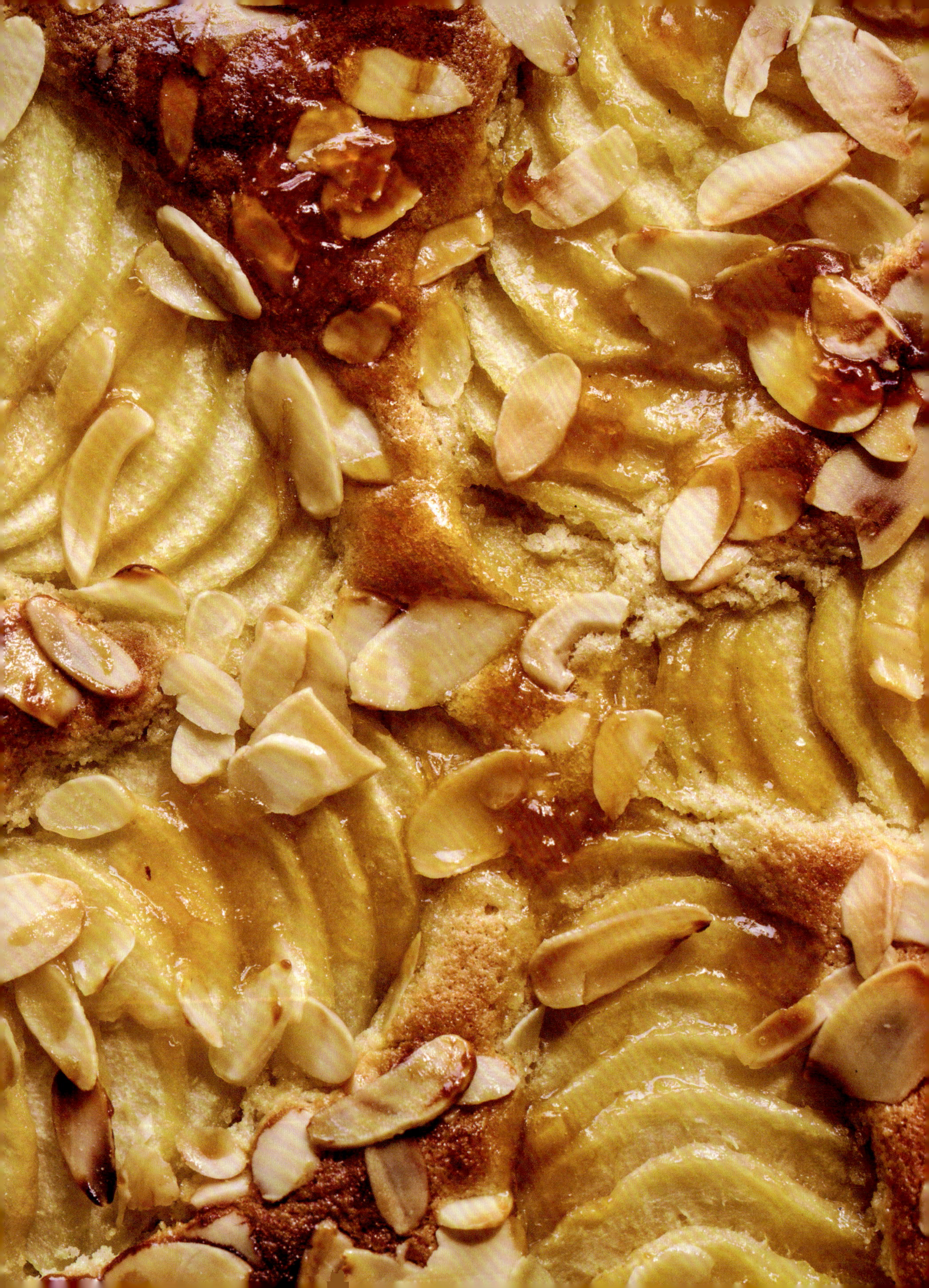

Fall is my favorite season for baking. It's all about warming spices and pure comfort food. At this time of year, we start thinking about hunkering down as the weather gets colder. Norwegians and Danes have captured that feeling so well – they call it *hygge*. It's like a warm, cozy hug next to a crackling fire. Put your slippers on, get comfy and watch your favorite boxset!

Early fall is when many countries celebrate harvest festival and you can see farmers everywhere gathering up their crops, preparing for the winter months ahead. It's almost like a mouse or squirrel going round gathering all the nuts and getting ready for hibernating. A wheatsheaf, like the one on page 168, is an intricate and beautiful bread made to celebrate the harvest and mark the move towards winter. You see them quite often in European bakeries, and I love making them.

In my own garden, the apple and pear trees are full at this time of year, and I love using the ripe fruit to make apple cakes, like the one on page 142, or my favorite Apple doughnuts (page 146). I also have a little vegetable patch at home and this is the season when it all starts coming through – parsnips, pumpkins and the sweetest carrots. I've used the best of the fall vegetables in my savory twist on the traditionally sweet roulade on page 160. It's creamy, delicious and a little bit unusual.

Dried fruits and spices also feature strongly in our baking around now. The Spiced loaf cake (page 145) and Chelsea buns (page 156) are both deeply spiced and perfect for an afternoon tea. In fact, I recently had the pleasure of delivering a big batch of Chelsea buns to the Royal Family at St James's Palace!

Each season is about embracing what's around at the time and finding ways to celebrate fruits and vegetables when they're at their best. It's one of the joys of baking seasonally, and for me fall is the highlight of the baking year.

Pear Bakewell Tart

Serves 8–10

Having spent some time around Bakewell, I wanted to include this classic British bake, which is traditionally made with cherries. Pears work beautifully with almond frangipane – it really is a marriage made in heaven. The freshness and intensity of the flavors make it far superior to store-bought versions.

Pie dough
1⅔ cups (200g) all-purpose flour, plus extra to dust
2 tbsp confectioners' sugar
7 tbsp (100g) chilled unsalted butter, diced
1 large egg
1 tsp lemon juice
2–3 tsp ice-cold water

Frangipane
7 tbsp (100g) unsalted butter, softened
½ cup (100g) superfine sugar
2 large eggs, at room temperature
⅓ cup plus 1 tbsp (50g) all-purpose flour
¾ cup (75g) almond flour
A drop of almond extract (optional)

To assemble
7 tbsp (100g) apricot preserves
1 × 15-oz (approx. 430g) can pear halves in juice, drained (6 pear halves needed)
¼ cup (20g) sliced almonds

1. To make the pie dough, mix the flour and confectioners' sugar together in a large bowl. Add the butter and rub in using your fingers until the mixture resembles fine breadcrumbs. Make a well in the center.

2. In a small bowl, beat the egg with the lemon juice and 2 tsp cold water then pour into the well and mix into the flour, using a dinner knife. Bring the dough together using one hand, adding a little more cold water if needed to do so.

3. Gently knead the pie dough into a ball and flatten to a disc. Wrap in plastic wrap and refrigerate for at least 20 minutes. Heat your oven to 400°F.

4. Roll out the pie dough on a lightly floured surface to a ⅛ inch thick and use to line a 9-inch loose-bottomed tart pan, leaving a little excess overhanging the edge.

5. Line the tart crust with parchment paper and fill with a layer of pie weights (or uncooked rice). Bake 'blind' for 12–15 minutes, until the crust is dry to the touch. Remove the paper and weights (or rice) and return the tart crust to the oven for about 5 minutes until it is very lightly colored. Using a small, sharp knife, trim away the excess dough from the edge. Turn the oven down to 350°F.

6. For the frangipane filling, beat the butter and sugar together until light and fluffy, then beat in the eggs one at a time. Stir in the flour, almond flour and almond extract, if using. Put the frangipane into a piping bag fitted with a ¾-inch plain piping tip.

7. Spread the apricot preserves over the base of the tart crust. Starting in the center, pipe the frangipane on top in a spiral, to fill the crust. Slice the pear halves and arrange the slices, overlapping, on the frangipane.

8. Bake the tart in the oven for 10 minutes, then scatter the sliced almonds evenly on top and bake for a further 15 minutes until golden. Transfer to a wire rack and leave to cool before releasing the tart from the pan. Cut into slices to serve.

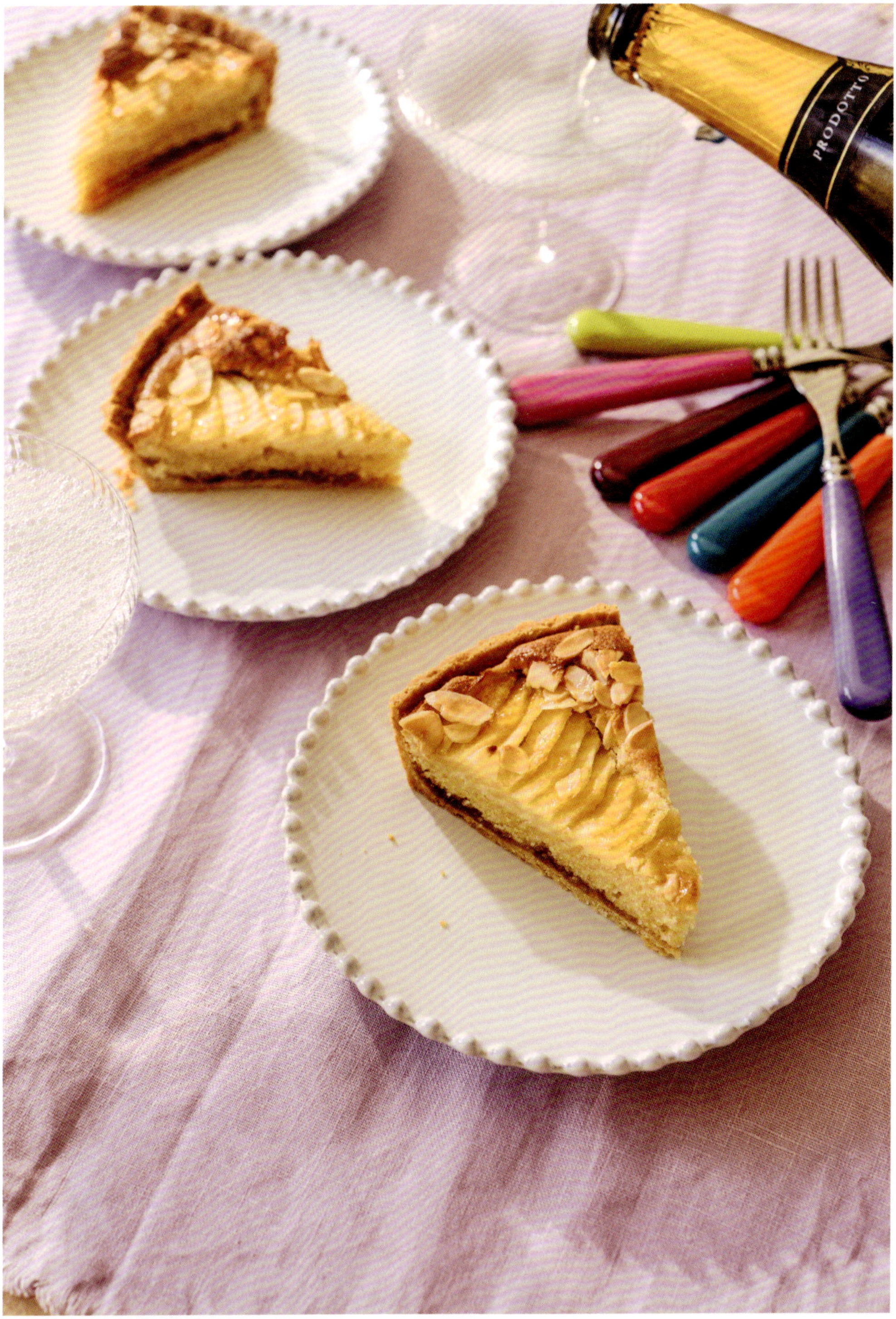
PRODOTTO

Almond and Amaretto Meringues

These are basically fancy, adult versions of meringues and cream that look very expensive! As with all meringues, whisk to properly stiff peaks and then incorporate the superfine sugar thoroughly, to ensure it is completely dissolved. Leave out the amaretto if you like, they'll be just as delicious.

Makes 12

⅔ cup (150g) egg whites (about 4 large eggs)
½ cup plus 1 tbsp (115g) superfine sugar
1 cup plus 1 tbsp (115g) confectioners' sugar
⅓ cup (50g) slivered almonds

Filling
1⅔ cups (400g) heavy cream
¼ cup (60g) amaretto liqueur

1. Heat your oven to 230°F. Line 2 baking sheets with parchment paper.

2. Put the egg whites into a large, clean bowl and beat using a hand mixer to stiff peaks. Whisk in the superfine sugar a tablespoon at a time, beating well after each addition and scraping down the sides of the bowl once or twice to pick up any loose grains of sugar. The meringue should be thick and glossy.

3. Sift one-third of the confectioners' sugar over the mixture, then gently fold it in, using a large metal spoon or spatula. Repeat to incorporate the remaining confectioners' sugar in two batches; the mixture should look smooth and billowy.

4. Transfer the mixture to a piping bag fitted with a ¾-inch plain piping tip and pipe 24 meringue kisses onto the prepared baking sheets. Sprinkle these with the slivered almonds. Bake in the oven for 1¼ hours until the meringues are dry, then turn the oven off and leave the meringues inside with the door slightly open until cooled completely.

5. For the filling, in a bowl, whip the cream to soft peaks and fold through the amaretto. Transfer to a piping bag fitted with a ½-inch star piping tip.

6. To assemble, pipe the amaretto cream onto half of the meringues, then sandwich together with the remaining meringues. Serve straight away.

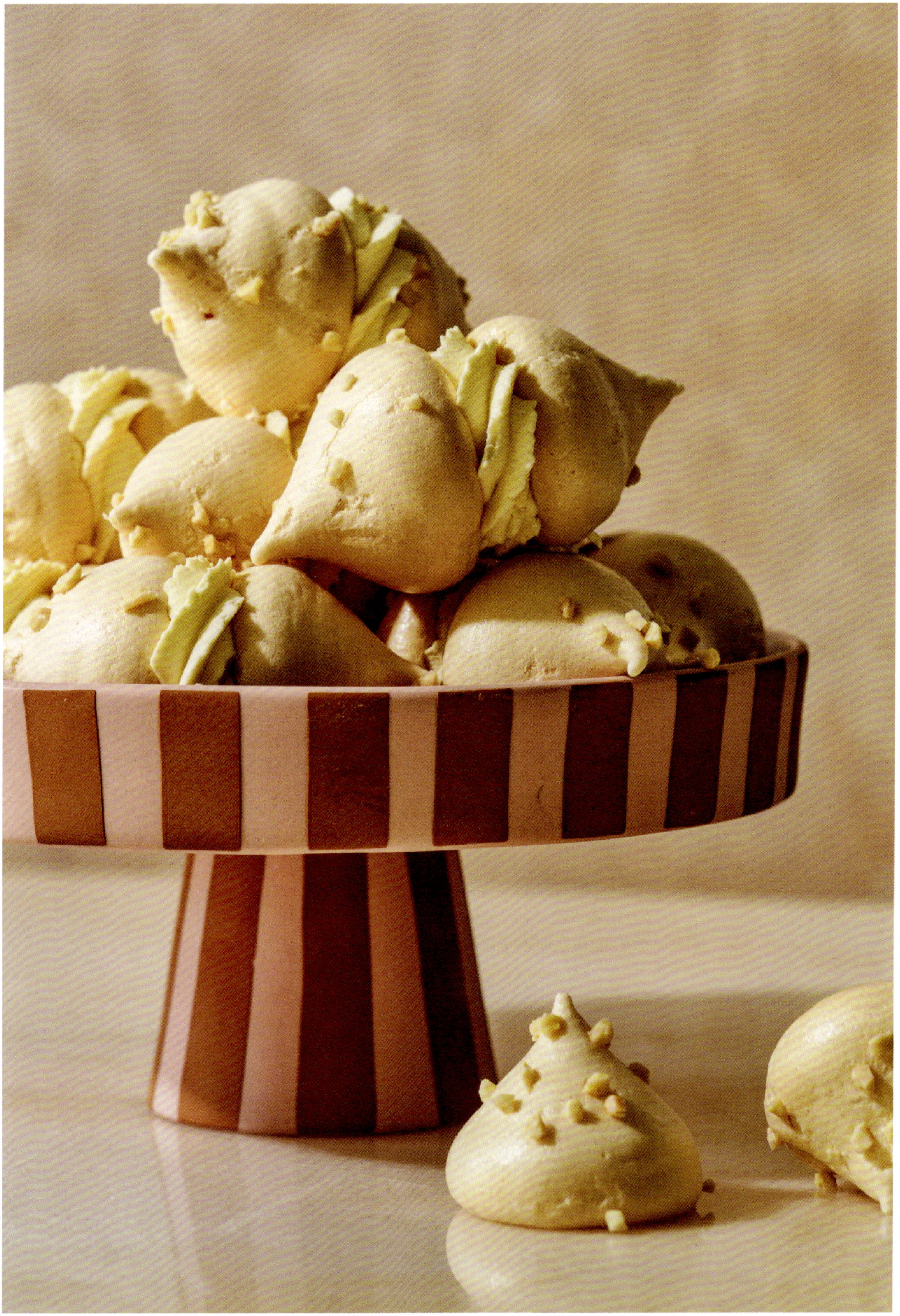

Blueberry Lattice Pie

An American classic, featuring one of my all-time favorite fruits. Blueberries have a natural thickener so they make a great pie filling. Make sure the pie dough for the lattice is chilled and weave it on a sheet of parchment paper, then lift it on top of your pie.

Serves 8

Cream cheese pie dough
7 tbsp (100g) unsalted butter, at room temperature
7 tbsp (100g) full-fat cream cheese, at room temperature
2 cups (250g) all-purpose flour, plus extra to dust
½ tsp fine salt
About 3 tbsp water

Filling
2 tbsp cornstarch
4½ tbsp superfine sugar
Finely grated zest of 1 lemon
A pinch of fine salt
scant 4 cups (500g) blueberries
1 tsp vanilla extract

To glaze
1 large egg, beaten

To serve
Heavy cream

1. To make the pie dough, put the butter and cream cheese into a food processor and blitz until smooth. Add the flour and salt and pulse to mix. Add just enough water to bring the dough together, continuing to pulse.

2. Transfer the pie dough to a lightly floured surface, gently knead into a ball and then flatten to a disc. Wrap the pastry in plastic wrap and rest in the fridge for an hour.

3. Divide the dough into 2 pieces: two-thirds and one-third. Re-wrap the smaller piece and chill for the lattice. On a lightly floured surface, roll out the larger piece to a ⅛-inch thick and use to line a 9-inch pie plate or dish. Trim the edges, leaving ½ inch of dough overhanging the rim. Chill in the fridge for 30 minutes.

4. Heat your oven to 400°F.

5. For the filling, in a large bowl, mix the cornstarch, 4 tbsp of the sugar, the lemon zest and salt together. Add the blueberries and vanilla extract and stir to mix then tip the filling into the pie crust.

6. Roll out the chilled portion of dough to a rectangle, at least 10 inches long and 8 inches wide, and cut into ½-inch wide strips. Weave the dough strips on a sheet of parchment paper dusted with flour to form a lattice. Brush the edge of the pie crust with water. Carefully invert the lattice on top of the pie and press the ends of the strips gently onto the rim of the crust to secure. Trim away the excess.

7. Carefully brush the pastry lattice with beaten egg and sprinkle with the remaining ½ tbsp sugar. Bake in the oven for 35–45 minutes until the pastry is golden and the filling is bubbling.

8. Place the pie dish on a wire rack and leave the pie to cool completely before serving, with plenty of heavy cream.

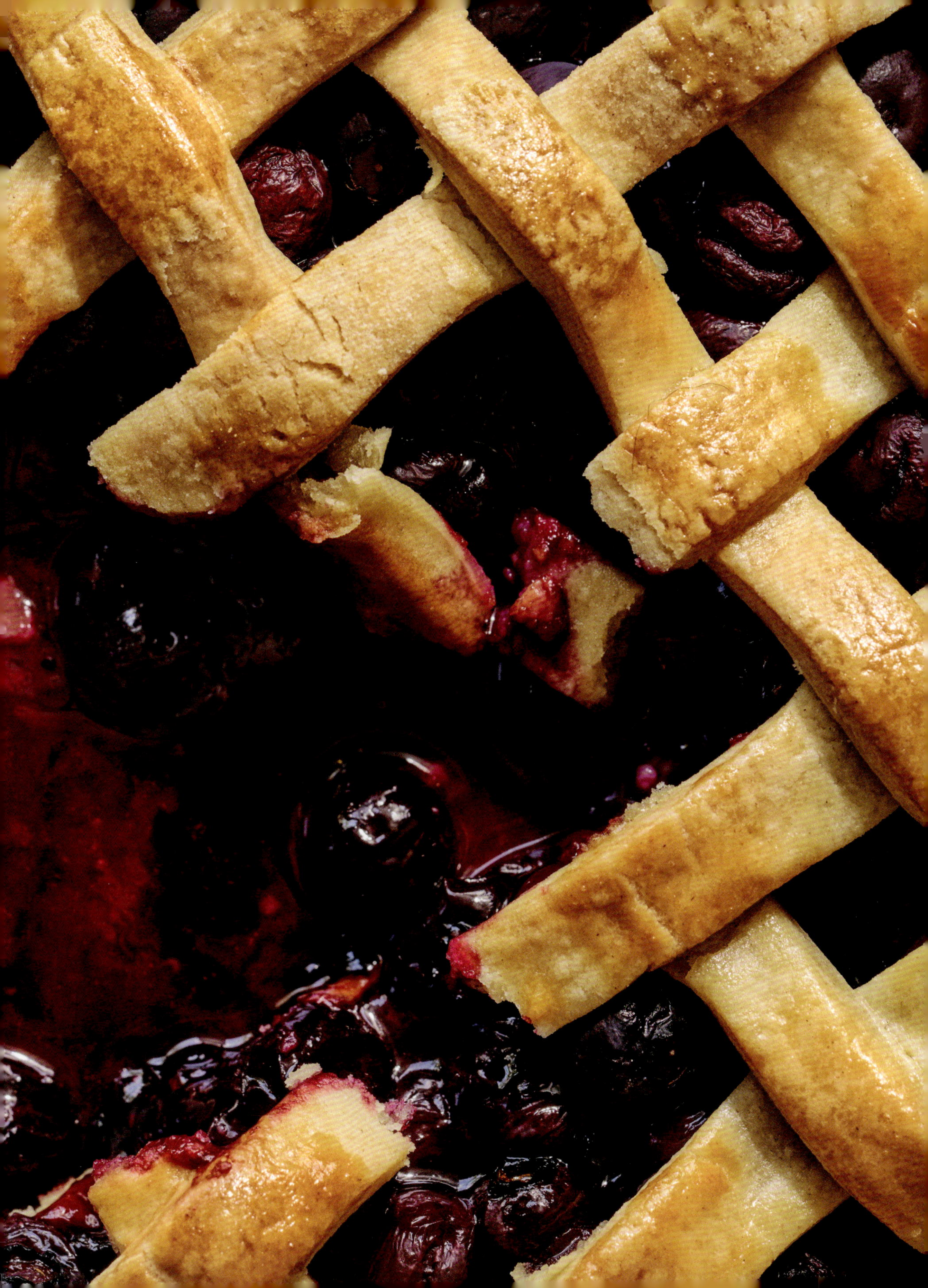

Candy Apple Cake

A robust apple sponge cake with a beautiful caramel flavor that's ideal for Halloween. The mini candy apples on top give it a professional finish, but if you don't fancy messing around with hot caramel, leave them off. You can forgo the frosting, too, and serve the cake with crème anglaise – as a perfect fall dessert.

9 squares

1¾ cups plus 1 tbsp (225g) all-purpose flour
2¾ tsp baking powder
½ tsp ground cinnamon
1 stick (110g) unsalted butter, in pieces, softened, plus extra to grease
2 medium-sized apples, such as Pink Lady or Gala
½ cup plus 1 tbsp (110g) light brown sugar
2 large eggs, at room temperature
2 tbsp milk
1 tbsp turbinado sugar

Mini candy apples
2 medium-sized apples (as above)
½ cup (100g) superfine sugar
1 tbsp glucose syrup
1½ tbsp water

Vanilla frosting
7 tbsp (100g) unsalted butter, softened
2 cups (200g) confectioners' sugar
1 tsp vanilla extract

To finish
Ground cinnamon, to dust

1. Heat your oven to 350°F. Grease and line a deep 8-inch square cake pan.

2. Sift the flour, baking powder and cinnamon together into a large bowl. Add the butter and rub in with your fingers until the mixture resembles fine breadcrumbs.

3. Peel, core and thinly slice the apples. Add them to the rubbed-in mixture with the light brown sugar and stir to mix. In another bowl, beat the eggs and milk together then add to the apple mixture and stir until well combined.

4. Transfer the mixture to the prepared pan, level the surface with the back of a spoon and sprinkle over the turbinado sugar. Bake in the oven for 40–50 minutes until the cake is risen and golden, and a cake tester inserted into the middle comes out clean.

5. Leave the cake in the pan for 10 minutes, then turn out and transfer to a wire rack. Leave to cool completely.

6. To make the mini candy apples, line a baking sheet with parchment paper. Peel the apples, then use a melon baller to scoop out 9 balls. Pat dry and place on the lined sheet. Insert a toothpick into each ball.

7. Heat the superfine sugar, glucose and water together in a small pan over a low heat, swirling the pan until the sugar dissolves; do not stir. Once dissolved, increase the heat and boil until the sugar syrup registers 285°F on a candy thermometer. Take the pan off the heat. Working quickly, tilt the pan and dip each apple in the caramel, turning it to coat all over. Return to the pan, toothpick pointing up. Leave to set.

8. To make the vanilla frosting, beat the butter, confectioners' sugar and vanilla extract together in a bowl until smooth.

9. To assemble, spread the frosting over the top of the cake and dust lightly with cinnamon. Cut into 9 squares and place a mini candy apple in the center of each square.

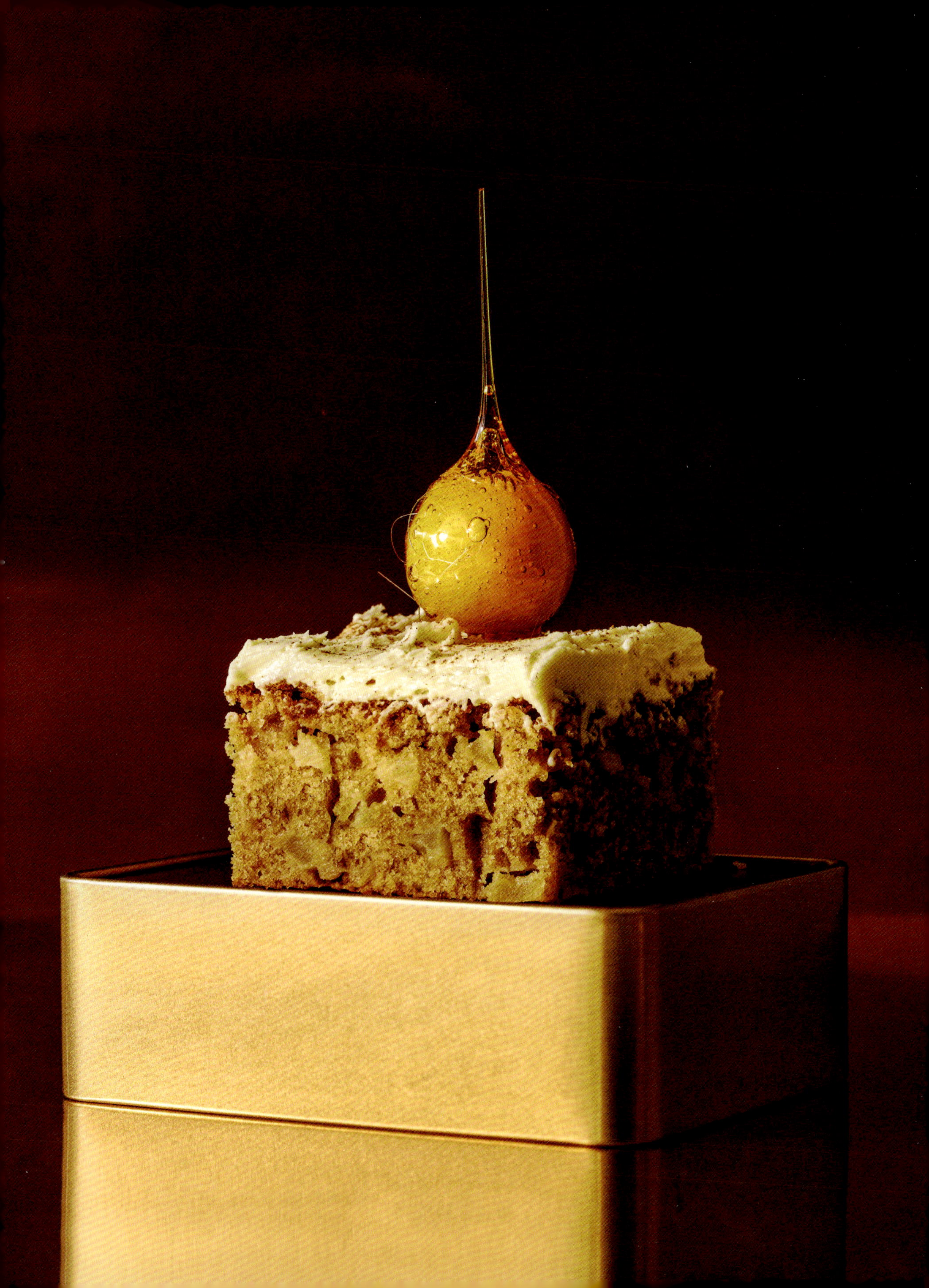

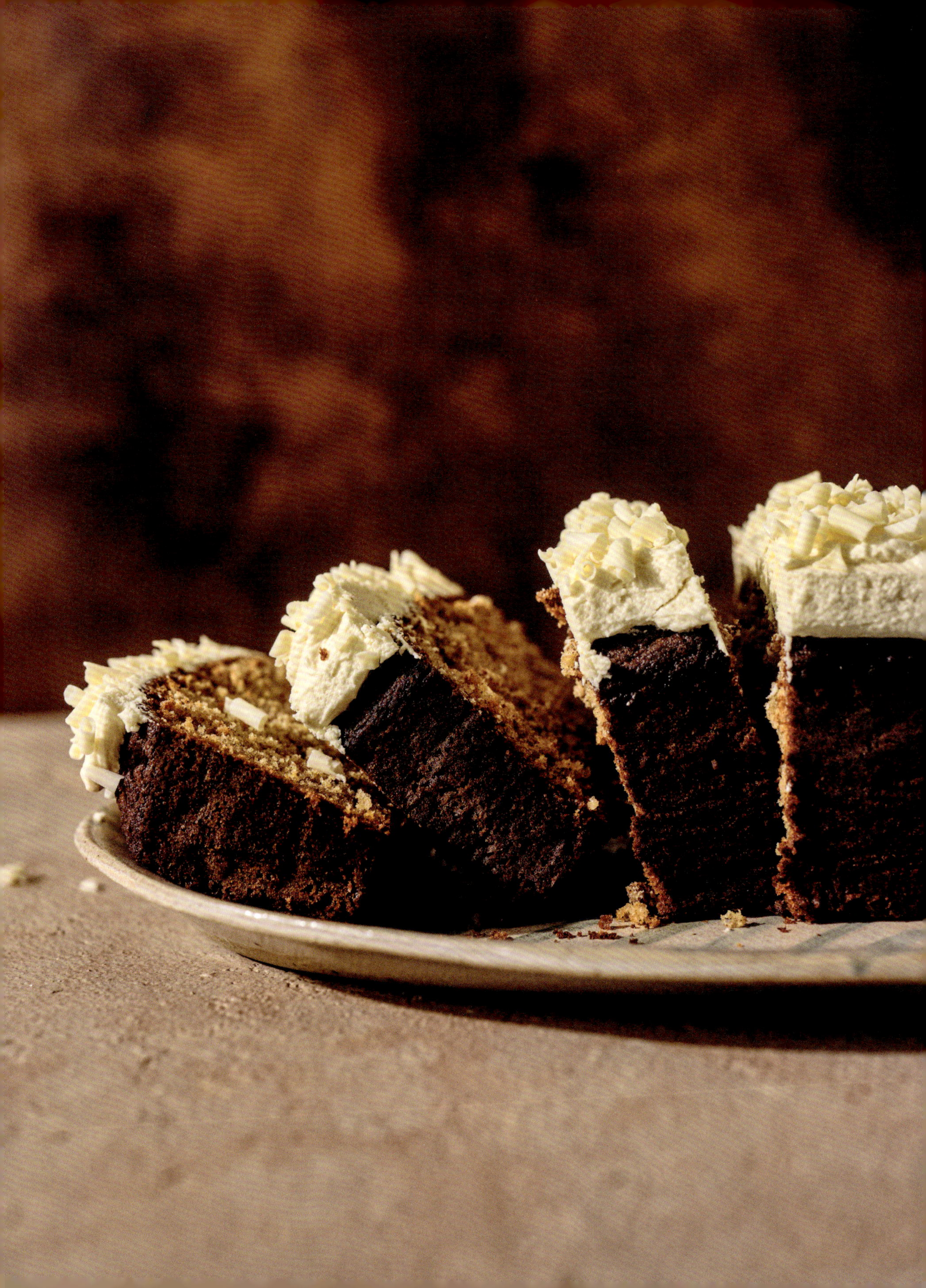

Spiced Loaf Cake

A slice of this classic spiced loaf cake with a cup of tea is the perfect fall afternoon treat. It's a recipe we used to make when I worked at The Dorchester, and with all those warming spices, it's one for when the colder weather is on its way.

10–12 slices

2 large eggs, at room temperature
½ cup (100g) superfine sugar
⅓ cup (65g) light brown sugar
½ cup (120g) vegetable oil, plus extra to oil the pan
½ cup (120g) whole milk, at room temperature
1 tsp vanilla extract
1⅔ cups (200g) all-purpose flour
2½ tsp baking powder
2 tsp ground cinnamon
1 tsp ground ginger
¼ tsp ground cloves
¼ tsp ground cardamom
A pinch of fine salt
Finely grated zest of 1 orange

White chocolate ganache
10 oz (300g) white chocolate, broken into small pieces
7 tbsp (100g) heavy cream

To decorate
2 tbsp small white chocolate curls

1. Heat your oven to 350°F. Lightly oil a 2-lb loaf pan and line with parchment paper.

2. Put the eggs and both sugars into a large bowl and beat with a hand mixer until light and creamy. Pour in the vegetable oil and milk, add the vanilla extract and beat until combined.

3. Sift the flour, baking powder, ground spices and salt together into a separate bowl. Add half of the flour mix to the whisked mixture and fold in gently until smoothly combined. Add the remaining flour mix, along with the orange zest, and fold together until combined.

4. Pour the mixture into the prepared loaf pan and bake in the oven for 45–50 minutes, until the cake is risen and golden, and a cake tester inserted into the middle comes out clean. Leave to cool in the pan for 10 minutes, then remove and let cool completely on a wire rack.

5. To make the ganache, put the white chocolate into a heatproof bowl. Heat the cream until it is almost boiling, then pour over the chocolate; do not stir. Leave to stand for 5 minutes, then stir until all the chocolate is melted and you have a smooth ganache. Let cool and thicken, then beat with a hand mixer to lighten.

6. Once the ganache is ready, spread it over the top of the cake and decorate with chocolate curls. Cut into slices to serve.

Apple Doughnuts

I love doughnuts – they're one of my absolute favorite things. I remember making my first apple doughnuts back in the eighties. In this version, I've stewed fresh apples with cinnamon and raisins for the filling… they taste incredible!

Makes 10

Dough
4 cups (500g) bread flour, plus extra to dust
1 tsp (5g) fine salt
1 × ¼-oz (7g) packet instant yeast
2 tbsp (30g) unsalted butter
2 large eggs, at room temperature, beaten
¼ cup (50g) superfine sugar
¾ cup plus 1 tbsp (200g) water

To cook
Vegetable oil, to deep-fry

Coating
½ cup plus 2 tbsp (120g) superfine sugar

Apple filling
6 medium-sized apples (Pink Lady work well)
2 tbsp water
⅓ cup (70g) superfine sugar
⅔ cup (80g) raisins
½ tsp ground cinnamon

1. Put all the ingredients for the dough into a large bowl and stir for 1 minute, using one hand or a wooden spoon, until the mixture comes together as a rough dough. Tip out onto a lightly floured surface and knead well for 10 minutes until silky and smooth.

2. Return the dough to the bowl, cover with a large plastic bag and leave for 2–3 hours until well risen.

3. Line a large baking sheet with parchment paper. Tip the dough out onto your work surface and divide into 10 pieces. Shape each into a smooth, tight ball, using your cupped hand. Place on the prepared baking sheet, cover with a large plastic bag to prevent the dough drying out and leave to proof for 1 hour.

4. Heat the oil in a deep-fryer or other deep, heavy saucepan (it should be no more than one-third full) over a medium heat to 350°F (check with an instant-read thermometer). Deep-fry the dough balls, 2 or 3 at a time, in the hot oil for 2–3 minutes, then turn over with a spoon, and deep-fry for a further 2 minutes or until golden brown all over.

5. Spread the sugar for coating out on a baking sheet. Remove the doughnuts from the pan, using a slotted spoon, and drain on paper towels then immediately roll in the sugar to coat all over. Place on a wire rack and leave to cool.

6. Meanwhile, to prepare the apple filling, peel, quarter, core and chop the apples. Put them into a saucepan with the water and place over a medium heat until they start to soften, then add the sugar, raisins and cinnamon. Continue to cook until the apples break down to form a purée. Set aside to cool.

7. Once cooled, make a hole in the side of each doughnut, using a piping tip or a sharp knife. Put the apple mixture into a piping bag fitted with a small plain piping tip and pipe an equal amount of apple filling into each doughnut through the hole. Your doughnuts are now ready to serve.

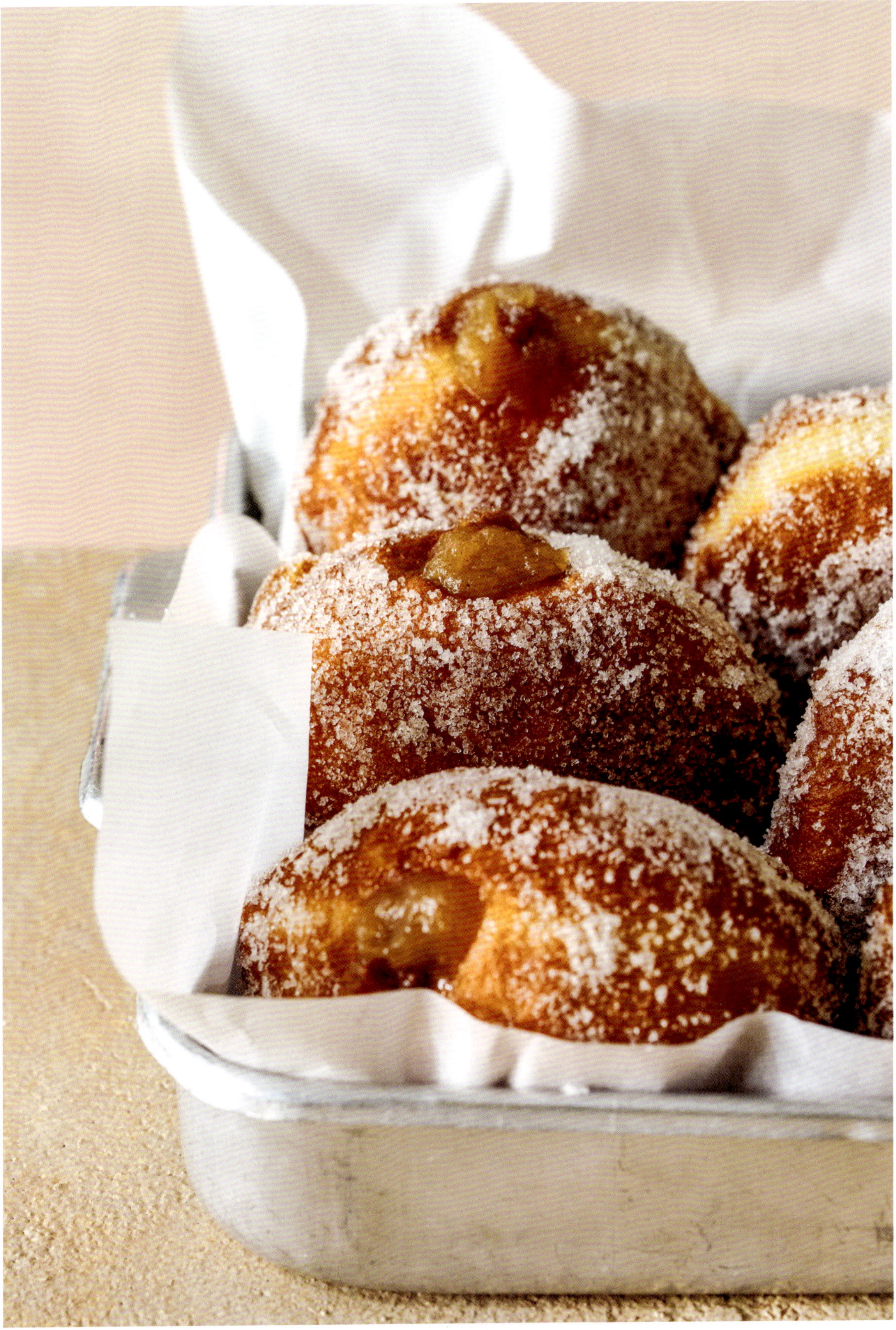

Pumpkin Spiced Macarons

These combine the popular American flavors of pumpkin spice with a classic French delicacy. It's unusual but it works really well! Rest the macarons for as long as you can before you bake them to help achieve the perfect crisp texture on the outside.

Makes 30

Macaron paste
3 large egg whites
2¾ cups (275g) almond flour
2¾ cups (275g) confectioners' sugar, sifted
Orange food gel coloring

Swiss meringue
3 large egg whites
1 cup plus 3 tbsp (240g) superfine sugar

Orange filling
1½ sticks (175g) unsalted butter, softened
4¾ cups (475g) confectioners' sugar, sifted
2 tsp pumpkin pie spice
Finely grated zest of 1 orange and 2 tbsp juice
Orange food gel coloring

To finish
Pumpkin pie spice, sifted, to sprinkle

1. Line 3 baking sheets with parchment paper. Using a biscuit cutter as a guide, draw circles, about 1¾ inches in diameter, on the paper, leaving a ¾-inch gap in between them. Turn the paper over and place on the baking sheet.

2. For the macaron paste, put the egg whites into a large bowl, add the almond flour and confectioners' sugar and mix to a thick paste. Transfer half to another bowl and color pale orange with a little food gel, mixing well.

3. For the Swiss meringue, put the egg whites and sugar into a heatproof bowl and set over a saucepan of simmering water, making sure the base of the bowl isn't touching the water. Using a balloon whisk, whisk vigorously until the sugar dissolves and the mixture registers 150°F on an instant-read thermometer.

4. Now, either transfer the mixture to a stand mixer fitted with the whisk attachment, or use a hand mixer, to whisk until it is cooled and you have a stiff, glossy meringue – this will take at least 5 minutes.

5. Fold half of the Swiss meringue into the orange macaron paste, a spoonful at a time. Gradually fold the rest into the plain macaron paste.

6. Spoon each macaron mixture into a piping bag fitted with a ½-inch plain piping tip. Pipe evenly over the marked circles on the baking paper. Leave the macarons to stand, uncovered, for at least 30 minutes, or until a skin forms. This helps prevent the surface from cracking.

7. Heat your oven to 300°F. Bake the macarons for 15 minutes, until risen and set. Leave to cool completely on the baking sheets.

8. To make the filling, using a hand mixer, beat the butter until soft, then beat in a few spoonfuls of the confectioners' sugar with the mixed spice. Beat in the rest of the confectioners' sugar, a spoonful at a time, adding the orange zest and juice with the final addition. Color deep orange with the gel. Place in a piping bag fitted with a small plain tip.

9. To assemble, pipe a little orange filling onto the plain macaron discs, leaving a narrow margin around the edge. Sandwich together with the orange discs and dust one half with the spice.

Also pictured overleaf

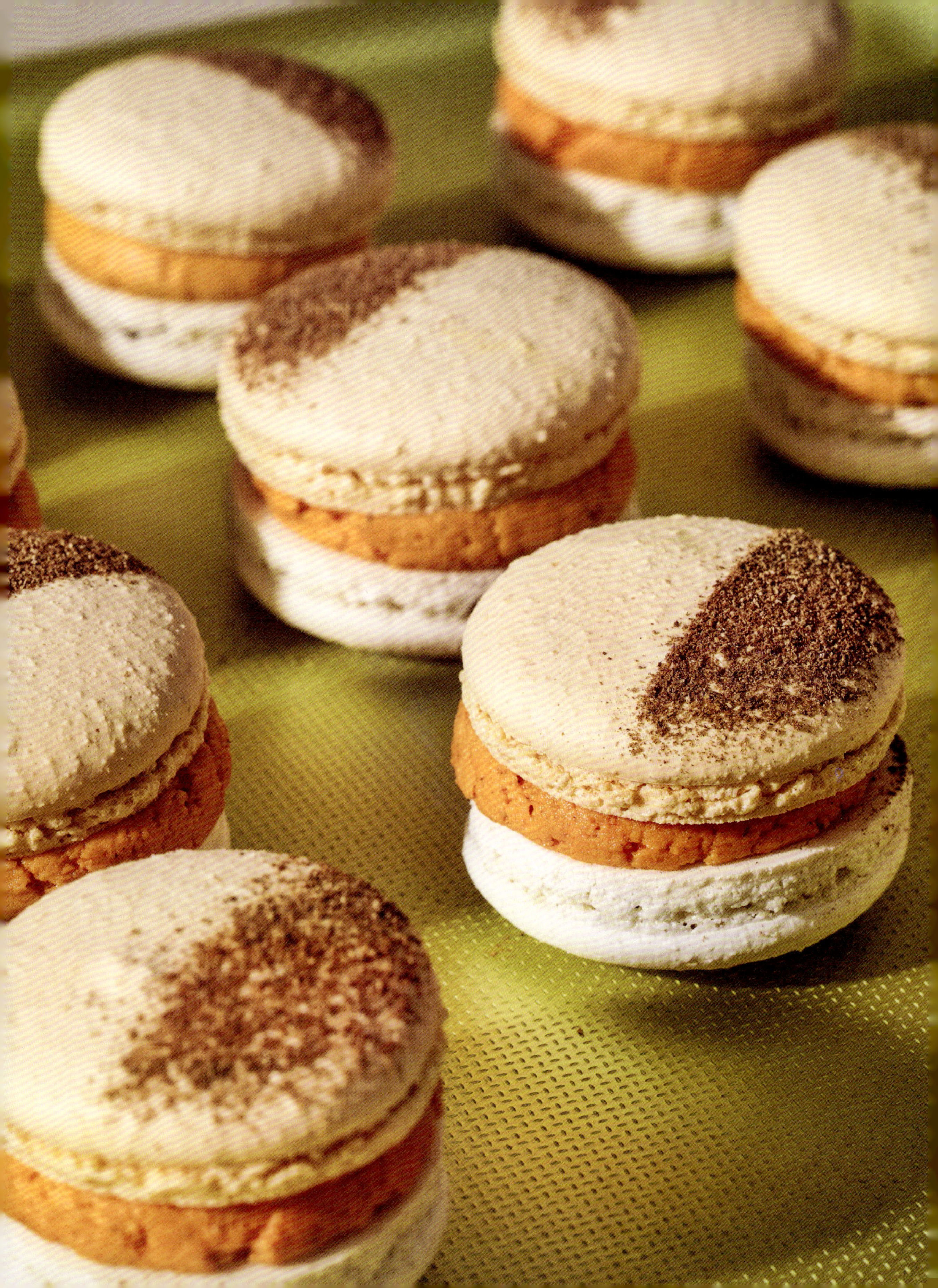

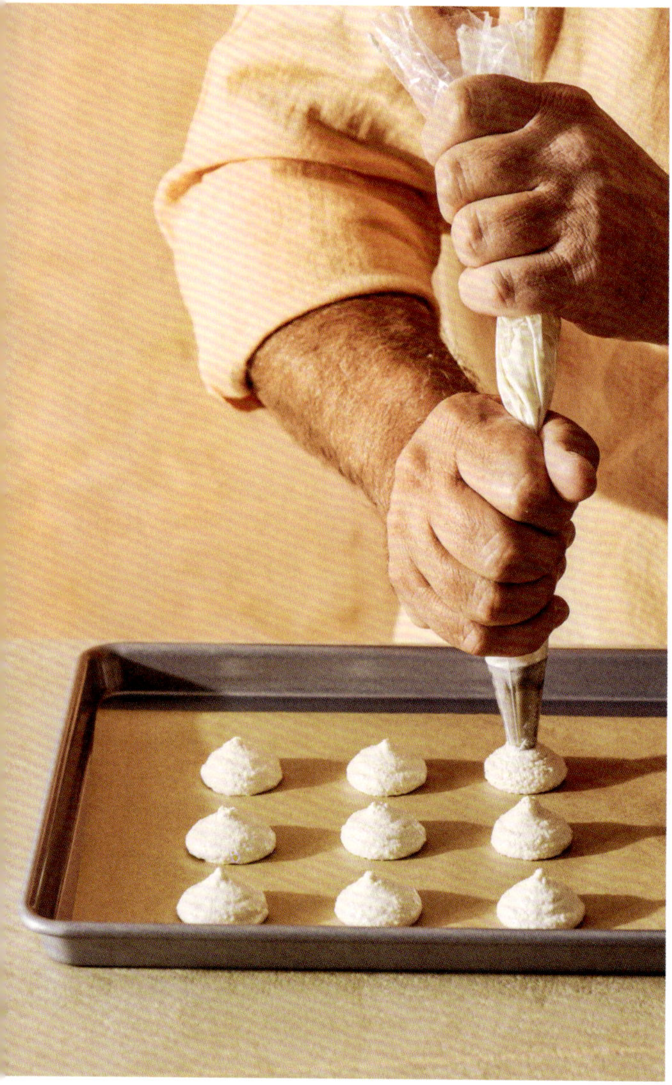
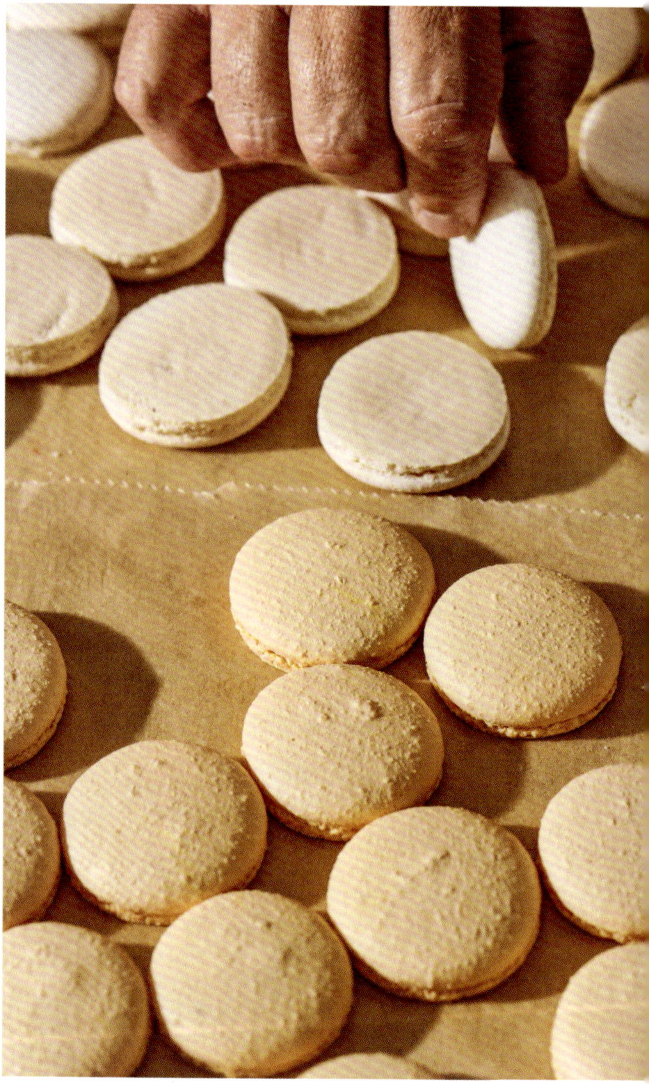

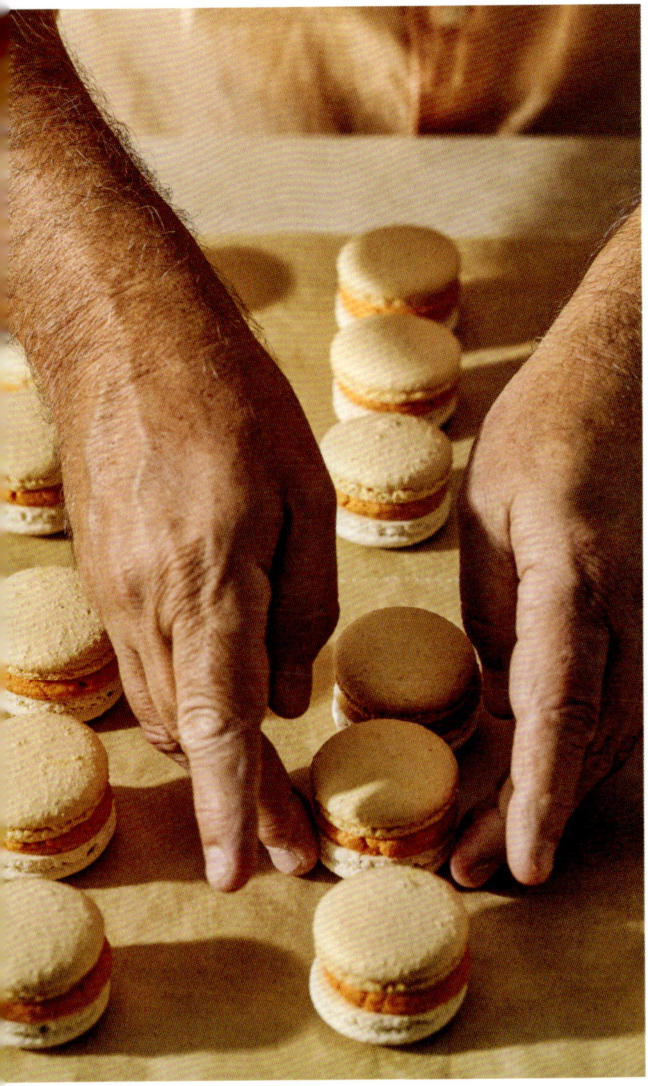

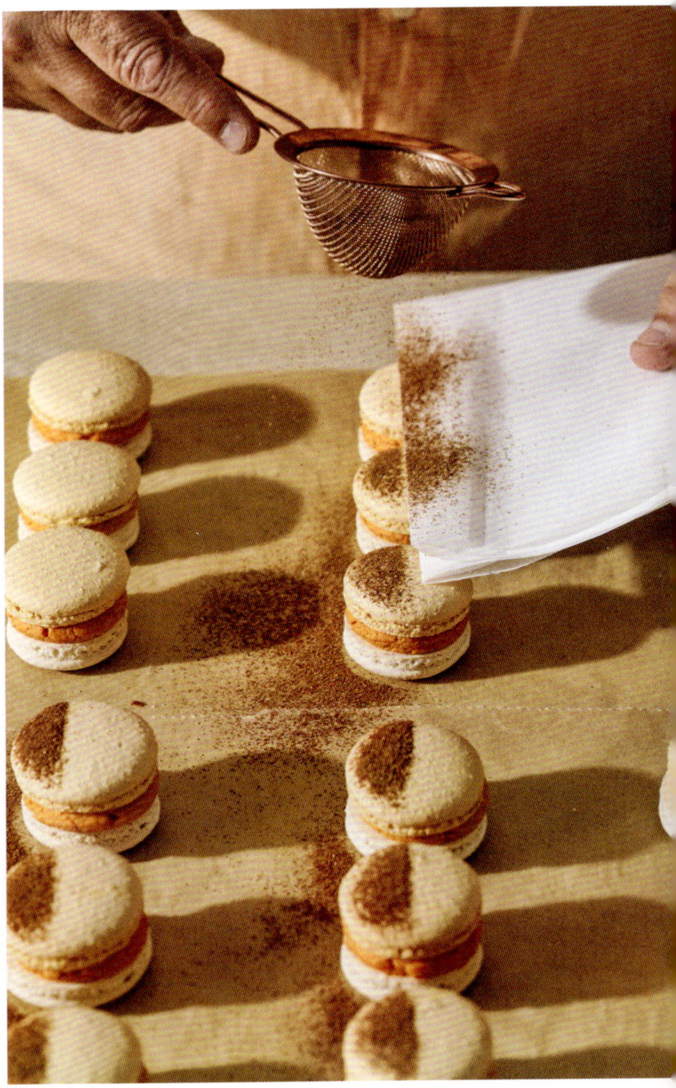

Peanut Butter Cookies

These are one of my all-time favorite cookies – the peanuts are king! The secret to the extra-soft filling is to freeze it in balls before wrapping in the cookie dough and baking.

Makes 16

Filling
1 cup (240g) creamy peanut butter

⅔ cup (60g) confectioners' sugar

Cookie dough
2¼ sticks (260g) unsalted butter, softened

⅔ cup plus 1 tbsp (175g) creamy peanut butter

⅔ cup (135g) light brown sugar

⅔ cup (135g) superfine sugar, plus extra for rolling

2 large eggs

2 cups plus 2 tbsp (275g) all-purpose flour

1 tsp baking powder

½ tsp fine salt

1. First make the filling: in a bowl, mix the peanut butter and confectioners' sugar together until smooth. Roll into 16 small balls, about 1¼ inches in diameter, between the palms of your hands. Place on a baking sheet and freeze until ready to use.

2. To make the cookie dough, put the butter, peanut butter and both sugars into a large bowl and beat using a hand mixer on medium speed until the mixture is light and fluffy. Add the eggs, one at a time, mixing until thoroughly combined.

3. Sift the flour, baking powder and salt together, then add to the peanut butter mixture and mix well to form a stiff dough.

4. Tip the dough onto a large sheet of parchment paper. Roll into a cylinder, about 3½ inches in diameter and 9½ inches long, and wrap in the paper. Place in the fridge for at least 2 hours to firm up.

5. Line 2 large baking sheets with parchment paper. Unwrap the dough and cut into slices, about ½ inch thick. Lay the slices flat on a clean surface and place a frozen peanut butter ball on each. Bring the edges of the dough up around the peanut butter ball and pinch them together to seal.

6. Transfer the dough balls to the baking sheets, seam side down, spacing them about 2 inches apart. Place in the fridge for 2 hours to firm up.

7. Heat your oven to 350°F.

8. Bake in the oven for 12–15 minutes until the cookies are golden on the bottom. They will still be soft when you take them from the oven, so leave on the baking sheets for a few minutes to firm up.

9. Transfer the cookies to a wire rack to finish cooling. Serve them still slightly warm from the oven, or cooled to room temperature.

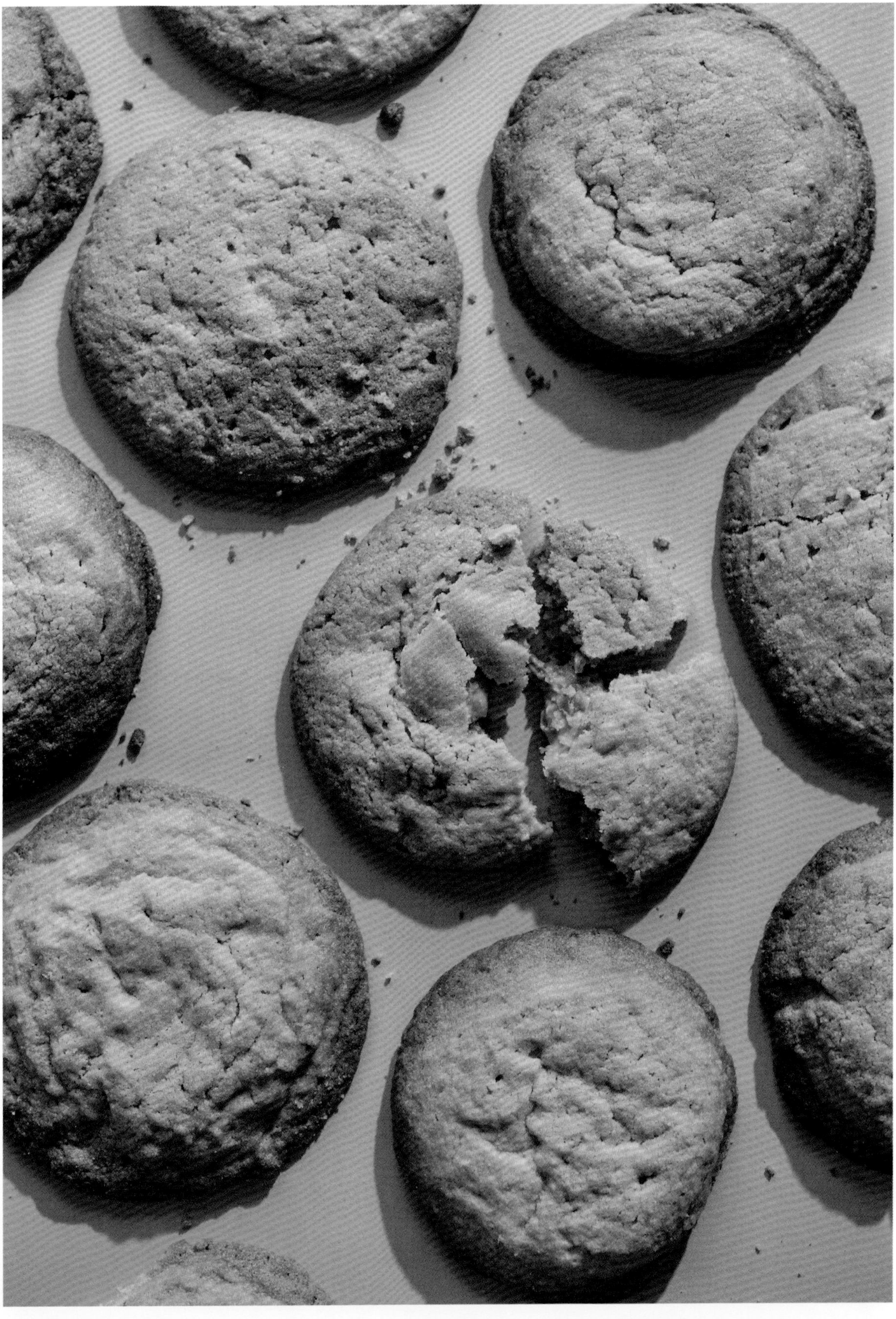

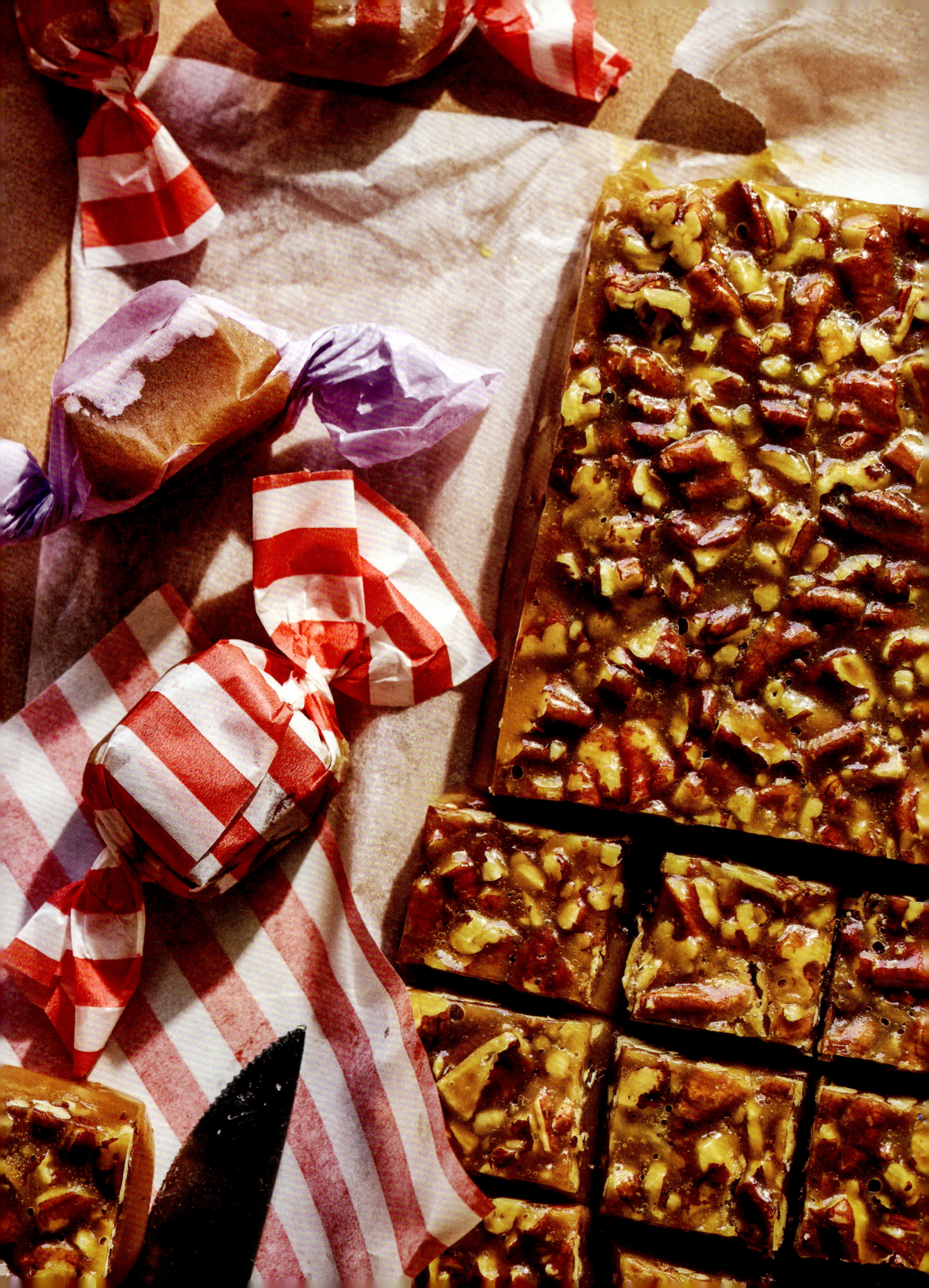

Pecan Fudge Bites

Great for Halloween, these little sticky, nutty fudge bites look beautiful and they are so easy to make. They keep well too, so you can make them well ahead.

Makes about 45

---

1 cup (100g) pecan nuts

7 tbsp (100g) unsalted butter, plus extra to grease

2¾ cups (550g) turbinado sugar

⅔ cup (200g) Lyle's golden syrup

1½ cups (350ml) heavy cream

1 tsp vanilla extract

½ tsp flaky sea salt

1. Heat your oven to 350°F. Grease a 9-inch square shallow baking pan and line with parchment paper.

2. Place the pecans on a baking sheet in a single layer and toast in the oven for 10 minutes. Tip onto a board and leave to cool, then roughly chop the nuts.

3. Put the butter, sugar, golden syrup and cream into a heavy-based deep saucepan and place over a medium-low heat, stirring occasionally, until the sugar is dissolved and the mixture comes to a simmer. Let simmer, stirring occasionally, until it registers 240°F on a candy thermometer.

4. Remove from the heat and beat in the vanilla extract and salt using a wooden spoon. Continue to beat until the mixture is thickened and no longer shiny. Stir in the chopped pecans.

5. Pour the mixture into the prepared pan, spread evenly and press down with the back of the spoon to level the surface. Leave to set.

6. Once the fudge has firmed up, cut into small squares and leave to cool completely. Store in an airtight container and eat within a couple of weeks.

Chelsea Buns

With an apricot, cinnamon and raisin filling, an apricot glaze and a zesty orange icing, these are a bit of a twist on the classic recipe. I don't like my Chelsea buns to be too square, so I leave them rounded and give them room to grow.

Makes 9

3⅔ cups (450g) bread flour, plus extra to dust

1 tsp fine salt

1 × ¼-oz (7g) packet instant yeast

1¼ cups (300g) milk

3 tbsp (40g) unsalted butter, plus extra to grease

1 large egg, at room temperature

Oil, to grease

Filling

2 tbsp (25g) unsalted butter, melted

Finely grated zest of 1 orange

⅓ cup (75g) light brown sugar

2 tsp ground cinnamon

1¼ cups (150g) raisins

1¼ cups (150g) chopped dried apricots

To finish

2 tbsp apricot preserves

1 cup (100g) confectioners' sugar, sifted

Finely grated zest of 1 orange

2 tbsp water

1. Put the flour, salt and yeast into a large bowl and stir to mix. Warm the milk and butter in a saucepan until the butter is melted and the mixture is lukewarm. Pour into the flour mix, with the egg, and stir until the mixture comes together as a smooth, soft dough. Tip onto a lightly floured surface and knead for 5 minutes until smooth and elastic. (Or use a stand mixer fitted with the dough hook, mixing on low speed until the dough comes together, then knead on medium speed for 3–5 minutes.)

2. Place the dough in an oiled bowl, cover and leave to rise for an hour or until doubled in size. Generously butter a 13 × 9-inch baking pan.

3. Tip the dough onto a lightly floured work surface and roll out to a rectangle, about 12 × 8 inches, with a long side facing you. Brush with the melted butter, then sprinkle evenly with the orange zest, then the brown sugar, cinnamon and dried fruit.

4. Tack down the long side of the dough nearest to you by pressing it down onto the surface with your thumb. Roll the opposite side of the dough towards you quite tightly. With a sharp knife, cut into 9 equal slices, about 1½ inches thick.

5. Place the buns, cut side up, on the greased baking pan, about ½ inch apart (i.e. close enough so that when they rise and bake, their sides will be touching). Leave to proof for about 30 minutes. Heat your oven to 375°F.

6. Once proofed, bake the buns in the oven for 20–25 minutes until golden brown, checking after 15 minutes or so and covering with foil if the tops are getting too brown.

7. Leave the buns to cool slightly in the pan. Warm the apricot preserves with a splash of water and pass through a sieve. Transfer the buns to a wire rack and brush with the preserves to glaze. Leave to cool.

8. Mix the confectioners' sugar, orange zest and water together in a bowl to make a smooth glacé. Drizzle the glacé over the cooled buns and leave to set before serving.

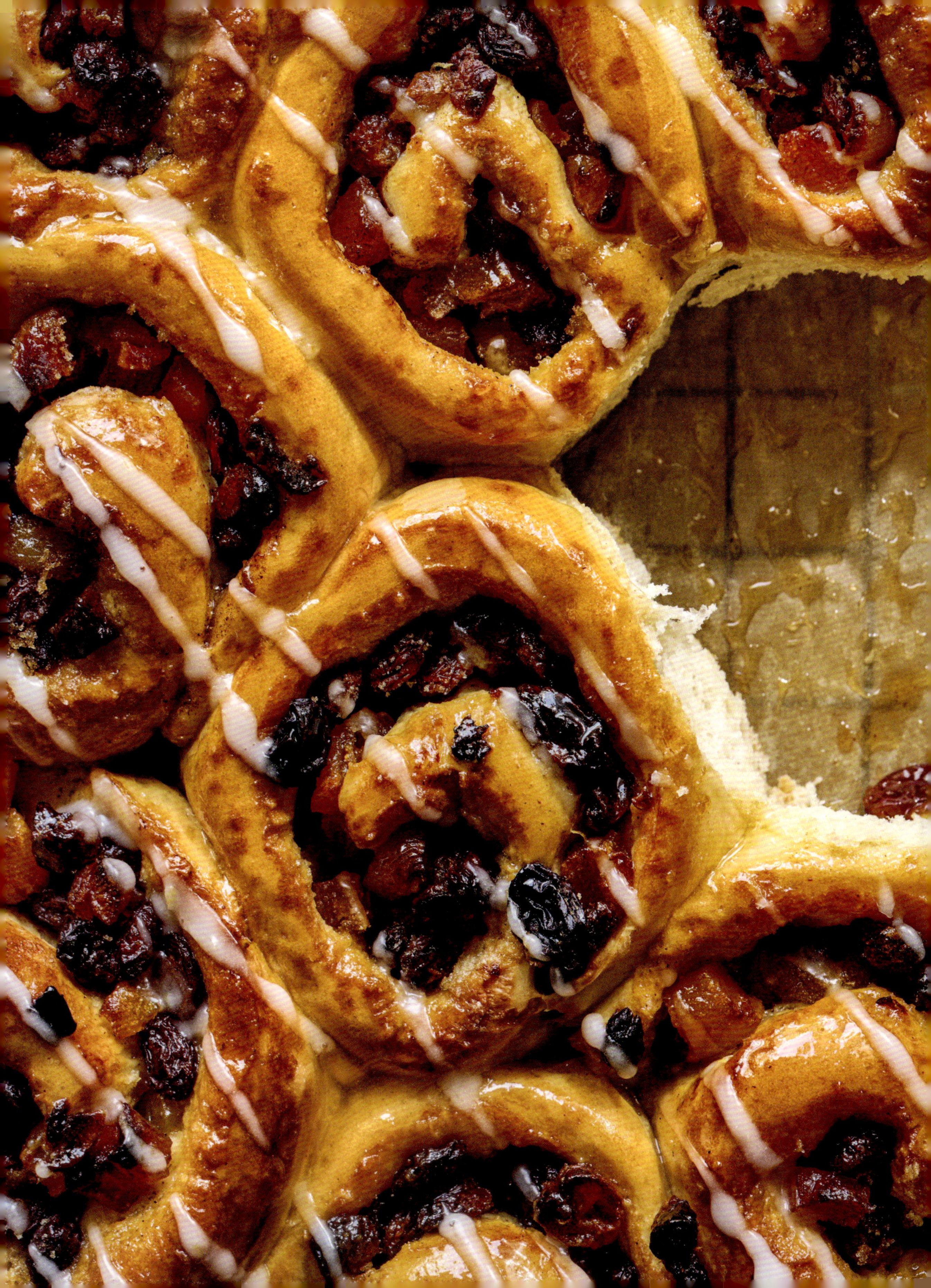

Maldivian Coconut Loaf

I first enjoyed this coconut cake for breakfast when I was on holiday in the Maldives, but I think it also works well for afternoon tea. It is made with rice flour, which is a popular ingredient on the islands. Rice flour absorbs more moisture than regular flour, hence the extra liquid in the mixture.

8–10 slices

Butter, to grease

3 cups (240g) unsweetened, shredded coconut

¾ cup plus 1 tbsp (120g) rice flour

½ cup (100g) superfine sugar

A good pinch of fine salt

¼ tsp ground cardamom (optional)

7 tbsp (100g) water

About ¾ cup plus 1 tbsp (200g) coconut milk

1. Heat your oven to 350°F. Grease a 1-lb loaf pan with butter and line with parchment paper.

2. In a large bowl, combine the shredded coconut, rice flour, sugar, salt and ground cardamom, if using, mixing well with a spoon. Make a well in the middle.

3. Pour the water and two-thirds of the coconut milk into the dry mixture, stirring to incorporate. Add as much of the remaining coconut milk as you need to achieve a thick batter consistency.

4. Transfer the batter to the prepared pan and spread evenly. Bake in the oven for 40 minutes or until golden and firm to the touch.

5. Leave the coconut loaf to cool in the pan for 10 minutes then transfer to a wire rack to cool. Serve cut into slices.

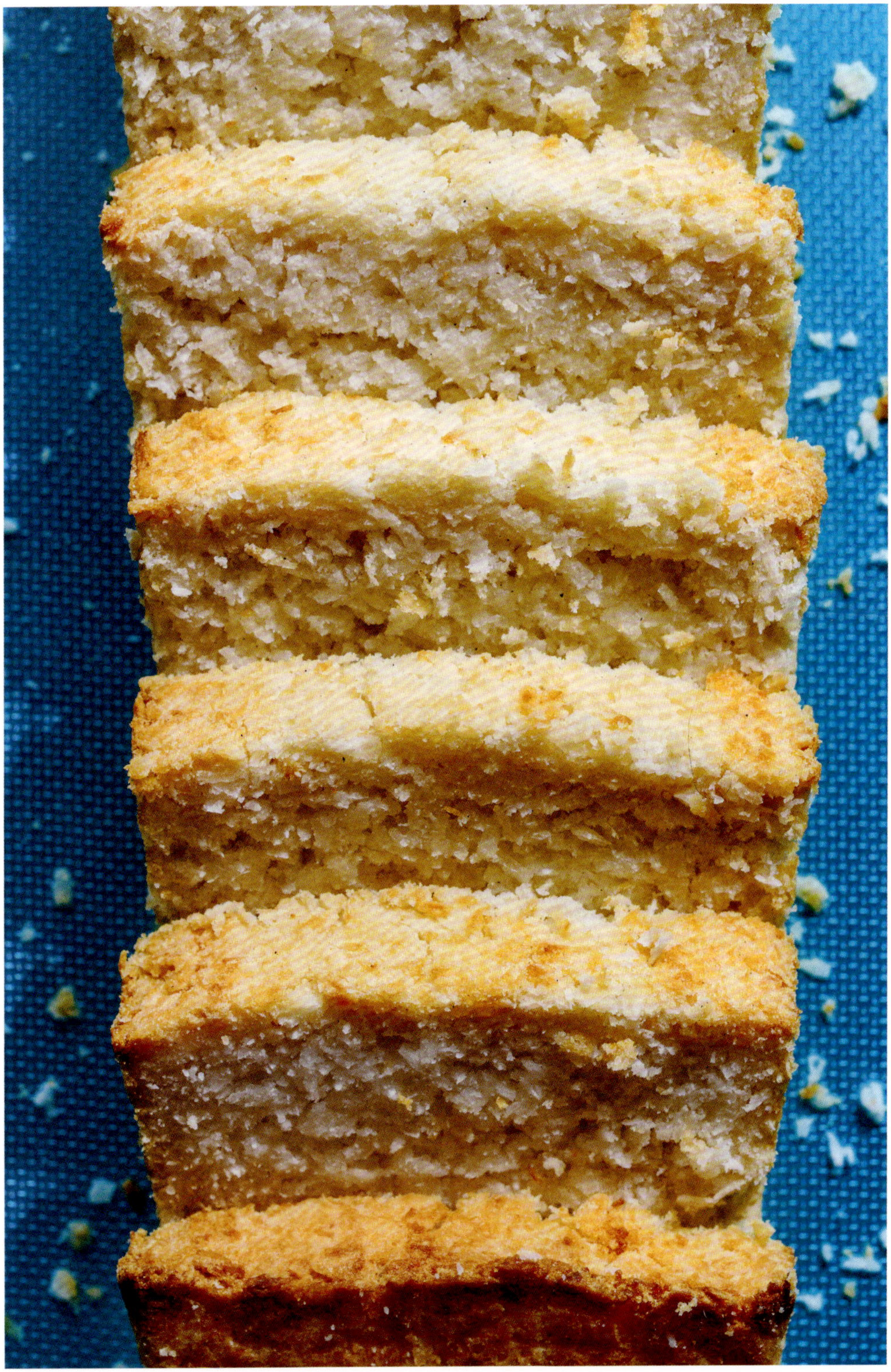

Hollywood Hot Dogs

I love hot dogs, but I wanted to find an easier way to hold them. I've encased the cooked sausage – with fried onions and ketchup – in my bread roll dough, and then cooked it all together. It will be the freshest hot dog you'll ever taste. And you won't lose bits of onion all over the floor!

Makes 12

Dough
4 cups (500g) bread flour, plus extra to dust
1 × ¼-oz (7g) packet instant yeast
1 tsp (5g) fine salt
1⅓ cups (330g) water

Filling
12 good-quality sausages of your choice
2 onions, chopped
A little vegetable oil, to fry
1 tbsp olive oil
A pat of unsalted butter
Tomato ketchup, yellow mustard, or a mixture of the two, to taste

To finish
1 large egg, beaten
⅔ cup (100g) sesame seeds

1. Place all of the ingredients for the dough in a stand mixer fitted with the dough hook. Mix on a low speed for 5 minutes, then increase the speed to medium and mix for a further 10 minutes until the dough is smooth and elastic.

2. Tip the dough into a large bowl, cover and leave to rise for 3 hours.

3. While your dough is rising, cook the sausages and onions. Heat a little vegetable oil in a medium frying pan and fry the sausages, turning to color on all sides, for about 15 minutes until golden brown and cooked through. Heat the olive oil and butter in a wide saucepan over a medium-low heat. Add the onions, cover and cook for 10–15 minutes until soft and golden. Leave the sausages and onions to cool.

4. Tip the dough onto a clean surface and punch down by folding the dough inwards repeatedly to knock out the air. Roll out to a rectangle, about 24 × 16 inches, with a long side facing you. Cut into strips, a little wider than your sausages. Place a sausage at the top end of each strip and spoon some onions along the length of each sausage. Dollop some tomato ketchup, yellow mustard, or both, on top.

5. Roll up the sausage and onions in enough of the dough strip to enclose them and overlap slightly. Cut away from the rest of the dough strip and press the edges to seal, trimming away any excess. Repeat to shape the rest of the hot dogs in the remainder of the dough strips.

6. Line 2 large baking sheets with parchment paper. Place the hot dogs, seam side down, on the pans, spacing them apart to give room for the dough to expand. Leave to proof for 30 minutes.

7. Heat your oven to 400°F.

8. Brush each hot dog with beaten egg and sprinkle generously with sesame seeds. Place the baking sheets in the oven and bake for 30 minutes until the hot dogs are golden brown. Eat while they are still warm.

Also pictured overleaf

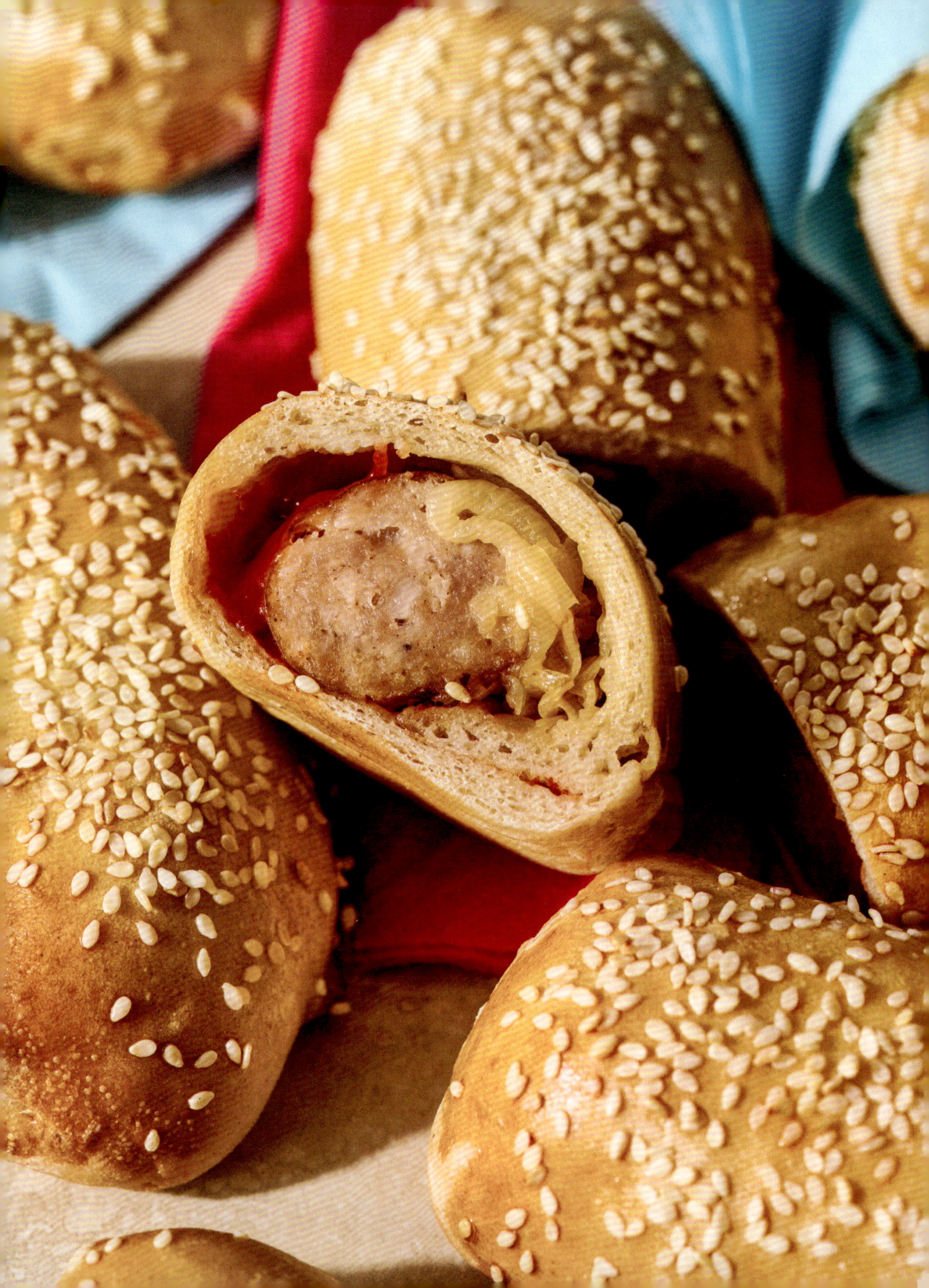

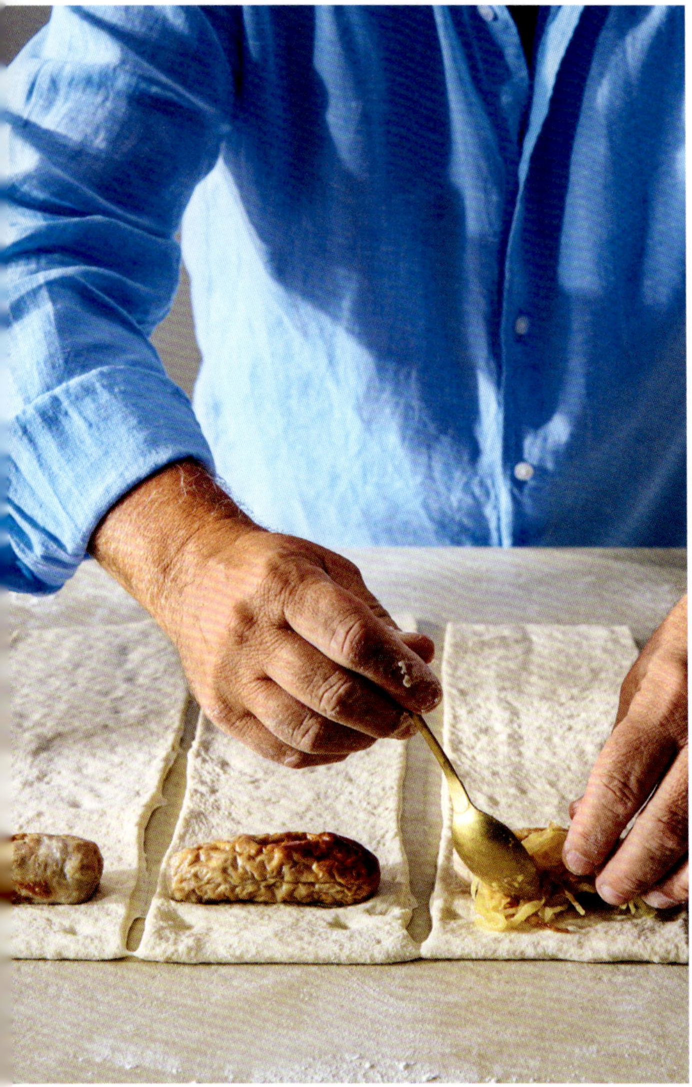
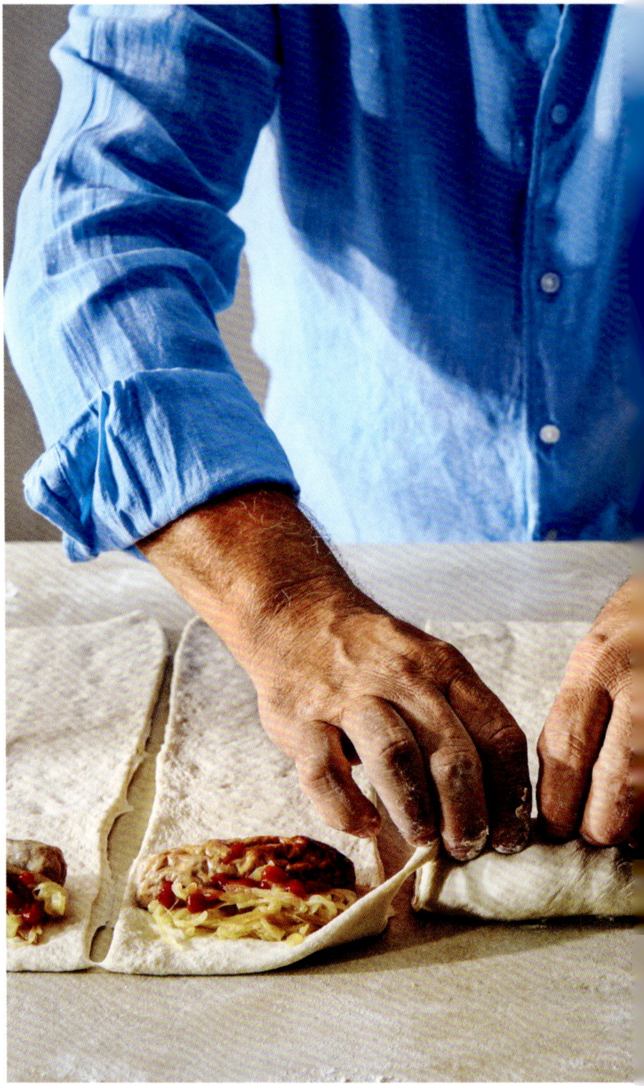

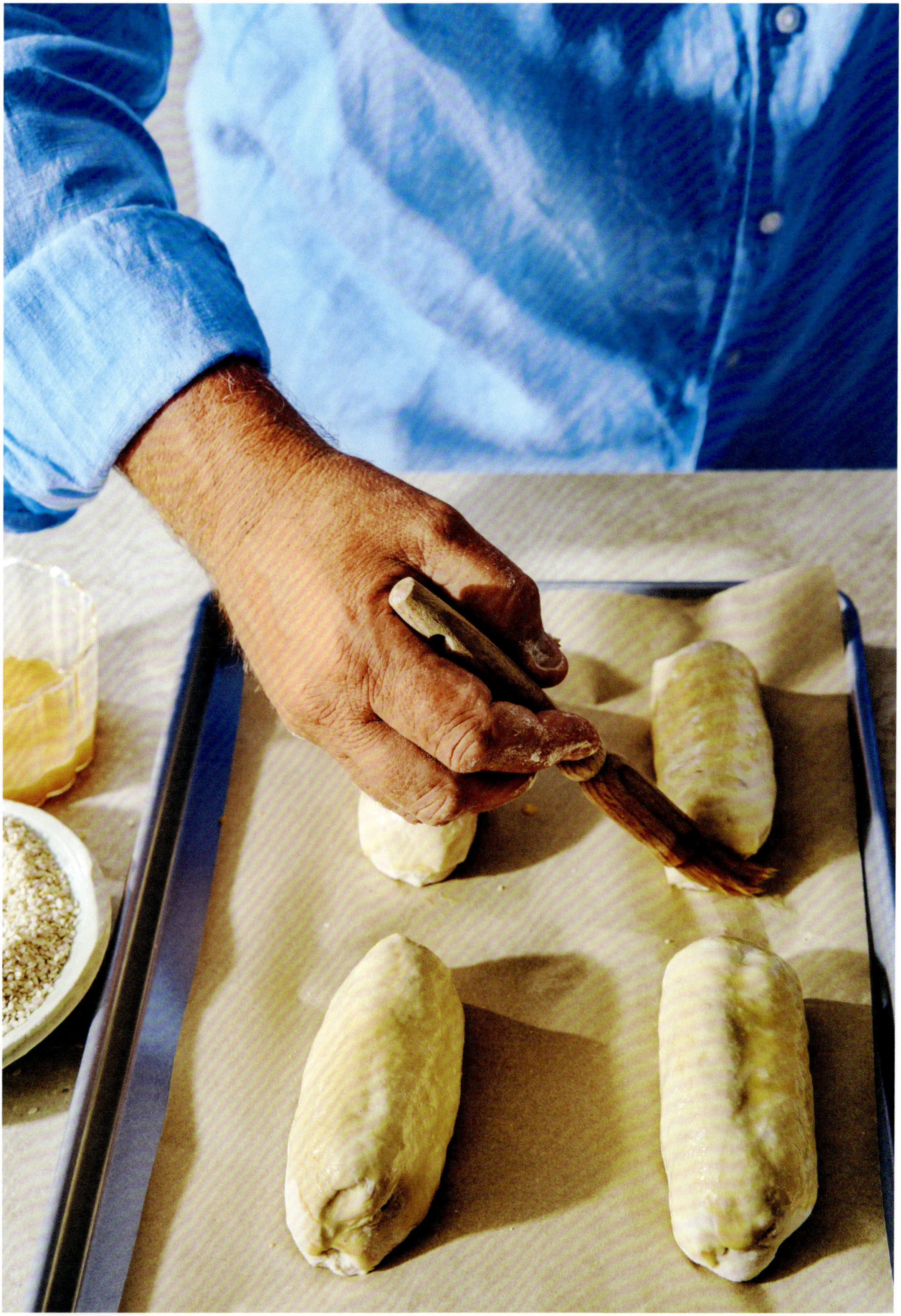

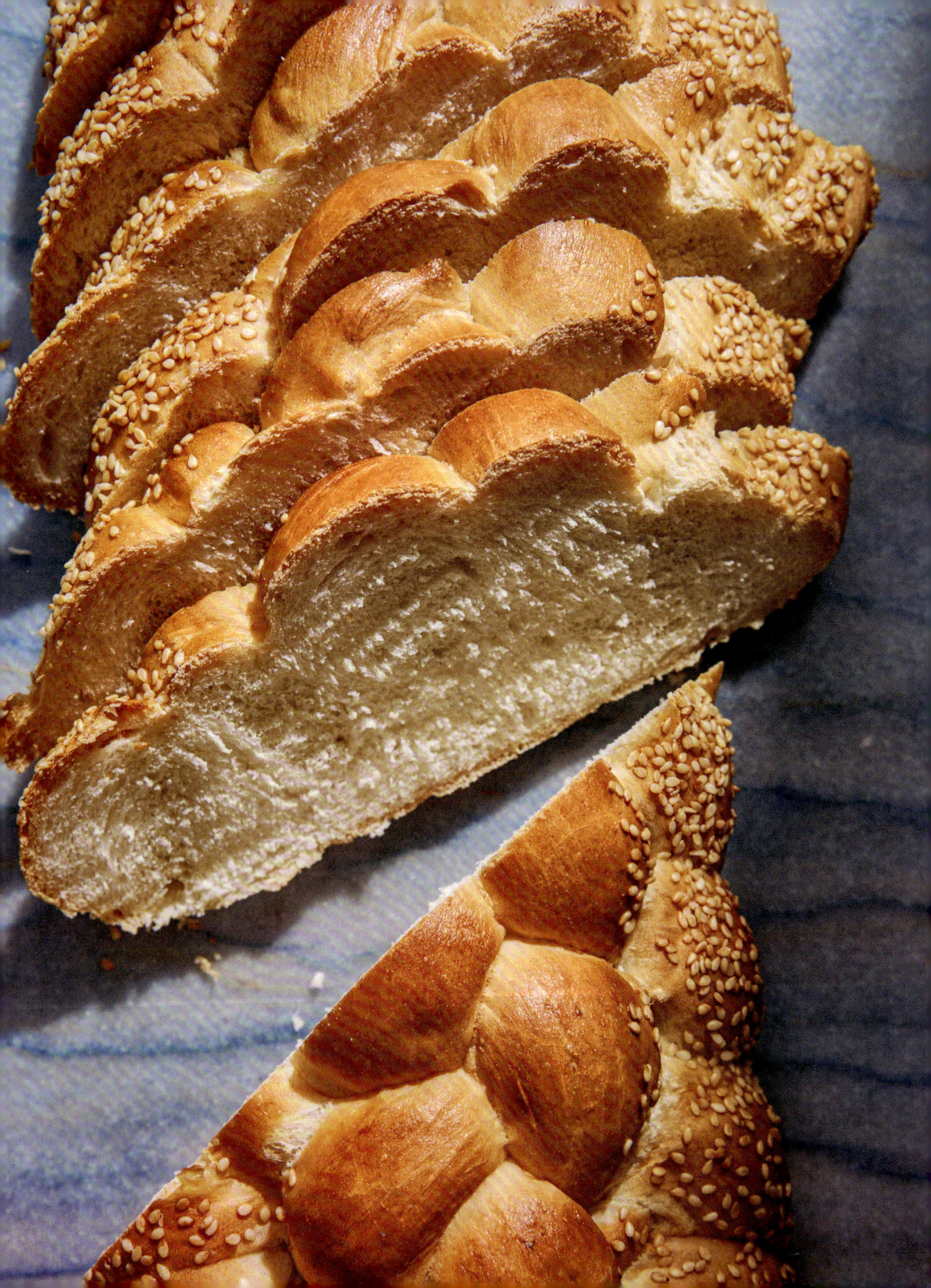

Challah

The perfect loaf to show off your braiding skills. I've gone for an eight-strand braid, but you can make an easier five- or three-strand braid if you prefer. Don't rush the proofing, and ensure the ropes you're braiding are equal sized – weigh them to be precise.

Makes 1 loaf

4 cups (500g) bread flour, plus extra to dust

heaping 1 tsp (6g) fine salt

1 × ¼-oz (7g) packet instant yeast

2 tbsp (30g) superfine sugar

3 tbsp (40g) olive oil, plus extra to oil

¾ cup plus 1 tbsp (200g) warm water

2 large eggs, at room temperature, beaten

A handful of sesame seeds, to finish

1. To make the dough, combine the flour, salt, yeast, sugar, olive oil, water and all except 1 tbsp of the beaten egg in a large bowl. Mix well to form a smooth dough that comes together in a ball. Turn the dough out onto a lightly floured surface and knead well for at least 10 minutes until smooth and elastic. (Alternatively, use a mixer fitted with the dough hook to mix and knead the dough, mixing on a low speed for 2 minutes, then kneading on medium speed for 7–8 minutes.)

2. Place the dough in an oiled bowl, cover and leave to rise for 2 hours.

3. Tip the dough onto a clean surface and punch down by folding the dough inwards repeatedly to knock out the air. Shape loosely into a ball by tucking the dough underneath itself then place back in the oiled bowl. Cover and leave to rise for a further 2 hours.

4. Tip the dough out onto a lightly floured surface and divide into 8 equal pieces. Roll each piece into a sausage and leave to rest for 2 minutes. Line a large baking sheet with parchment paper.

5. Now roll each sausage out to a rope, 20 inches in length. Press the ropes together at one end to join them and spread the ropes out (to resemble an octopus). Dust them with a little flour.

6. Now it's time to braid the ropes to form an 8-strand braid. Number each rope of dough 1–8, from left to right. First, take 8 under 7 then over 1. Then repeat the following sequence until the plait is complete: take 2 under 3 then over 8; 1 over 4; 7 under 6 then over 1; 8 over 5.

7. Place the braid on the lined baking sheet. Cover with plastic wrap and leave to rise for 1–2 hours until almost doubled in size.

8. Heat your oven to 400°F.

9. Brush the braided loaf with the remaining beaten egg and sprinkle the edges with sesame seeds. Bake in the oven for 35 minutes until golden brown. Transfer to a wire rack and leave to cool before serving.

Wheatsheaf

My uncle was a vicar and the first time I came across a wheatsheaf was in his church. Over the years, I've made a lot of them for harvest festivals. They take time and require a bit of skill but look so impressive.

Makes 1

8 cups (1kg) bread flour, plus extra to dust
1 tbsp (15g) fine salt
1¼ tsp (3g) instant yeast
2⅔ cups (640g) water

To glaze
2 large eggs, beaten

To finish (optional)
1 raisin

1. Place the flour, salt, yeast and water in a stand mixer fitted with the dough hook. Mix on a low speed for 5 minutes to combine, then increase the speed to medium and mix for a further 10 minutes to knead the dough until it is smooth and elastic.

2. Tip the dough into a bowl, cover and leave to rest in the fridge for 1 hour. Lightly flour the largest baking sheet you have that will fit inside your oven.

3. To create your wheatsheaf, start by rolling out about one tenth (200g) of the dough and cut a keyhole shape, about 8 inches at its widest point and 12 inches long. Place on the prepared baking sheet.

4. From the rest of the dough, pull off pieces and roll these into long, thin grissini or breadsticks (the thinner the better); these will be the strands of wheat.

5. From the middle of the wheatsheaf, position the strips of dough down to the bottom of the keyhole starting from the sides then working in to cover the whole base. You need to overlap the bottom but keep the middle line straight; trim where necessary.

6. Now roll another 3 pieces of dough into long strands, at least 16 inches. Press these together at one end and braid the strands neatly to make a classic braid (*as pictured on page 172*). Place your braid underneath the middle of the keyhole, leaving the ends of the braid strands spreading out left and right of the keyhole. This will become the tie!

7. Now rip off small pieces of the remaining dough and roll into balls, about 1¼ inches in diameter, in your hand. On a lightly floured surface, roll each into a tiny roll with a tapered end, resembling a mini petit pain. Using a pair of scissors, snip 3 small cuts in each side of the rolls and 3 nicks across the top.

8. Begin to position these 'ears of wheat' around the dome at the top of the keyhole. Continue, concentrically, to cover the domed part of the keyhole. Once completely covered, draw in the two ends of the braid to tie around the middle, where the strips meet the wheat shapes.

Continued overleaf

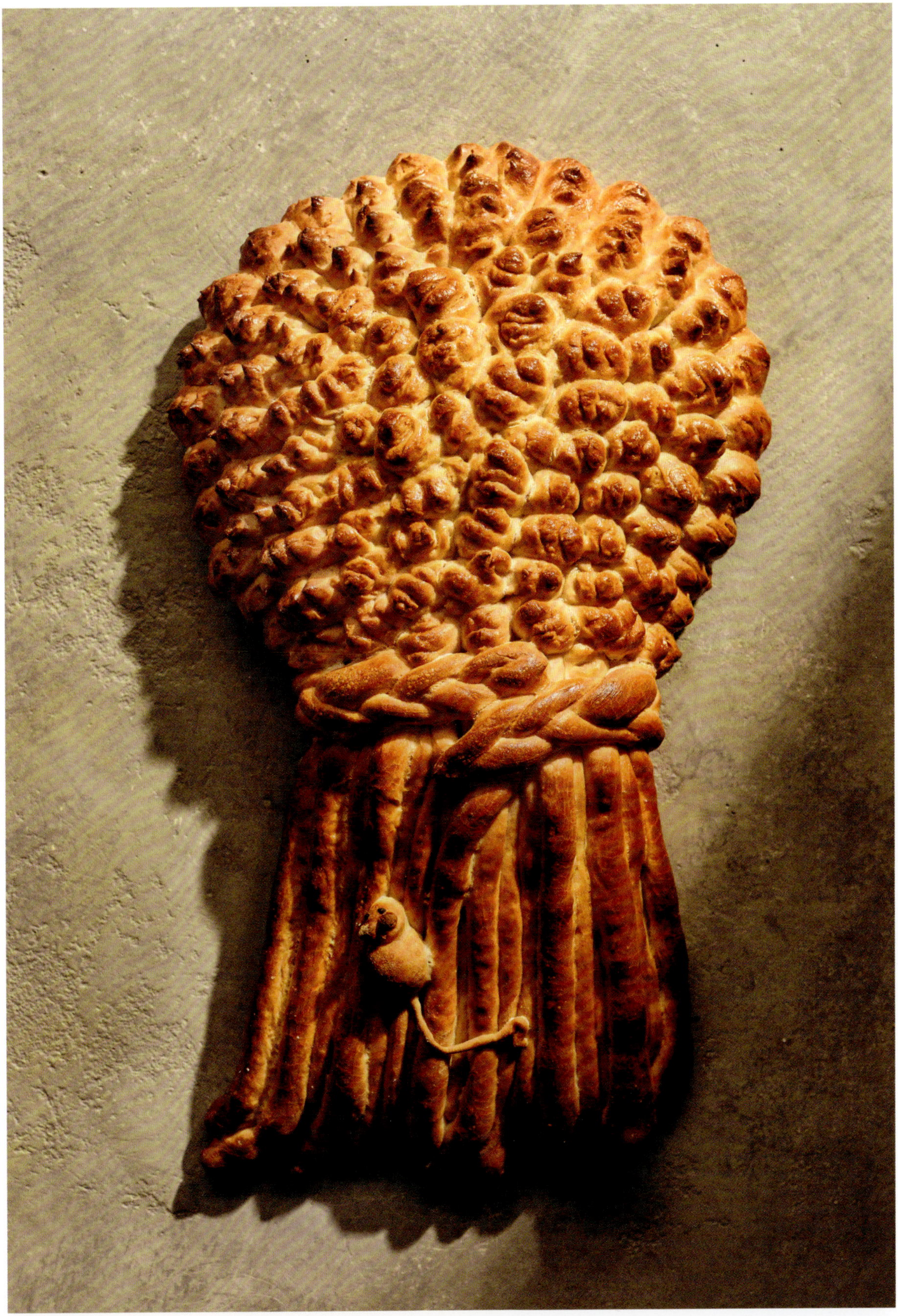

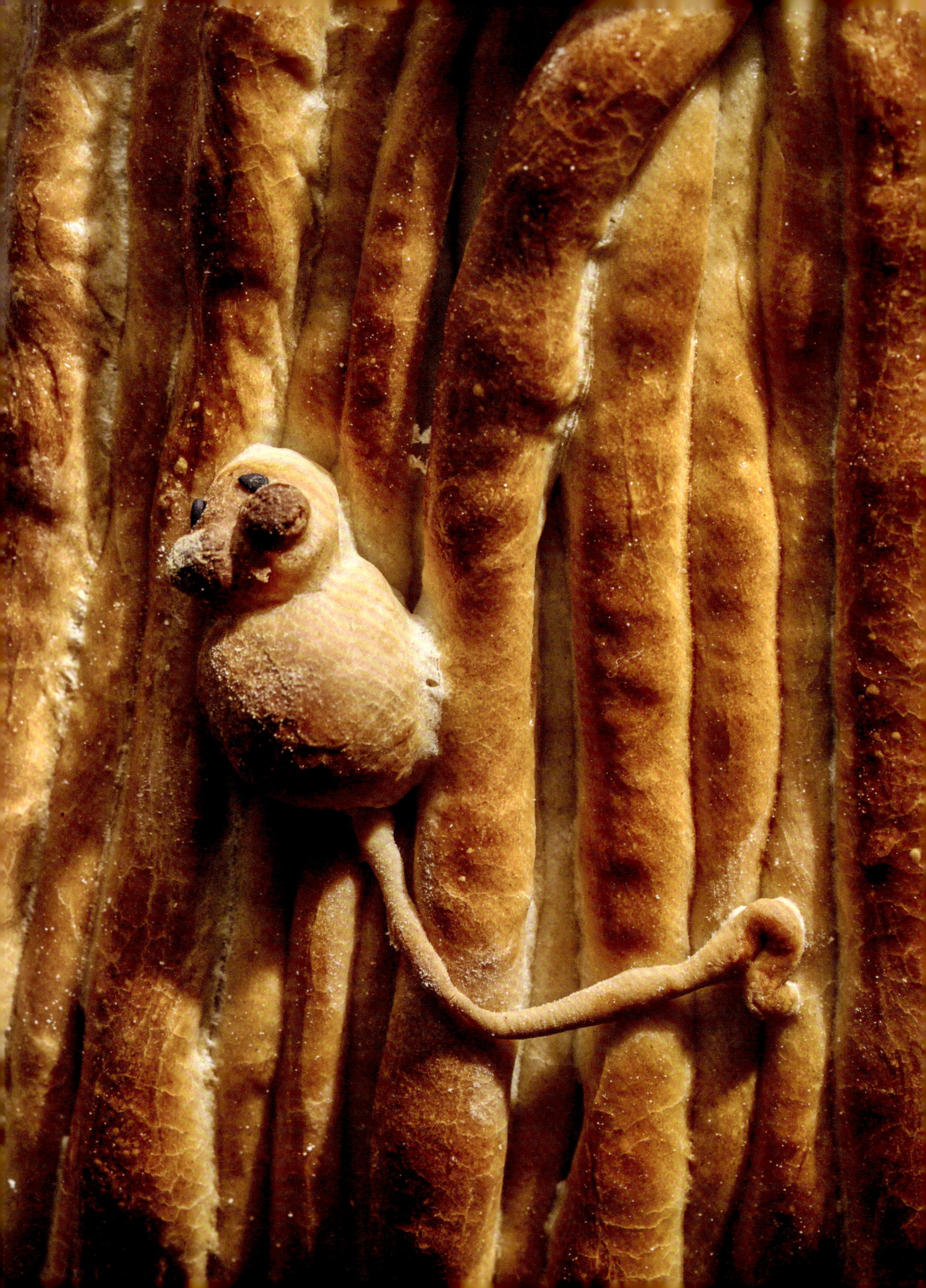

Continued from page 168

9   To make a mouse climbing up your wheatsheaf, if you like, simply roll out a tail, a body and a smaller piece for the head. Position the mouse on the strips, pressing the parts together. Shape 2 little ears from very small pieces and position these. Finally, cut up a raisin and use 2 little pieces as eyes.

10 Heat your oven to 400°F.

11 Brush the wheatsheaf all over with beaten egg. If you've made a mouse, position it on top of the wheat and brush with egg glaze. Bake in the oven for 40 minutes until golden brown. Cool on a wire rack.

Also pictured overleaf

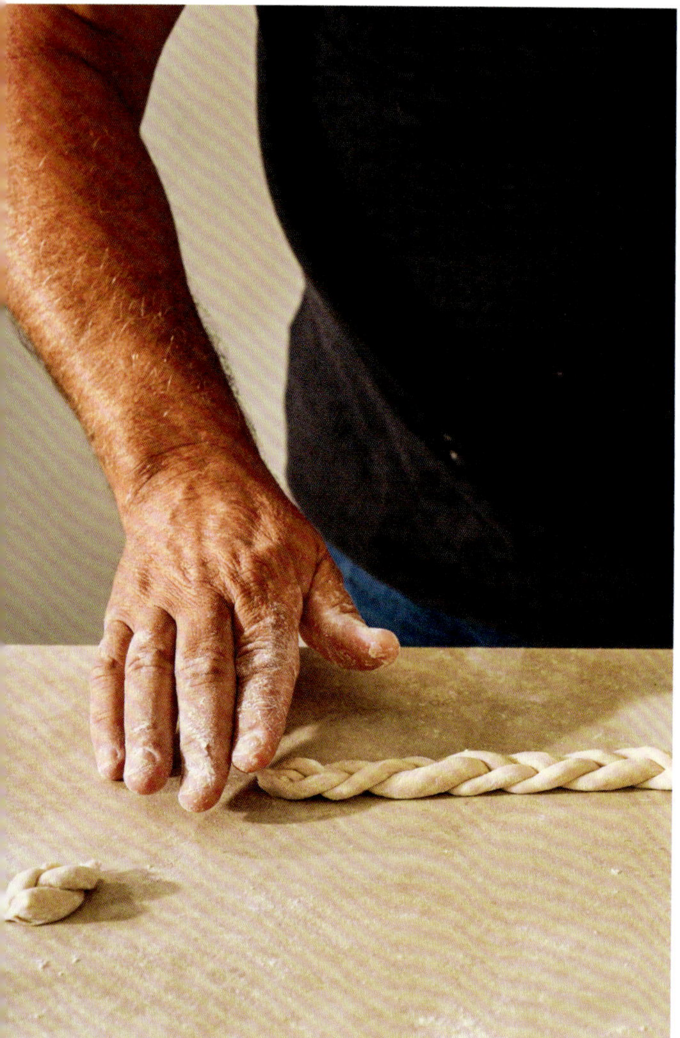
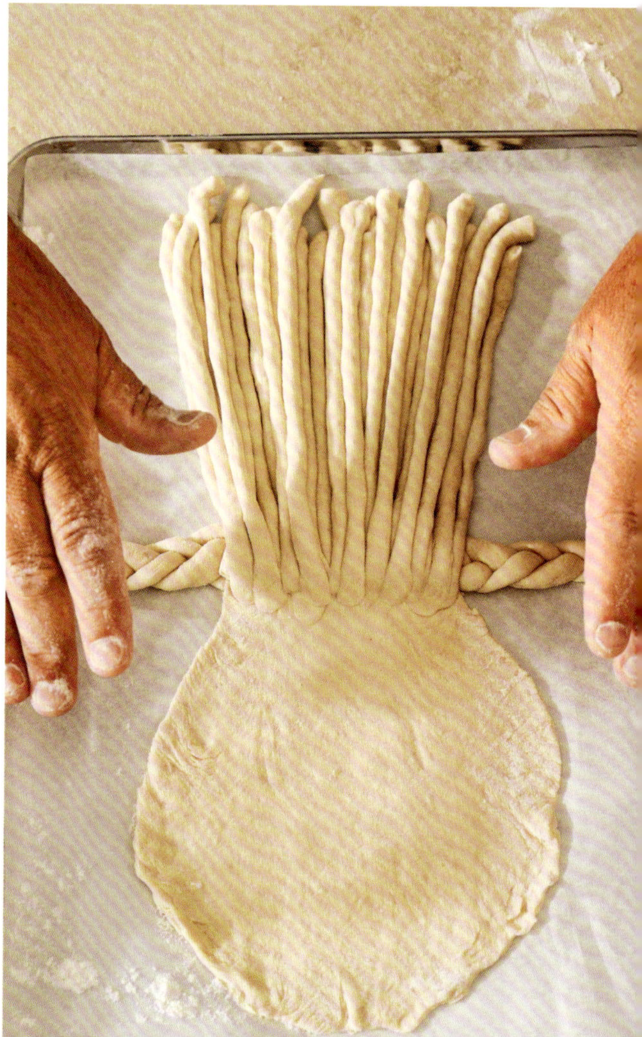

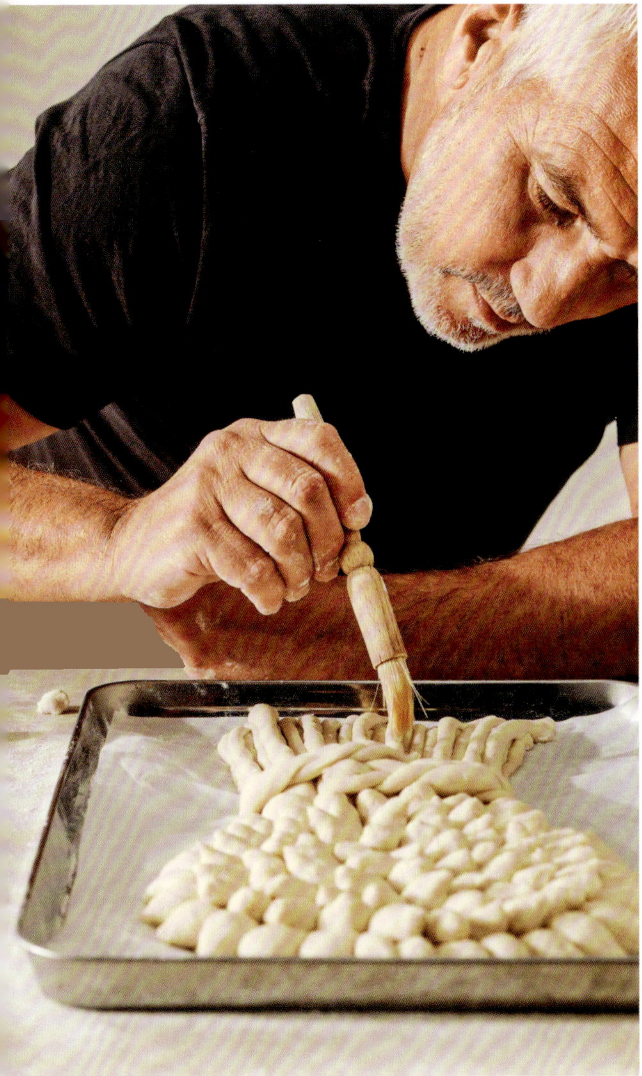
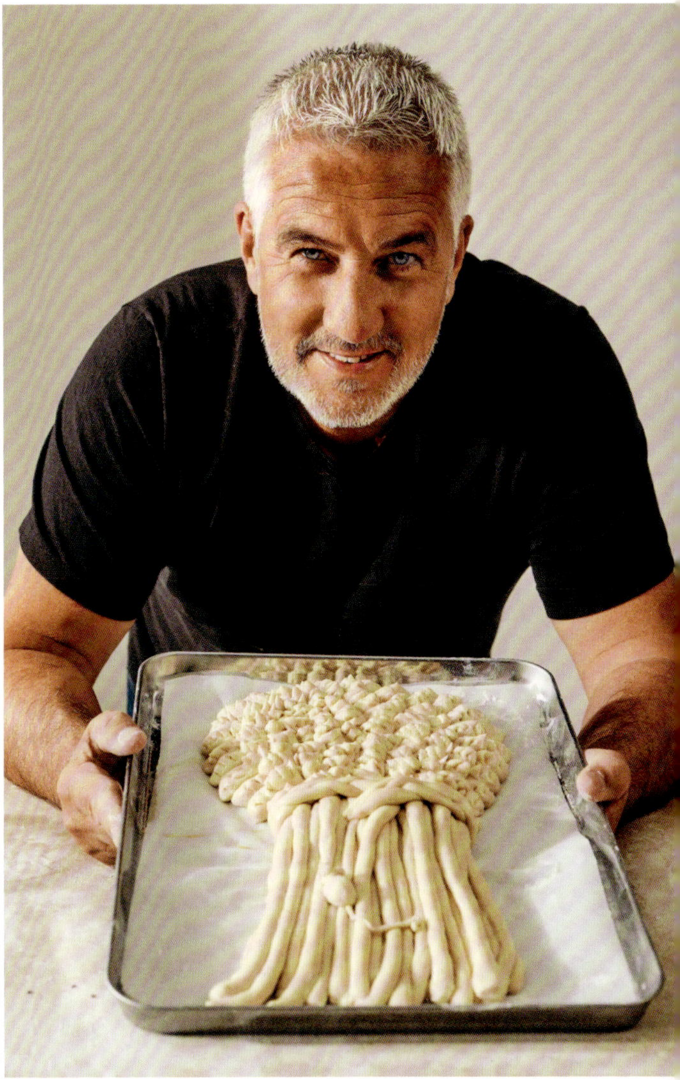

Winter

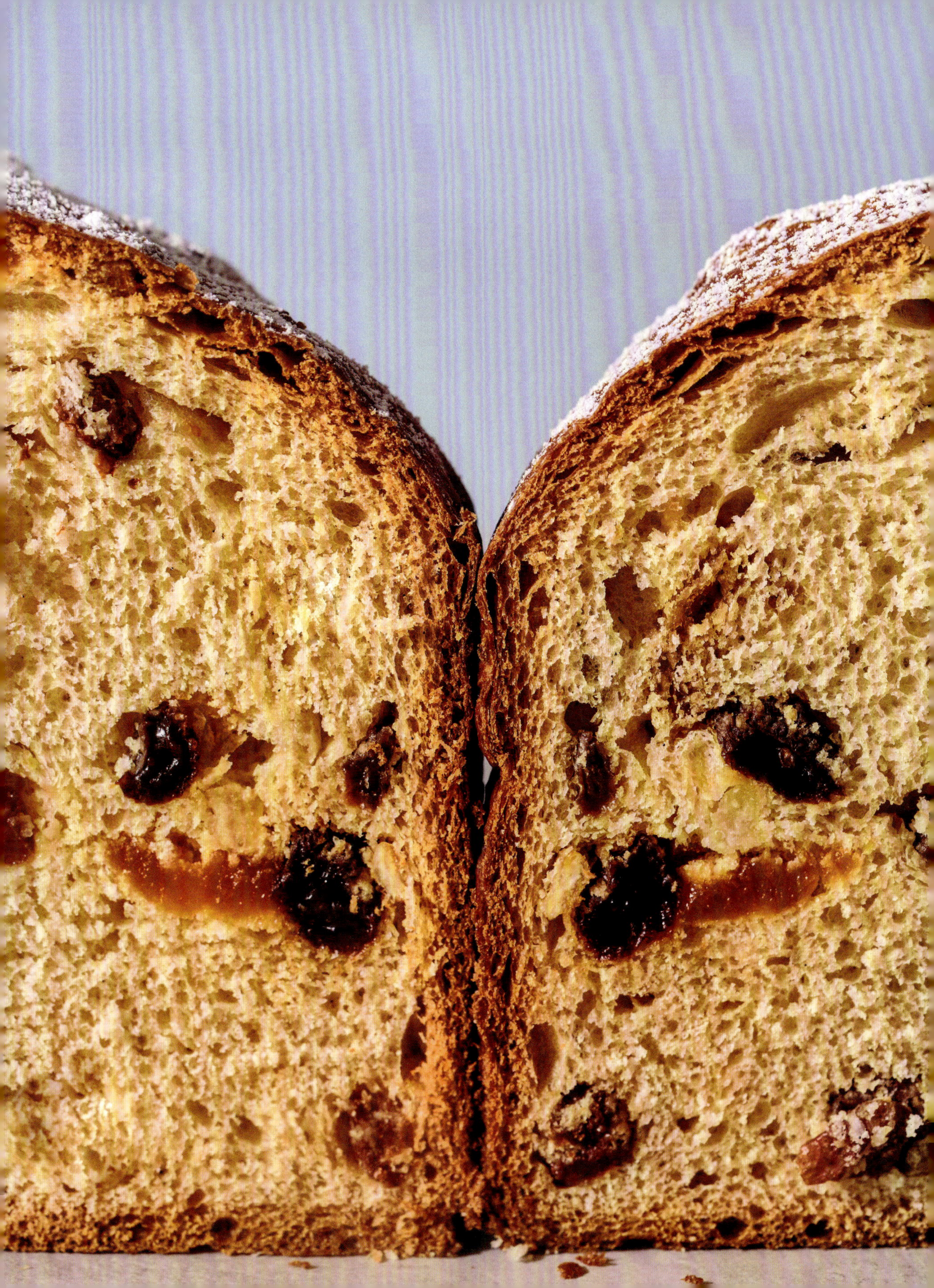

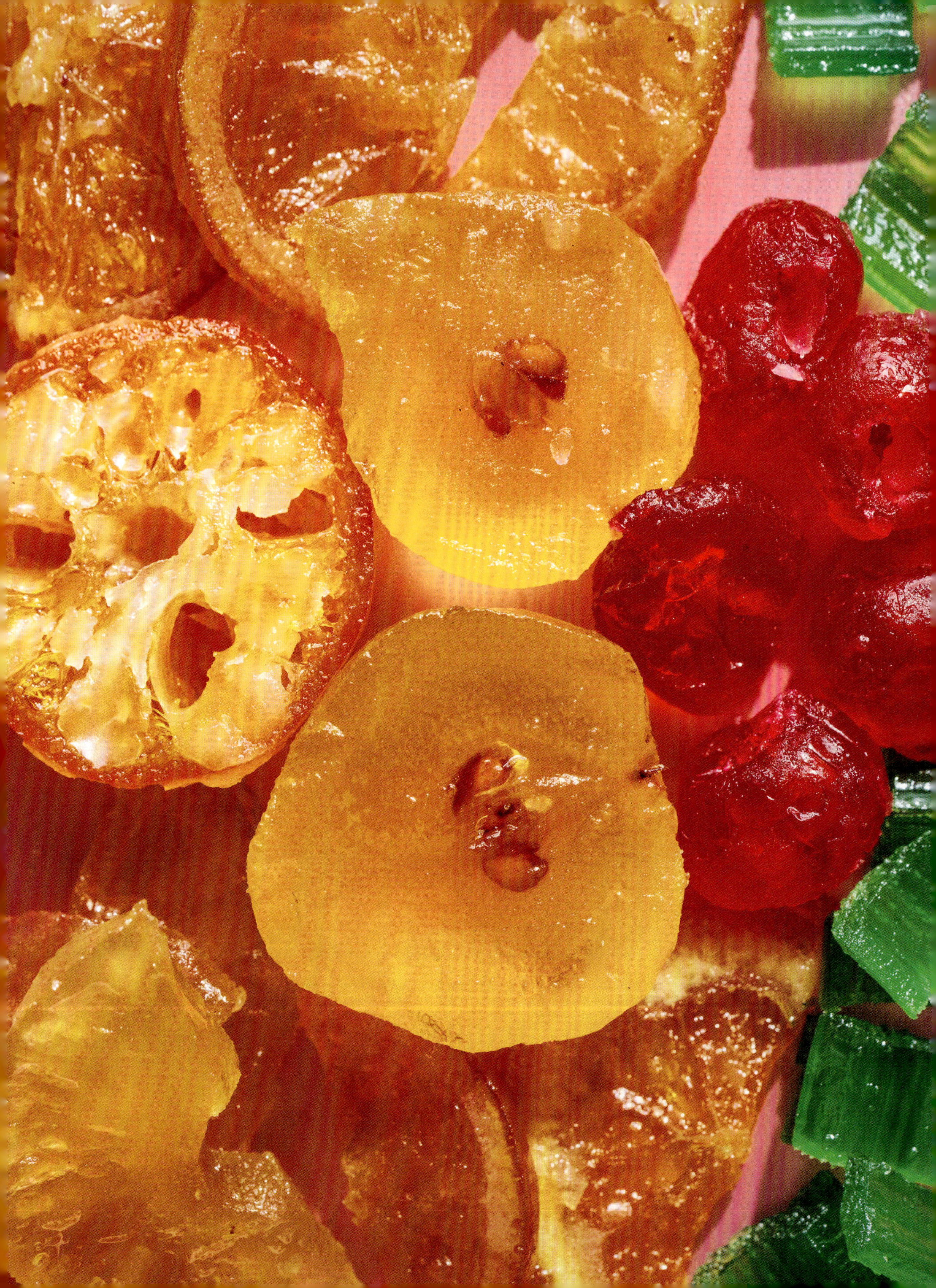

As soon as we reach December, I start making sheets of mince pies ready for when people visit. It just wouldn't be Christmas for me without them. I like to serve the pies warm with lots of cream to help cool them down. I've been adding clementine and apple to the filling (see page 182) since I used to work as a chef in hotels. It's tradition for me now, and I wouldn't do it any other way.

You'll find that a lot of recipes made to celebrate the end of the year and the start of the new one are steeped in long-held traditions or rituals like this. They conjure up so many memories, and it's usually why we love them so much. But that doesn't mean you always have to stick to them or bake the same festive treats as everyone else!

Start creating your own traditions in what you bake to share with friends and family, perhaps including some European favorites. Why not try Italian panettone (page 178), French Christmas couronne (page 180) or the traditional Spanish Roscón de Reyes (page 194), which celebrates the journey of the three kings? And if you're bored of pies or Christmas pudding (page 185), serve up Chocolate mini logs (page 188) instead. These are your celebrations, so make them your own.

In the winter there's not very much going on when it comes to fresh ingredients, which is why you'll see dried fruits and spices in a lot of baking now, often with a bit of citrus to give it a lift. They add a touch of luxury and incredible flavors. The Panforte (page 186) is rich and sticky, packed with dried ingredients and heavily spiced; it makes a stunning winter afternoon treat with a cup of tea.

When it's dark outside and the weather is rubbish, not much can beat the smell of freshly baked cookies, cakes or bread. The recipes in this chapter will help you enjoy (and even celebrate!) the cold winter months.

Panettone

Aromatic from all the preserved fruit, this traditional Italian sweet yeast bread is eaten at Christmas time. I like to toast slices lightly and spread them with butter. If you have any panettone left over, it makes an incredible bread pudding or summer pudding.

10–12 slices

4 cups (500g) bread flour, plus extra to dust

1 tsp (5g) fine salt

½ cup (100g) superfine sugar

2 tsp (8g) instant yeast

¾ cup (180g) warm whole milk

4 large eggs, at room temperature

2 tsp (10g) vanilla bean paste

1¼ sticks (150g) unsalted butter, in pieces, softened, plus extra to grease

Finely grated zest of 1 orange

Finely grated zest of ½ lemon

½ cup (80g) diced candied peel (preferably a mixture of orange and lemon)

½ cup (60g) golden raisins

½ cup (60g) raisins

½ cup (60g) chopped dried apricots

To finish

Confectioners' sugar, to dust

1. Put the flour, salt, sugar, yeast, warm milk, eggs and vanilla paste into a stand mixer fitted with the dough hook and mix on a low speed for 5 minutes. Increase the speed to medium, add the softened butter and mix for a further 10 minutes until you have a very soft, silky, stretchy dough. Cover the bowl and leave the dough to rise for 2 hours.

2. Add the citrus zests, candied peel and dried fruits to the dough and mix on a low speed for 3 minutes until evenly incorporated. Re-cover and leave to rise for another 2 hours.

3. Grease a deep 8-inch springform pan and line the base and sides with parchment paper.

4. Tip the dough out onto a lightly floured surface and punch down by folding the dough inwards repeatedly to knock out the air. Shape into a ball and place in the prepared pan.

5. Cover and leave to proof for a further 1–2 hours until the dough is well risen and starting to dome above the top of the pan. It should be light to touch.

6. Heat your oven to 375°F.

7. Once the dough is proofed, place the pan in the oven and bake for about 40 minutes until the panettone is risen and golden.

8. Leave to cool in the pan for 10 minutes, then turn out and place on a wire rack. Let the panettone cool completely. Dust with confectioners' sugar before serving.

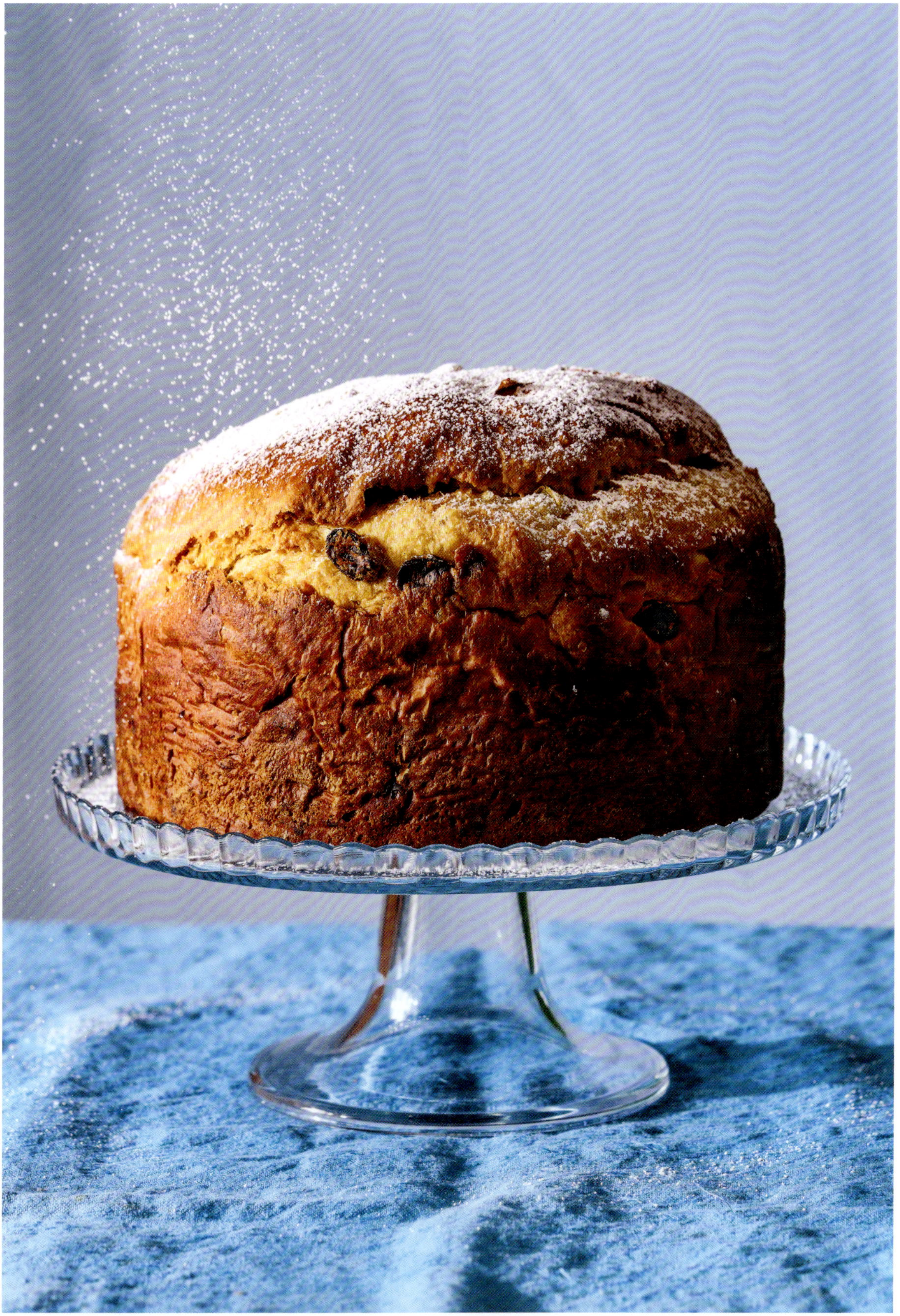

Christmas Couronne

This is a classic French enriched sweet dough, which you slice open to reveal a frangipane and apricot filling, then twist together again before baking. It's finished with an apricot glaze and decorated with a thin lemon glacé.

12–15 slices

Dough

5⅔ cups (700g) bread flour, plus extra to dust

2 tsp (10g) fine salt

3¾ tsp (10g) instant yeast

3 tbsp (50g) unsalted butter, in pieces, softened

2 large eggs, at room temperature

¼ cup plus 1 tbsp (60g) superfine sugar

Finely grated zest of 2 oranges

1 cup (250g) water

¾ cup plus 1 tbsp (200g) warm whole milk

Frangipane filling

7 tbsp (100g) unsalted butter, softened

¼ cup (45g) superfine sugar

2 large eggs, at room temperature

⅓ cup (75g) all-purpose flour

½ tsp baking powder

1 cup (100g) almond flour

1 tsp almond extract

⅔ cup plus 1 tbsp (100g) skinned almonds, toasted

1¼ cups (150g) chopped dried apricots

To finish

3 tbsp apricot preserves

1 cup (100g) confectioners' sugar

Finely grated zest and juice of 1 lemon

1 cup (100g) sliced almonds, toasted

1. Place all of the dough ingredients, except the milk, in a stand mixer fitted with the dough hook. Mix on a slow speed for 4 minutes, slowly adding the milk as you do so. Increase the speed to medium and mix for a further 10 minutes until the dough is smooth and elastic. Tip the dough into a bowl, cover and leave to rise for 3 hours.

2. Meanwhile, make the frangipane. Whisk the butter and sugar together until light and fluffy, then beat in the eggs one at a time, adding a spoonful of flour with each. Add the rest of the flour, the baking powder, almond flour and almond extract and beat well to combine.

3. Tip the risen dough out onto a lightly floured surface and roll out to a rectangle, 16 × 10 inches, with a long side facing you. Spread the frangipane over the dough and scatter the toasted almonds and dried apricots evenly on top.

4. Starting at a long side, roll the dough up tightly to enclose the filling (like a jelly roll). Press the edges with your fingers and roll the dough slightly until it is sealed and an even thickness, about 18 inches in length.

5. Transfer the roll to a sheet of parchment paper and cut it in half lengthwise. Place the halves next to each other, cut sides facing up. Now twist them neatly around each other and form into a ring. Press the ends together to seal.

6. Slide the twisted dough ring, on the paper, onto a baking sheet. Cover with a kitchen towel and leave to proof for 2 hours. Heat your oven to 400°F.

7. Bake the couronne in the oven for 30 minutes until risen and golden. Transfer to a wire rack and let cool slightly. Meanwhile, in a small saucepan, warm the apricot preserves with a splash of water then pass through a strainer. Brush the warm glaze all over the warm couronne then leave to cool.

8. Mix the confectioners' sugar with the lemon zest and juice to make a thin icing. Drizzle this icing all over the couronne and sprinkle with the toasted almonds. Leave to set before serving.

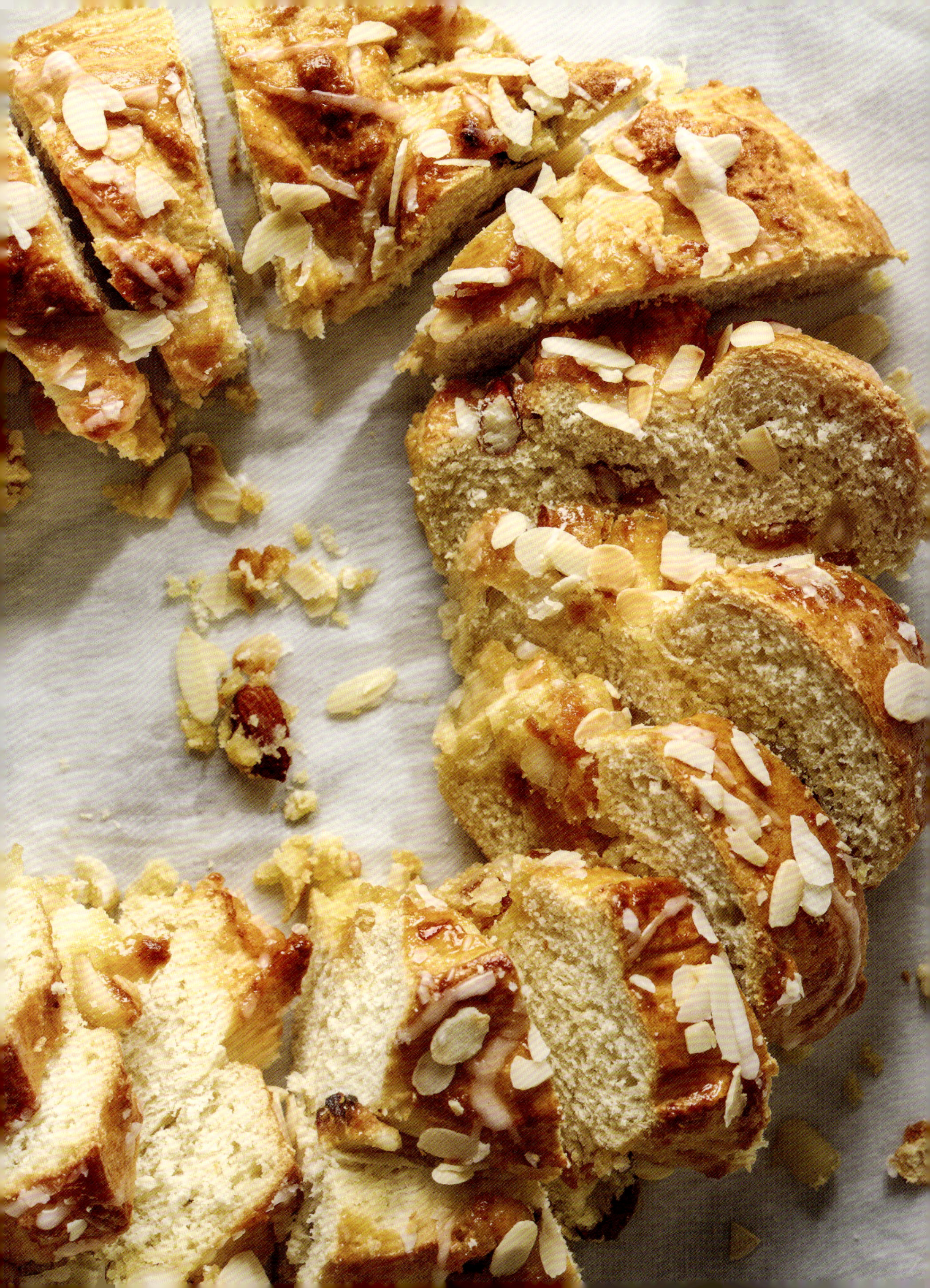

Paul's Classic Mince Pies

I start making big batches of these mince pies the first week in December, for people to enjoy when they drop in. The sweet, shortbread-like crust is luxurious, while the clementine and apple filling takes the humble mince pie to another level. You can add a splash of Cognac to the filling too, if you like.

Makes 12

Sweet pie dough
2⅔ cups (330g) all-purpose flour, plus extra to dust

1 stick plus 3 tbsp (165g) chilled unsalted butter, diced, plus extra to grease

¼ cup (50g) superfine sugar, plus extra to sprinkle

1 large egg

Filling
1 × 14-oz (400g) jar mincemeat

1 clementine

1 medium-sized apple, such as Pink Lady or Fuji

Topping
1¾ sticks (200g) unsalted butter, softened

1⅔ cups (200g) all-purpose flour

5 tbsp (40g) cornstarch

5 tbsp (40g) confectioners' sugar

1. To make the pie dough, put the flour into a large bowl, add the butter and rub in using your fingers until the mixture resembles fine breadcrumbs. Stir in the sugar and make a well in the center. In a small bowl, beat the egg together with a splash of cold water then pour into the well and mix into the flour, using a dinner knife.

2. Bring the pie dough together with one hand; do not overwork the dough. Gently knead the dough into a ball and flatten to a disc. Wrap in plastic wrap and refrigerate for at least 20 minutes.

3. Lightly grease a 12-cup muffin pan with butter. On a lightly floured surface, roll out the dough to a ⅛ inch thick. Using a 4¼-inch biscuit cutter, cut out 12 circles and use to line the muffin pan. Re-roll the dough trimmings to cut more circles as needed. Place in the fridge to rest while you prepare the filling.

4. To make the filling, put the mincemeat into a bowl. Finely grate the zest from the clementine over the mincemeat, then peel and chop the clementine, discarding any seeds. Peel, core and chop the apple and add to the mincemeat with the chopped clementine. Stir to mix well. Spoon the mincemeat mixture into the pie crusts, to three-quarters fill them.

5. For the topping, in a bowl beat the butter using a hand mixer until it is very soft. Add the flour, cornstarch and confectioners' sugar and mix until you have a smooth paste, like a thick buttercream. Put into a piping bag fitted with a large star piping tip and pipe a neat spiral on top of each mince pie. Chill in the fridge for 30 minutes before baking.

6. Heat your oven to 400°F.

7. Bake the mince pies in the oven for 20 minutes. Leave them to cool slightly in the pans for about 5 minutes then transfer to a wire rack to cool. Serve warm or at room temperature.

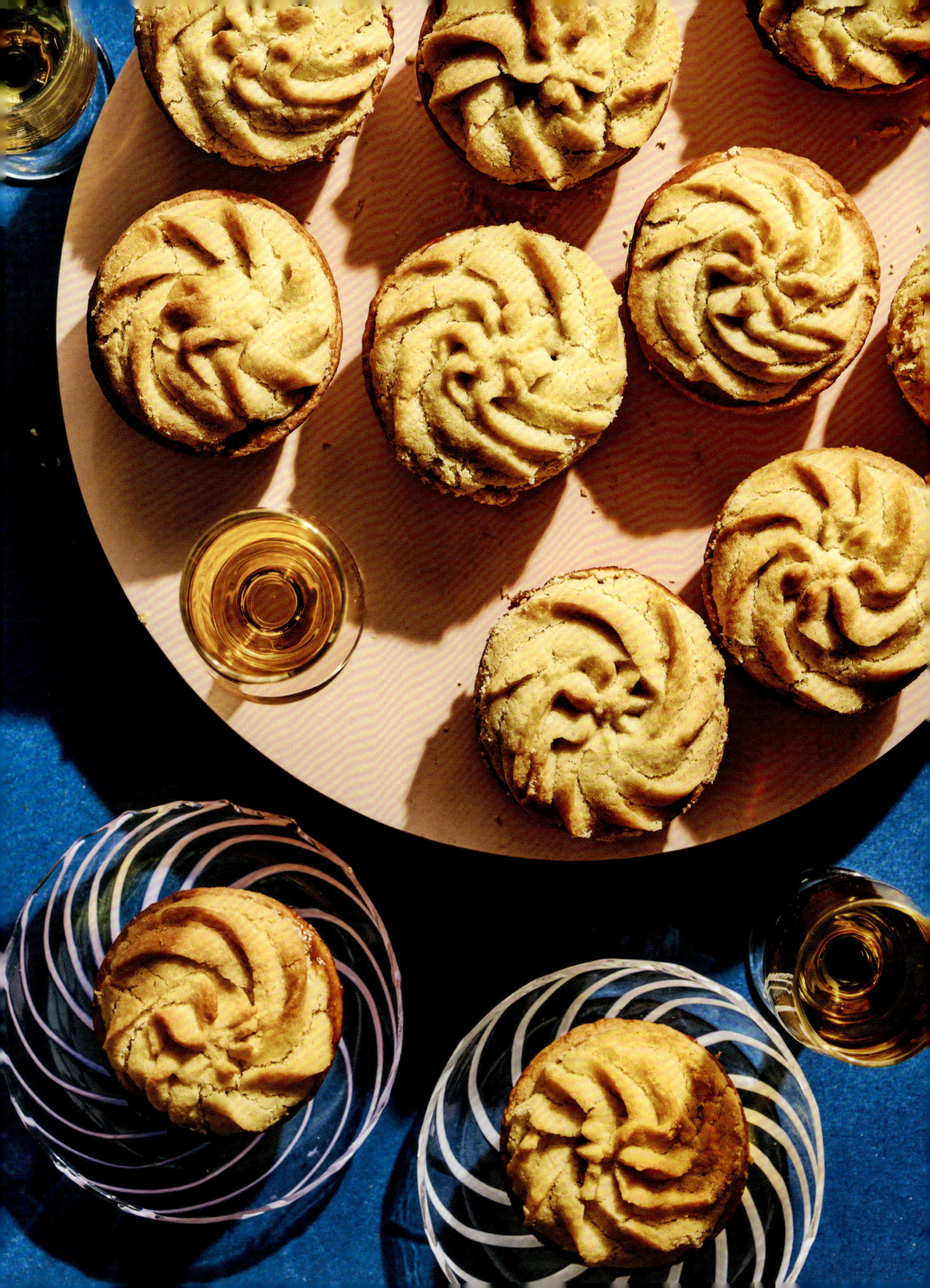

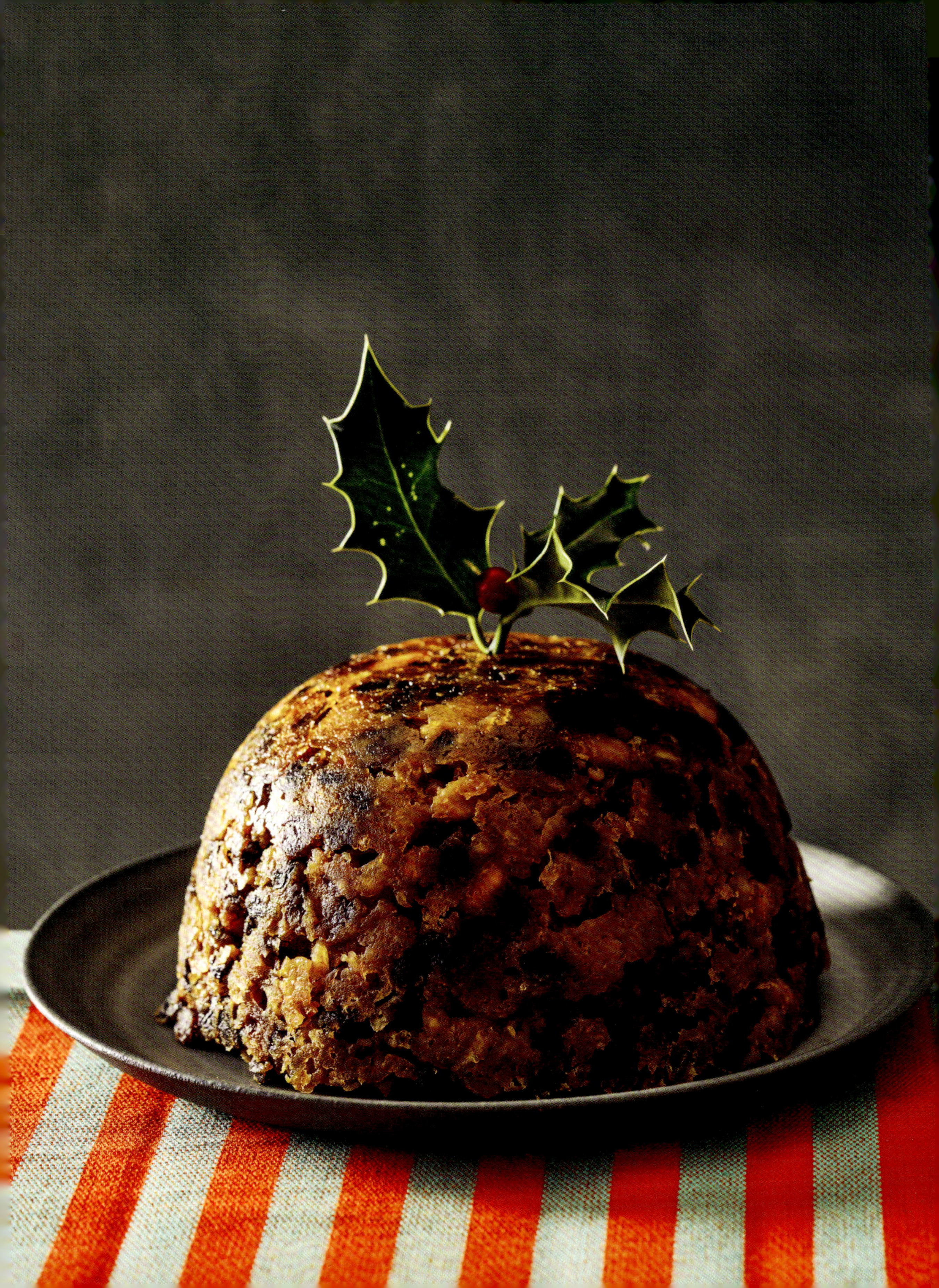

Christmas Pudding

When I worked at The Dorchester, we'd make these a year in advance and keep them in the cellar. If you can, get organized and aim to prepare them by at least mid-November, to give them time to mature – but even a week before Christmas would be fine.

Serves 8

---

1 cup (120g) zante currants

1 cup (120g) raisins

¾ cup plus 1 tbsp (100g) golden raisins

⅓ cup (50g) diced candied peel (preferably a mixture of orange and lemon)

3 tbsp (50g) Cognac, plus an extra 3–4 tbsp to flambé

Finely grated zest and juice of 1 orange

Finely grated zest and juice of 1 lemon

1 cup (100g) shredded suet, or ½ cup chilled vegetable shortening or butter, grated

1 cup (50g) fresh breadcrumbs

½ cup plus 1 tbsp (110g) light brown sugar

1¼ cups (125g) grated apple

½ cup plus 1 tbsp (75g) all-purpose flour

¼ cup plus 1 tbsp (40g) skinned almonds

2 large eggs, beaten

½ tsp fine salt

1 tsp ground cinnamon

Butter, to grease

To serve

Crème anglaise, cream or hard sauce

1. Put all the dried fruit and the candied peel into a bowl and pour on the Cognac, lemon juice and orange juice. Stir to mix, then cover and leave to soak overnight.

2. Put all the remaining ingredients into a large bowl, including the citrus zests. Mix thoroughly, using a large spoon or your hands. Add the soaked fruit together with any liquid and stir to combine. Grease a 1-quart heatproof glass mixing bowl or pudding basin with butter.

3. Spoon the pudding mixture into the basin or bowl to fill it to ¾ inch from the top. Cover the surface closely with a disc of parchment paper. To cover the basin, place a piece of parchment paper on a sheet of foil and make a large pleat in the middle. Lay, paper side down, over the basin or bowl and secure under the rim with string, looping the end of the string over the pudding to create a handle for lifting the pudding out once it is cooked. Trim away any excessive paper and foil.

4. Stand the pudding basin or bowl in a large saucepan and pour in enough boiling water to come halfway up the side of the basin. Cover with a tight-fitting lid and bring to a boil over a medium heat. Lower the heat to maintain a simmer and cook for 8 hours, topping up the boiling water as necessary; don't let the pan boil dry. You can also cook the pudding in a steamer.

5. When cooked, carefully lift the pudding out of the pan and leave to cool completely then replace the pleated foil and paper with fresh coverings. Store in a cool, dry place.

6. To serve, steam the pudding, as above, for 2 hours to reheat. Lift out the pudding, uncover and run the tip of a knife around the edge to help release it. Invert a serving plate over the top then, holding the plate and basin tightly together, turn them upside down to unmold the pudding onto the plate.

7. Warm the 3–4 tbsp Cognac in a small saucepan (or the microwave), pour over the pudding and set alight. Bring to the table and serve with crème anglaise, cream or hard sauce.

Panforte

A rich, sticky Tuscan Christmas treat that's packed with so many aromatic winter flavors. There's a lot going on, but panforte is actually simple to make and looks beautiful. Use good-quality candied citrus peel – it will make all the difference to this bake.

12–15 slices

A little oil, to grease
¾ cup plus 1 tbsp (125g) skinned almonds
¾ cup plus 1 tbsp (125g) whole, raw almonds
1 cup (100g) walnut halves
6 oz (150g) mixed candied lemon and orange peel
4 oz (100g) soft dried figs (about 10)
1 cup (125g) all-purpose flour
3 tbsp unsweetened cocoa powder
1 tsp ground cinnamon
½ tsp freshly grated nutmeg
½ tsp black pepper
½ tsp ground cloves
¾ cup (150g) superfine sugar
½ cup (150g) honey
Confectioners' sugar, to finish

1. Heat your oven to 400°F. Oil an 8-inch springform pan and line with parchment paper.

2. Place all the nuts on a baking sheet and toast in the oven for 5 minutes. Remove and let cool. Lower the oven temperature to 325°F.

3. Tip one-third of the nuts into a food processor and blitz until they are fairly finely chopped. Coarsely chop the other two-thirds with a knife. Chop the candied peel and figs into small pieces.

4. Put the flour, cocoa and spices into a large heatproof bowl and whisk to combine. Add all of the chopped nuts, candied peel and figs and stir to mix thoroughly.

5. Put the sugar and honey into a medium saucepan and heat gently until the sugar is dissolved. Continue to cook until the syrup registers 240°F on a candy thermometer. Immediately pour the syrup onto the fruit and nut mixture and mix until well combined.

6. Transfer the mixture to the prepared pan, flatten the surface and press down to flatten with damp hands. Bake in the oven for about 30 minutes until just firm. Leave to cool in the pan.

7. Once cooled, turn out the panforte and transfer to a serving plate. Dust heavily with confectioners' sugar to serve.

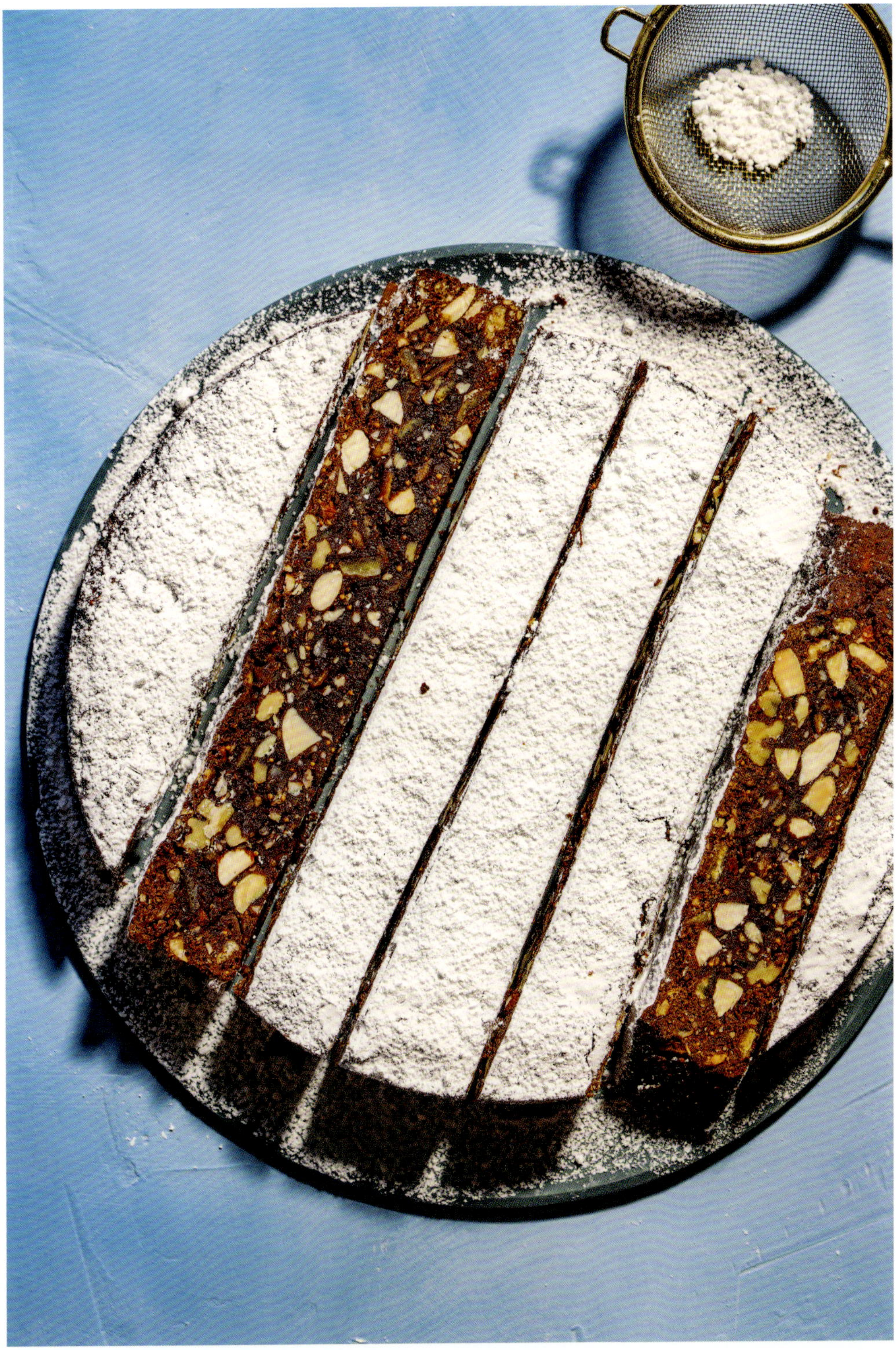

Chocolate Mini Logs

Using mostly store-bought ingredients, these mini yule logs are easy to whip up. A great festive treat for kids, they look impressive too. You'll need four 4-inch square boards and a tiny holly leaf cutter.

Makes 5

---

7 oz (200g) marzipan (page 209, or use good-quality store-bought)

Confectioners' sugar, to dust

5 cream-filled Swiss rolls

2 tbsp warmed, strained apricot preserves

5 tbsp royal icing (store-bought or make your own, see page 202)

6 oz (150g) milk chocolate

¾ oz (20g) green rolled fondant icing

¼ oz (5g) red rolled fondant icing

1. Roll out three quarters of the marzipan on a surface lightly dusted with confectioners' sugar to ¼ inch thick. Trim the edges to neaten. Sit a Swiss roll at one edge and cut a rectangle of marzipan large enough to wrap around it. Brush this marzipan rectangle with apricot preserves and then roll it around the Swiss roll to cover it, positioning the join underneath.

2. Repeat to cover all the Swiss rolls, re-rolling the trimmings to cut more as necessary. Save the final marzipan trimmings.

3. Place each roll on a 4-inch cake board, positioning it diagonally across the board and securing it with a dab of royal icing.

4. Melt the chocolate in a heatproof bowl set over a saucepan of simmering water, making sure the base of the bowl is not in direct contact with the water. Once melted, remove the bowl from the heat, stir the chocolate until smooth and set aside to cool slightly.

5. Paint each marzipan-covered Swiss roll thickly with melted chocolate. From the marzipan trimmings, shape 10 chunks, ½ inch in diameter and about 1¼ inch long. Position one on each side of the logs towards each end (to resemble gnarly bits). Paint these with chocolate. Once the chocolate begins to set, use a fork to mark a bark pattern along each chocolate log.

6. Roll out the remaining marzipan on a surface lightly dusted with confectioners' sugar to a rectangle, 9 × 4 inches, with a long side facing you. Brush lightly with melted chocolate. Starting from a long side, roll up tightly and cut into ¾-inch lengths. Roll the slices into discs and stamp out neat rounds, using a 1-inch biscuit cutter. Stick one on each end of the logs, using a little royal icing. Leave to set.

7. Spread royal icing on the boards around the logs to cover, swirling the icing with an offset spatula to create a snow effect.

8. On a surface lightly dusted with confectioners' sugar, roll out the green rolled fondant and cut out 10 holly leaves, using a small holly leaf cutter. Pinch tiny amounts of the red paste and roll these into 15 berries. Position 2 holly leaves and 3 berries on each chocolate log. Dust the chocolate logs and holly with confectioners' sugar to finish.

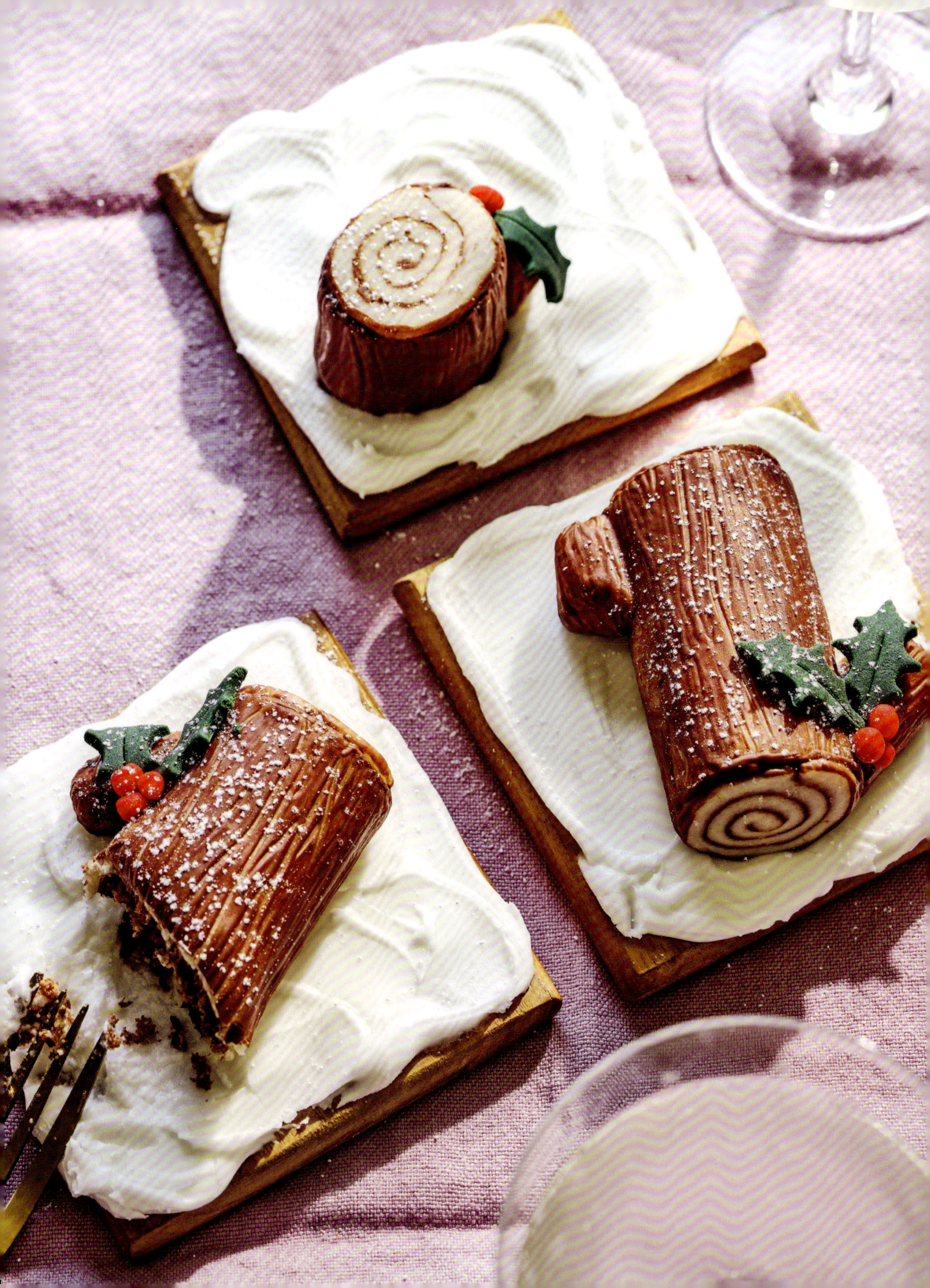

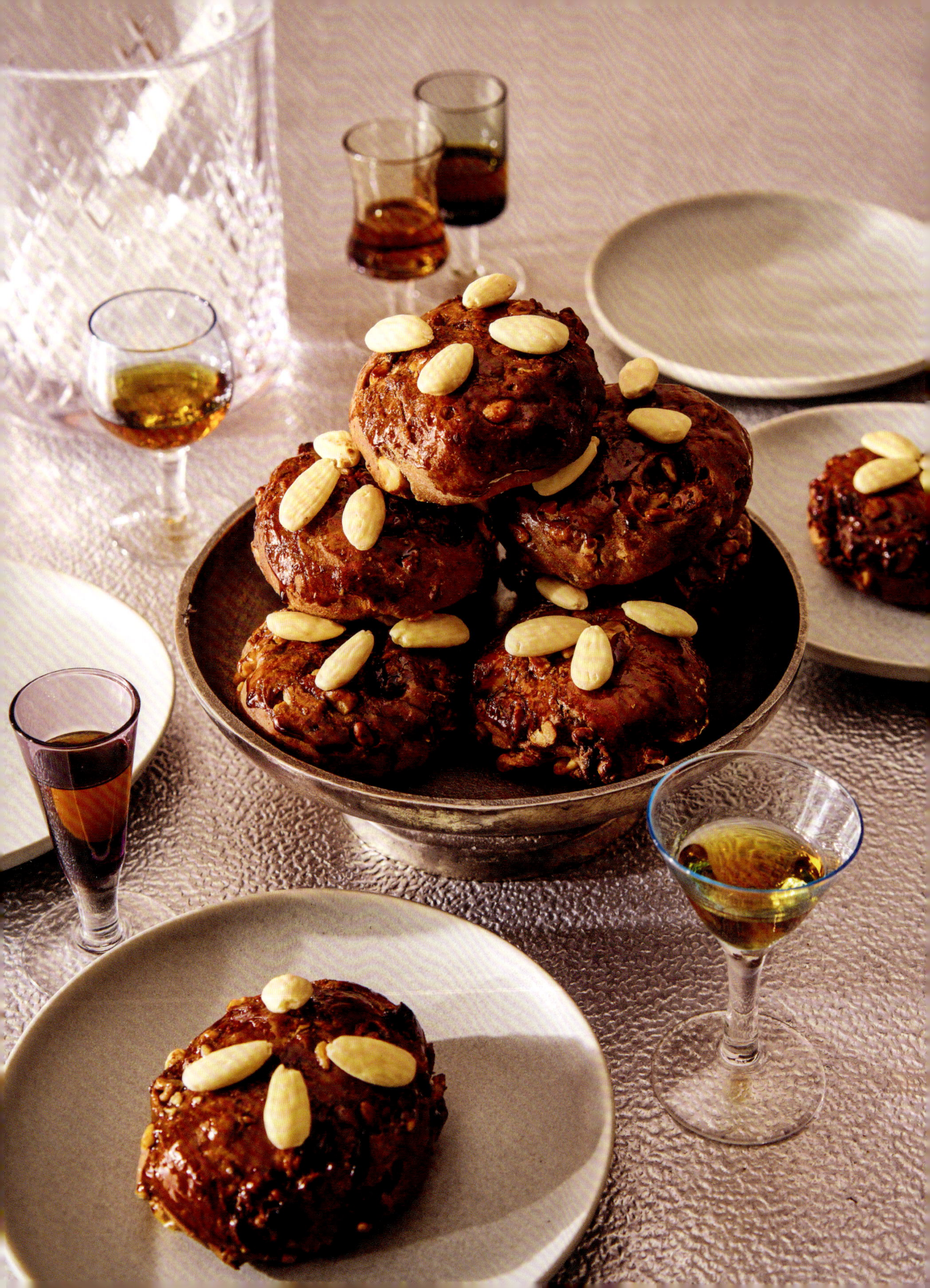

Pan'e Saba

My friend Nino gave me this recipe for a very sweet, rich dessert enjoyed in Sardinia during the festive season. It uses sapa, a syrupy reduced grape juice, which acts as a thickener and has an incredible intense flavor.

Makes 14

4 cups (500g) bread flour, plus extra to dust
3¾ tsp (10g) instant yeast
1 cup (300g) sapa
7 tbsp (100g) warm water
1⅔ cups (200g) raisins
2 cups (200g) walnut halves, chopped
¼ cup plus 1 tbsp (50g) pine nuts
⅓ cup (50g) skinned almonds
¾ tbsp ground cinnamon
A pinch of fine salt

To finish
2–3 tbsp sapa, to brush
A handful of skinned almonds

1. Put the flour into a stand mixer fitted with the dough hook and add the yeast, sapa and warm water. Mix on a low speed for 5 minutes to form a dough. Add the raisins, walnuts, pine nuts, almonds, cinnamon and salt and mix for a couple of minutes until evenly combined. (Alternatively, you can mix the dough by hand.)

2. Cover the bowl and leave the dough to rise for 3 hours.

3. Line a large baking sheet with parchment paper. Divide the risen dough into 14 pieces, shape into balls and flatten slightly. Place on the lined baking sheet, spacing them apart to give room for spreading, and leave to proof for 1½–2 hours until doubled in size.

4. Heat your oven to 350°F.

5. Bake the yeast cakes in the oven for about 40 minutes until slightly risen and deep golden brown.

6. As you remove the sheet from the oven, brush the yeast cakes with sapa and top with almonds. Transfer to a wire rack to cool.

Valentine Chocolate and Cherry Loaf

I've been making this morello cherry and chocolate loaf cake for more than 30 years. It's delicious sliced on its own, or spread with a little butter. Using bittersweet chocolate means it's not as sweet as you think it's going to be, and the cherries turn the enriched dough a fantastic pink color.

16 slices

Dough
4½ cups (560g) bread flour, plus extra to dust
2 tsp (8g) instant yeast
2 large eggs, at room temperature
1 tsp (5g) fine salt
1⅓ cups (320g) water

Filling
1 cup (180g) pitted morello cherries (the type in syrup that are sold in jars)
½ cup (60g) bread flour
⅔ cup plus 1 tbsp (150g) good-quality bittersweet chocolate chips

To finish
¼ cup (50g) good-quality bittersweet chocolate chips
¼ cup (50g) good-quality white chocolate chips

1. Put all of the dough ingredients into a stand mixer fitted with the dough hook and mix on a low speed for 5 minutes. Increase the speed to medium and mix for a further 15 minutes. Cover the bowl and leave the dough to rise for 3 hours.

2. Add the morello cherries to the dough, along with the ½ cup flour (which will absorb the extra moisture from them) and mix on a low speed for 5 minutes. Add the chocolate chips and mix until evenly incorporated. Re-cover and leave to rise for a further 1 hour.

3. Line a large baking sheet with parchment paper. Tip the dough out onto a lightly floured surface and punch down by folding the dough inwards repeatedly to knock out the air. Divide in half and roll each piece into a rope, about 24 inches long, tapering the ends slightly.

4. Twist the ropes together and then shape into a heart on the prepared baking sheet, joining the end pieces at the top of the heart, in the middle. Cover and leave to proof for about 2 hours until well risen and light to touch.

5. Heat your oven to 400°F.

6. Bake the loaf in the oven for 30 minutes until golden. Transfer to a wire rack and leave to cool before decorating.

7. To finish, melt the bittersweet and white chocolate in separate bowls over saucepans of simmering water, making sure the bases of the bowls aren't in contact with the water. Stir until smooth, then remove from the heat and leave to cool and thicken slightly.

8. Put the melted bittersweet chocolate into a paper piping bag and snip off the end to create a ¼-inch opening. Pipe a band of chocolate on top of the loaf to fashion a chocolate heart. Put the white chocolate into a small paper piping bag and snip off the tip. Drizzle this decoratively over the bittersweet chocolate heart. Leave to set before serving.

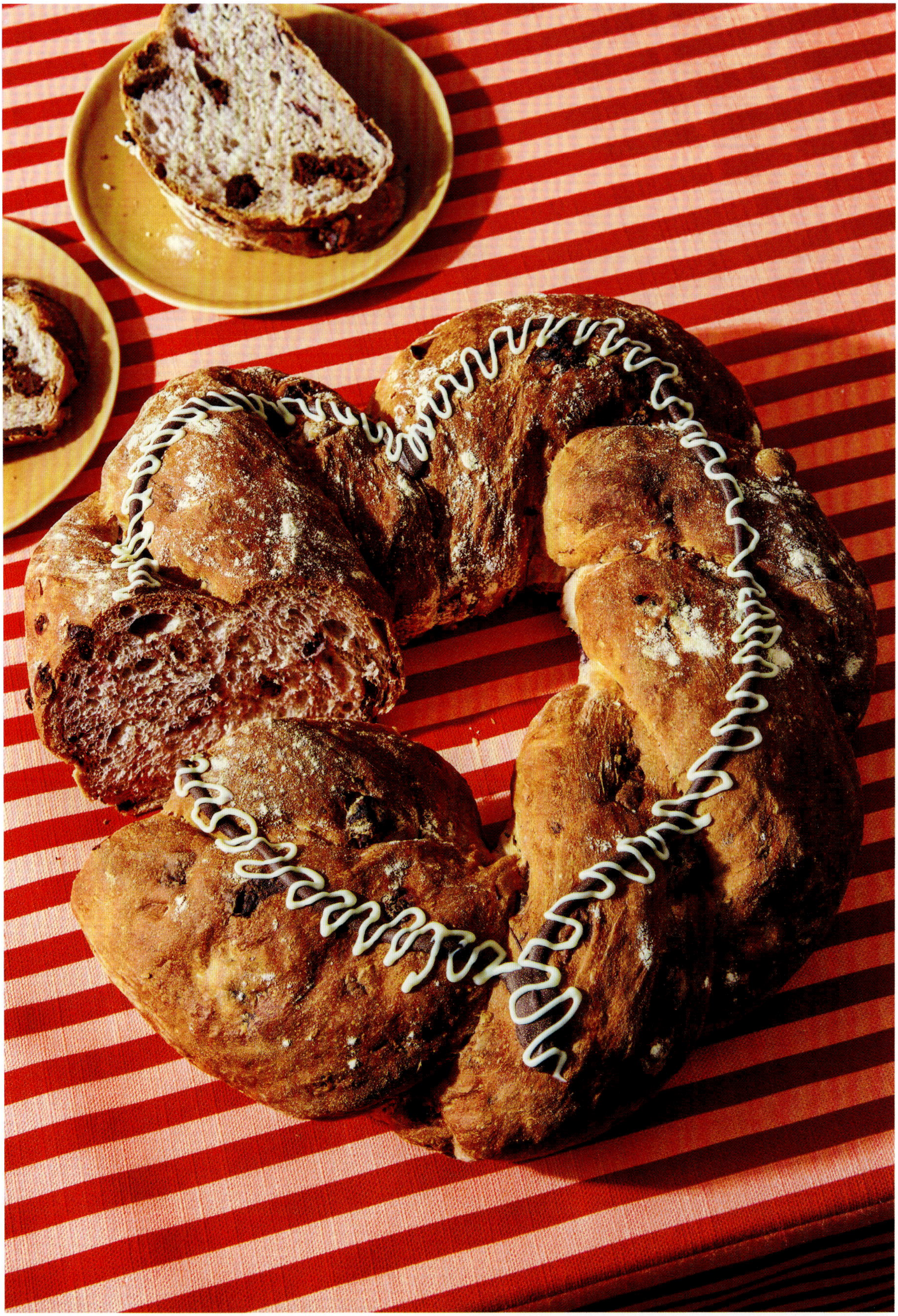

Roscón De Reyes

My friend Omar made this cake for me when I was in Madrid. It's eaten at Epiphany on January 6 and is the Spanish version of the French *galette des rois*. **Traditionally, a little ceramic figure is hidden inside and whoever finds it is crowned king for the day.**

8–10 slices

Dough
4 cups (500g) bread flour, plus extra to dust

1 tsp (5g) fine salt

2 tsp (8g) instant yeast

2 large eggs, at room temperature

½ cup (100g) superfine sugar

⅔ cup (150g) warm whole milk

Finely grated zest of 1 orange

7 tbsp (100g) unsalted butter, in pieces, softened

¾ cup plus 1 tbsp (120g) diced candied peel (preferably a mixture of orange and lemon)

Topping
½ cup (120g) apricot preserves

1 cup (100g) sliced almonds, toasted

Candied fruits, to decorate

Icing
1 cup (100g) confectioners' sugar

Finely grated zest and juice of 1 orange

To finish
Confectioners' sugar, to dust

1. Put all the dough ingredients, except the butter and candied peel, into a stand mixer fitted with the dough hook and mix on a low speed for 5 minutes. Increase the speed to medium and mix for a further 10 minutes, adding the butter a little at a time until it is all in and then incorporate the mixed peel.

2. Cover the bowl and leave the dough to rise for 3 hours.

3. Tip the dough out onto a lightly floured surface and flatten into a rectangle, 12 × 8 inches, with a long side facing you. Fold in the edges and then, starting at a long side, roll the dough up tightly into a sausage. Join the edges together to form a ring.

4. Grease a 10-inch savarin mold and place the ring of dough in it. Cover with a sheet of parchment paper and leave to proof for 2 hours.

5. Heat your oven to 400°F.

6. Once proofed, bake the dough in the oven for 30 minutes until risen and golden. Transfer to a wire rack to cool.

7. In a small saucepan, heat the apricot preserves with a little water, then pass through a strainer. Brush the cooled loaf all over with the apricot glaze and then sprinkle with the toasted sliced almonds. Arrange the candied fruits decoratively on top.

8. For the glacé icing, in a bowl, mix the confectioners' sugar with the orange zest and juice to make a thin icing. Transfer to a paper piping bag and snip off the end. Drizzle the glacé decoratively all over the top of the sweet bread. Leave to set on the wire rack.

9. Just before serving, sift confectioners' sugar over the surface of the sweet bread to finish.

Also pictured overleaf

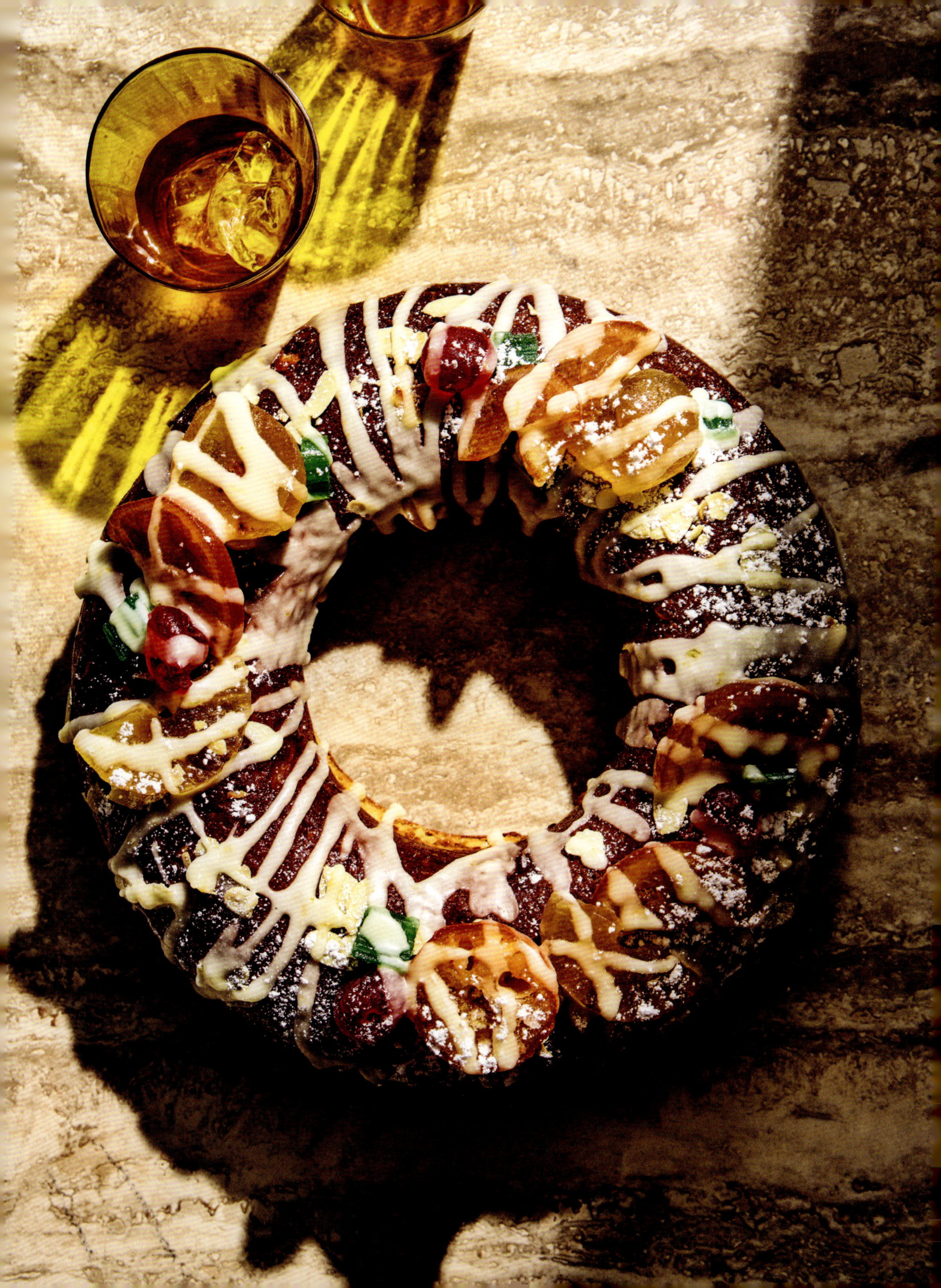

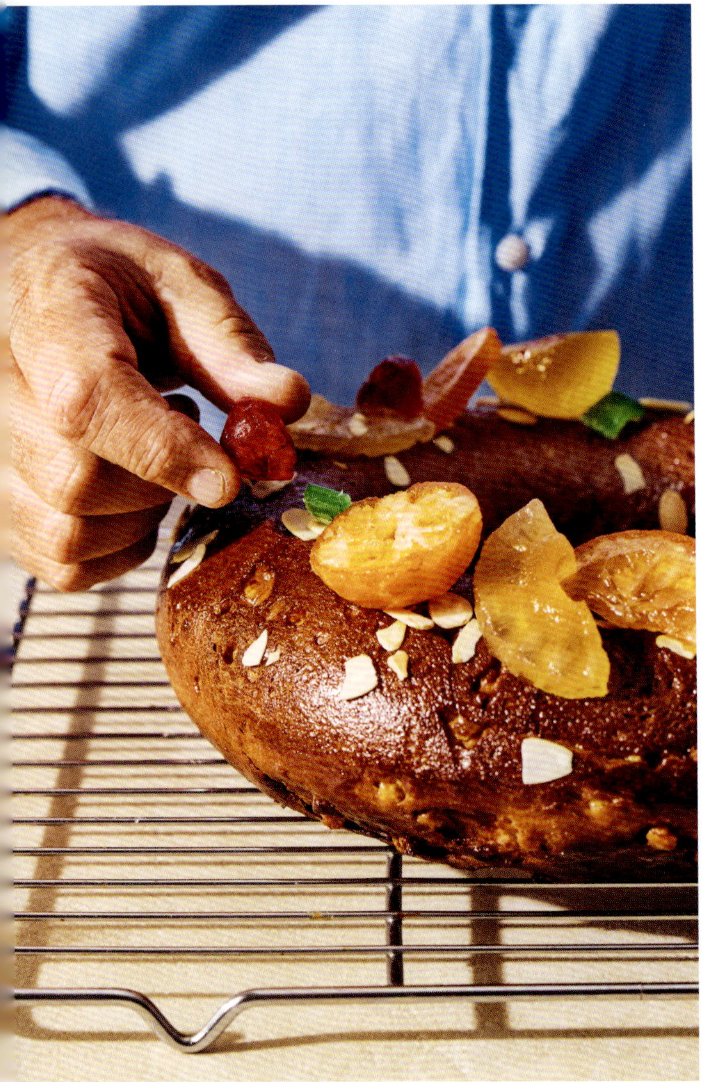
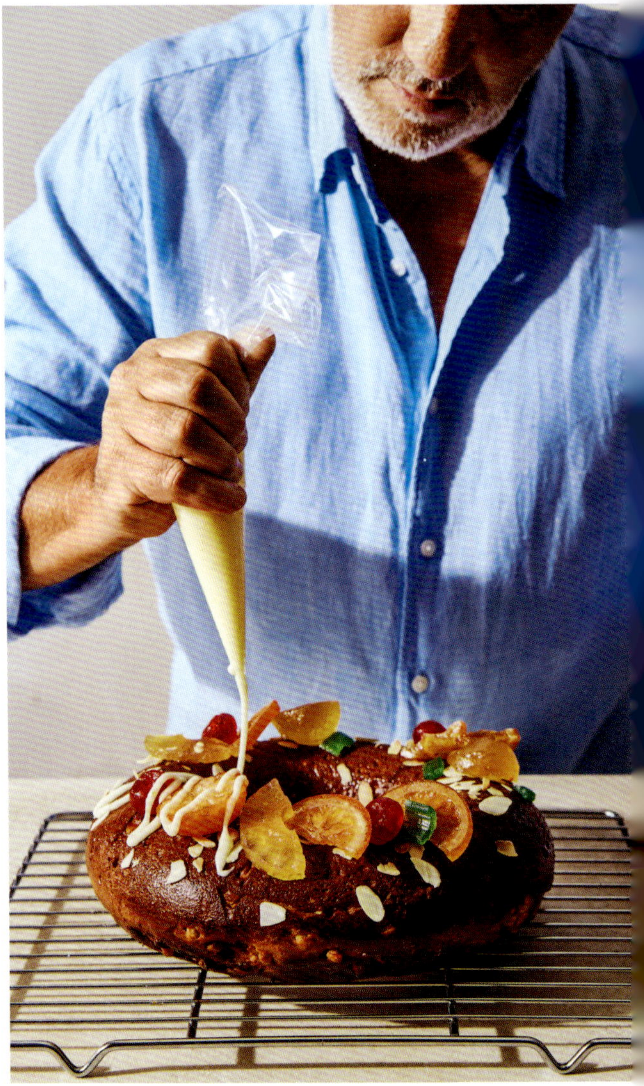

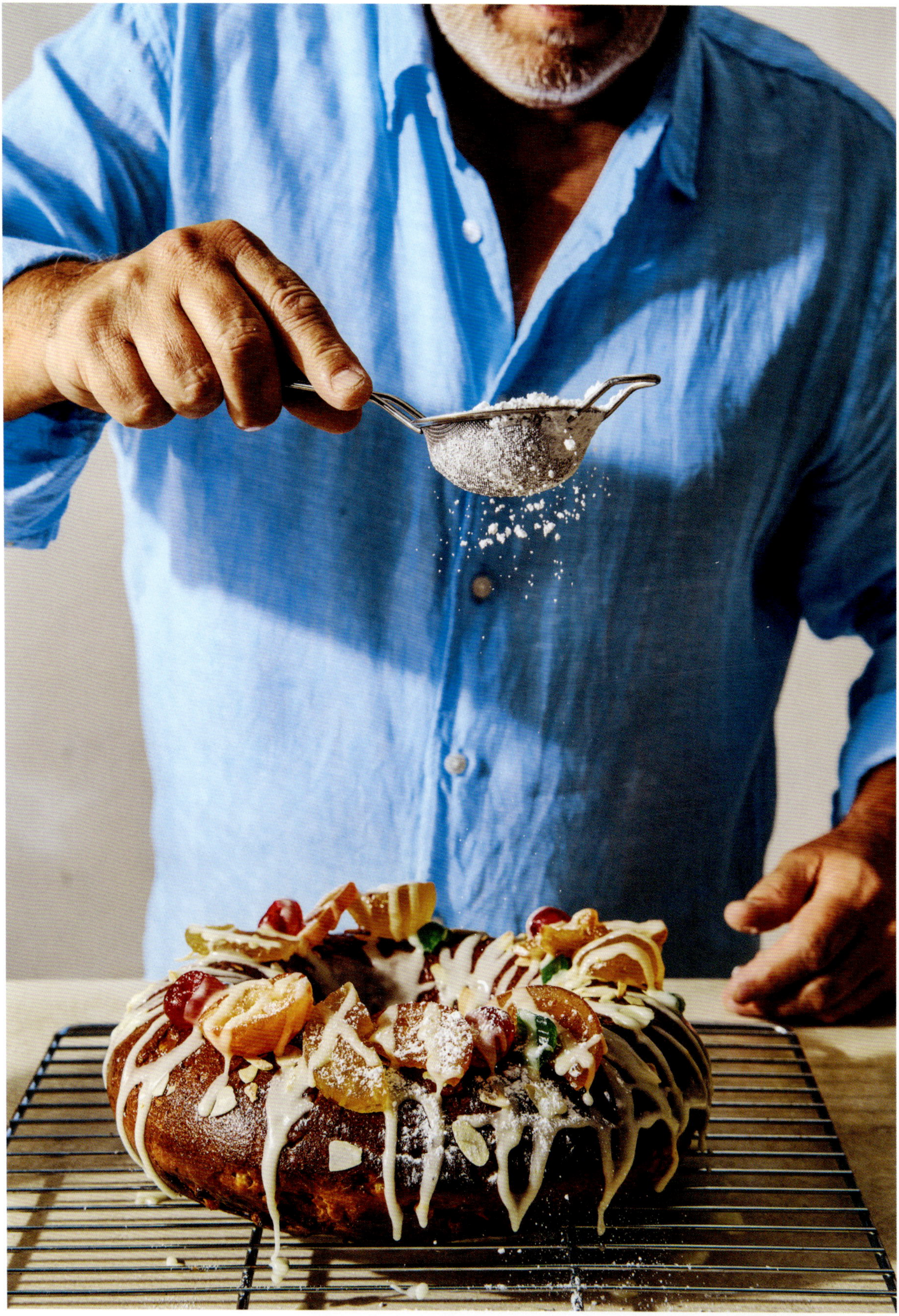

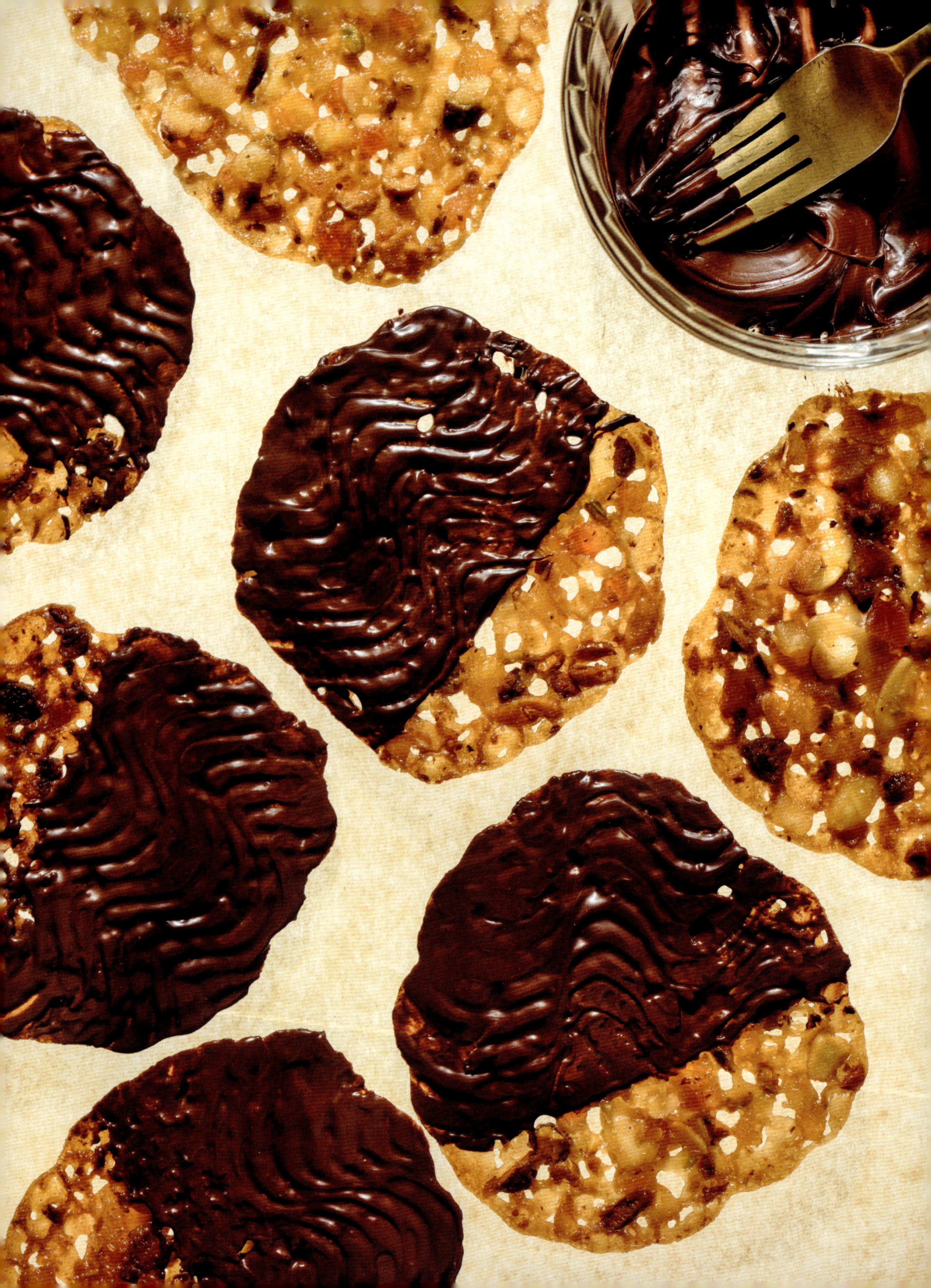

Florentines

Piled in a little stack at the end of a meal with your coffee or as part of an afternoon tea, Florentines are beautiful to look at. Packed with candied fruit and chopped nuts, and dipped in bittersweet chocolate, they are delicious to eat, too!

Makes 15

3 tbsp (50g) unsalted butter
¼ cup (50g) light brown sugar
3 tbsp (50g) Lyle's golden syrup
⅓ cup plus 1 tbsp (50g) all-purpose flour
4 candied cherries, finely chopped
⅓ cup (50g) diced candied peel (preferably a mix of orange and lemon)
2 tbsp (25g) shelled pistachio nuts, roughly chopped
¼ cup (25g) sliced almonds
7 oz (200g) bittersweet chocolate, broken into small pieces

1. Heat your oven to 350°F. Line 3 baking sheets with parchment paper.

2. Put the butter, sugar and golden syrup into a small saucepan and heat gently until the butter is melted. Remove from the heat and add the flour, candied cherries, candied peel and nuts. Stir to combine.

3. Scoop heaping teaspoonfuls of the mixture onto the prepared baking sheets, spacing them well apart to give plenty of room for spreading on baking, so just 5 Florentines on each baking sheet. Press them flat with the back of a spoon.

4. Bake in the oven, one baking sheet at a time, for 8–10 minutes, until golden brown and bubbling. Leave the Florentines on the baking sheets to cool and firm up for a few minutes, then transfer to wire racks to finish cooling.

5. Melt half of the chocolate in a heatproof bowl set over a pan of simmering water, making sure the base of the bowl isn't in contact with the water. Remove the bowl from the pan and add the remaining chocolate. Stir until it is melted and smoothly incorporated.

6. Partially coat each Florentine with melted chocolate and place on a wire rack. Mark decorative wavy lines on the chocolate with a fork and leave to set before serving. The Florentines will keep for up to a month in an airtight container.

White Chocolate, Dried Cranberry and Nut Cookies

In the middle of winter, we all need a bit of comfort food, so make yourself a cup of tea and enjoy proper luxury in a home-baked cookie. Use good-quality white chocolate, as it will hold its shape better and won't fully melt on baking, so you can bite into little chocolatey pieces in the finished cookie.

Makes 16

1¼ sticks (150g) unsalted butter, softened

¾ cup (150g) superfine sugar

½ cup (100g) light brown sugar

1 large egg

2 cups plus 2 tbsp (275g) all-purpose flour

1 tsp baking powder

½ tsp fine salt

Heaping ⅓ cup (75g) good-quality white chocolate chips

¼ cup (40g) dried cranberries

⅓ cup (40g) macadamia nuts, chopped

1. In a large bowl, using a hand mixer, cream the butter and both sugars together until light and fluffy. Add the egg and beat to incorporate.

2. Add the flour, baking powder and salt and mix well on a low speed to form a stiff dough. Initially, it will seem as though there is too much flour but beat slowly and the dough will come together. Add the white chocolate chips, dried cranberries and chopped macadamia nuts and mix slowly until evenly combined.

3. Tip the dough onto a large piece of parchment paper and roll into a cylinder, 11 inches long and 2½ inches in diameter. Wrap in the paper, twist the ends to seal and chill in the fridge for 2 hours.

4. Heat your oven to 350°F. Line 2 baking sheets with parchment paper.

5. Unwrap the dough and cut into 16 equal slices. Place on the prepared baking sheets, leaving space in between to give room for spreading.

6. Bake in the oven for 12–15 minutes until risen and golden; the cookies will still be soft when you remove them from the oven. Leave to firm up on the baking sheets for a few minutes before carefully transferring to a wire rack to cool completely.

7. These cookies will keep for up to 2 weeks in an airtight container.

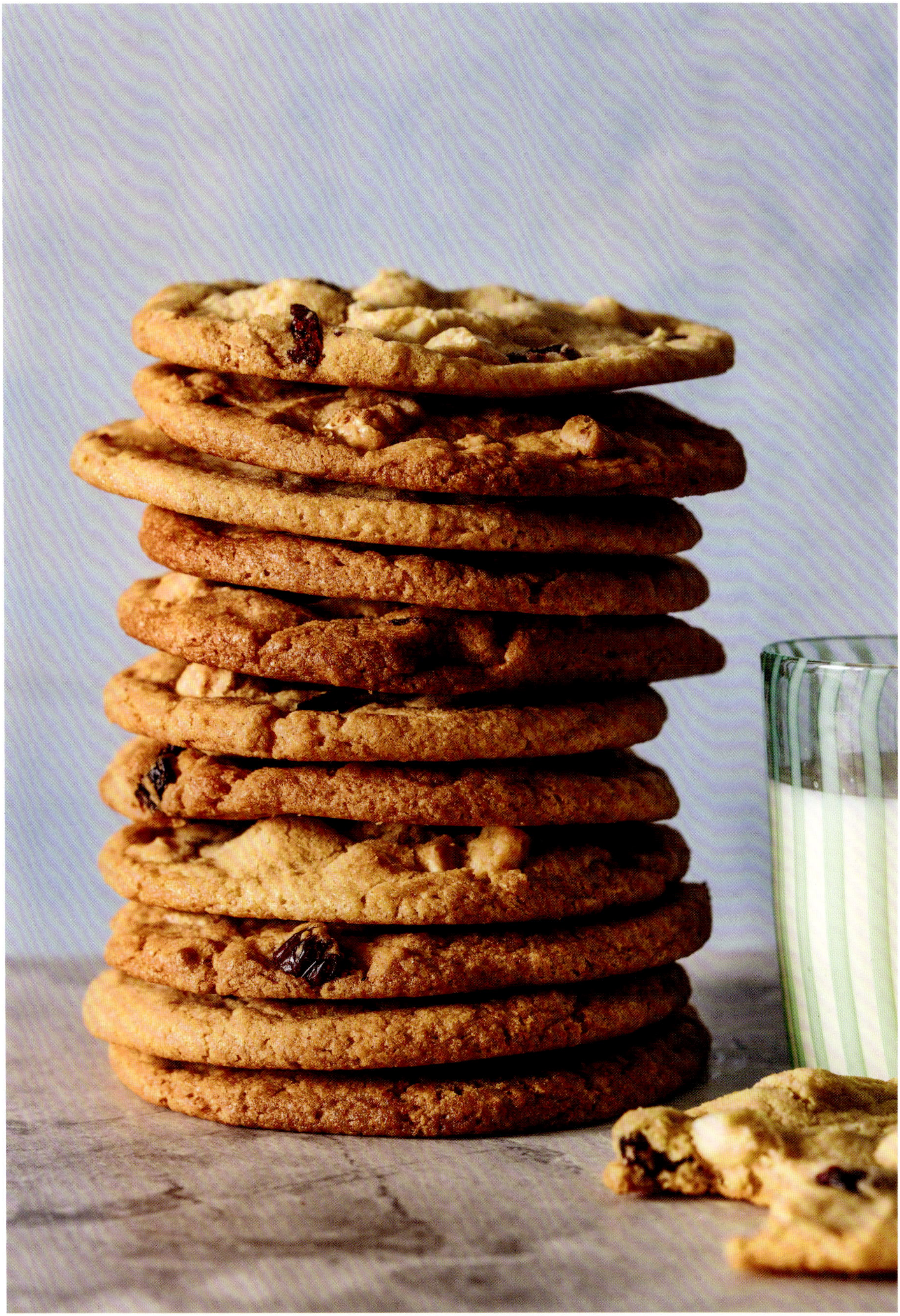

Valentine Love Heart Cookies

A fun cookie to make for Valentine's Day – and a great way to practice your piping skills! These use a classic vanilla dough, but you can add a few drops of rosewater or orange extract, or some lemon or orange zest if you like. Chill the dough before baking the cookies, to help keep their neat shape.

Makes 28

1¾ sticks (200g) unsalted butter, softened
1 cup (200g) superfine sugar
1 tsp vanilla extract (or orange or rose extract)
1 large egg, beaten
3¼ cups (400g) all-purpose flour

To decorate
1 × 1 lb (450g) box confectioners' sugar
About 5 tbsp (75g) water
Pastel gel food coloring (a few shades)
Red writing icing (in a tube)

1. In a large bowl, using a hand mixer, beat the butter and sugar together until the mixture is pale and creamy. Add the vanilla extract (or other flavoring) with the egg and beat until smoothly combined. Finally, with the mixer on a low speed, gradually add the flour.

2. Once the flour is all incorporated, gather the dough with one hand and form it into a ball. Flatten slightly into a disc, wrap in plastic wrap and refrigerate for at least 1 hour.

3. Line 2 baking sheets with parchment paper. Roll out the dough between 2 sheets of parchment paper to a ¼-inch thick then lift off the top sheet of paper. Using a heart-shaped cutter, stamp out hearts. Carefully transfer the dough hearts to the lined baking sheets with a spatula, spacing them apart to give room for spreading. Chill in the fridge for at least 30 minutes.

4. Heat your oven to 350°F.

5. Bake the cookies in the oven for 10–12 minutes until golden brown. Leave them on the baking sheets to firm up for 5 minutes then transfer to a wire rack to cool completely.

6. These cookies will keep in an airtight container for up to 2 weeks; they are best decorated within a day of serving.

7. To make the royal icing, in a large bowl using the electric whisk, beat the confectioners' sugar with enough water to give a smooth consistency that holds its shape but is still slightly fluid. Divide the icing between a few small bowls and color each with a few drops of your chosen food coloring, mixing until well blended.

8. To decorate the cookies, spoon a little of each icing into a small paper piping bag and snip off the tip. Pipe an outline of icing around the edge of each cookie and leave to dry for a few minutes.

Continued overleaf

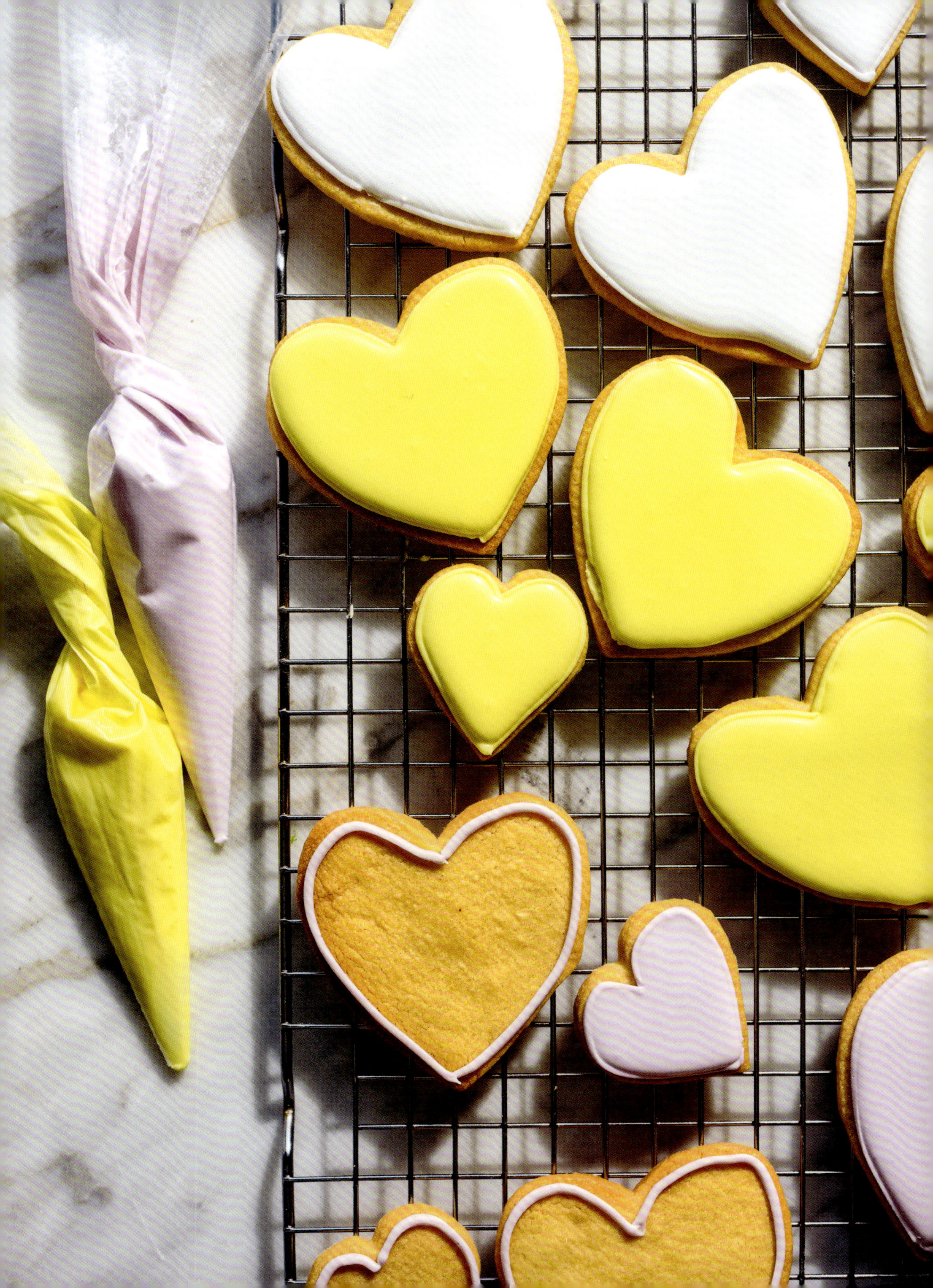

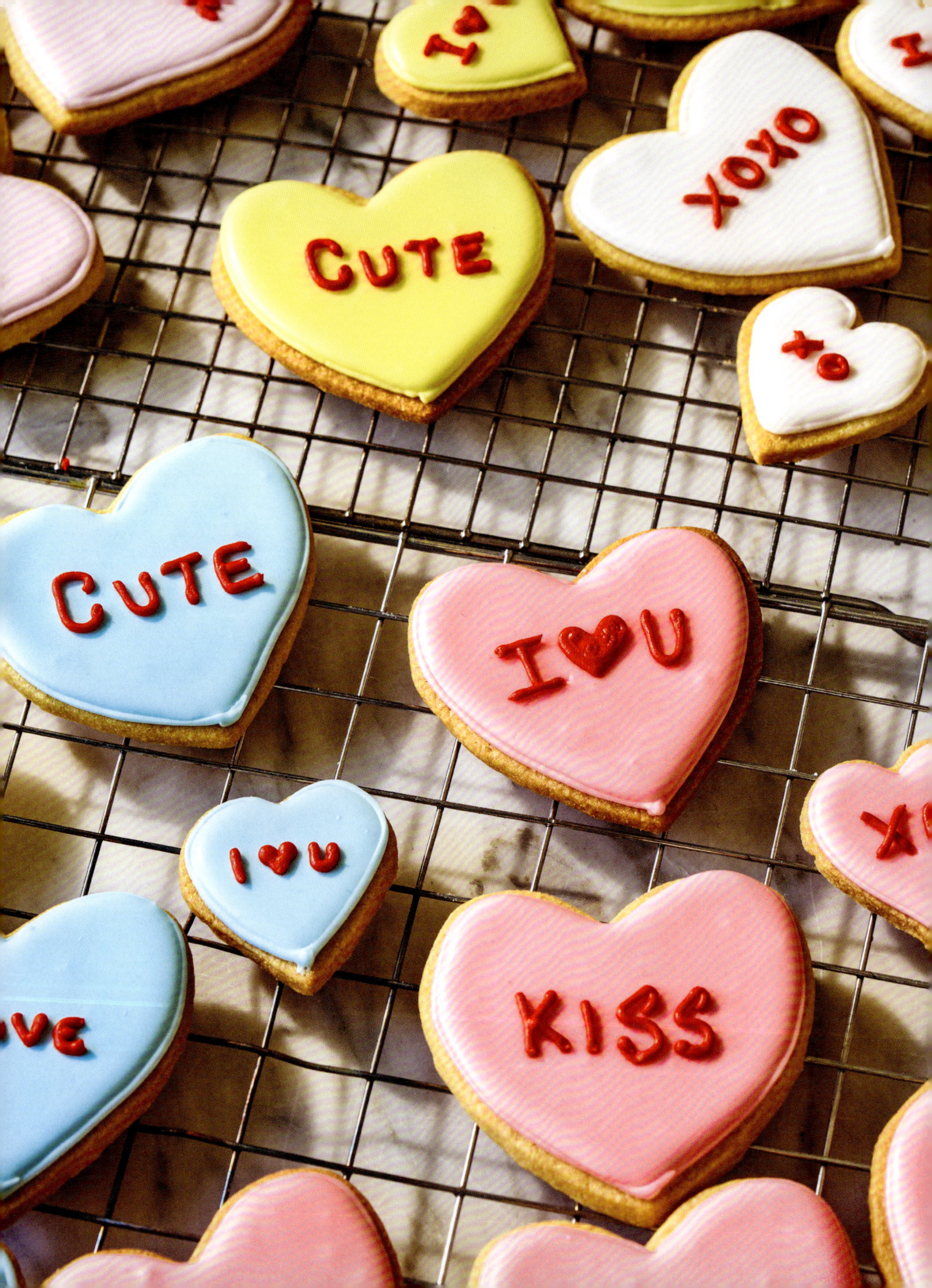
CUTE
XOXO
XO
CUTE
I ♥ U
I ♥ U
KISS

Continued from page 202

9   You can either use the same color icing or a contrasting color to 'flood' the cookies. Add a few drops of water to the remaining icing in each bowl to make it slightly runny. Spoon a little of this thin icing into the center of a cookie and spread to fill the area within the piped line. Repeat with the rest of the cookies.

10   Place the cookies on a wire rack and leave until the icing is set.

11   To finish the cookies, write messages on the set icing, using the red writing icing. Touch the starting point with the tip of the tube and slowly squeeze out the icing, lifting the tube a little away from the surface as you write – use a constant pressure and let the line of icing fall naturally into place as you guide it. As you come to the end, stop squeezing and drop the line, touching the finish point. Leave to set on the wire rack before serving.

Igloo Cake

A novelty cake that looks complicated but is quite easy, if you follow the instructions carefully. Make the rolled fondant decorations at least a day ahead, so they have time to set, and keep all the modeling pastes wrapped so they don't dry out. You'll need a 12-inch cake board, turntable and fondant smoother.

24–30 slices

Pre-made decorations
4 oz (100g) black rolled fondant icing (for the penguins)
Cornstarch, to dust
9 oz (250g) ready-to-use white flower and cake modeling paste (for the igloo tunnel, skis, penguin feet, post)
Edible glue
Food coloring gels: orange, brown and black
1 oz (25g) red rolled fondant icing (for the hats)

Madeira cake
3⅔ cups (450g) all-purpose flour
3½ tsp baking powder
2 cups (400g) superfine sugar
3½ sticks (400g) unsalted butter, softened
7 large eggs, at room temperature
3½ tbsp milk

Royal icing
2 tbsp plus 2 tsp meringue powder
⅔ cup (150g) water
4 cups (400g) confectioners' sugar, sifted

Buttercream
1¼ sticks (145g) unsalted butter, softened
2¾ cups (285g) confectioners' sugar
3 tbsp milk

1. To make the penguins, take some black rolled fondant and roll into a ball the size of a walnut. Make a snip in each side, lift this and stretch to form wings. Insert a toothpick through the middle. Roll another ball the size of a cherry to form the head and sit on top of the body. Repeat to make 3 penguins in total.

2. Dust your work surface with cornstarch and roll out a piece of white modeling paste to ⅛ inch thick. Cut out bellies for the penguins, using a ¾-inch cutter, and stretch to ovals. Using edible glue, attach to the front of the penguins. Stamp out faces, using the base of a ½-inch plain piping tip, and stick to the front of the penguins' heads.

3. For the feet and beaks, color a small piece of white modeling paste with orange gel. Shape 6 feet and set aside. Roll out the rest of the orange paste very thinly and cut 3 beaks, ½ inch long and 1/16 inch across. Trim the ends to a point. Insert a piece of toothpick in the center then press the beaks onto the penguin's faces.

4. Shape hats out of red rolled fondant and sit on top of the penguins' heads. Roll eyes out of black rolled fondant and stick onto the faces, using edible glue.

5. To form the igloo tunnel, roll out some modeling paste to ⅛ inch thick and cut a rectangle, 8 × 4 inches. Using a knife, score a brickwork pattern on the surface. Lift and bend over a metal ring (or a cleaned 14-oz can, paper removed) to shape a tunnel.

6. To make the signpost, color a piece of modeling paste brown. Roll out one strip, 4 × ½ inch, and another 3¼ inch × ½ inch. Score both with a bark pattern and stick together at right angles to make a signpost.

7. For the skis, color a piece of modeling paste gray, using a little black gel. Roll out and cut 6 skis, 3¼ inch × ¼ inch. Trim one end to a point and gently bend to form the end of the ski.

8. Leave all the modeling paste decorations in a cool, dry place to dry and set overnight.

Continued overleaf

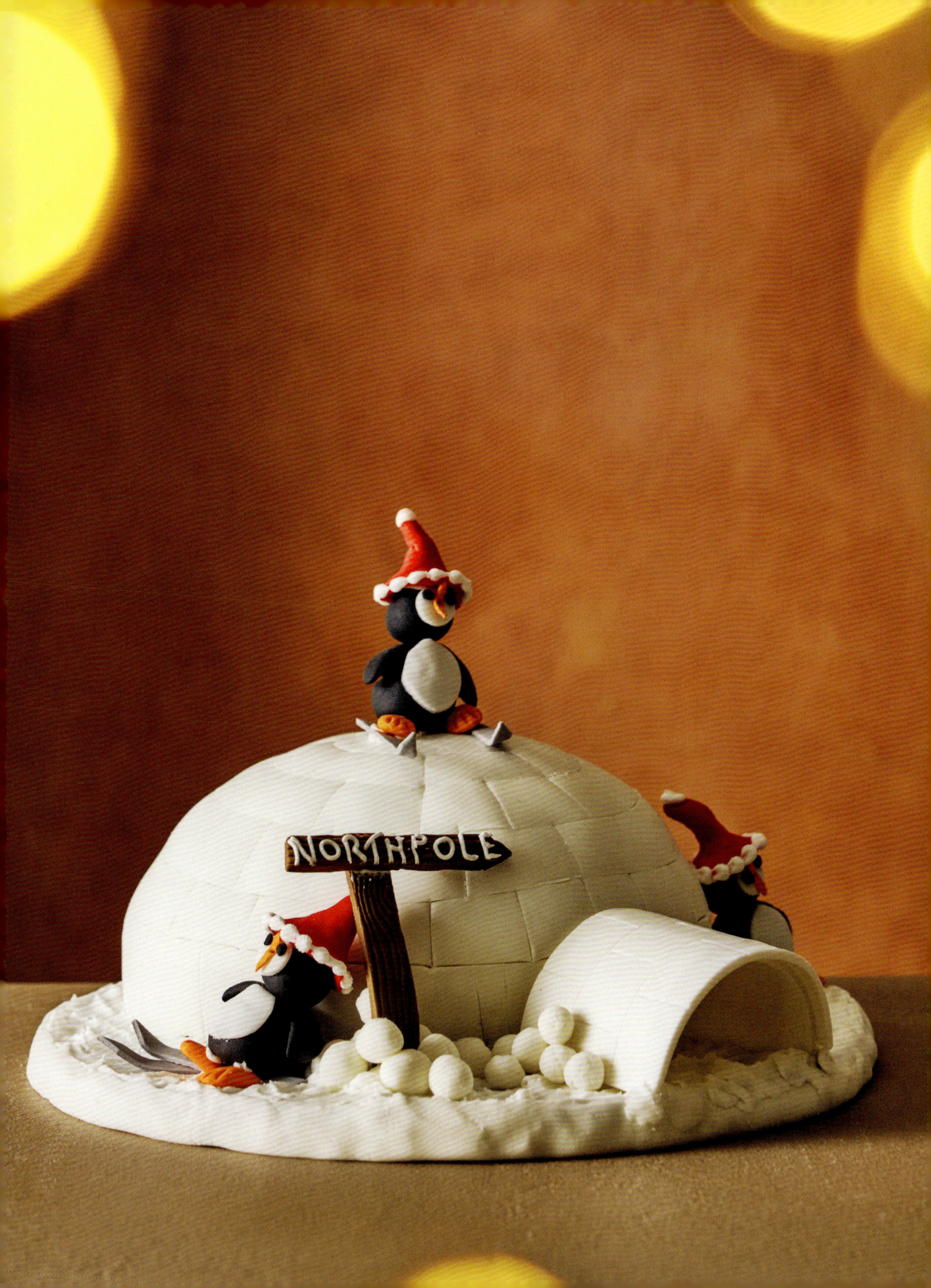
NORTHPOLE

Continued from page 206

To assemble

2 tbsp raspberry preserves

14 oz (400g) Marzipan (page 209, or use good quality store bought)

Confectioners' sugar, to dust

1 lb (450g) white rolled fondant icing

9 To make the cake, grease a 9-inch hemisphere (dome-shaped) cake pan with non-stick baking spray if you have it (or wipe with oiled paper towel). Heat your oven to 300°F.

10 Place all the cake ingredients in a stand mixer and mix on a low speed. Once smoothly combined, increase the speed to medium and beat for 1 minute. Transfer the mixture to the prepared pan and smooth the top to level. Bake in the center of the oven for 1¾–2 hours until golden brown and a cake tester inserted into the center comes out clean.

11 While the cake is in the oven, make the royal icing. In a small bowl, mix the meringue powder with the water until fully dissolved. Transfer to a stand mixer fitted with the paddle attachment and add half the confectioners' sugar. Mix on a slow speed until fully incorporated, then add the remaining confectioners' sugar and continue to mix on a low speed until the royal icing is smoothly combined. Increase the speed to medium and beat until it forms stiff peaks. Cover until ready to use.

12 When the cake is cooked, leave it to cool in the pan for 10 minutes, then remove and place on a wire rack. Leave to cool completely.

13 To make the buttercream, in a large bowl, beat the butter with a hand mixer until very soft. Gradually whisk in the confectioners' sugar until it is all incorporated. Add the milk and beat for 2 minutes until light and fluffy; it should be the consistency of thick whipped cream.

14 Place the cake on a board, dome side down, and trim a slice from the base to level it. Trim around the edge to remove the lip. Sit the cake upright (dome side up).

15 Slice the cake horizontally 1¼ inches from the base and remove the top. Spread the bottom with a ½-inch layer of buttercream. Cut another 1¼-inch slice from the bottom of the dome and position on the base. Using a clean offset spatula, spread with raspberry preserves. Position the top of the dome on the preserves layer. Clean your work surface, removing any crumbs.

16 Place 3 heaping tbsp of buttercream on top of the cake and spread thinly with an offset spatula to cover the entire surface of the cake.

17 Knead the marzipan until pliable and roll out on a surface lightly dusted with confectioners' sugar to a large circle, ⅛ inch thick. Lift the marzipan over the domed cake to cover it, using your hands to smooth the marzipan around the side. Trim to within ⅛ inch of the bottom edge.

18. Transfer the cake to a 12-inch cake board. Clean and dry your work surface then dust with confectioners' sugar. Roll out the white rolled fondant to a large circle, big enough to cover the cake, and press lightly all over with a fondant smoother until smooth and shiny.

19. Very lightly dampen the marzipan, so the rolled fondant will stick to it. Lift the rolled fondant over the marzipan-covered cake and gently smooth down. Lift the bottom edges to avoid pleats forming. Trim the edges then lift the cake board onto the turntable. Hold the fondant smoother vertically against the side of the cake, while turning the turntable with the other hand, to create a smooth, even finish. Gently move the igloo cake to the back of the board.

20. To mark the brickwork on the igloo, take a 3-inch biscuit cutter and press lightly on top of the cake to indent a circle. Using a sharp knife, below this circle mark another 3 circles around the cake, at 1-inch intervals. Mark vertical lines between the circles to create the brickwork.

21. Place some royal icing on your confectioners'-sugar-dusted surface and use your offset spatula in a forwards and backwards motion to smooth it and remove any air. Spread the royal icing over the board around the cake to cover it completely and use the offset spatula to make peaks that resemble snow.

22. Lift the modeling paste tunnel off its mold and position centrally in front of the igloo.

23. To finish the cake, put a little royal icing into a piping bag fitted with a no.2 piping tip and write North Pole on the signpost. Stick the signpost, penguins and skis in position on the cake, using royal icing. To stabilize the signpost, roll snowballs of white rolled fondant and secure them around the base of the signpost.

To make your own marzipan
Put scant ½ cup (90g) superfine sugar, 1⅓ cups (140g) confectioners' sugar and 2 cups plus 2 tbsp (220g) almond flour into a large bowl and stir together. Make a well in the middle and add the finely grated zest and juice of 1 orange, 1 tsp almond extract and 1 beaten large egg. Mix well to combine and bring together with one hand. Tip the marzipan onto a surface dusted with confectioners' sugar and knead briefly. Form into a ball, flatten to a disc and wrap in plastic wrap. Refrigerate for 15 minutes or until ready to use.

Celebrate

Pistachio, Lemon and Ginger Biscotti

Biscotti are twice-baked little Italian cookies that are perfect for dunking in your coffee in the morning. Once you've got the hang of them, you can play with the flavors – almonds and pine nuts are traditional, but you can also use hazelnuts or peanuts, and orange zest instead of lemon.

Makes 24

1⅓ cups (165g) all-purpose flour, plus extra to dust

½ tsp baking powder

½ tsp ground ginger

A pinch of fine salt

¾ cup plus 1 tbsp (165g) superfine sugar

2 large eggs, beaten

Finely grated zest of 1 lemon

½ cup (60g) shelled pistachio nuts

¼ cup (40g) finely chopped preserved stem ginger (drained of syrup), or crystallized ginger

1. Heat your oven to 350°F. Line 2 large baking sheets with parchment paper.

2. Mix the flour, baking powder, ground ginger, salt and sugar together in a large bowl. Make a well in the center and add the beaten eggs, lemon zest, pistachios and chopped ginger. Mix together until evenly combined to form a dough. If the dough is too sticky to hold its shape, incorporate a little more flour.

3. Turn the dough out onto a lightly floured surface and divide in two. Form each portion into a log shape, about 9 inches long, and press gently to flatten. Transfer the biscotti lengths to the prepared sheets and bake in the oven for 20 minutes until golden brown.

4. Remove the dough logs from the oven and leave them to cool and firm up on the baking sheets for 5 minutes. Lower the oven setting to 300°F.

5. Lift the biscotti logs onto a board and cut them into ½-inch thick slices, using a serrated knife. Lay the slices on the baking sheets. Return to the oven and bake for 15 minutes until golden brown.

6. Transfer the biscotti to a wire rack and leave them to cool completely. The biscotti will keep for a couple of weeks in an airtight container.

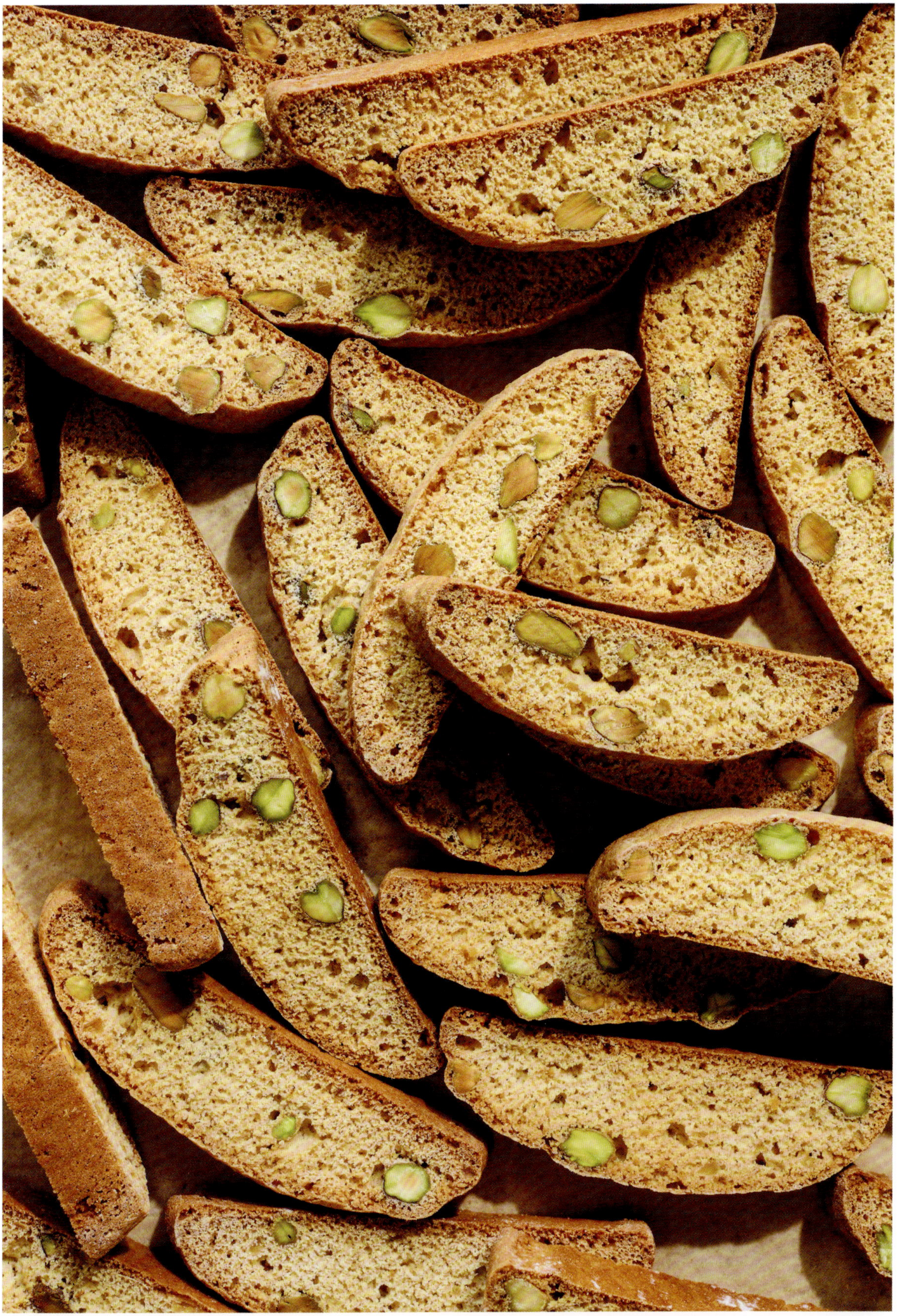

Turkey and Stuffing Pies

These individual pies are a great way of using up the leftovers after Thanksgiving or Christmas. You can add almost anything to them – if you have any cranberry sauce, get a bit of that in there too! The shortening in the pastry gives it a nice flake and helps to create a seal.

Makes 6

Pie dough
2⅓ cups plus 1 tbsp (300g) all-purpose flour, plus extra to dust
A pinch of fine salt
3 tbsp (50g) chilled unsalted butter, diced
¼ cup (50g) chilled vegetable shortening, diced
2–3 tbsp cold water

Stuffing topping
1 tbsp olive oil
1 onion, finely diced
2 cups (100g) fresh white breadcrumbs
2 tbsp chopped sage
1 tbsp chopped parsley
3 tbsp (50g) unsalted butter, diced

Filling
4 tbsp (65g) unsalted butter
5 oz (125g) pancetta, diced
2 leeks, trimmed, well washed and chopped
2 sprigs of thyme
7 tbsp (100g) white wine
⅓ cup plus 1 tbsp (50g) all-purpose flour
2 cups (500g) chicken broth
4 cups (about 300g) leftover cooked turkey, cut into bite-sized pieces
Salt and black pepper

1. To make the pie dough, put the flour and salt into a large bowl, add the butter and vegetable shortening and rub in using your fingers until the mixture resembles fine breadcrumbs. Add just enough cold water to bring the dough together. Turn out onto a lightly floured surface and knead briefly until smooth. Wrap in plastic wrap and chill in the fridge for 30 minutes.

2. For the stuffing topping, heat the olive oil in a small frying pan, add the onion and fry until soft and translucent. Combine the breadcrumbs and chopped herbs in a bowl, add the onion and toss to mix. Set aside.

3. To make the filling, heat the butter in a large wide saucepan, then add the pancetta, leeks and thyme. Season with salt and pepper and sauté for a few minutes, then pour in the wine. Cook over a medium heat until the wine has evaporated and the leeks are tender.

4. Sprinkle over the flour and stir until the leeks are coated. Now gradually add the broth, stirring as you do so to make a sauce. Add the turkey and fold through. Leave to cool completely.

5. Heat your oven to 400°F and put a baking sheet in the oven to heat up.

6. To assemble the pies, roll out the pie dough on a lightly floured surface to ⅛ inch thick. Cut out 6 rounds and use to line 6 individual foil pie pans, 5 inches in diameter and 1½ inches deep. Stand on a baking sheet.

7. Divide the turkey filling between the pie crusts. Spoon the stuffing mix evenly on top and dot with the diced butter.

8. Bake the pies on the preheated baking sheet in the oven for 30 minutes, or until the topping is golden brown and the turkey filling is piping hot. Serve hot.

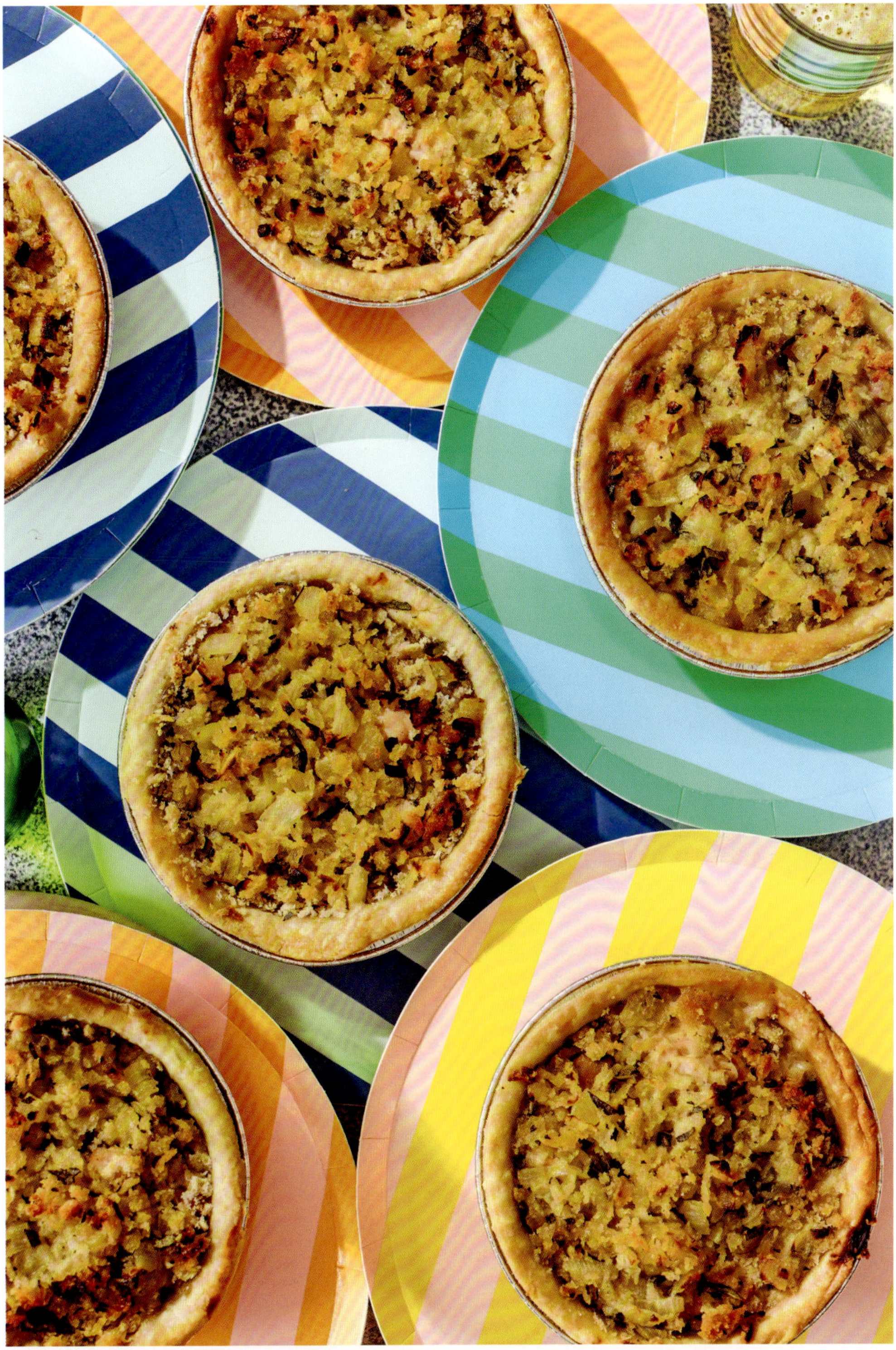

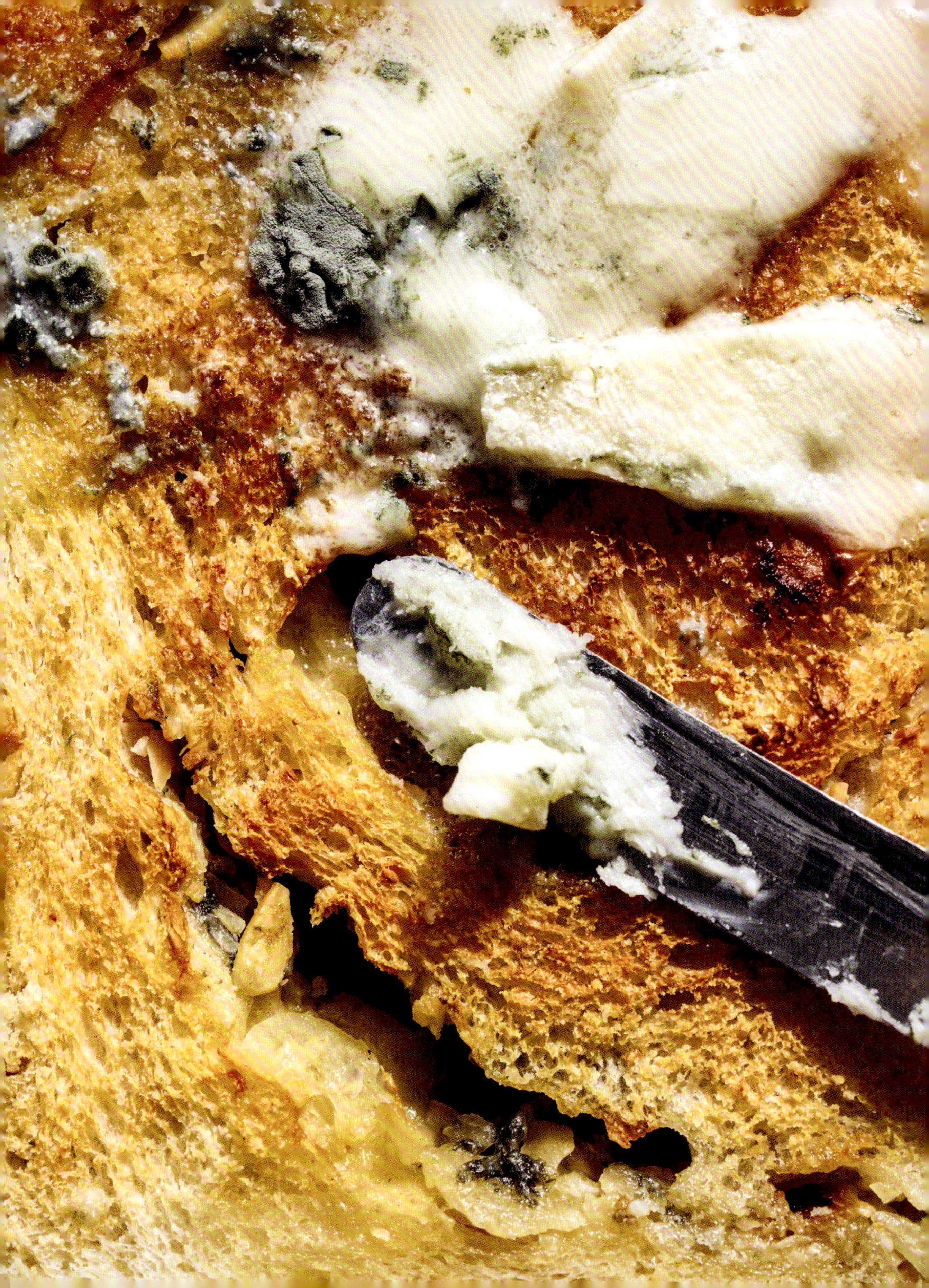

Christmas Cheese Loaf

Sliced and toasted, this Roquefort and almond loaf is beautiful as part of a cheese board. Toasted, it crisps up until it's almost like a cracker. I once made a sourdough version to sell in Harrods – it was nicknamed the Rolls Royce of breads! You can use Stilton instead of the Roquefort if you prefer.

Makes 1 loaf

Sponge
1⅔ cups (200g) bread flour
¾ cup (180g) water
1¼ tsp (3g) instant yeast

Dough
2⅓ cups plus 1 tbsp (300g) bread flour, plus extra to dust
¾ cup (170g) water
1½ tsp (4g) instant yeast
A little oil, to grease the pan

Filling
1¾ cups (180g) crumbled Roquefort
1¾ cups (180g) sliced almonds, toasted

1. To prepare the sponge, put the ingredients into a stand mixer fitted with the dough hook and mix on a low speed for 5 minutes. Cover and leave to rise for 3 hours.

2. Add the dough ingredients to your sponge and mix on medium speed for 10 minutes until smoothly combined to form a dough. Cover and leave to rise for a further 2 hours.

3. Lightly oil a 2-lb loaf pan. Tip the risen dough out onto a floured surface and roll out to a rectangle, 16 × 8 inches, with a short side facing you. Sprinkle the Roquefort evenly over the surface and then sprinkle the toasted almonds over the top. Roll up the dough, from a short side, into a sausage, so it is around 8 inches in length.

4. Place the dough in the prepared loaf pan, with the join underneath. Now put the loaf pan inside a large plastic bag and leave to proof for 2 hours until doubled in size.

5. Heat your oven to 400°F.

6. Remove the loaf pan from the bag. Spray the top of the loaf with water and then dust (or rub) with flour. Using a razor blade or very sharp knife, slash deep lines across the top of the dough.

7. Bake the loaf in the oven for 40 minutes until golden brown and cooked through. Tip it out of the pan and cool on a wire rack.

Also pictured overleaf

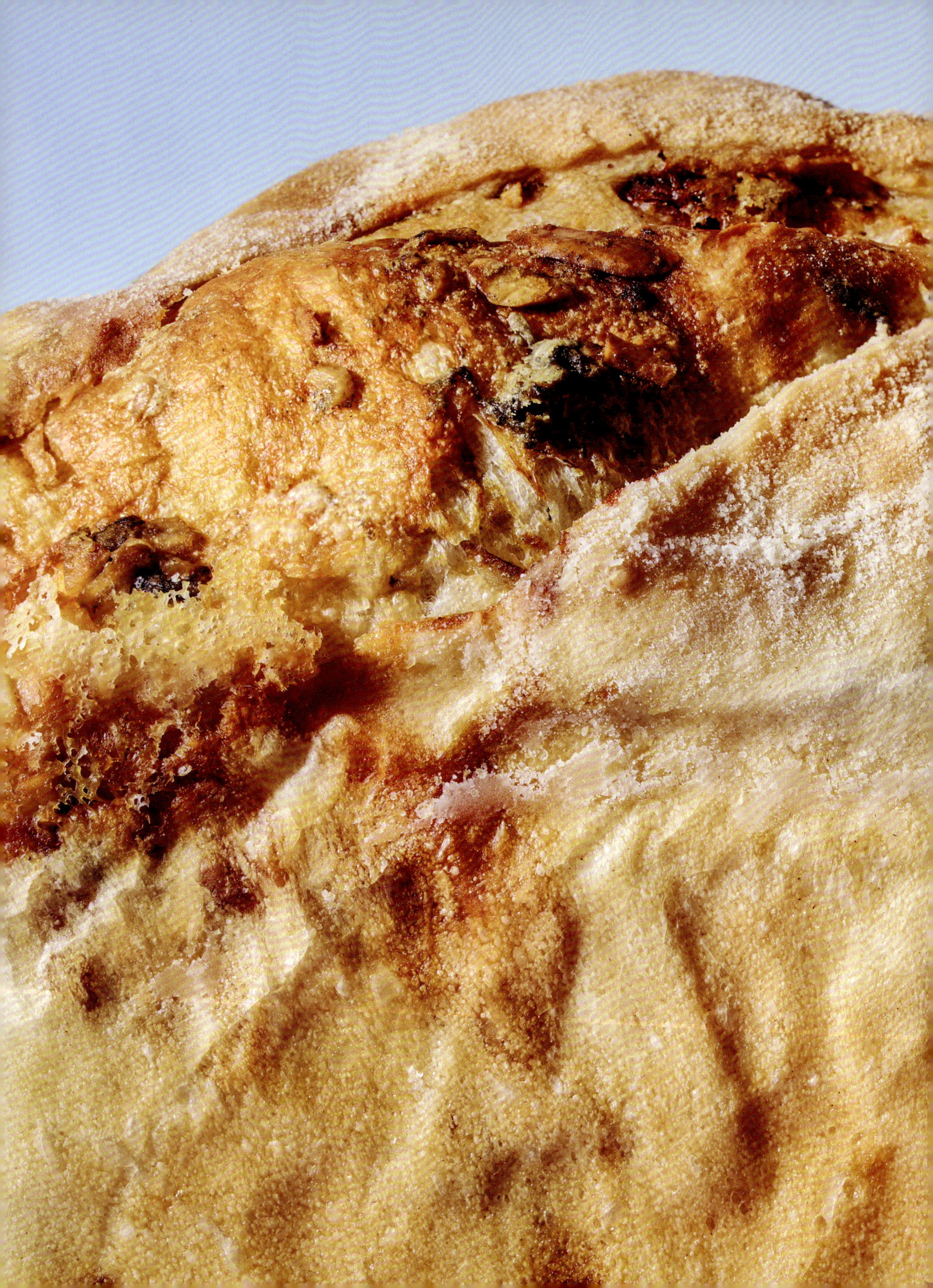

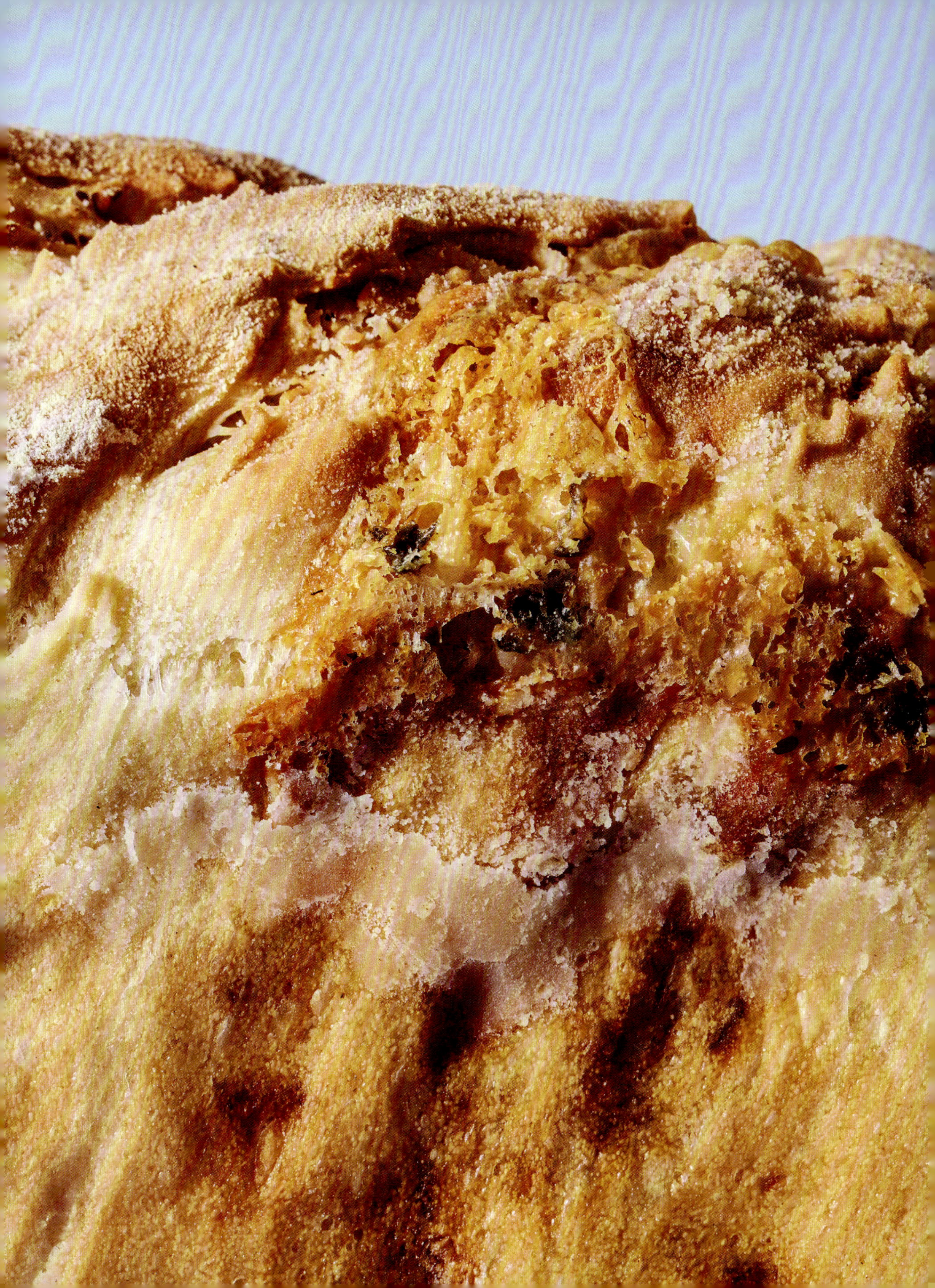

Shokupan

A Japanese loaf that I learned to make in Tokyo. It uses a yudane – a mix of flour and boiling water that you leave overnight – which results in the softest, lightest bread I've ever eaten. A ham and cucumber sandwich in slices of this loaf is perfection. Toasted, shokupan is out of this world!

Makes 1 loaf

Yudane
⅔ cup (80g) bread flour
⅓ cup (80g) boiling water

Dough
2⅓ cups plus 1 tbsp (300g) bread flour, plus extra to dust
¾ cup plus 3 tbsp (225g) warm milk
2 tbsp (25g) superfine sugar
1 × ¼-oz (7g) packet instant yeast
1½ tbsp (20g) unsalted butter, in pieces, softened
1 tsp (5g) fine salt
A little oil, to grease the pan

1. For the yudane, mix the flour and boiling water together in a medium bowl for 3 minutes until smoothly combined. Cover and leave to stand for at least 2 hours, or overnight in the fridge if you have time.

2. Transfer the yudane to a stand mixer fitted with the dough hook and add all the dough ingredients. Mix on low speed for 5 minutes until smoothly combined to form a dough. Increase the speed to medium and mix for a further 10 minutes to knead the dough until it is soft and elastic.

3. Cover the bowl and leave the dough to rise for 2–3 hours until doubled in size.

4. Lightly oil a 2-lb loaf pan. Tip the dough out onto a lightly floured surface and knock back by folding it inwards repeatedly to punch down the air. Divide into 3 equal pieces.

5. Shape each piece of dough into a ball and place side by side in the loaf pan. Put the pan inside a large plastic bag and leave the dough to proof for 2–3 hours until at least doubled in size.

6. Heat your oven to 400°F.

7. Bake the loaf in the oven for 30 minutes or until golden brown and cooked through. To check, tip the loaf out of the pan and tap the base – it should sound hollow. Transfer to a wire rack to cool.

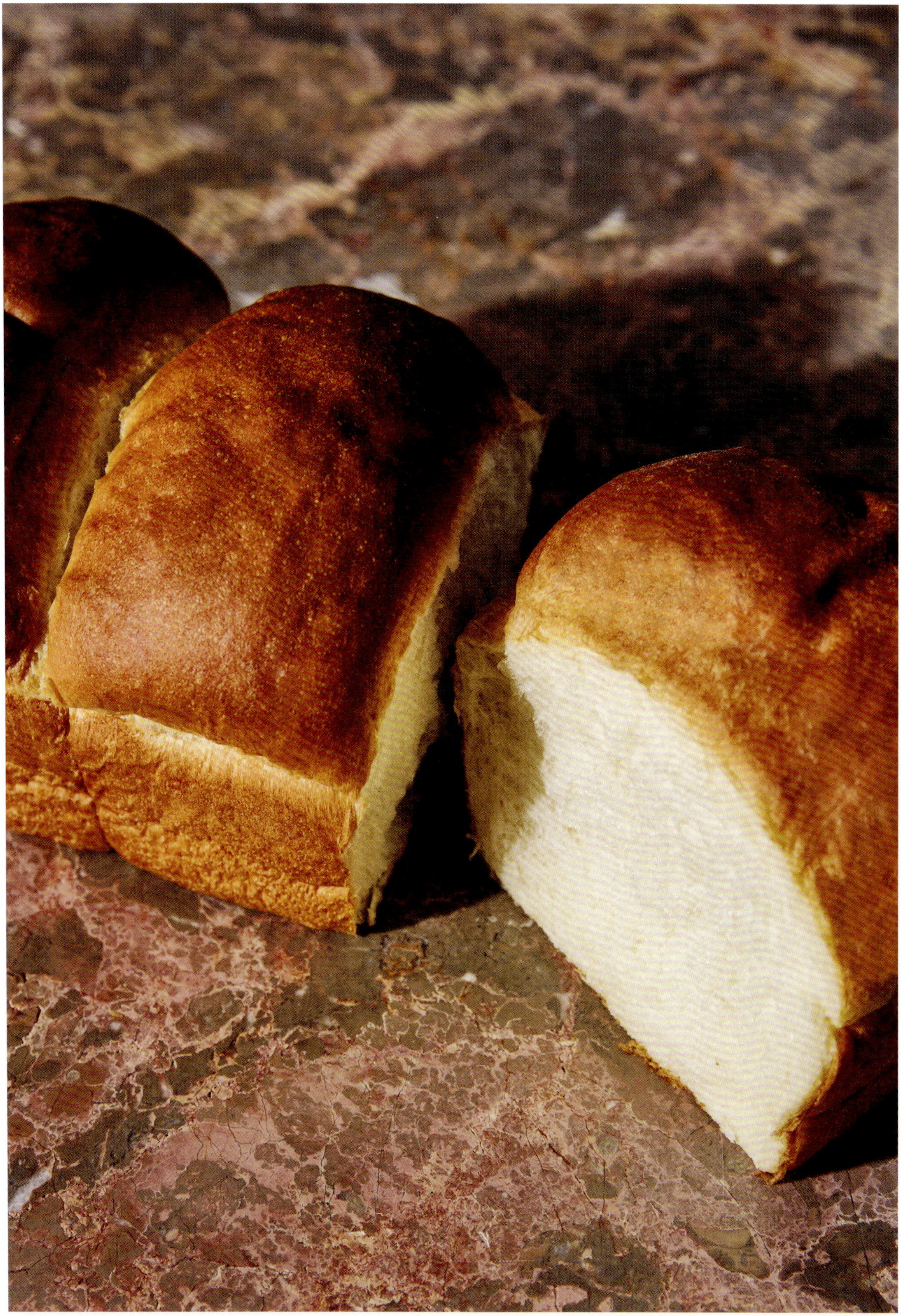

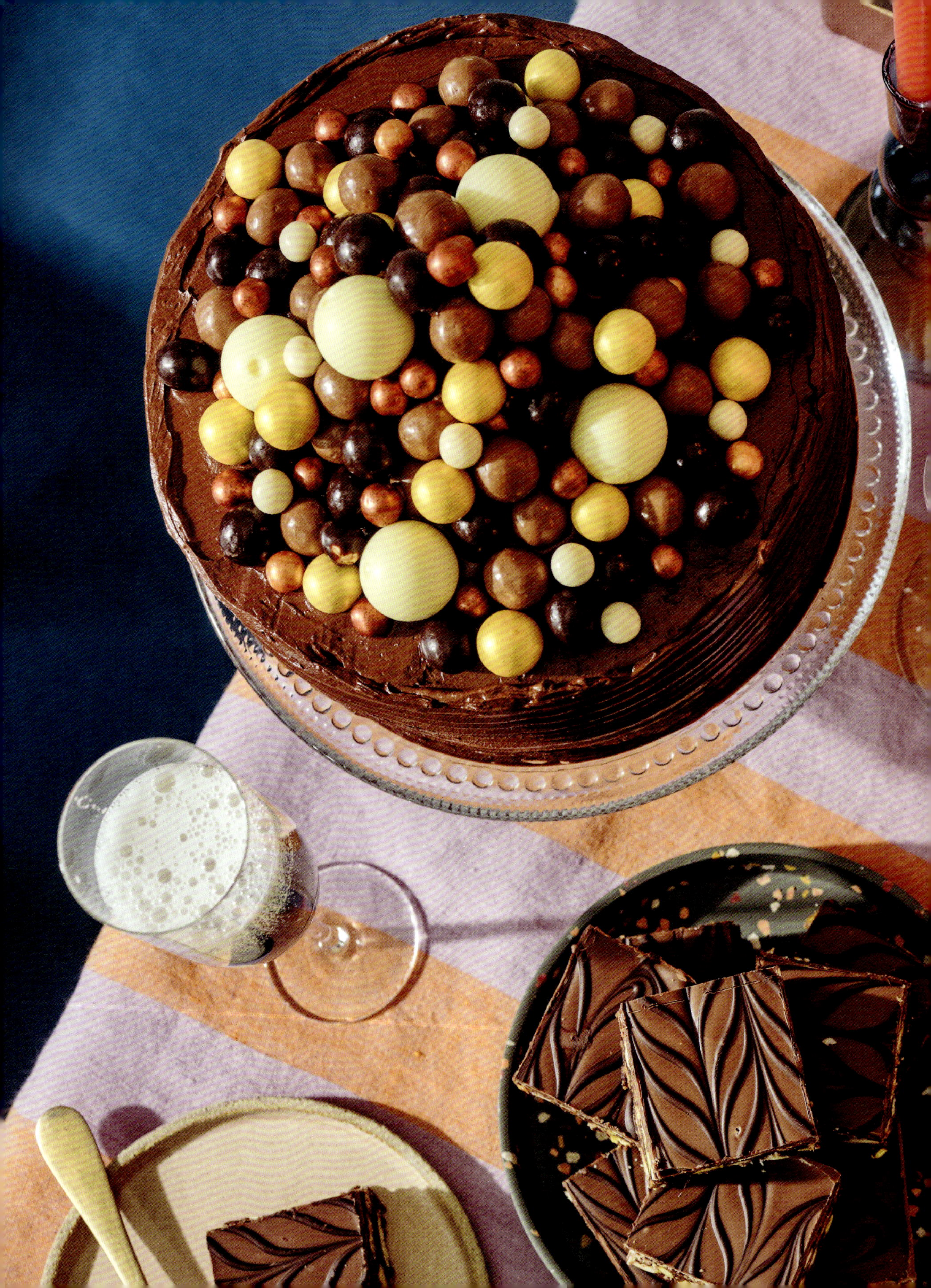

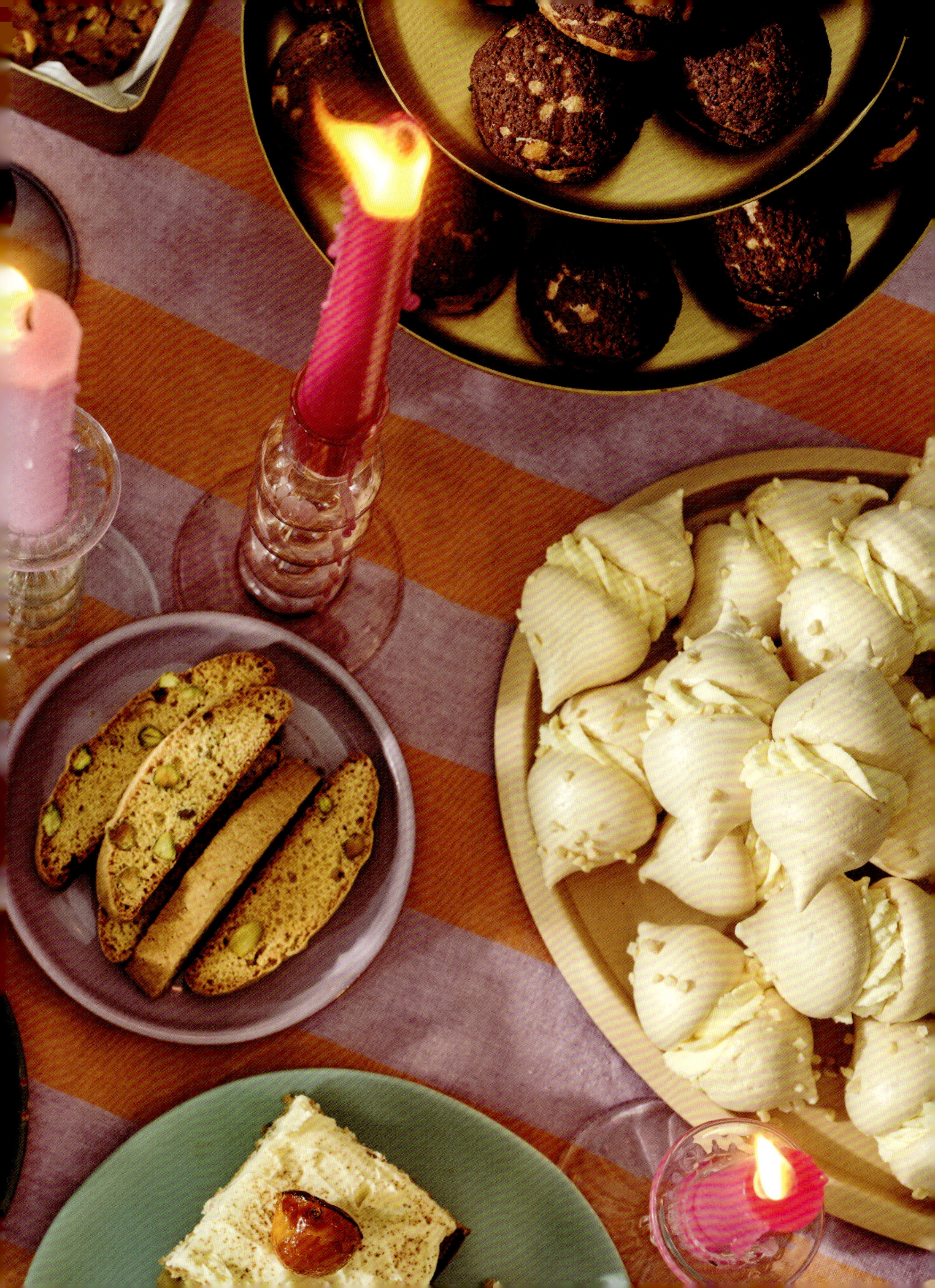

Party

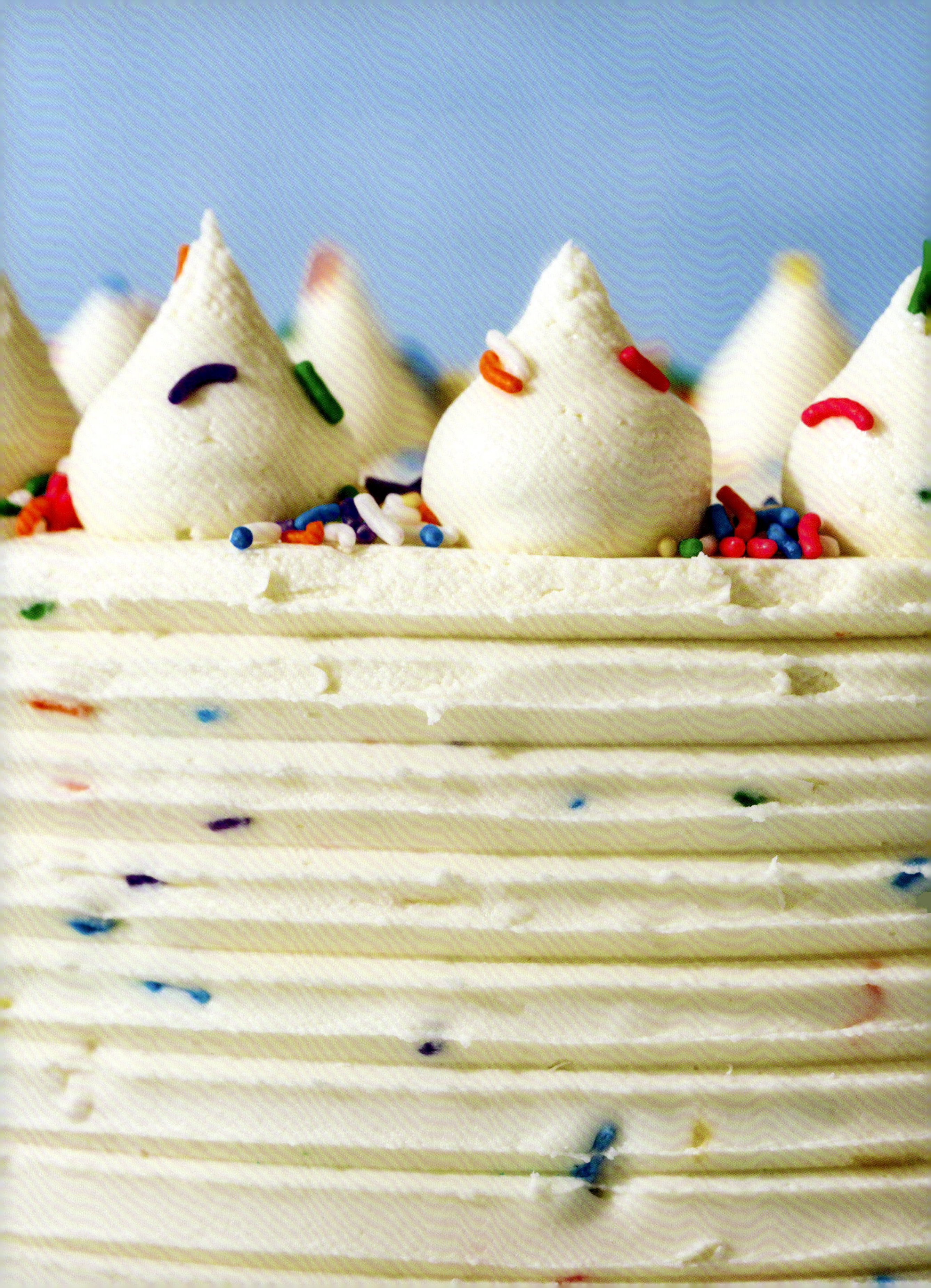

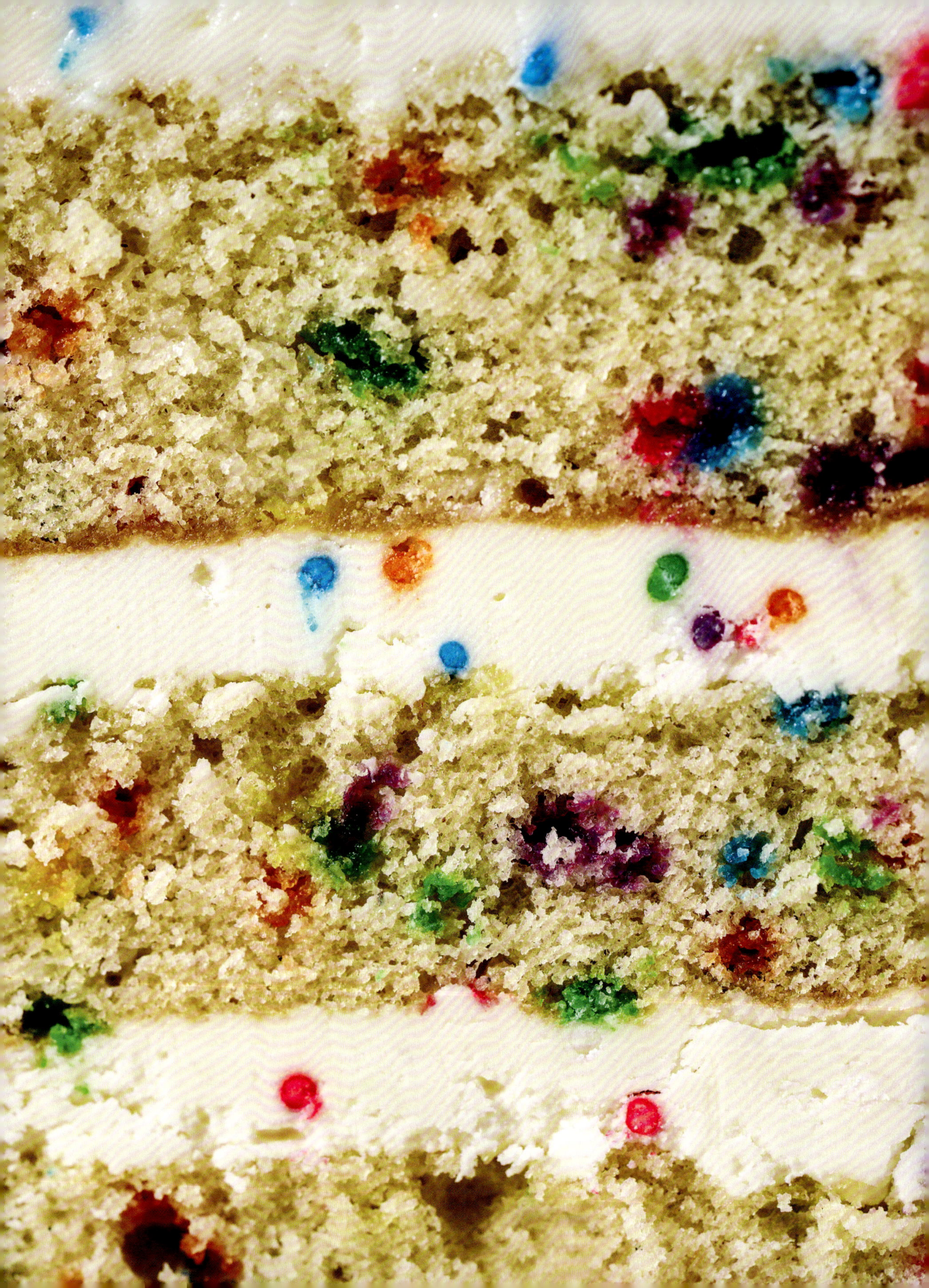

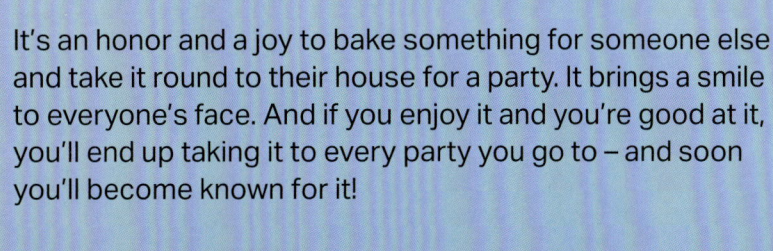

It's an honor and a joy to bake something for someone else and take it round to their house for a party. It brings a smile to everyone's face. And if you enjoy it and you're good at it, you'll end up taking it to every party you go to – and soon you'll become known for it!

The recipes in the book so far have covered lots of the regular festivals and events throughout the year, as well as bakes to mark your own seasonal celebrations, but the recipes in this chapter are the ones I turn to all year round, whatever the season and whatever the occasion. They are guaranteed crowd-pleasers that everyone will love.

I'm a seventies kid at heart and I've got to be honest and say that one of my favorite kinds of party food these days is retro party food – you just can't go wrong with a bit of cheese-and-pineapple on a stick, as part of a buffet!

So, there are plenty of classics from my childhood to enjoy, like the Sprinkletti cake (page 226), Ultimate rocky road (page 228), Chicken and leek vol-au-vents (page 245) and Sausage braid (page 250). I've given some of them a bit of an upgrade, maybe with additional flavors or by using a slightly different technique, but they're all based on the classic recipes I remember as a child. Take a look at the Rainbow gelatin crown on page 234… it will be the talking point at any party, whether you're five or ninety-five!

There are canapés to serve with cocktails, like the Miso and sesame cheese twists (page 242), more substantial party snacks like my Savory couronne (page 254) and Sweet potato and black bean empanadas (page 260), and incredible sweet party treats, including a No-bake speculoos cheesecake on page 232, with Biscoff in every layer. So, whatever kind of party it is, and whoever it's for, start making these recipes part of your own family favorites.

Sprinkletti Cake

Decorated and dotted throughout with sprinkles, this cake is all about having a bit of fun and it's great for children's birthday parties. Just make sure you use jimmies sprinkles, so they keep a good color and shape when they're cooked.

10–12 slices

---

2 sticks plus 1 tbsp (250g) unsalted butter, softened

1¼ cups (250g) superfine sugar

5 large eggs, at room temperature

1 tsp vanilla bean paste

2 cups (250g) all-purpose flour

3 tsp baking powder

⅓ cup (80g) rainbow jimmies cake sprinkles

Vanilla buttercream

1½ sticks (175g) unsalted butter, softened

3½ cups (350g) confectioners' sugar

1 tsp vanilla bean paste

2 tbsp boiling water

A drop of purple food coloring (optional)

To decorate

Cake sprinkles

1. Heat your oven to 350°F. Grease 3 × 8-inch round cake pans with parchment paper.

2. Using a stand mixer fitted with the paddle attachment, beat the butter and sugar together until the mixture is pale and fluffy. Scrape down the sides of the bowl with a spatula and beat again.

3. In a separate bowl, beat the eggs with the vanilla paste. With the mixer running on a low speed, slowly pour the beaten egg mix into the creamed mixture until it is all incorporated. Sift the flour and baking powder together over the mixture and then beat on a medium-low speed, until just smoothly combined.

4. Using a spatula, carefully fold the rainbow sprinkles through the mixture and then divide equally between the prepared pans. Bake for 20–25 minutes until the cakes are risen, golden and slightly shrunk away from the sides of the pan. Leave in the pans for 5 minutes then remove and place on wire racks to cool completely.

5. To make the vanilla buttercream, using the stand mixer fitted with the whisk attachment, beat the butter until very soft. Slowly add the confectioners' sugar, mixing well between each addition. Once it is all incorporated, add the vanilla paste and boiling water and mix until soft and fluffy. To make your buttercream extra white, add a tiny speck of purple food coloring and mix well.

6. To assemble the cake, place one cake layer on a serving plate or cake stand and spread with one-quarter of the buttercream. Place a second cake layer on top and spread with another quarter of the buttercream. Sit the final cake layer on top and cover the top and side of the cake with half of the remaining buttercream. Use a warm serrated cake decorating comb to get a neat finish around the side.

7. Put the remaining buttercream into a piping bag fitted with a ¾-inch plain piping tip and pipe a decorative border around the top of the cake. To finish, press a band of sprinkles around the bottom inch of the cake and scatter some sprinkles on top of the cake.

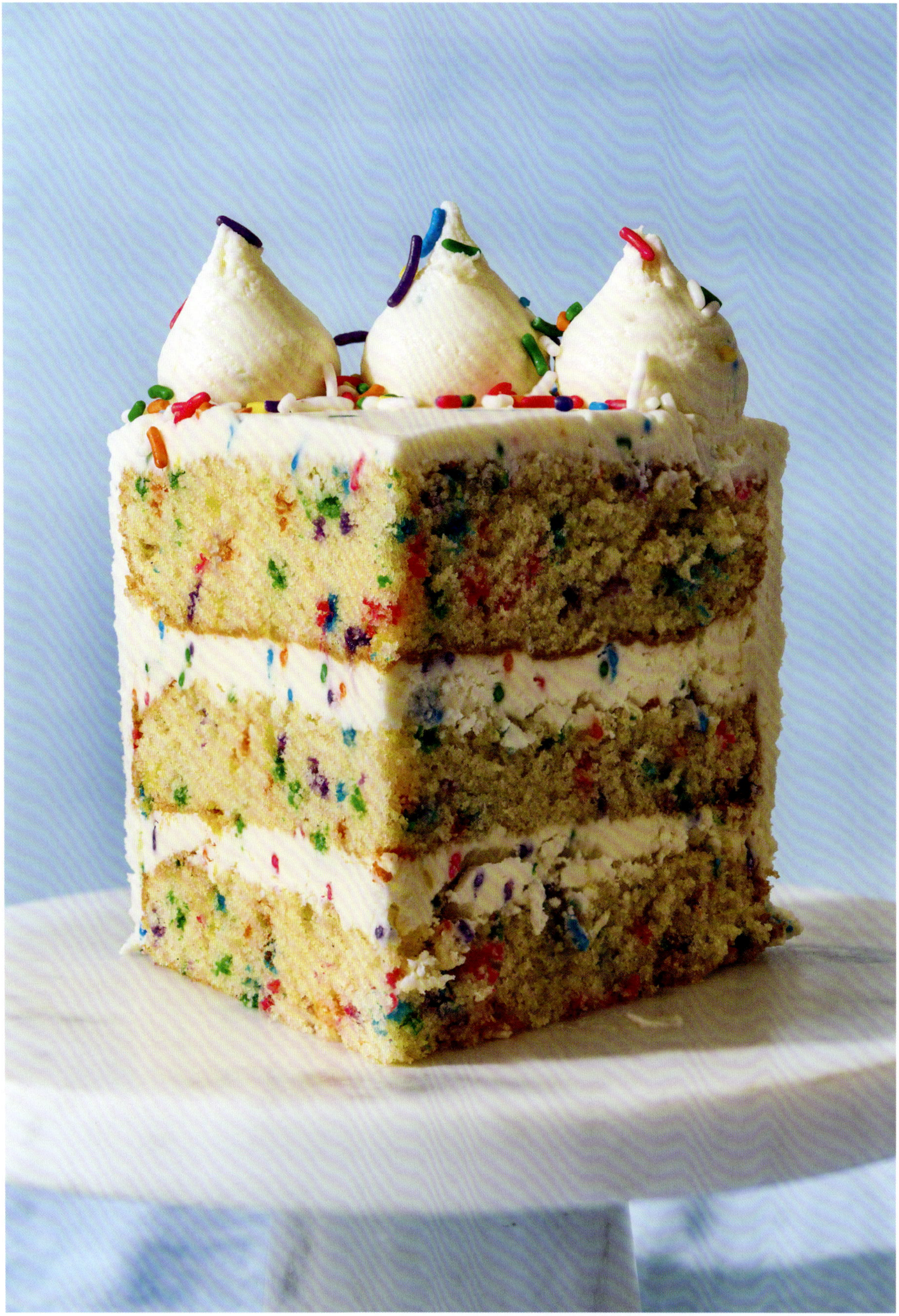

Ultimate Rocky Road

Everyone should learn how to make rocky road. This is quite a sophisticated version, but you can throw in whatever ingredients you like. It's a great way to finish up leftover bits too. Mix it well and give it plenty of time to cool and set, so you get a bit of everything in each mouthful.

16 squares

1¾ stick (200g) unsalted butter

½ cup (140g) Lyle's golden syrup

¾ cup (70g) unsweetened cocoa powder

7 oz (200g) digestive biscuits or graham crackers (about 13 sheets)

7 oz (200g) chocolate-coated honeycomb candy

½ cup plus 1 tbsp (90g) raw almonds

¾ cup (90g) shelled pistachio nuts

⅔ cup (80g) chopped dried apricots

Topping

10 oz (280g) milk chocolate, broken into small pieces

2 oz (50g) bittersweet chocolate, broken into small pieces

1   Line a an 8-inch square cake pan with parchment paper.

2   Melt the butter and golden syrup together in a medium saucepan. Remove from the heat, add the cocoa powder and stir until well combined. Set aside to cool down.

3   Put the digestive biscuits or graham crackers and honeycomb candy into a sturdy plastic bag and bash with a rolling pin to break into a mix of small pieces and crumbs. Tip into a large bowl and add the almonds, pistachios and dried apricots. Pour on the melted mixture and stir to combine.

4   Press the mixture into the prepared pan and spread out evenly, leveling the surface with the back of a spoon. Place in the fridge to chill for 2 hours.

5   Melt the milk chocolate and bittersweet chocolate separately in heatproof bowls over pans of simmering water, making sure the base of the bowls is not in direct contact with the water. Remove from the heat and let cool slightly.

6   Turn the rocky road out of the pan and place on a board. Spread half of the milk chocolate over the surface and leave it to set for a few minutes. Put the melted dark chocolate into a small paper piping bag and snip off the tip.

7   Spread the remaining milk chocolate over the rocky road and immediately pipe thin parallel lines of dark chocolate, ¾ inch apart, across the surface. Using a skewer or toothpick, drag the melted chocolate in alternate directions to create a feathered pattern.

8   Leave the chocolate to set before cutting the rocky road into squares to serve.

Also pictured overleaf

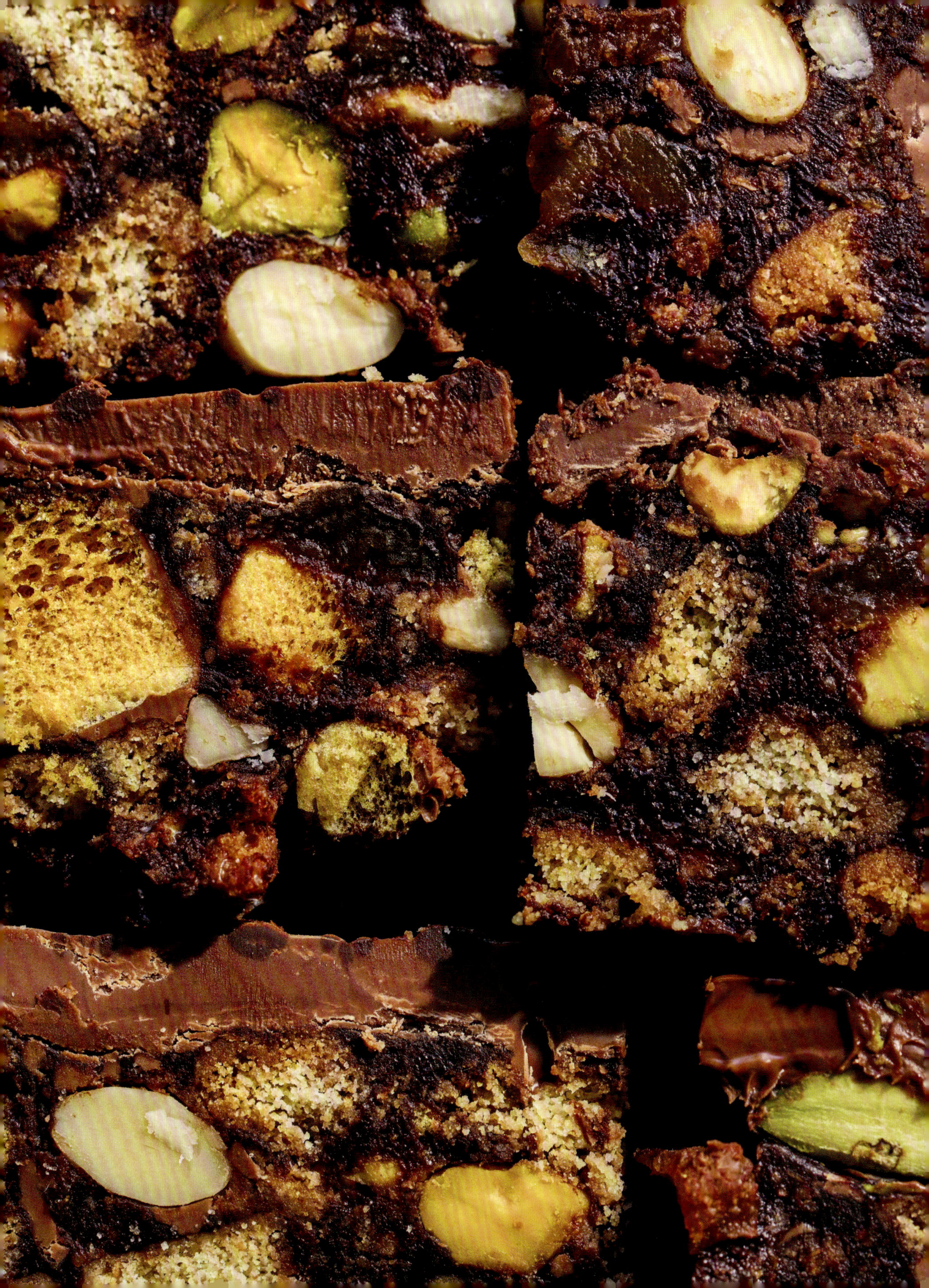

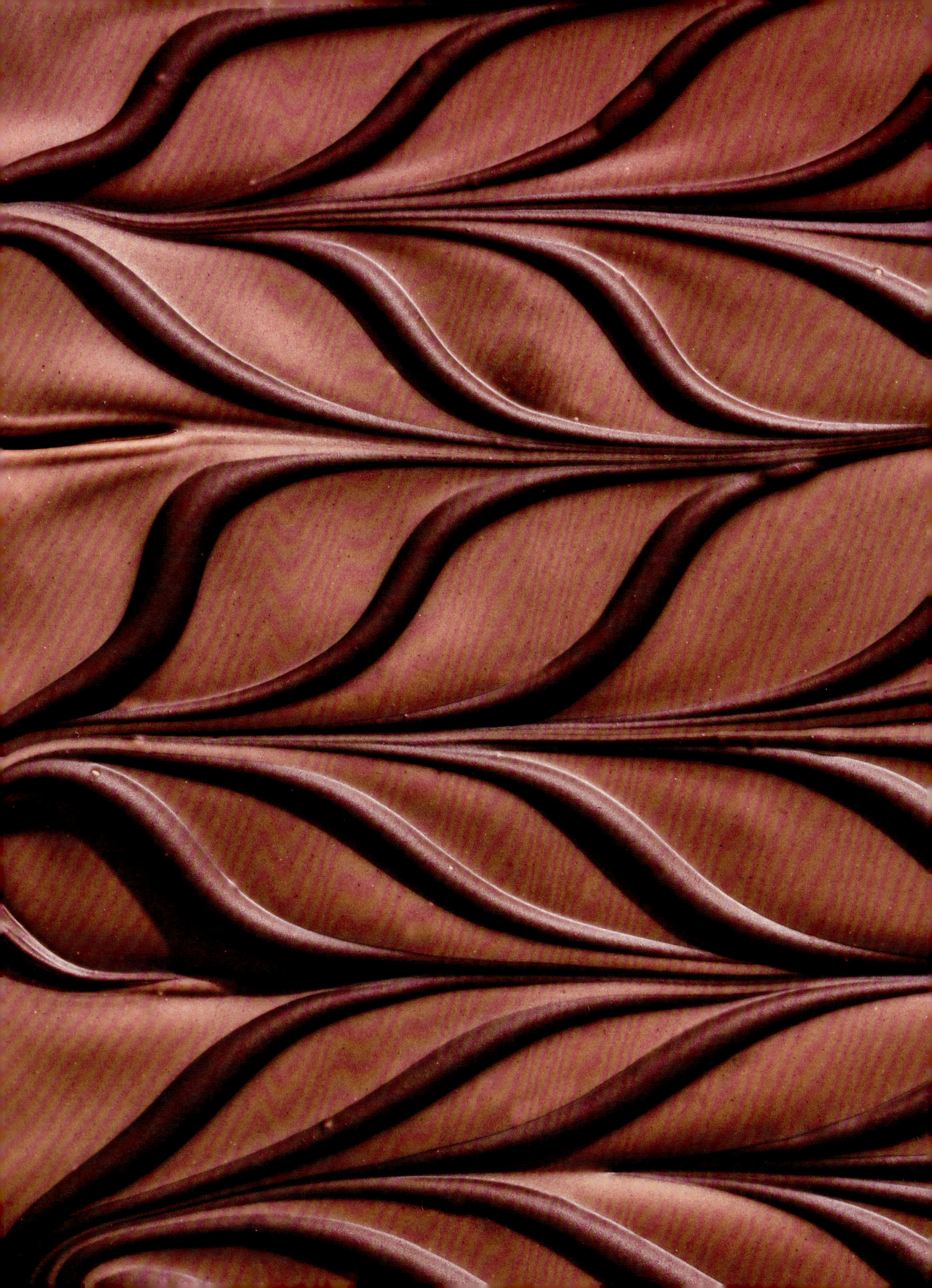

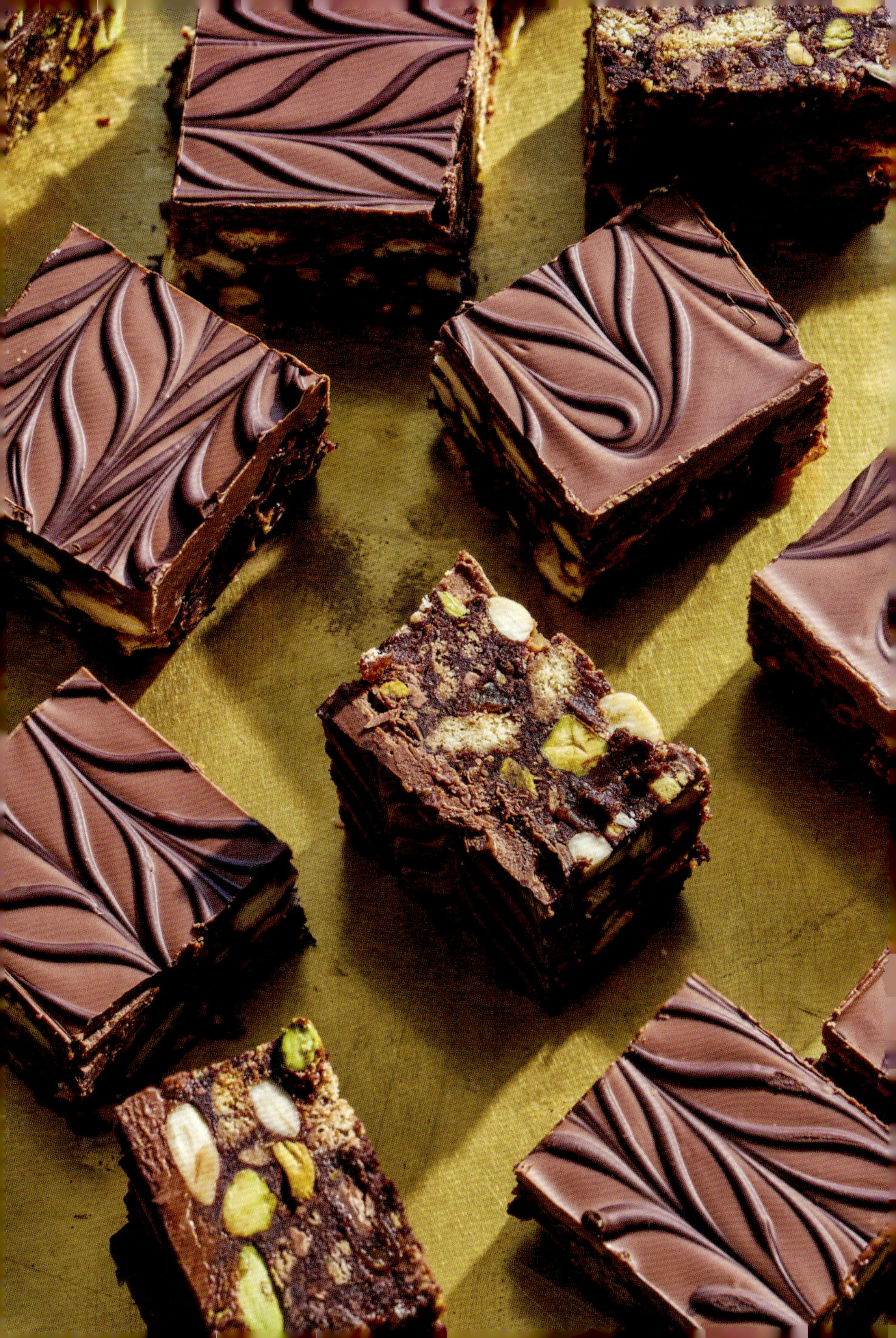

No-bake Speculoos Cheesecake

With a Biscoff cookie base and Biscoff spread in the filling, this delicious cheesecake is all about warm, lightly spiced caramel flavors. Press the base down nice and firmly, so it holds the filling on top and you get a nice snap when you slice into it, but not so firmly that it will be hard to cut through.

Serves 12

Base
7 oz (180g) Lotus Biscoff cookies (about 23 cookies)

6 tbsp (90g) unsalted butter, melted

Filling
1¼ cups (10 oz/300g) full-fat cream cheese

¾ cup plus 1 tbsp (200g) mascarpone

¾ cup (75g) confectioners' sugar

1¼ cups (300g) heavy cream

⅔ cup (150g) Biscoff cookie butter (creamy or crunchy)

Topping
¾ cup plus 1 tbsp (200g) creamy Biscoff cookie butter

3 Biscoff cookies, finely crushed

8 Biscoff vanilla cream sandwich cookies, halved

1. For the base, blitz the cookies in a food processor to a sand-like texture. Tip the cookie crumbs into a bowl, add the melted butter and stir to combine. Transfer to an 8-inch springform pan and spread evenly, right to the edge of the pan. Press firmly onto the base, using the back of a spoon. Chill in the fridge for 30 minutes, or until required.

2. To prepare the filling, beat the cream cheese, mascarpone and confectioners' sugar together in a large bowl until smooth. Pour in the cream and whisk until the mixture is thick enough to hold its shape.

3. Melt the Biscoff cookie butter in a small saucepan over a low heat (or in a bowl in the microwave on low) until it is a pourable consistency. Add to the creamy mixture and swirl through. Spoon the mixture over the set cookie base and spread evenly.

4. For the topping, melt the Biscoff cookie butter (as above), then pour over the filling and smooth the top to level.

5. Place the cheesecake in the fridge for at least 6 hours, preferably overnight, to set and chill thoroughly.

6. To serve, sprinkle the crushed cookies around the edge of the cheesecake to make a border. Carefully release from the pan and transfer to a serving plate. Decorate with the halved vanilla cream sandwich cookies.

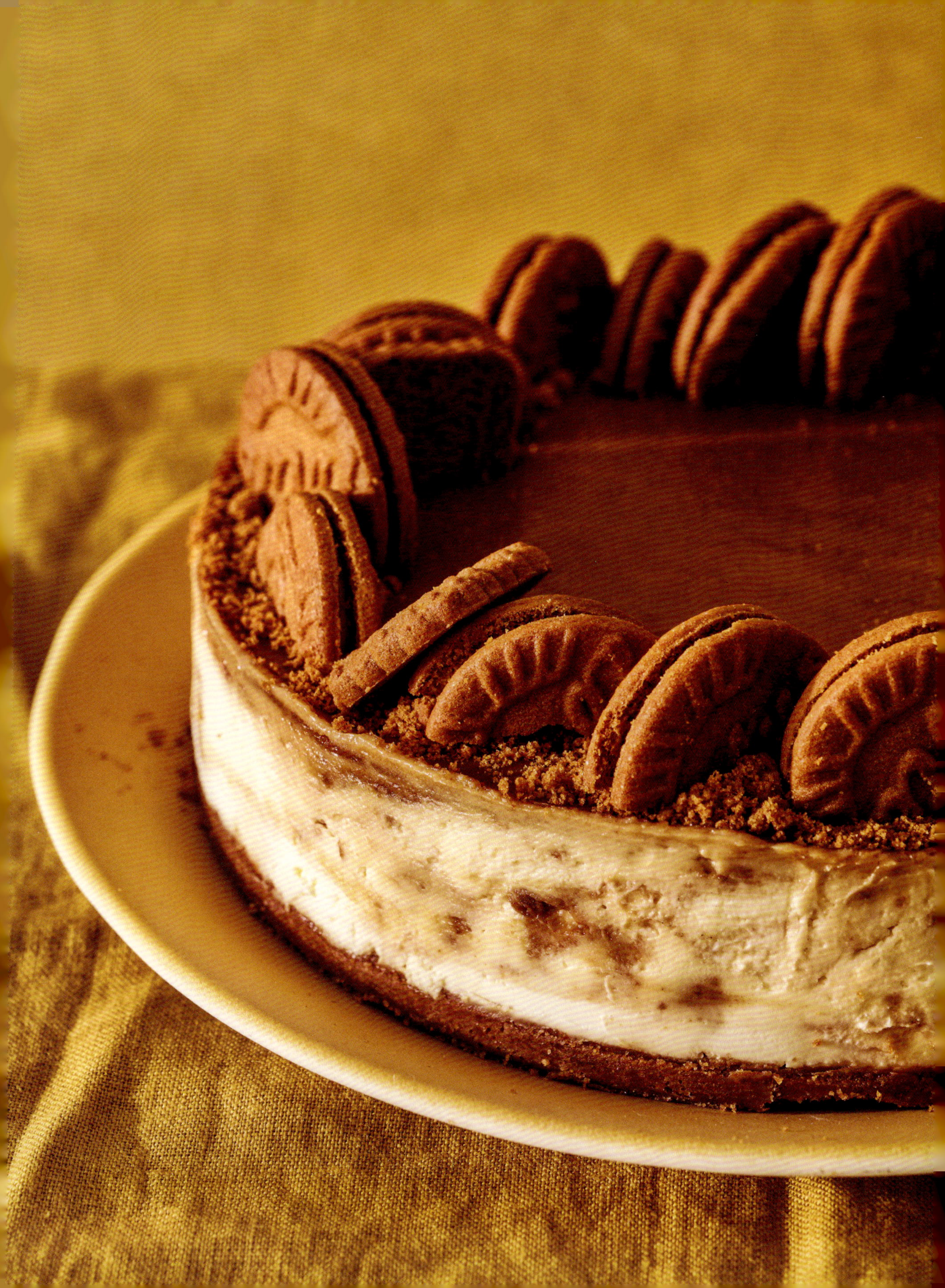

Rainbow Gelatin Crown

A dessert that's guaranteed to impress your guests when you bring it to the table! It takes a bit of time for the layers of jelly to set, but it's absolutely worth the effort.

Serves 16

A little vegetable oil, to oil

4 × 3-oz packages gelatin dessert (lemon, lime, orange and black cherry)

1⅓ cups (14 oz/400g) sweetened condensed milk

5¾ tsp unflavored powdered gelatin

4¾ cups just boiled water

¼ cup cold water

1 Using a piece of paper towel, wipe the inside of a 2-quart gelatin mold with a tiny bit of oil.

2 To make your first gelatin layer, place the lemon gelatin dessert powder in a pitcher. Pour over 1 cup just-boiled water and stir until dissolved. Pour into the gelatin mold and place in the fridge for 1 hour until almost set. The secret to layering up the gelatin is never to let the previous layer fully set. It should still be wobbly, or the next layer won't stick to it.

3 While your first layer is setting in the fridge, make the white layer. Put ¼ cup cold water into a shallow bowl and sprinkle over the unflavored gelatin powder. Let stand for 5 minutes to hydrate. Pour ¾ cup just-boiled water into a pitcher, add the hydrated gelatin and stir until fully dissolved. Stir in the sweetened condensed milk.

4 Once the lemon gelatin layer is sufficiently set, pour one-third of the condensed milk mixture on top to create a thin layer and place in the fridge to set for 30 minutes. Meanwhile, stand the pitcher in a pan of warm water to prevent the rest of the mixture setting.

5 Repeat these layers, preparing the next gelatin while your mold is in the fridge and adding a thin layer of the condensed milk mixture once it is sufficiently set. Once your mold is full you will have a striking stripy dessert of alternating colors separated by thin white layers. Place in the fridge until set.

6 To turn out the gelatin crown, partially dip the mold in a bowl of hot water for a few seconds, then invert a serving plate over the mold. Holding the plate and mold tightly together, turn them upside down to unmold the gelatin crown onto the plate.

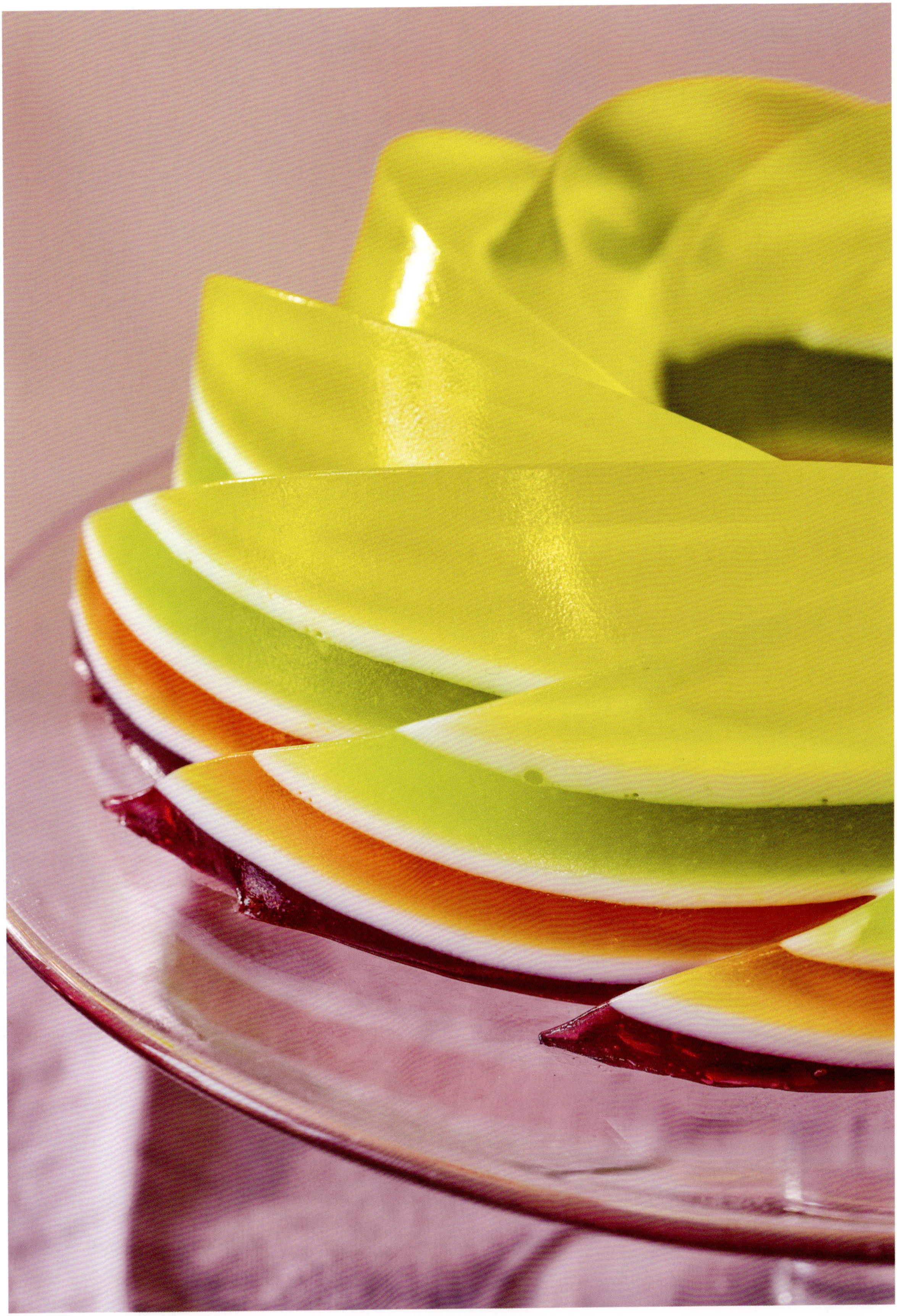

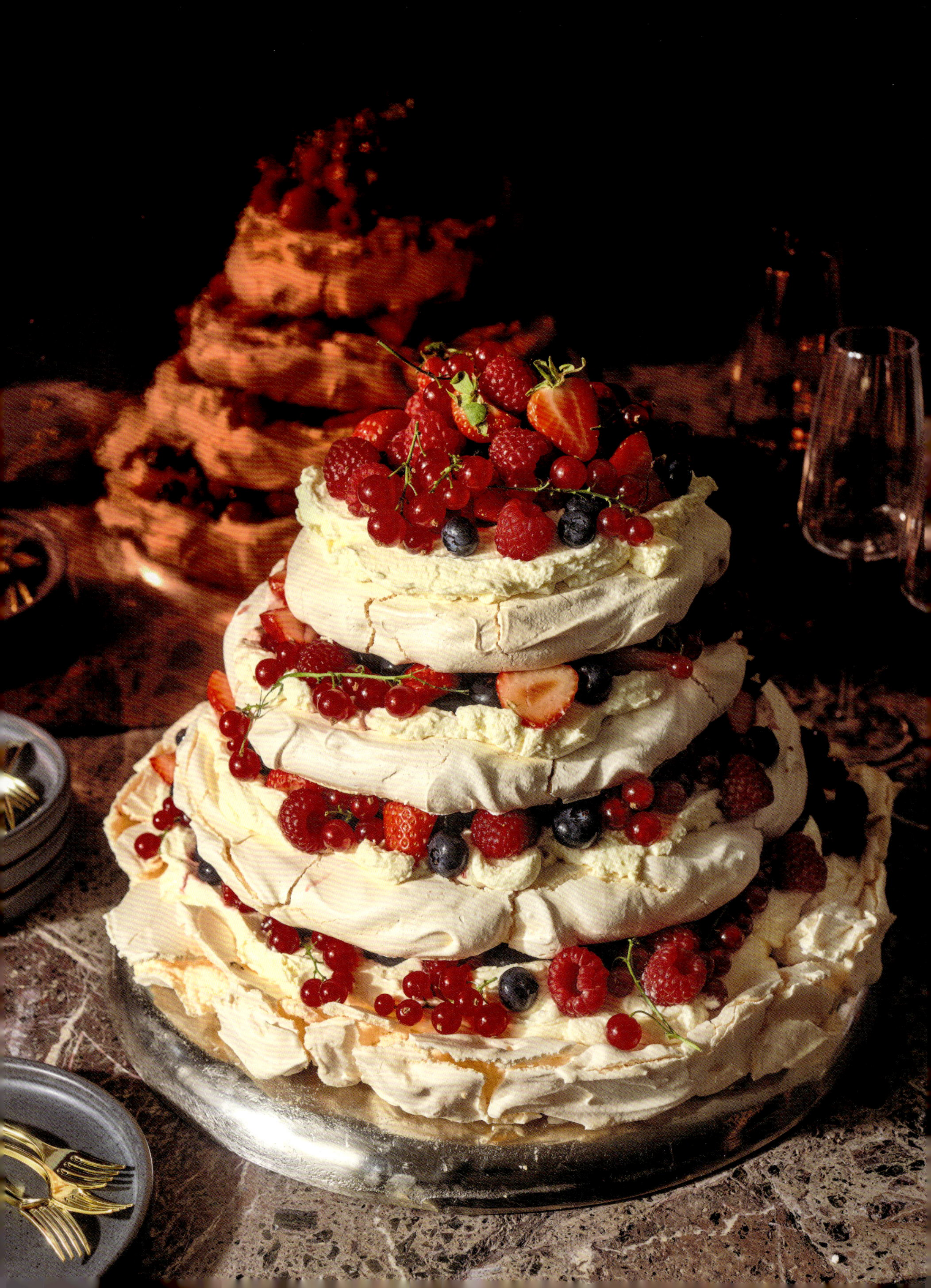

Tiered Pavlova and Boozy Berries

A gorgeous showstopper of a dessert! Make sure you spread the meringue layers neatly and evenly, then bake them low and slow in the oven, so you get that satisfying crispness on the outside and soft marshmallow-like texture inside.

Serves 40

Pavlova base
6 large egg whites
1¾ cups (350g) superfine sugar
1 tsp white wine vinegar
1 tsp cornstarch

Meringue tiers
6 large egg whites
1¾ cups (350g) superfine sugar
1 tsp white wine vinegar
1 tsp cornstarch

Filling
1½ lbs (700g) strawberries, hulled and halved
1 lb 2 oz (500g) blueberries
2 tbsp superfine sugar
¾ cup (200g) crème de cassis liqueur
6¼ cups (1.5kg) heavy cream
2 cups (500g) whole milk Greek yogurt
Finely grated zest of 1 lemon
1½ lbs (700g) raspberries
10 oz (300g) red currants

1. Heat your oven to 325°F. Line a large baking sheet with parchment paper, draw a 12-inch circle on it and turn the paper over.

2. To make the pavlova base, in a large clean bowl using a hand mixer or in a stand mixer, whisk the egg whites until they form stiff peaks. Now gradually whisk in the sugar on full speed, a spoonful at a time, until it is fully dissolved and the meringue is thick and glossy. Add the wine vinegar and cornstarch and fold through.

3. Spread the meringue over the marked circle on the lined baking sheet; it should be 2 inches thick. Place in the oven and immediately lower the setting to 300°F. Bake for 1 hour, then turn the oven off and leave the pavlova inside to cool slowly and dry out for at least an hour.

4. To make the pavlova tiers, heat your oven to 325°F and line 2 baking sheets with parchment paper. On one draw a 10-inch circle; on the other draw an 8-inch and a 5-inch circle. Turn the paper over.

5. Make the meringue as for the pavlova base. Spread over the 3 marked circles on the lined baking sheets, making them the same depth. Place the baking sheet holding the largest circle in the oven and immediately lower the oven setting to 300°F. Bake for 15 minutes, then add the other sheet with the two smaller meringue rounds to the oven. Bake for 45 minutes, then turn the oven off and leave the 3 meringue rounds inside to dry out for at least an hour.

6. For the filling, put the strawberries and blueberries into a large bowl, sprinkle with the sugar and pour on the cassis. Stir, then set aside. Whip the cream in a bowl to firm peaks, then fold through the yogurt and lemon zest. Add the raspberries and red currants to the macerated fruit and toss to mix.

7. Place the pavlova base on a flat serving plate and cover with a layer of the whipped cream mix. Scatter over a third of the fruit. Carefully place the largest meringue tier on top and cover with more cream and fruit. Repeat to layer the other 2 tiers and finish with the last of the cream and fruit. To serve, lift each meringue tier off and cut into wedges.

Chocolate Choux Buns

Choux buns are all about being precise with the ingredients, which is why I measure the eggs. Most often you see them as chocolate profiteroles, but these are topped with craquelin. This gives them a professional look and adds a lovely sweet, crunchy texture, but keep the craquelin nice and thin, so it doesn't inhibit the rise of the choux.

Makes 30

Chocolate craquelin
- ½ cup plus 1 tbsp (75g) all-purpose flour
- 2 tbsp (15g) cocoa powder
- 5 tbsp (75g) unsalted butter, softened
- scant ½ cup (90g) superfine sugar

Chocolate crème pâtissière
- 2 cups (500g) whole milk
- 2 tsp vanilla bean paste
- ½ cup (120g) egg yolks (about 6 yolks)
- ½ cup (100g) superfine sugar
- ⅓ cup (40g) all-purpose flour
- 5 tbsp (40g) unsweetened cocoa powder
- 2 oz (50g) bittersweet chocolate, broken into small pieces

Choux pastry
- ¼ cup plus 1 tsp (65g) water
- ¼ cup plus 1 tsp (65g) whole milk
- 4 tbsp plus 1 tsp (65g) unsalted butter
- 1 tsp superfine sugar
- ⅔ cup (80g) all-purpose flour
- A pinch of fine salt
- ½ cup (125g) beaten eggs (about 3 large), at room temperature

1. First make the craquelin. Sift the flour and cocoa powder together. Beat the butter and sugar together in a bowl until smooth and creamy. Gradually add the flour mixture and combine thoroughly to form a dough, using one hand to bring it together. (Alternatively, you can use a stand mixer fitted with the paddle attachment to mix the dough.)

2. Roll out the craquelin dough thinly between 2 sheets of parchment paper to a 1/16–1/8 inch thick. Lift the dough on the paper onto a baking sheet and chill in the fridge until needed.

3. To make the chocolate crème pâtissière, heat the milk and vanilla paste in a small saucepan over a low heat and slowly bring to a boil. Meanwhile, whisk the egg yolks and sugar together in a bowl for 2 minutes until the mixture turns pale and thickens. Add the flour and cocoa powder and mix again until smooth. Now gradually pour in the warm milk, whisking as you do so.

4. Pass the crème pâtissière through a strainer into a clean saucepan and bring to a simmer over a medium-low heat. Cook, stirring continuously, until thickened. Remove from the heat, add the chocolate and stir until melted. Pour into a bowl, press a piece of plastic wrap onto the surface to prevent a skin forming and leave to cool.

5. To make the choux pastry, put the water, milk, butter and sugar into a medium saucepan over a medium heat. Once the butter has melted, increase the heat. As soon as the mixture comes to a boil, remove from the heat and tip in the flour and salt. Beat well with a wooden spoon until combined.

6. Return to a low heat and beat well until the dough forms a ball that leaves the side of the pan. Transfer the mixture to a bowl and leave to cool slightly, for about 5 minutes.

7. Now slowly add the beaten eggs, mixing until the dough is smooth and shiny; it should just drop off a spoon but be of a pipeable consistency.

Continued overleaf

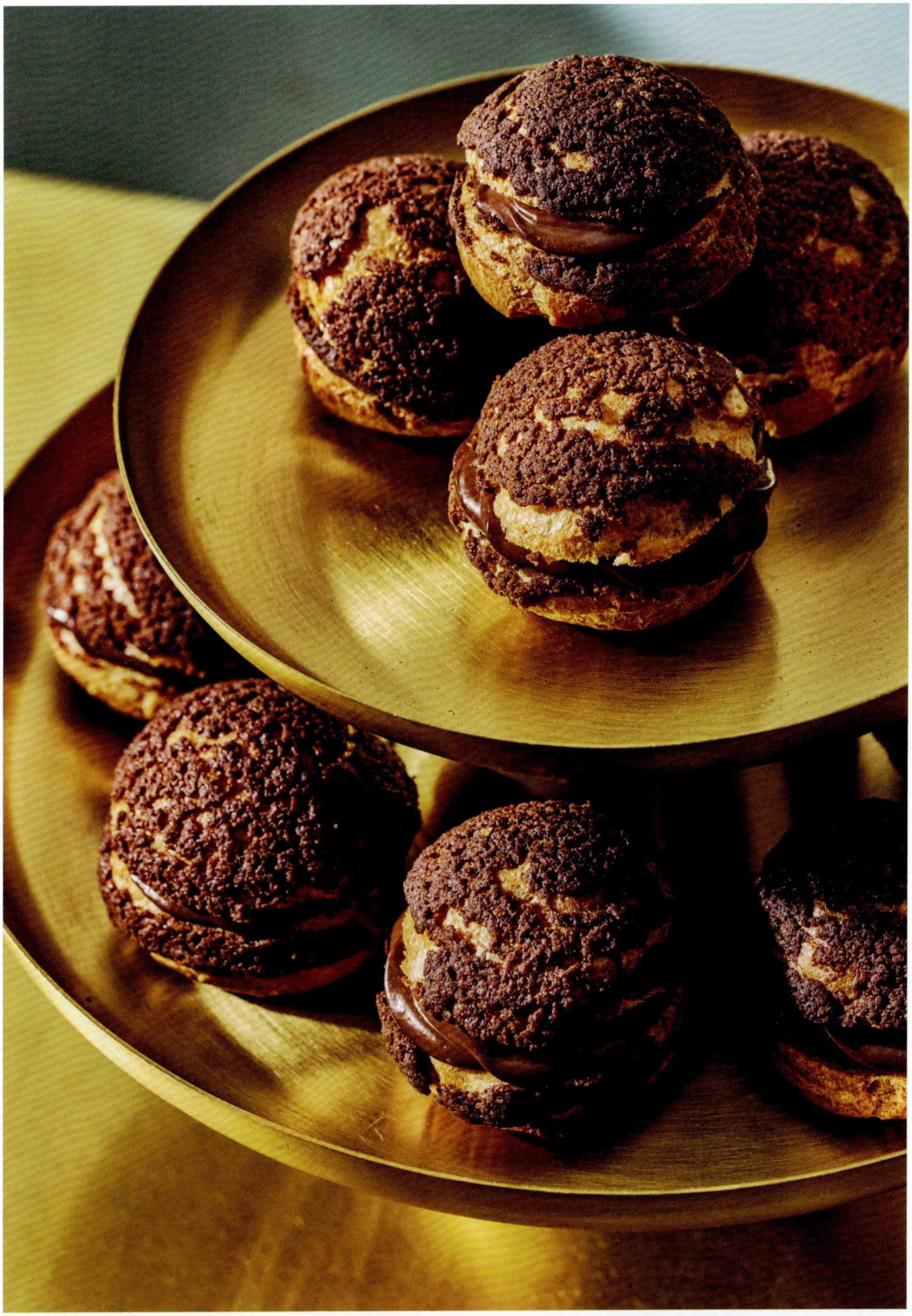

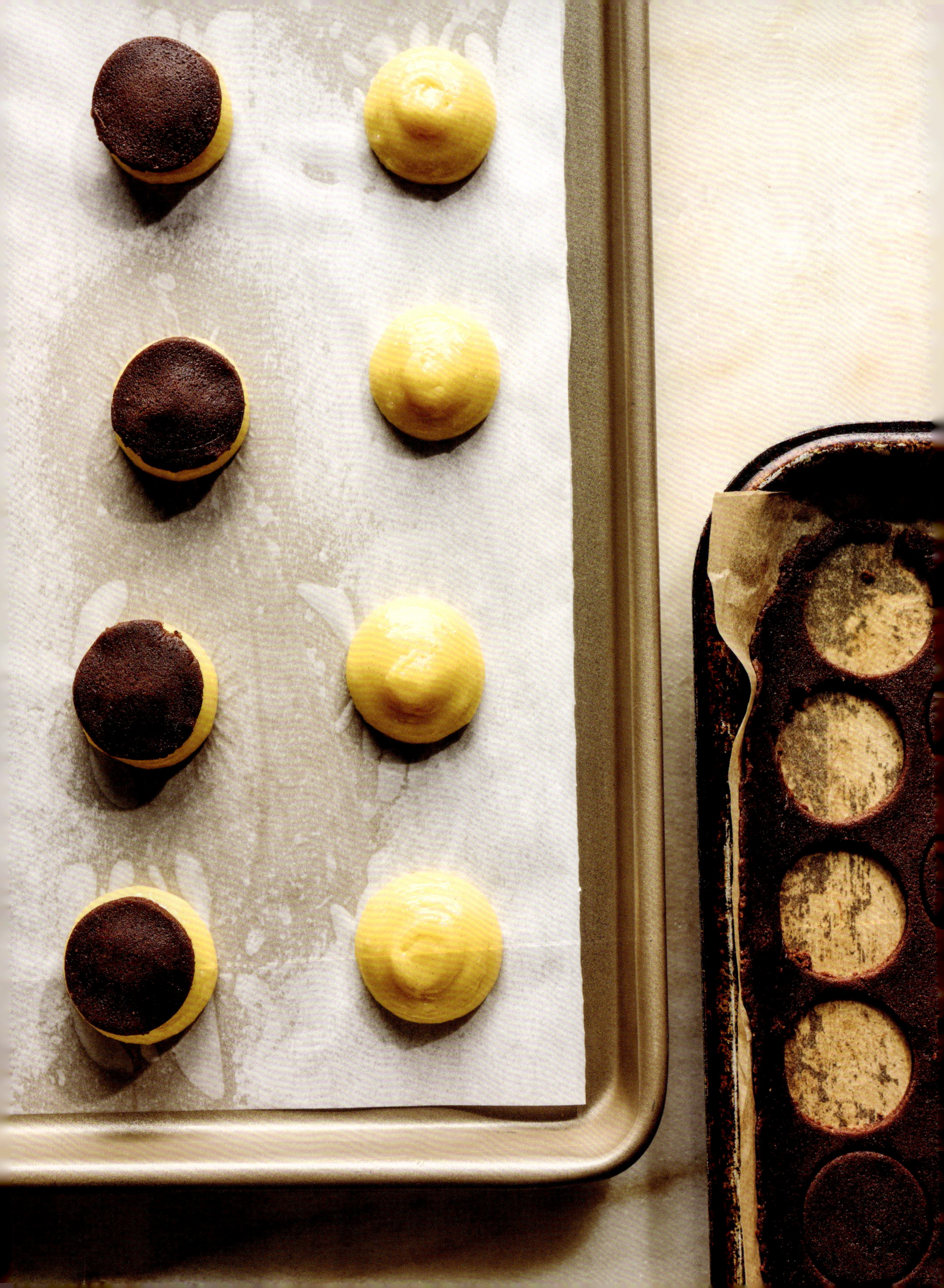

Continued from page 238

8   Heat your oven to 400°F and line a large baking sheet with parchment paper.

9   Transfer the choux pastry to a piping bag fitted with a ⅜-inch plain piping tip and pipe 30 small buns, 1/16 inch in diameter, onto the prepared baking sheet, leaving plenty of space in between them. Take the sheet of craquelin from the fridge and peel away the top sheet of paper. Cut out 30 discs, each ¾ inch in diameter, and place one on top of each choux bun.

10 Bake the choux buns for 15 minutes then lower the oven setting to 350°F and cook for a further 6 minutes. The choux will expand and the craquelin will melt over the top, forming a glaze. Using a spatula, carefully transfer the choux buns to a wire rack and leave to cool.

11 Once the buns are fully cooled, put the chocolate crème pâtissière into a piping bag fitted with a ¼-inch plain piping tip. Cut the choux buns in half and pipe the chocolate cream pâtissière onto the bases. Carefully sandwich together with the tops and serve.

Baking tip
One little secret I have to making perfect choux buns is to spray a little water into the oven before you bake them. This stops the choux cooking too quickly, letting the buns rise up, and helps open up the texture so they become beautifully light and puffy.

Miso and Sesame Cheese Twists

Topped with sesame seeds, these little savory pastry twists make brilliant party canapés to serve with a cocktail, or you can cut them a little bigger and treat them like a snack. Either use a good-quality store-bought puff pastry or, if you're up for it, make your own, and keep everything as cool as possible.

Makes 16–20

---

10 oz (300g) puff pastry (page 244, ½ quantity, or 2 sheets store-bought, thawed if frozen)

All-purpose flour, to dust

1½ tbsp white miso

1 tbsp honey

⅔ cup (60g) grated sharp cheddar

1 large egg, beaten

1 tbsp black sesame seeds

1 tbsp white sesame seeds

1. Heat your oven to 400°F and line 2 baking sheets with parchment paper.

2. On a lightly floured surface, roll out the puff pastry to a 14 × 9-inch rectangle and cut in half lengthwise, to give two 7 × 9-inch rectangles. If using store-bought puff pastry, use a sharp knife to trim each sheet to 7 × 9 inches.

3. Mix the miso and honey together and spread over one of the pastry rectangles. Sprinkle the grated cheese evenly over the top and then roll a flour-dusted rolling pin over the surface to press the cheese into the miso.

4. Place the other puff pastry rectangle on top and gently roll to press the two sheets together. Brush the surface with beaten egg and sprinkle the black and white sesame seeds evenly over the surface.

5. Using a pizza wheel, cut the filled dough into ½-inch wide strips. Twist the individual strips and lay on the prepared baking sheets, spacing them apart to give room for expansion on cooking.

6. Bake the cheese straws in the oven for 12–15 minutes until crisp and deep golden brown. Transfer them to a wire rack and let cool before serving.

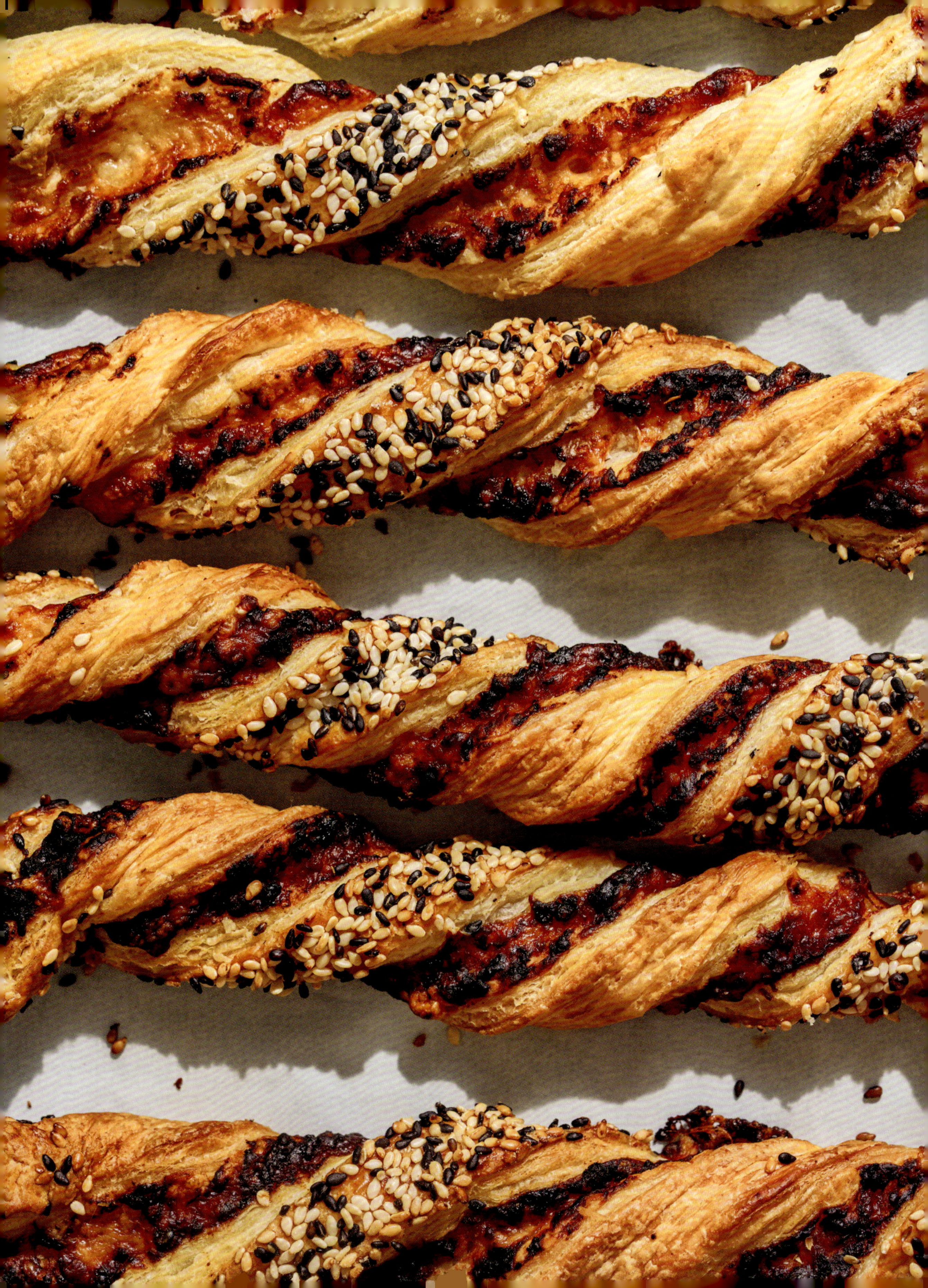

Puff Pastry

Making puff pastry can be fiddly, but don't be put off. It's a big challenge and a real accomplishment. Take your time over it, and make your folds as neat as you can. One tip is to chill the flour in the fridge for 24 hours beforehand; the colder the ingredients, the easier it will be to laminate the dough.

Makes about 22 oz (600g)

1 cup plus 2 tbsp (150g) chilled bread flour

1 cup plus 2 tbsp (150g) chilled all-purpose flour, plus extra to dust

A pinch of fine salt

2 large eggs, beaten

7 tbsp (100g) cold water

2 sticks plus 1 tbsp (250g) chilled unsalted butter (preferably good-quality European-style butter)

1. Put the flours, salt, beaten eggs and water into a large bowl and gently mix to an even dough with your fingers. Transfer the dough to a lightly floured surface and knead for 5–10 minutes until smooth; it should feel a little tight at this stage. Shape the dough into a ball, put it inside a plastic bag and chill in the fridge overnight, or for at least 7 hours.

2. Flatten the butter into a rectangle, about 16 × 7½ inches, by battering it down with your rolling pin. (You may find this easier to do if you sandwich the butter between 2 sheets of plastic wrap.) Place the butter in the fridge for an hour to harden again.

3. Roll out your dough on a lightly floured surface to a rectangle, about 24 × 8 inches. Place the butter rectangle on the dough so it covers the bottom two-thirds; make sure it is positioned neatly and extends almost to the edges.

4. Lift the exposed top third of dough down over half of the butter, then fold the butter-covered third up over the top. You will now have a sandwich of two layers of butter and three of dough. Pinch the edges together to seal. Put it back into the plastic bag and chill for 1 hour.

5. Place the dough on a lightly floured surface with a short side towards you. Roll out to a rectangle as before, keeping the edges as even as possible. Fold the top quarter down and the bottom quarter up so they meet neatly in the center. Then fold the dough in half along the center line: this is called a book turn. Chill in the plastic bag for 1 hour.

6. Transfer the dough to a lightly floured surface with the short end towards you and roll into a rectangle as before. This time, fold down one-third of the dough, then fold up the bottom third to make a neat square: this is called a single turn. Chill in the plastic bag for 1 hour.

7. Bring your dough out again and do a single turn as previously. Chill in the plastic bag overnight.

8. The next day, your puff pastry is ready to use. When you roll it out, the butter should be marbled throughout – this is an indication of a good pastry that's going to rise beautifully in the oven.

Chicken and Leek Vol-au-Vents

I'm a seventies kid and vol-au-vents remind me of sitting on the stairs watching through the banisters as my mother served these up at Tupperware parties. They were quite posh back then! They've had a bit of a revival recently and this classic filling is so delicious, I defy anyone to eat just one.

Makes 20

2 × quantity puff pastry (page 244, or 4 sheets store-bought puff pastry, thawed if frozen)

All-purpose flour, to dust

1 large egg, beaten, to glaze

Filling

1 large leek, trimmed and well washed

3 tbsp (45g) unsalted butter

2 tbsp (25g) all-purpose flour

⅔ cup (150g) chicken broth

5 tbsp (75g) heavy cream

2 tsp chopped chives

6 oz (150g) cooked chicken, shredded

Salt and white pepper

1. Line a large baking sheet with parchment paper. Roll out half of the puff pastry on a lightly floured surface to ¼ inch thick (or unroll 2 sheets of store-bought puff pastry) and use a 2½-inch biscuit cutter to stamp out 20 rounds. Use a 1½-inch biscuit cutter to cut the middles from these rounds. (The little rounds will form the vol-au-vent tops, while the rings become the sides.)

2. Roll out the other piece of pastry to ⅛ inch thick (or unroll the remaining sheets of puff pastry) and cut out 20 rounds, using the 2½-inch cutter for the vol-au-vent bases. Place the bases and tops on the prepared baking sheet. Prick the bases with a fork, then brush the edge of each with beaten egg and position a pastry ring on top. Brush the rings and little tops with beaten egg, then chill everything in the fridge for 30 minutes.

3. Heat your oven to 400°F.

4. Bake the vol-au-vent cases for 15–20 minutes until risen, crisp and golden. Meanwhile, make the filling. Finely chop the leek. Heat 1 tbsp of the butter in a frying pan over a low heat until melted and foaming. Add the leek and cook gently for about 10 minutes until it is soft but not browned. Remove from the heat.

5. Once baked, transfer the vol-au-vent cases and tops to a wire rack. Leave until cool enough to handle.

6. Melt the remaining 2 tbsp butter in a small saucepan over a medium-low heat then stir in the flour. Gradually add the chicken broth, stirring as you do so, to make a smooth sauce. Stir through the cooked leek and cream and season with salt and pepper to taste. Fold through the chives and cooked chicken.

7. Spoon the filling into the cooked vol-au-vent cases, top with the little lids and serve warm.

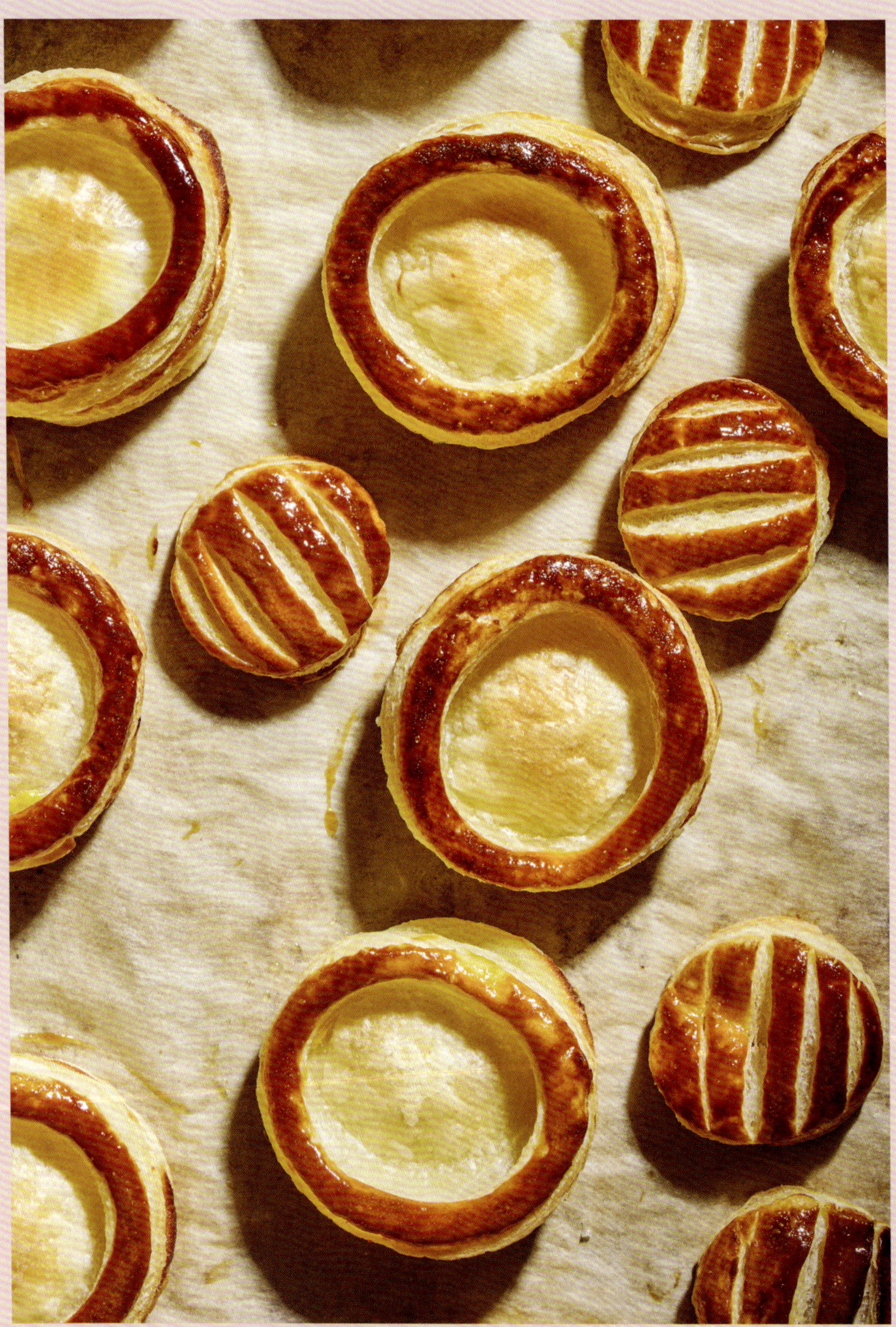

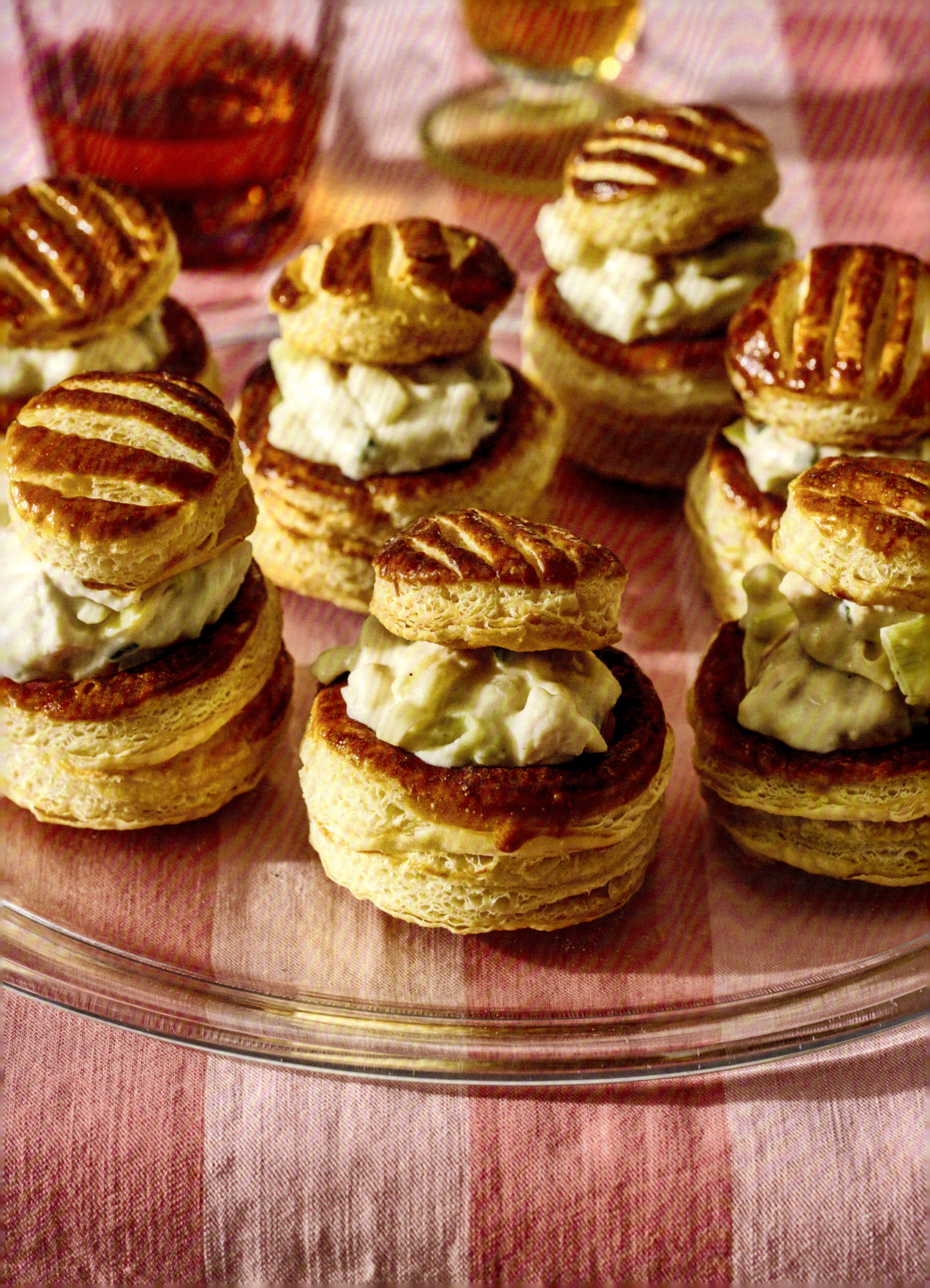

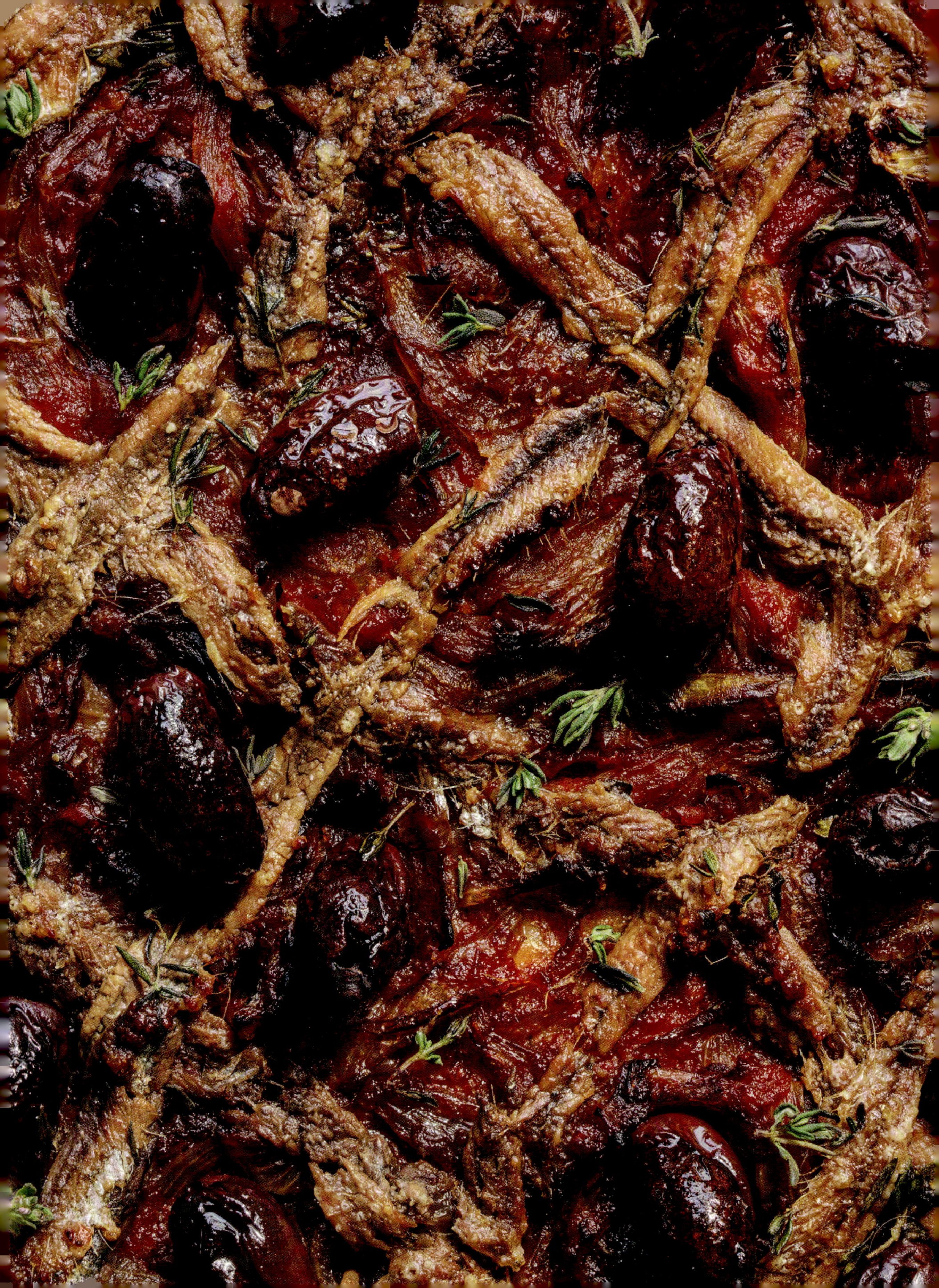

Paul's Pissaladière

With onions, tomatoes, anchovies and black olives, pissaladière looks striking and tastes incredible. Traditionally, it has a bread dough base, but I've made it with cheat's puff pastry for its buttery flavor and fantastic texture. Serve this pissaladière as a canapé, or cut into larger slices for lunch.

10-12 slices

Cheat's puff pastry base

2⅓ cups plus 1 tbsp (300g) all-purpose flour, plus extra to dust

A pinch of fine salt

3 tbsp (50g) chilled diced unsalted butter

5 tbsp cold water

1¼ sticks (150g) unsalted butter, frozen and grated

Topping

2 tbsp olive oil

2 tbsp (25g) unsalted butter

4 medium onions, thinly sliced

A few sprigs of thyme, leaves picked and chopped

1 × 14-oz (400g) can diced tomatoes

2 × 2-oz (50g) cans anchovy fillets in olive oil, drained

20 pitted black olives

Salt and black pepper

Extra virgin olive oil, to drizzle

1. To make the cheat's puff pastry, mix the flour and salt together in a bowl and rub in the diced butter with your fingers until the mixture resembles breadcrumbs. Add the water and mix well to form a smooth dough. Wrap in plastic wrap and leave to rest in the fridge for 1 hour.

2. Unwrap the pastry dough and roll out on a lightly floured surface to a rectangle, about 16 × 8 inches, with a short side facing you. Scatter half of the grated butter over the lower two-thirds of the dough then fold the top one-third down. Now fold the butter-topped bottom third of the dough up over the top, as if folding a letter. You should now have 3 layers of dough and 2 layers of butter.

3. Turn the dough 90° and roll out to a rectangle as before. Scatter the remaining butter over the lower two-thirds, then fold as before. Wrap the dough in plastic wrap and chill in the fridge for at least 30 minutes.

4. To make the topping, heat the olive oil and butter in a large, wide saucepan over a medium-low heat. When the butter is melted and foaming, add the sliced onions and cook gently for at least 10 minutes until softened and golden.

5. Add the chopped thyme to the pan and tip in the diced tomatoes. Season with salt and pepper and lower the heat to a simmer. Cook for 15 minutes until reduced and thickened then remove from the heat and set aside to cool.

6. Heat your oven to 400°F. Have ready a 12 × 8-inch baking sheet.

7. Roll out the puff pastry on a lightly floured surface to the dimensions of your baking sheet and about ¼ inch thick. Transfer it to the sheet.

8. Spread the tomato and onion mixture over the surface of the pastry, leaving a ½-inch margin all the way around. Arrange the anchovies on top in a crisscross pattern. Place a black olive in each of the diamonds and drizzle over a little olive oil. Bake in the oven for about 30 minutes. I like to eat this pissaladière still slightly warm, but it's great cold, too.

Sausage Braid

I grew up with sausage rolls in my dad's bakery and they're still probably my all-time number one food! This elaborate braided version is a great way to show off your pastry skills. The sausage meat is flavored with roasted red peppers, fennel seeds and red pepper flakes, but you can leave out these extras and just use your favorite sausages – it'll still taste amazing.

Serves 10

1 quantity puff pastry (page 244, or 2 sheets store-bought puff pastry, thawed if frozen)

All-purpose flour, to dust

Filling

1 tbsp olive oil

1 onion, finely chopped

2 garlic cloves, crushed or grated

2 tsp fennel seeds

½ tsp crushed red pepper flakes

1¾ lbs (800g) good-quality sausages

1 × 16-oz jar (450g) roasted red peppers (about 2 cups)

To finish

1 large egg, beaten, to glaze

A small handful of poppy seeds

1. For the filling, heat the olive oil in a small frying pan, add the onion and cook over a medium-low heat for 7–10 minutes until softened. Add the garlic, fennel seeds and red pepper flakes and sauté for another minute. Transfer to a medium bowl and leave to cool.

2. Peel away the skins from the sausages and then add the sausage meat to the cooled onion mix. Mix well with your hand until the ingredients are thoroughly combined.

3. Heat your oven to 425°F. Line a large baking sheet with parchment paper.

4. Drain the roasted red peppers, cut them lengthwise to open them up and pat dry on paper towels.

5. On a lightly floured surface, unroll one of the sheets of puff pastry. Unroll the second sheet and stack it directly on top of the first sheet. Press down slightly to stick the two sheets together, then roll out the puff pastry to a 14 × 16-inch rectangle. Arrange half of the roasted peppers down the center of the pastry. Now form the sausage mix into a log that will cover the center third of the pastry. Lay the sausage log on top of the peppers and then arrange the remaining peppers on top.

6. Using a small knife, make diagonal cuts in the pastry down either side of the sausage filling, spacing them ½–¾ inch apart. Fold the strips in over the filling alternately to create a braid and seal the ends.

7. Brush the pastry with beaten egg and sprinkle with poppy seeds. Bake the braid in the oven for 35–45 minutes until crisp and piping hot. Leave to stand for 10 minutes before slicing. It is delicious hot or cold.

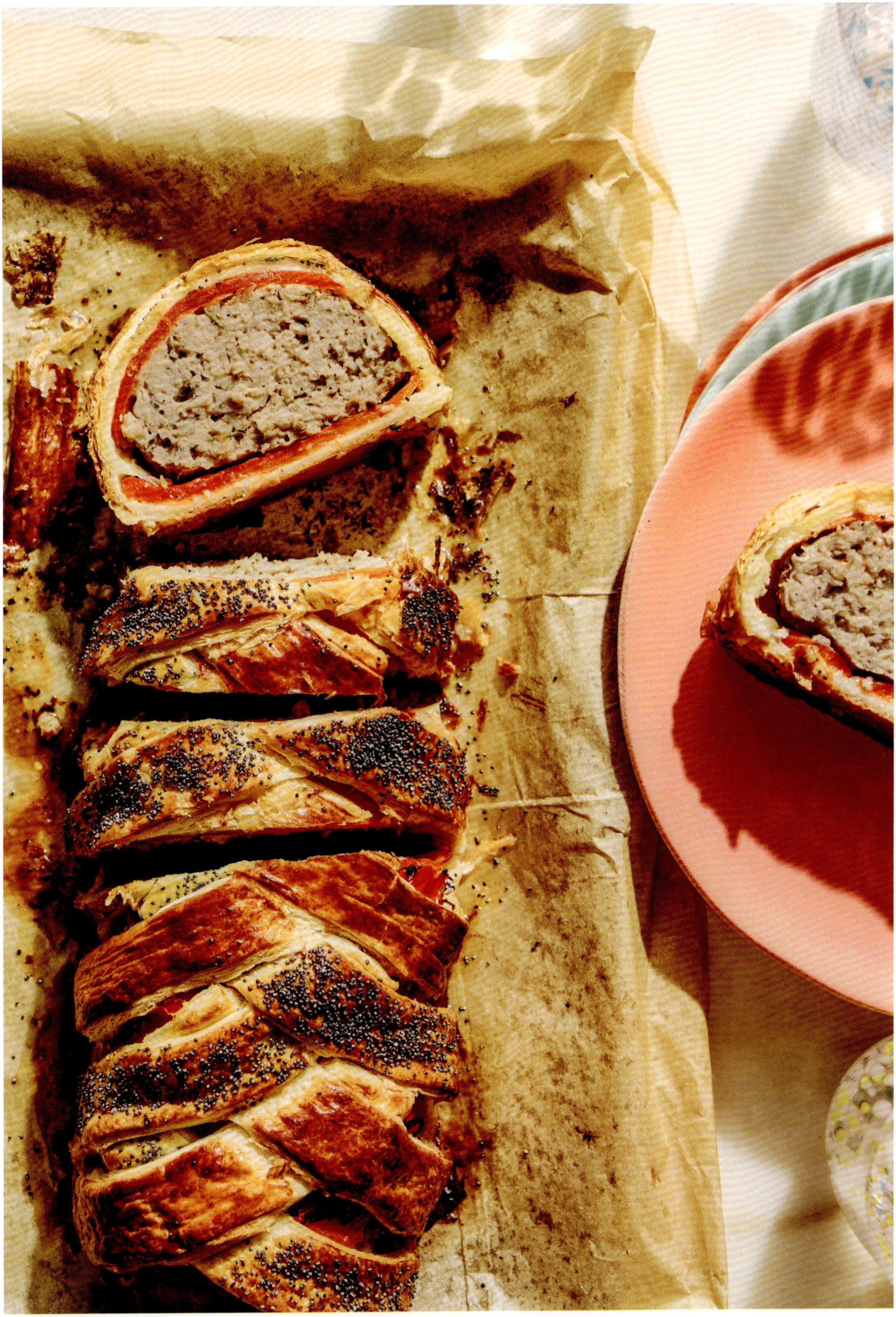

Vakkaru Bis Keemiya

Maldivian cooking doesn't hold back when it comes to flavor and these little pies really pack a spicy punch. The chef at the Vakkaru Hotel where I was staying in the Maldives kindly gave me the recipe. Shredded cabbage is the more traditional filling for Bis Keemiya, but this meaty version is delicious.

Makes 16

Dough
3¼ cups (400g) bread flour, plus extra to dust
½ tsp fine salt
4 tbsp (65g) unsalted butter, diced
⅔ cup (160g) water
1 medium egg, beaten

Filling
8 oz (225g) ground beef or chicken (raw)
1 onion, finely chopped
2 potatoes, boiled and mashed
2 jalapeño chiles, seeded and finely chopped
1 tsp hot curry powder
Salt and black pepper

To cook
Vegetable oil, to deep-fry

1. To make the dough, mix the flour and salt together in a bowl and rub in the diced butter with your fingers until the mixture resembles breadcrumbs. Make a well in the middle and add the water and beaten egg. Mix well to combine and form a soft dough. Tip out onto a lightly oiled surface and knead well until smooth. (Alternatively, you can use a stand mixer fitted with the dough hook to mix and knead the dough, adding the water and egg once the butter is fully incorporated.)

2. Cover the bowl and leave the dough to rest for 2 hours.

3. To make the filling, in a bowl, mix the ground meat, onion, mashed potatoes, chiles and curry powder together well and season generously with salt and pepper.

4. Divide the dough into 16 small balls. Roll out each ball of dough on a lightly floured surface to a round, 3-4 inches in diameter.

5. Place a heaping tablespoonful of the filling in the middle of each round. Fold in the sides of the dough over the filling, then fold the top and bottom over to make a parcel. Seal by pressing a fork on the seams.

6. Heat the oil in a deep-fryer or other deep, heavy saucepan (it should be no more than one-third full) over a medium heat to 350°F (check with an instant-read thermometer).

7. Deep-fry the parcels, 3 or 4 at a time, in the hot oil for 4–5 minutes, then turn them over with a spoon, and deep-fry for a further 4–5 minutes or until golden brown all over. Remove with a slotted spoon and drain on paper towels. Serve warm.

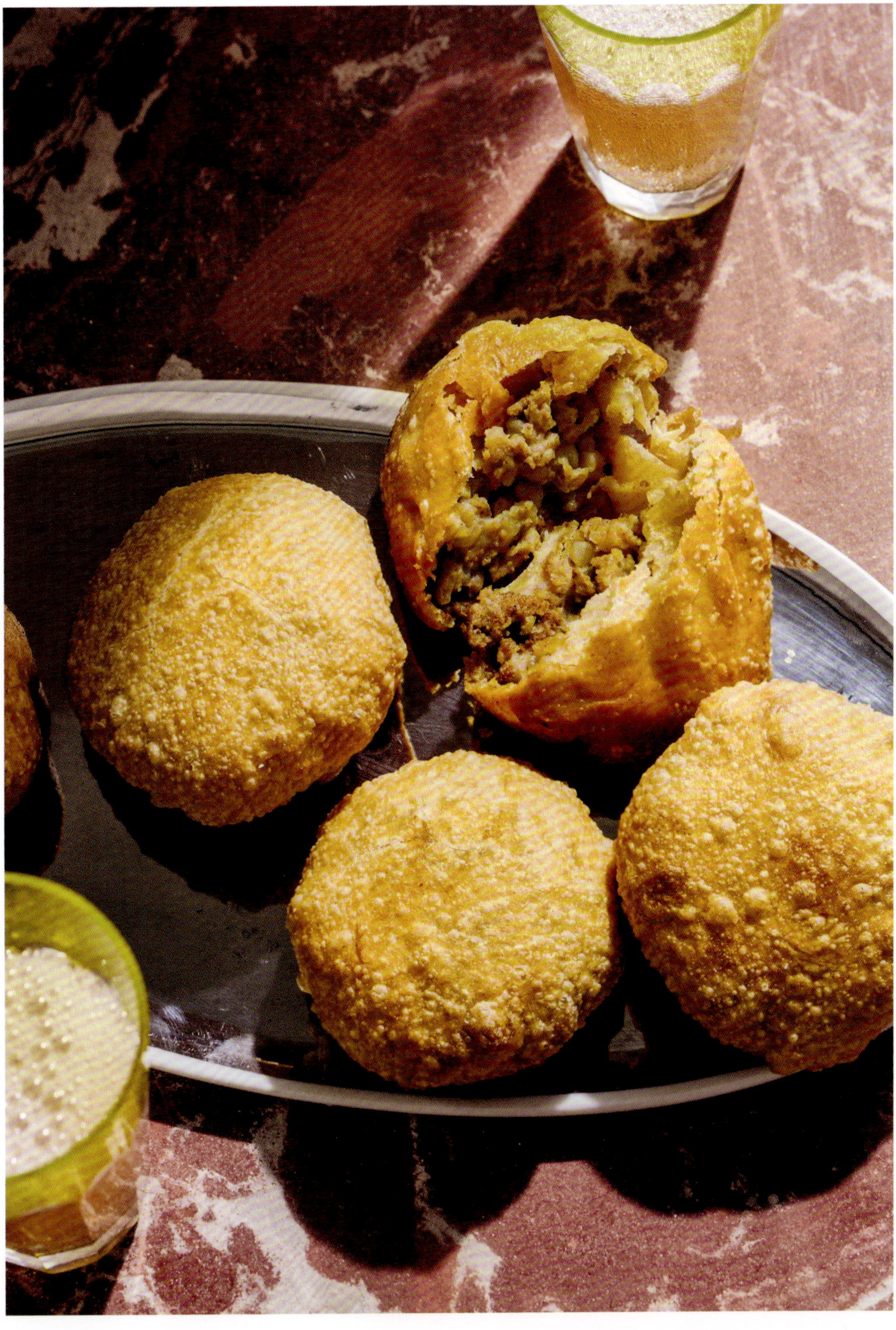

Savory Couronne

A French couronne (meaning 'crown') is usually sweet, filled with dried fruit and nuts and eaten at Christmas (as on page 180). I love the technique and it looks impressive, so I've also made a savory version packed with onions, mushrooms, bell peppers and Parmesan to enjoy all year round.

Serves 10–12

Dough
4 cups (500g) bread flour, plus extra to dust
1¼ tsp (7g) fine salt
4 tbsp (60g) unsalted butter, plus extra to grease
1 × ¼-oz (7g) packet instant yeast
1 large egg
1⅓ cups (320g) water

Filling
1–2 tbsp olive oil
1 onion, thinly sliced
2 red bell peppers, halved, cored, seeded and chopped
4 oz (100g) white mushrooms, sliced
4 oz (100g) Parmesan, freshly grated (about 1 cup), plus extra to finish

To glaze
1 large egg, beaten

1. Place all of the dough ingredients in a stand mixer fitted with the dough hook. Mix on a low speed for 5 minutes, then increase the speed to medium and mix for a further 10 minutes until the dough is smooth and elastic.

2. Tip the dough into a bowl, cover and leave to rise for 3 hours.

3. Meanwhile, prepare the filling. Heat the olive oil in a medium frying pan and add the onion and bell peppers. Sauté for 5 minutes, then add the mushrooms and sauté for another 5 minutes or until all the vegetables are softened. Tip onto a plate and set aside to cool.

4. Tip the risen dough out onto a floured surface and roll out to a rectangle 16 × 8 inches, with a long side facing you. Scatter the sautéed vegetables evenly over the dough and spread out to ½ inch from the edges, then sprinkle with the grated Parmesan.

5. Starting at a long side, roll the dough up tightly to enclose the filling (like a jelly roll). Press the edges with your fingers and roll the dough slightly to seal. Cut the roll in half lengthwise and place the halves next to each other, cut sides facing up. Now twist the halves neatly around each other. Form into a ring and press the ends together to seal.

6. Grease a 10-inch savarin mold and place the ring of dough in the mold. Cover with a sheet of parchment paper and leave to proof for 2 hours.

7. Heat your oven to 400°F.

8. Brush the couronne with beaten egg then, using scissors, cut nicks all over the surface. Sprinkle over a little grated Parmesan. Bake in the oven for 30 minutes or until risen and golden. Transfer to a wire rack to cool. Serve slightly warm from the oven, or cooled.

Note
The filling bursts out slightly from the twisted dough on baking, so it caramelizes in the oven, giving an extra layer of flavor.

Also pictured overleaf

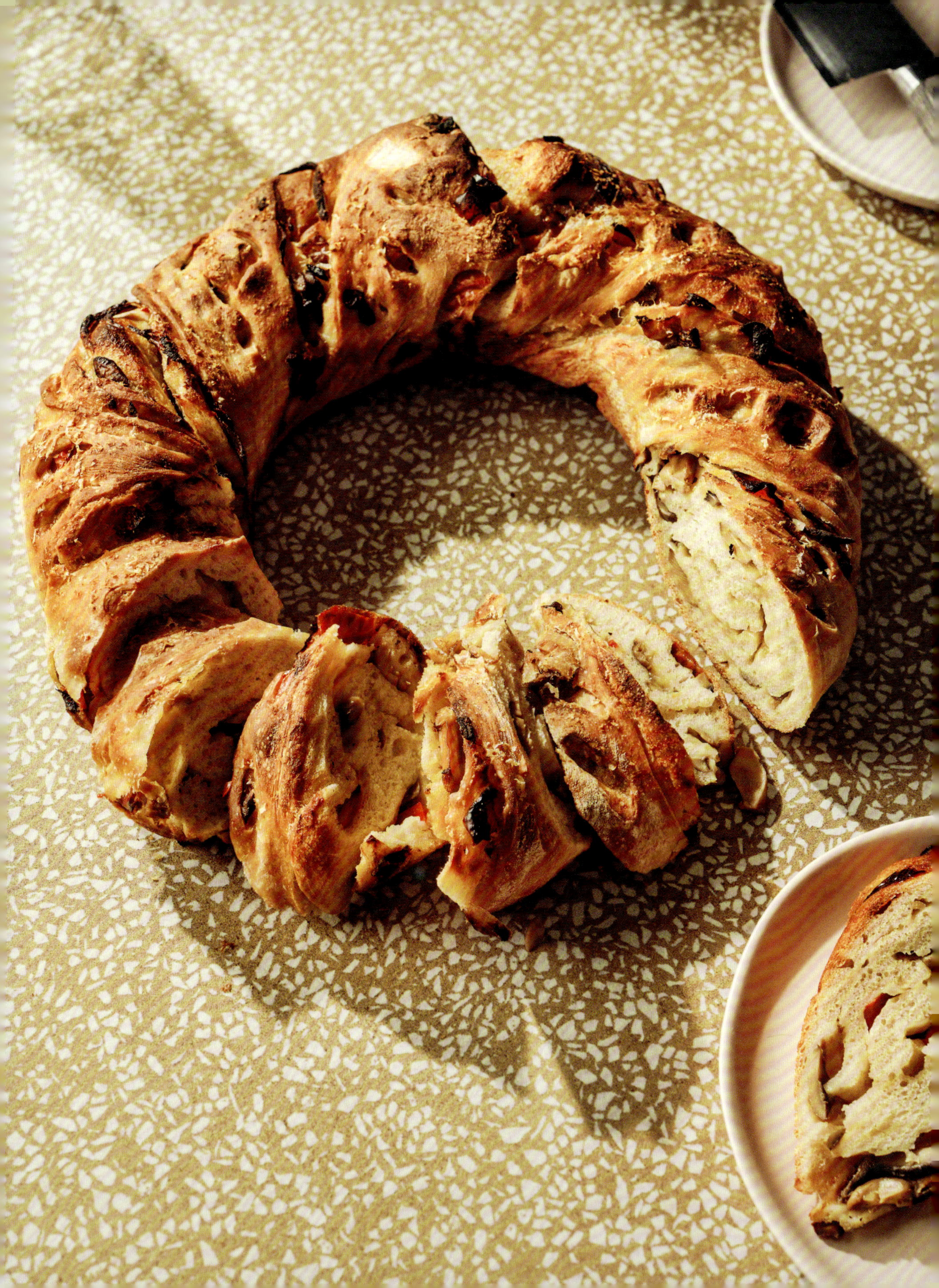

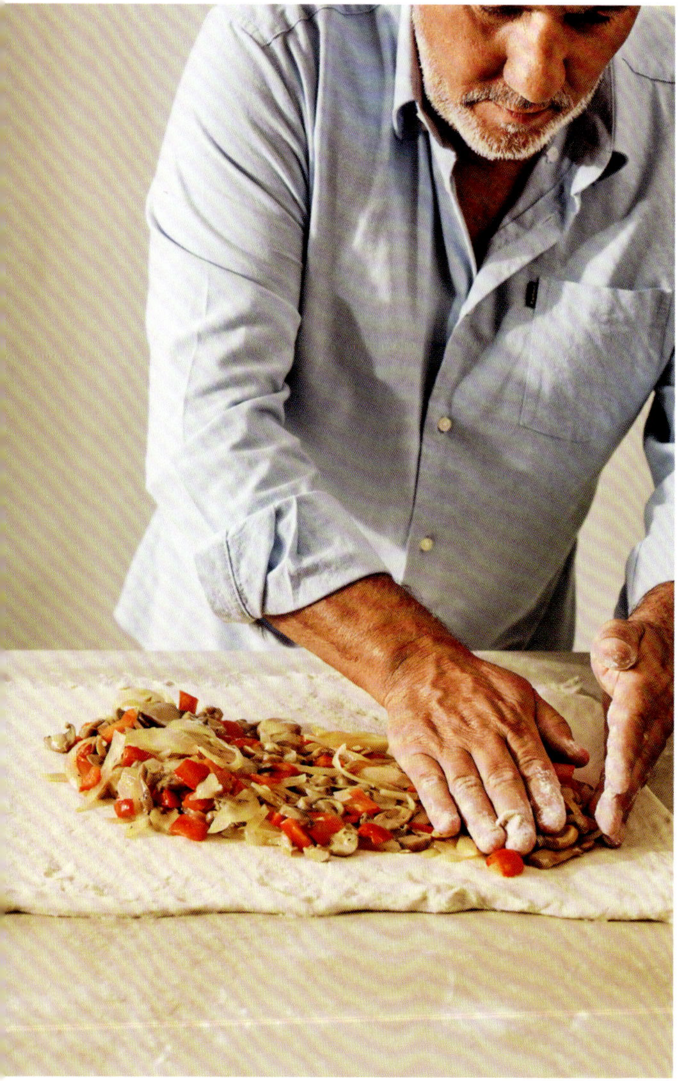

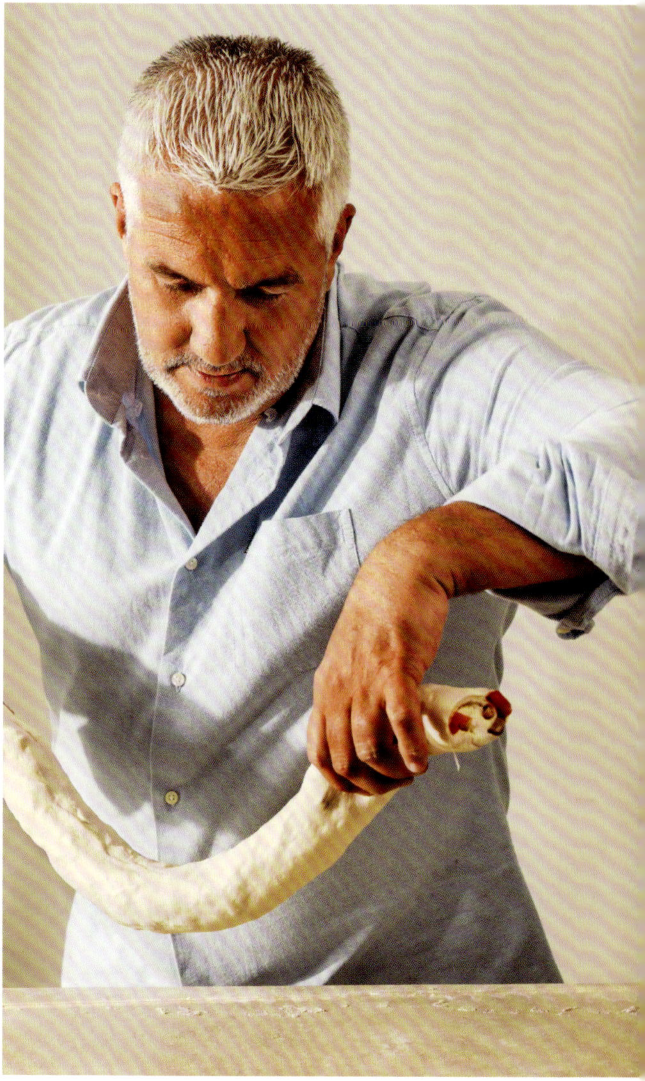

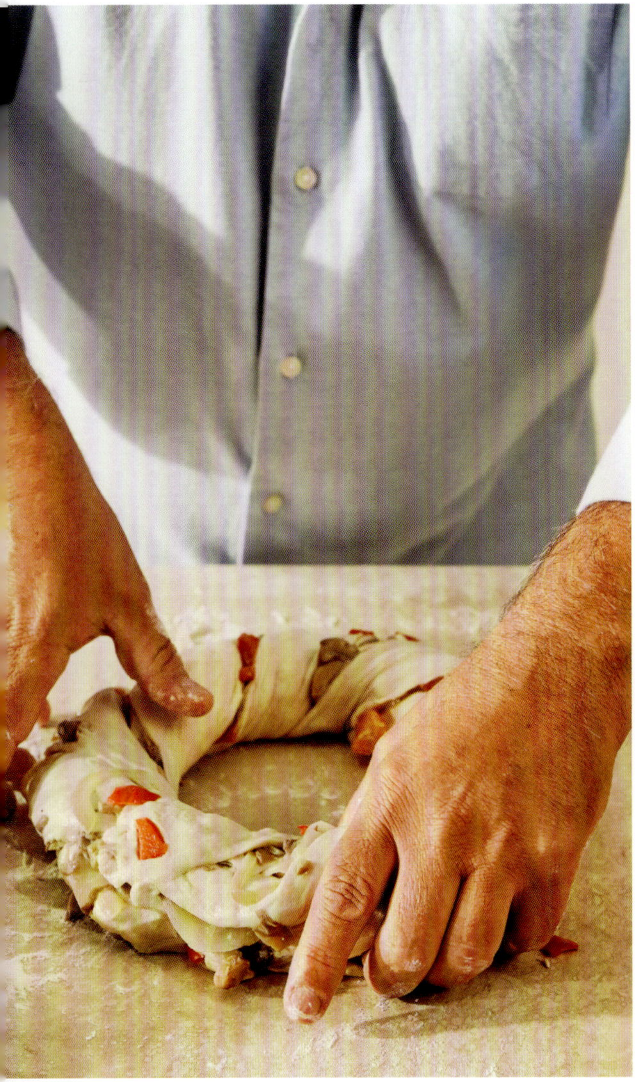
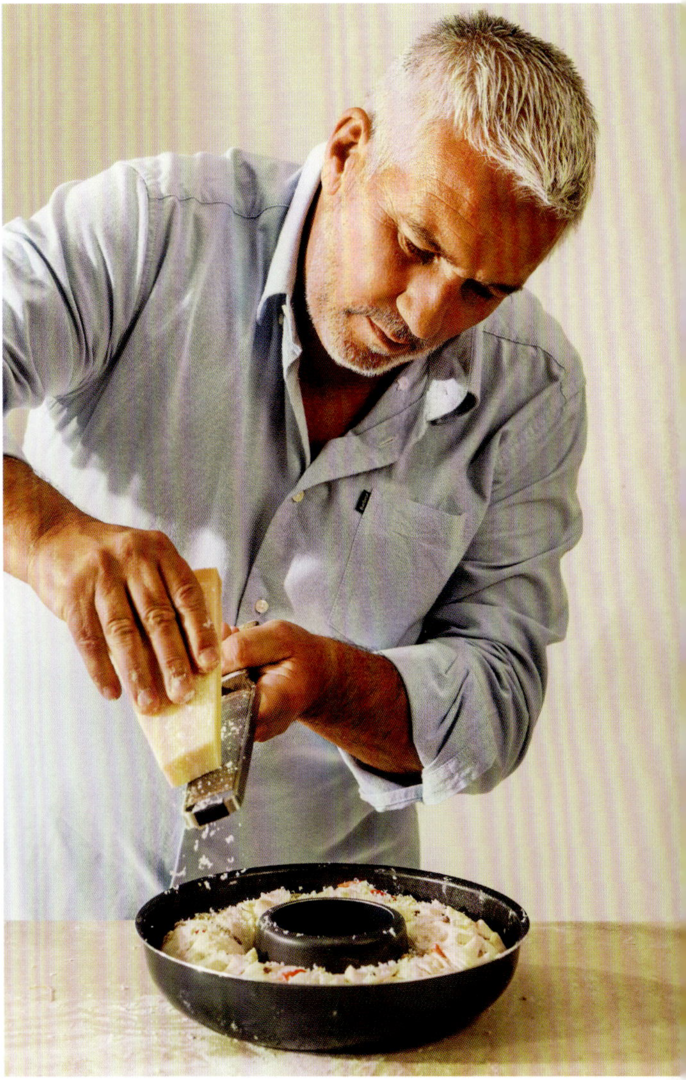

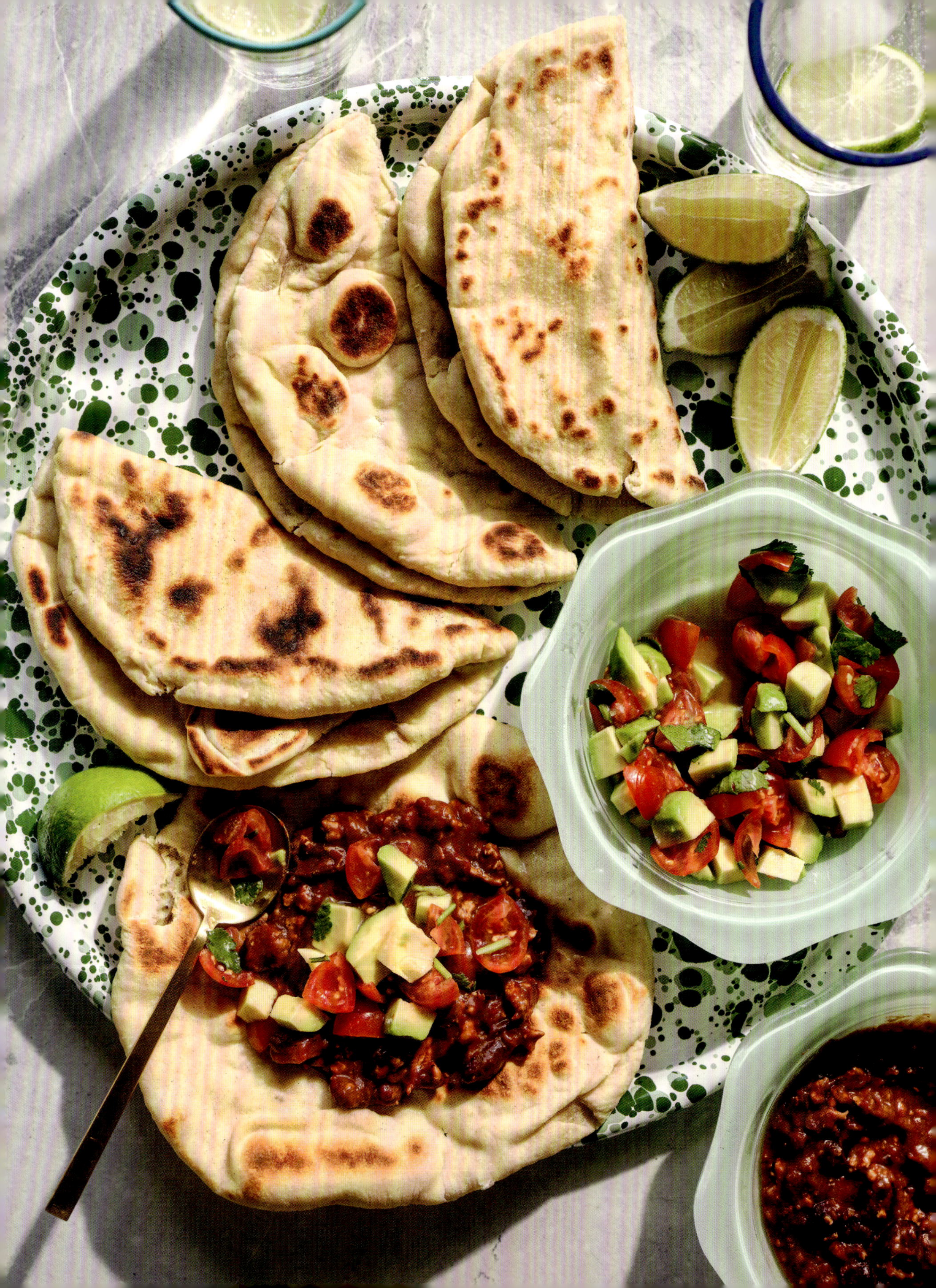

Gorditas

I learned to make gorditas when I was in Mexico City where they are a popular street food. Essentially, a gordita is a Mexican flatbread but it's sometimes eaten more like a pita – folded around a savory filling. They're great as a snack with guacamole, or served with a rich beef chili ragu.

Makes 5

———

2 cup (250g) bread flour
½ tsp (3g) fine salt
2 tsp (10g) baking powder
¾ cup (180g) whole milk

1 Mix the flour, salt and baking powder together in a large bowl and make a well in the center. Gradually add the milk and mix to form a soft, pliable dough. Divide the dough into 5 equal balls (each about 100g) and roll each out to a 7-inch circle.

2 Heat a dry non-stick frying pan over a medium-high heat. Cook the dough rounds, one at a time, for a couple of minutes or so, until they are puffed up, form golden brown patches on the underside, and bubbles appear on the surface. Flip them over and cook for 2–3 minutes on the other side.

3 As you remove each gordita from the pan, fold it in half and wrap in a kitchen towel to keep warm and soft while you cook the rest. Serve the folded breads filled with chili or other savory fillings, fajita style.

Sweet Potato and Black Bean Empanadas

I made empanadas with my Spanish friend, Omar, when we were in the famous San Miguel food market in Madrid. We were trying to impress each other with our different fillings and this is one I made for him. They're incredibly versatile – you can fill them with almost anything, and make them in any size.

Makes 10

Filling

1 tbsp olive oil

1 onion, finely chopped

1 carrot, cut into small dice

1 large sweet potato, peeled and cut into small dice

1 garlic clove, crushed

1 tbsp tomato paste

1 tsp ground cumin

1 tsp hot smoked paprika

Heaping ¾ cup (100g) frozen corn

⅔ cup (100g) well-drained tinned black beans

A handful of cilantro leaves, chopped

Juice of 1 lime

Salt and black pepper

Dough

2⅓ cups plus 1 tbsp (300g) all-purpose flour, plus extra to dust

½ tsp ground turmeric

A large pinch of fine salt

3 tbsp olive oil

⅔–¾ cup (150–175g) warm water

To glaze

1 large egg, beaten

---

1. For the filling, heat the olive oil in a wide saucepan over a medium-low heat. Add the onion, carrot, sweet potato and garlic and fry gently for 10–15 minutes until softened.

2. Meanwhile, make the dough. Mix the flour, turmeric and salt together in a large bowl and make a well in the center. Add the olive oil then gradually incorporate enough warm water to form a sticky, wet dough. Bring it together with one hand – it's more like bread dough than pie dough. (You can make it in a food processor if you prefer.)

3. Turn the dough out onto a clean work surface and knead gently for a few minutes until smooth. Return it to the bowl, cover and leave to rest while you finish preparing the filling.

4. Add the tomato paste, cumin and smoked paprika to the softened vegetables and stir well. Add the frozen corn and black beans and cook for a further 5 minutes. Season with salt and pepper to taste.

5. Transfer half the filling to a bowl and crush with a fork then return to the pan. Add the chopped cilantro and lime juice and stir to combine. The filling should have texture but bind together.

6. Heat your oven to 400°F and line a large baking sheet with parchment paper.

7. Roll out the dough on a lightly floured surface to ⅛ inch thick. Using a 4½-inch biscuit cutter (or an inverted small bowl as a guide), cut out rounds. Re-roll the offcuts and cut more rounds.

8. Divide the filling evenly between the rounds of dough. Dampen the edges of the dough rounds with water and then fold over one half to enclose the filling and make a semicircular parcel. Press the edges together firmly then crimp or press the edges with a fork.

9. Place the empanadas on the baking sheet and brush with beaten egg. Bake for 15–20 minutes or until golden brown. Eat them warm from the oven, on their own or with chili sauce on the side.

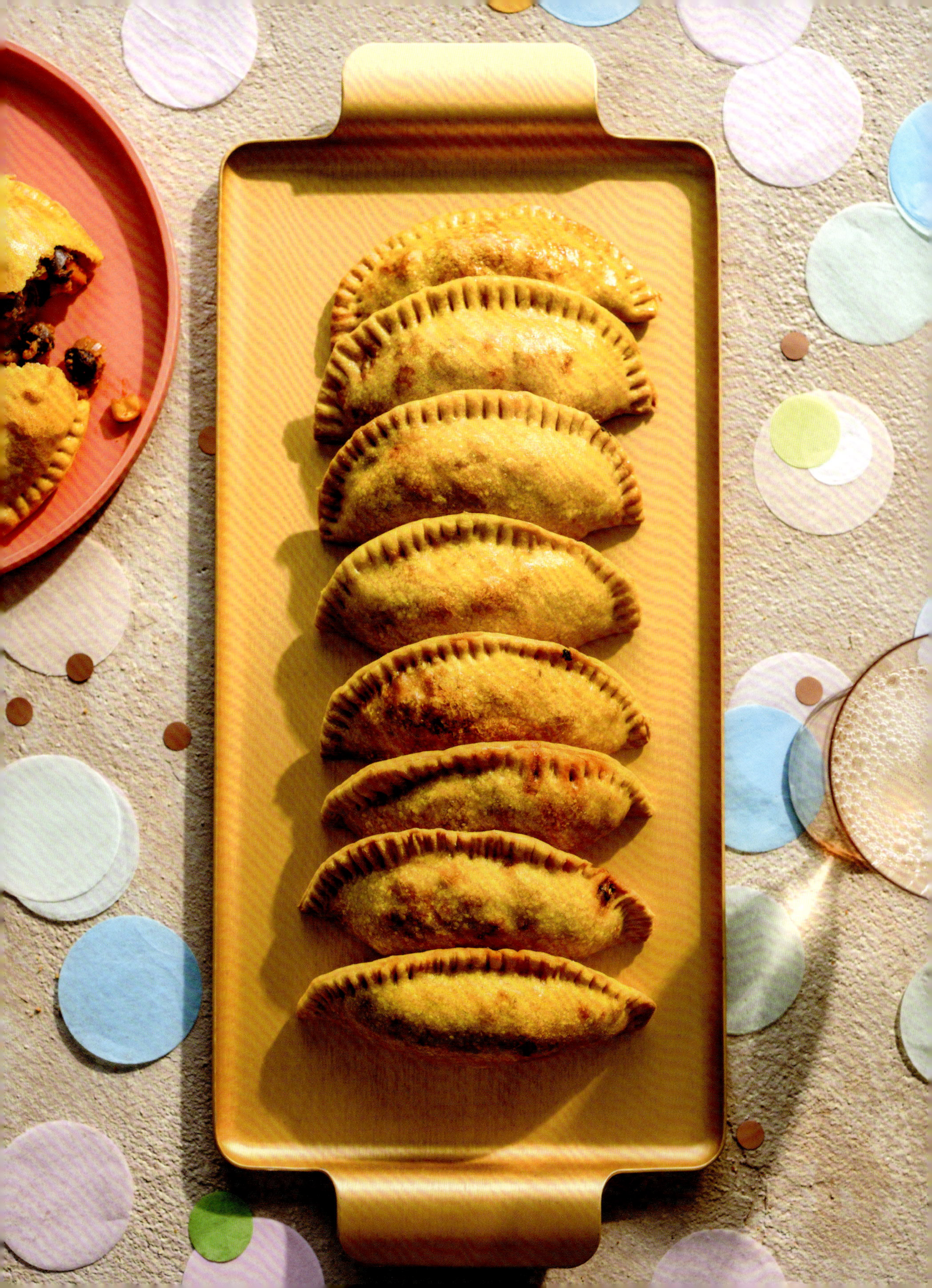

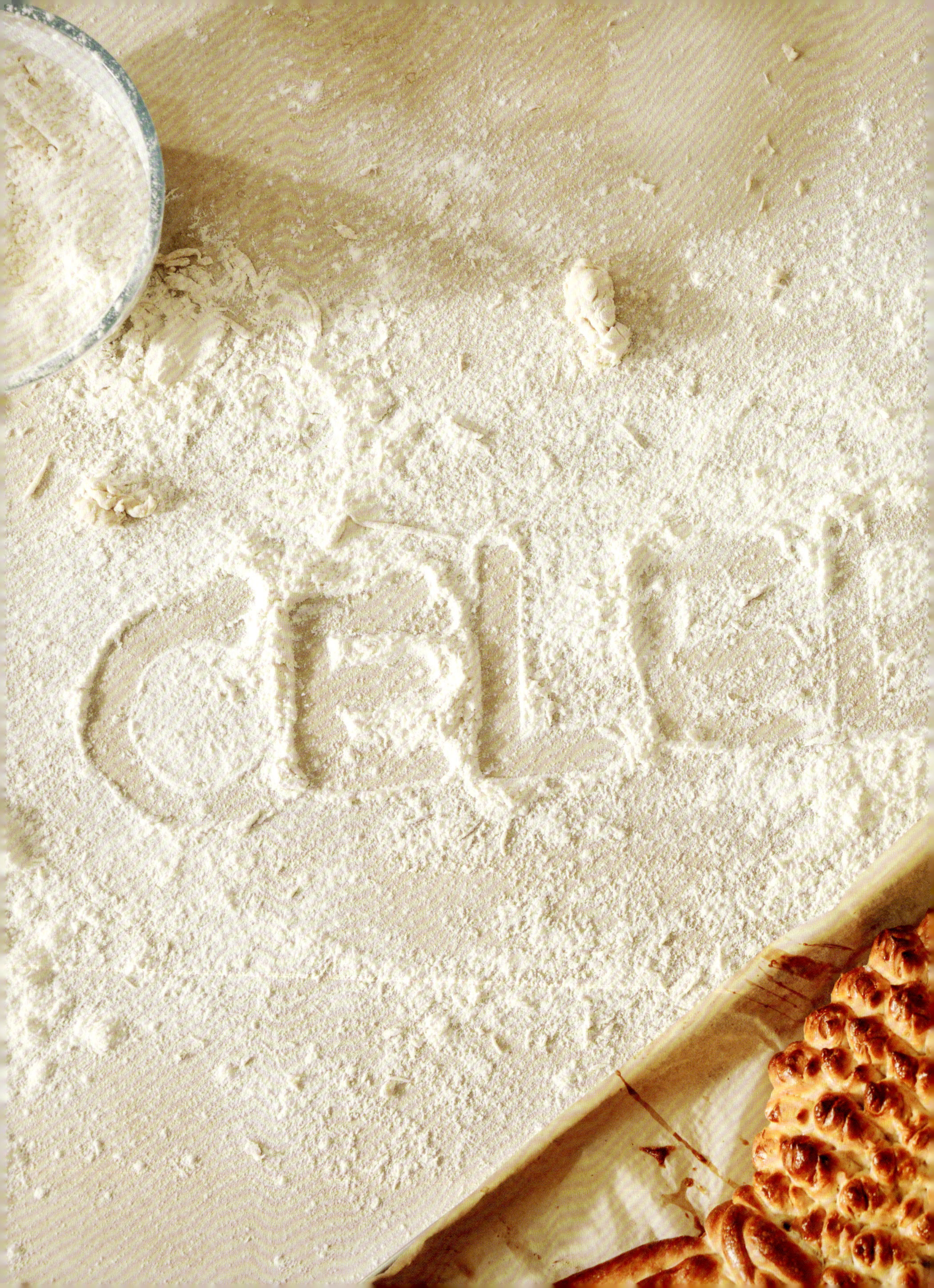

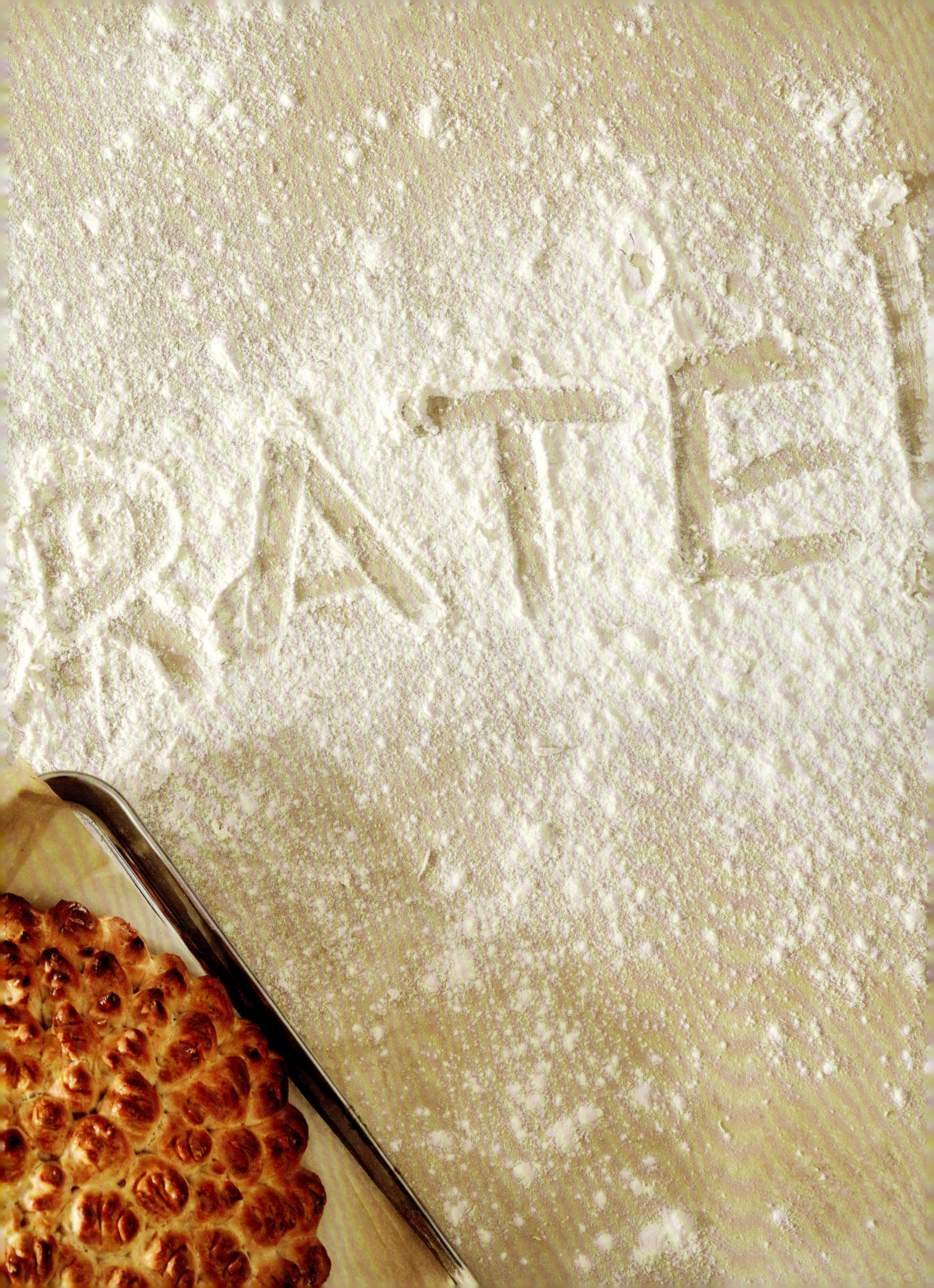

Index

A

almonds: almond and amaretto meringues 138
  cherry marble cake bars 26
  Christmas cheese loaf 215
  Christmas couronne 180
  Christmas pudding 185
  Florentines 199
  marzipan 209
  pan'e saba 191
  panforte 186
  pear Bakewell tart 136
  pumpkin spiced macarons 148
  roscón de reyes 194
  ultimate rocky road 228
amaretto liqueur: almond and amaretto meringues 138
anchovies: Paul's pissaladière 249
apples: apple doughnuts 146
  candy apple cake 142
  Christmas pudding 185
  hot cross bun loaf 63
  Paul's classic mince pies 182
  rhubarb and apple crumble 70
apricot jam: pear Bakewell tart 136
  roscón de reyes 194
apricots (dried): Chelsea buns 156
  panettone 178
  ultimate rocky road 228
asparagus, feta and phyllo tart 56

B

babka, Polish Easter 58
bagels 82
Bakewell tart, pear 136
beans: sweet potato and black bean empanadas 260
beef: hand-held beef pies 122–5
  Vakkaru bis keemiya 252
Biscoff spread: no-bake speculoos cheesecake 232
black beans: sweet potato and black bean empanadas 260
blueberries: blueberry lattice pie 140
  tiered pavlova and boozy berries 237

bread: challah 167
  Christmas cheese loaf 215
  Christmas couronne 180
  classic sandwich bread 126
  garlic and onion focaccia 130
  gorditas 259
  lemon Easter bread 60
  panettone 178
  Polish Easter babka 58
  St Patrick's Day loaf 84
  savory couronne 254
  shokupan 218
  summer pudding 94
  taboon bread 129
  tsoureki 80
  Valentine chocolate and cherry loaf 192
  wheatsheaf 168–71
brownie bars 74
bundt cake, spiced maple 48
buns, Chelsea 156
butter, garlic 130
buttercream 36–9, 206–9
  lemon buttercream 73
  lime and mint buttercream 106
  orange buttercream 33–4
  vanilla buttercream 20–3, 226
  see also icing
buttermilk: St Patrick's Day loaf 84

C

cakes 14–51
  brownie bars 74
  candy apple cake 142
  cherry marble cake bars 26
  chocolate fudge cake 18
  chocolate mini logs 188
  coconut and passion fruit cake bars 30
  drip cake 20–3
  elderflower cupcakes 42
  fraisier cake 99–100
  hazelnut and orange cake 33–4
  igloo cake 206–9
  lemon drizzle loaf cake 73
  Maldivian coconut loaf 158

mojito cupcakes 106
pan'e saba 191
Paul's chocolate cake 44
Polish Easter babka 58
rainbow cake 36–9
roscón de reyes 194
spiced loaf cake 145
spiced maple bundt cake 48
sprinkletti cake 226
tiramisu ice cream cake 96
zucchini and lime cake 110
candied peel: Christmas pudding 185
   Florentines 199
   hot cross bun loaf 63
   panettone 178
   panforte 186
   roscón de reyes 194
caramel: candy apple cake 142
   chocolate craquelin 238–41
cardamom: solboller 115
celery root: savory fall roulade 160
challah 167
cheese: asparagus, feta and phyllo tart 56
   Christmas cheese loaf 215
   miso and sesame cheese twists 242
   savory autumn roulade 160
   savory couronne 254
   zucchini, feta and fava bean quiche 118
   see also cream cheese; mascarpone; ricotta
cheesecakes: Japanese cheesecake 24
   no-bake speculoos cheesecake 232
Chelsea buns 156
cherries: cherry marble cake bars 26
   Valentine chocolate and cherry loaf 192
chicken and leek vol-au-vents 245
chilies: Vakkaru bis keemiya 252
chocolate: brownie bars 74
   chocolate choux buns 238–41
   chocolate craquelin 238–41
   chocolate crème pâtissière 238–41
   chocolate Easter nests 78
   chocolate frosting 44
   chocolate fudge cake 18

chocolate icing 18
chocolate mini logs 188
crostata pasquale 64
Florentines 199
ganache 44, 145
Paul's chocolate cake 44
tiramisu ice cream cake 96
ultimate rocky road 228
Valentine chocolate and cherry loaf 192
white chocolate, dried cranberry and nut cookies 200
white chocolate ganache 145
choux buns, chocolate 238–41
Christmas cheese loaf 215
Christmas couronne 180
Christmas pudding 185
cinnamon: solboller 115
classic sandwich bread 126
coconut: coconut and passion fruit cake bars 30
   Maldivian coconut loaf 158
coffee: tiramisu ice cream cake 96
Cognac: Christmas pudding 185
condensed milk: crostata pasquale 64
   Key lime pie 102
   rainbow gelatin crown 234
Cookies: brownie bars 74
   no-bake speculoos cheesecake 232
   peanut butter cookies 152
   pistachio, lemon and ginger biscotti 210
   ultimate rocky road 228
   Valentine love heart cookies 202–5
   white chocolate, dried cranberry and nut cookies 200
couronnes: Christmas couronne 180
   savory couronne 254
cranberries (dried): white chocolate, dried cranberry and nut cookies 200
craquelin, chocolate 238–41
cream: almond and amaretto meringues 138
   crème diplomat 99–100
   custard tarts 68
   Eton mess 92
   ganache 44

Celebrate

Key lime pie 102
  no-bake speculoos cheesecake 232
  pecan fudge bites 155
  tiered pavlova and boozy berries 237
  white chocolate ganache 145
  see also sour cream
cream cheese: cream cheese pastry 140
  Japanese cheesecake 24
  no-bake speculoos cheesecake 232
crème de cassis liqueur: tiered pavlova and boozy berries 237
crème diplomat: fraisier cake 99–100
crème pâtissière: chocolate crème pâtissière 238–41
  solboller 115
crostata pasquale 64
crumble, rhubarb and apple 70
cupcakes: elderflower cupcakes 42
  mojito cupcakes 106
currants: Christmas pudding 185
custard tarts 68

D

dehydrated orange slices 33–4
digestive biscuits: Key lime pie 102
  ultimate rocky road 228
doughnuts, apple 146
dried fruit: Polish Easter babka 58
  see also apricots (dried), raisins etc
drip cake 20–3

E

Easter: chocolate Easter nests 78
  crostata pasquale 64
  lemon Easter bread 60
  Polish Easter babka 58
  tsoureki 80
eggs: tsoureki 80
elderflower cupcakes 42
empanadas, sweet potato and black bean 260
Eton mess 92

F

fava beans: zucchini, feta and fava bean quiche 118
figs (dried): panforte 186
Florentines 199
focaccia, garlic and onion 130
frangipane: Christmas couronne 180
  pear Bakewell tart 136
fraisier cake 99–100
fritters: Vakkaru bis keemiya 252
frosting, chocolate 44
fruit: Eton mess 92
  summer pudding 94
  see also apples, dried fruit, raspberries etc
fudge: chocolate fudge cake 18
  pecan fudge bites 155

G

ganache 44
  white chocolate ganache 145
garlic and onion focaccia 130
gelatin: fraisier cake 99–100
  rainbow gelatin crown 234
genoise sponge: fraisier cake 99–100
ginger: pistachio, lemon and ginger biscotti 210
golden syrup: chocolate Easter nests 78
  pecan fudge bites 155
  ultimate rocky road 228
gorditas 259
graham cracker: Key lime pie 102
  ultimate rocky road 228
Guinness: St Patrick's Day loaf 84

H

hand-held beef pies 122–5
hazelnut and orange cake 33–4
Hollywood hot dogs 162
honey: panforte 186
honeycomb: ultimate rocky road 228
hot cross bun loaf 63
hot dogs, Hollywood 162
hot water crust pastry 122–5

I

ice cream: tiramisu ice cream cake 96
icing: chocolate frosting 44
   chocolate icing 18
   ganache 44, 145
   maple icing 48
   royal icing 202–5, 206–9
   rum icing 58
   vanilla icing 142
   see also buttercream
igloo cake 206–9

J

jam: pear Bakewell tart 136
   roscón de reyes 194
   strawberry heart scones 112
Japanese cheesecake 24

K

Key lime pie 102

L

leeks: chicken and leek vol-au-vents 245
   turkey and stuffing pies 212
lemon: lemon buttercream 73
   lemon curd filling 60, 73
   lemon drizzle loaf cake 73
   lemon Easter bread 60
   pistachio, lemon and ginger biscotti 210
limes: coconut and passion fruit cake bars 30
   Key lime pie 102
   lime and mint buttercream 106
   rum syrup 106
   zucchini and lime cake 110
love heart cookies 202–5

M

macadamia nuts: white chocolate, dried cranberry and nut cookies 200
macarons, pumpkin spiced 148
Madeira cake: drip cake 20–3
   igloo cake 206–9
Maldivian coconut loaf 158
maple syrup: spiced maple bundt cake 48

marmalade: hazelnut and orange cake 33–4
Marsala wine: tiramisu ice cream cake 96
marzipan 209
   chocolate mini logs 188
   igloo cake 206–9
mascarpone: coconut and passion fruit cake bars 30
   no-bake speculoos cheesecake 232
   tiramisu ice cream cake 96
meringue: almond and amaretto meringues 138
   Eton mess 92
   pumpkin spiced macarons 148
   tiered pavlova and boozy berries 237
milk: chocolate crème pâtissière 238–41
   crème diplomat 99–100
   crème pâtissière 115
   custard tarts 68
mince pies, Paul's classic 182
mint: lime and mint buttercream 106
miso and sesame cheese twists 242
mojito cupcakes 106
molasses: St Patrick's Day loaf 84
morello cherries: Valentine chocolate and cherry loaf 192
mushrooms: savory couronne 254

N

nigella seeds: taboon bread 129
no-bake speculoos cheesecake 232

O

oats: rhubarb and apple crumble 70
   St Patrick's Day loaf 84
olive oil: garlic and onion focaccia 130
olives: Paul's pissaladière 249
onions: garlic and onion focaccia 130
   Paul's pissaladière 249
oranges: dehydrated orange slices 33–4
   hazelnut and orange cake 33–4
   hot cross bun loaf 63
   orange buttercream 33–4
   pumpkin spiced macarons 148
Oreos: brownie bars 74

Celebrate

P

pancetta: turkey and stuffing pies 212
pan'e saba 191
panettone 178
panforte 186
parsnips: savory fall roulade 160
pasquale, crostata 64
passion fruit: coconut and passion fruit cake bars 30
pastries: Chelsea buns 156
   miso and sesame cheese twists 242
   sausage braid 250
   solboller 115
   see also pies; tarts
pastry 64, 68, 136, 212
   cheat's puff pastry base 249
   choux pastry 238–41
   cream cheese pastry 140
   hot water crust pastry 122–5
   puff pastry 244
   shortcrust pastry 118
   sweet pastry 182
Paul's chocolate cake 44
Paul's classic mince pies 182
Paul's pissaladière 249
pavlova and boozy berries 237
peanut butter cookies 152
pear Bakewell tart 136
pecan fudge bites 155
penguin decorations 206–9
peppers: sausage braid 250
   savory couronne 254
phyllo pastry: asparagus, feta and phyllo tart 56
pies: blueberry lattice pie 140
   hand-held beef pies 122–5
   Paul's classic mince pies 182
   sweet potato and black bean empanadas 260
   turkey and stuffing pies 212
   see also pastries; tarts
pine nuts: pan'e saba 191
pissaladière, Paul's 249
pistachio nuts: Florentines 199
   pistachio, lemon and ginger biscotti 210
   ultimate rocky road 228

Polish Easter babka 58
popcorn crunch 48
poppy seeds: bagels 82
potatoes: Vakkaru bis keemiya 252
puff pastry 244
   cheat's puff pastry base 249
   miso and sesame cheese twists 242
   sausage braid 250
pumpkin spiced macarons 148

Q

quail's eggs: tsoureki 80
quiche: zucchini, feta and fava bean 118

R

rainbow cake 36–9
rainbow gelatin crown 234
raisins: apple doughnuts 146
   Chelsea buns 156
   Christmas pudding 185
   hot cross bun loaf 63
   pan'e saba 191
   panettone 178
raspberries: Paul's chocolate cake 44
   tiered pavlova and boozy berries 237
red currants: tiered pavlova and boozy berries 237
rhubarb and apple crumble 70
rice flour: Maldivian coconut loaf 158
ricotta: crostata pasquale 64
rocky road 228
roscón de reyes 194
roulade, savory fall 160
royal icing 202–5, 206–9
rum: icing 58
   mojito cupcakes 106
   rum syrup 58, 106

S

St Patrick's Day loaf 84
sandwich bread 126
sapa (reduced grape juice): pan'e saba 191
sausages: Hollywood hot dogs 162
   sausage bread 250

savoiardi sponges: tiramisu ice cream cake 96
savory fall roulade 160
savory couronne 254
scones, strawberry heart 112
sesame seeds: bagels 82
   challah 167
   Hollywood hot dogs 162
   miso and sesame cheese twists 242
   taboon bread 129
   tsoureki 80
   wheatsheaf 168–71
shokupan 218
shortcrust pastry 118
Shredded Wheat: chocolate Easter nests 78
soda bread: St Patrick's Day loaf 84
solboller 115
sour cream: chocolate fudge cake 18
   Paul's chocolate cake 44
spiced loaf cake 145
spiced maple bundt cake 48
sprinkletti cake 226
strawberries: Eton mess 92
   fraisier cake 99–100
   strawberry heart scones 112
   tiered pavlova and boozy berries 237
stuffing: turkey and stuffing pies 212
suet: Christmas pudding 185
sugar syrup 63
summer pudding 94
sweet pastry 182
sweet potato and black bean empanadas 260
sweetcorn: sweet potato and black bean empanadas 260
Swiss meringue: pumpkin spiced macarons 148
syrup: rum syrup 58, 106
   sugar syrup 63

T
taboon bread 129
tangerines: Paul's classic mince pies 182
tarts: asparagus, feta and phyllo tart 56
   crostata pasquale 64
   custard tarts 68
   Key lime pie 102
   pear Bakewell tart 136
   zucchini, feta and fava bean quiche 118
   see also pastries; pies
tiered pavlova and boozy berries 237
tiramisu ice cream cake 96
tomatoes: Paul's pissaladière 249
tsoureki 80
turkey and stuffing pies 212

U
ultimate rocky road 228

V
Vakkaru bis keemiya 252
Valentine chocolate and cherry loaf 192
Valentine love heart cookies 202–5
vanilla: crème pâtissière 115
   vanilla buttercream 20–3, 226
   vanilla icing 142
vol-au-vents, chicken and leek 245

W
walnuts: pan'e saba 191
   panforte 186
wheatsheaf 168–71
white chocolate, dried cranberry and nut cookies 200
white chocolate ganache 145

Y
yeast: pan'e saba 191
   roscón de reyes 194
   see also bread
yogurt: Eton mess 92
   tiered pavlova and boozy berries 237

Z
zucchini: zucchini and lime cake 110
   zucchini, feta and fava bean quiche 118

Thanks

To the team at Bloomsbury: Rowan Yapp, Lena Hall, Laura Brodie, Shunayna Vaghela, Rob Cox, Helen Upton and Rose Brown. You are brilliant, thank you for your support and expertise.

To the incredible Claire Bassano and Lola Brandelli, you're the best. Thanks for all your long hours baking.

Liz and Max Haarala Hamilton, you are legends behind the camera, thank you so much.

To Nikki Dupin and Jen Kay, you've made the book look very special, thank you.

Janet Illsley and Laura Bayliss, thank you very much for all your hard work, again.

To my team Geraldine Woods, Anna Bruce and Kate Cooper, thanks for always being there.

And to my amazing wife, Melissa x

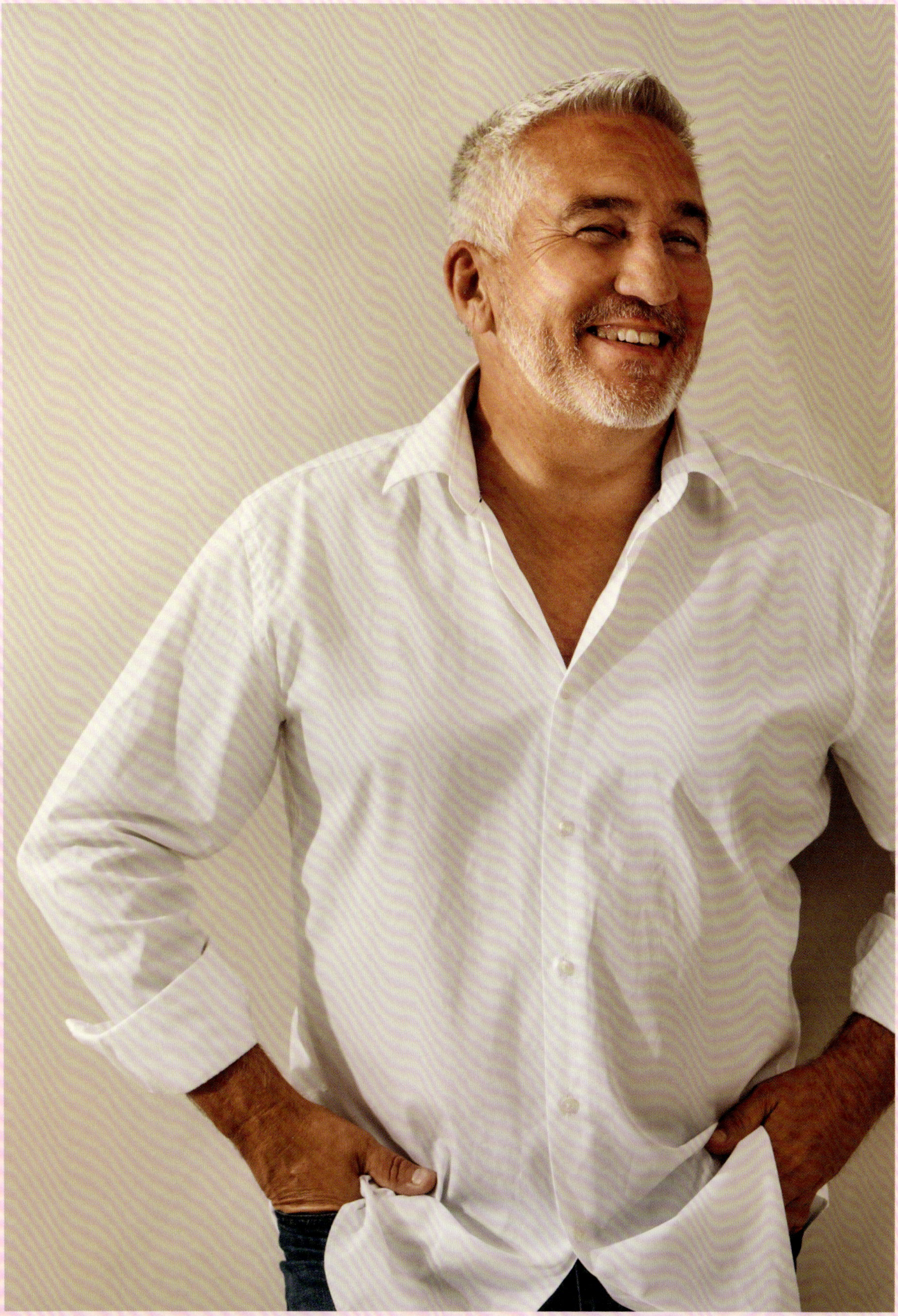

BLOOMSBURY PUBLISHING
Bloomsbury Publishing Inc
1359 Broadway, New York, NY 10018, USA
50 Bedford Square, London, WC1B 3DP, UK
Bloomsbury Publishing Ireland Limited
29 Earlsfort Terrace, Dublin 2, Ireland

BLOOMSBURY, BLOOMSBURY PUBLISHING and the Diana logo are trademarks of Bloomsbury Publishing Plc

First published in Great Britain 2025
First published in the United States 2025

Text © Paul Hollywood, 2025
Photographs © Haarala Hamilton, 2025

Paul Hollywood and Haarala Hamilton have asserted their right under the Copyright, Designs and Patents Act, 1988, to be identified as author and photographer, respectively, of this work

For legal purposes the Acknowledgements on p.270 constitute an extension of this copyright page

All rights reserved. No part of this publication may be: i) reproduced or transmitted in any form, electronic or mechanical, including photocopying, recording, or by means of any information storage or retrieval system without prior permission in writing from the publishers; or ii) used or reproduced in any way for the training, development, or operation of artificial intelligence (AI) technologies, including generative AI technologies. The rights holders expressly reserve this publication from the text and data mining exception as per Article 4(3) of the Digital Single Market Directive (EU) 2019/790.

While every effort has been made to ensure the accuracy of the information contained in this book, in no circumstances can the publisher or the author accept any legal responsibility or liability for any loss or damage (including damage to property and/or personal injury) arising from any error in or omission from the information contained in this book, or from the failure of the reader to properly and accurately follow any instructions contained in the book. The author and publisher specifically disclaim, as far as the law allows, any responsibility from any liability, loss or risk (personal or otherwise) which is incurred as a consequence, directly or indirectly, of the use and applications of any of the contents of this book

ISBN: HB: 978-1-63973-503-7; eBook: 978-1-63973-504-4

Library of Congress Cataloging-in-Pubication Data is available

2 4 6 8 10 9 7 5 3 1

Project editor: Janet Illsley
Art Direction & Design: Nikki Dupin at Studio Nic + Lou
Photography: Liz and Max at Haarala Hamilton
Food Styling: Claire Bassano, assisted by Lola Brandelli
Prop Styling: Jennifer Kay
Indexer: Hilary Bird
Americanization: Caroline Stearns

Printed and bound in China by C&C Offset Printing Co., Ltd.

To find out more about our authors and books visit www.bloomsbury.com and sign up for our newsletters

Bloomsbury books may be purchased for business or promotional use. For information on bulk purchases please contact Macmillan Corporate and Premium Sales Department at specialmarkets@macmillan.com
For product safety–related questions contact productsafety@bloomsbury.com

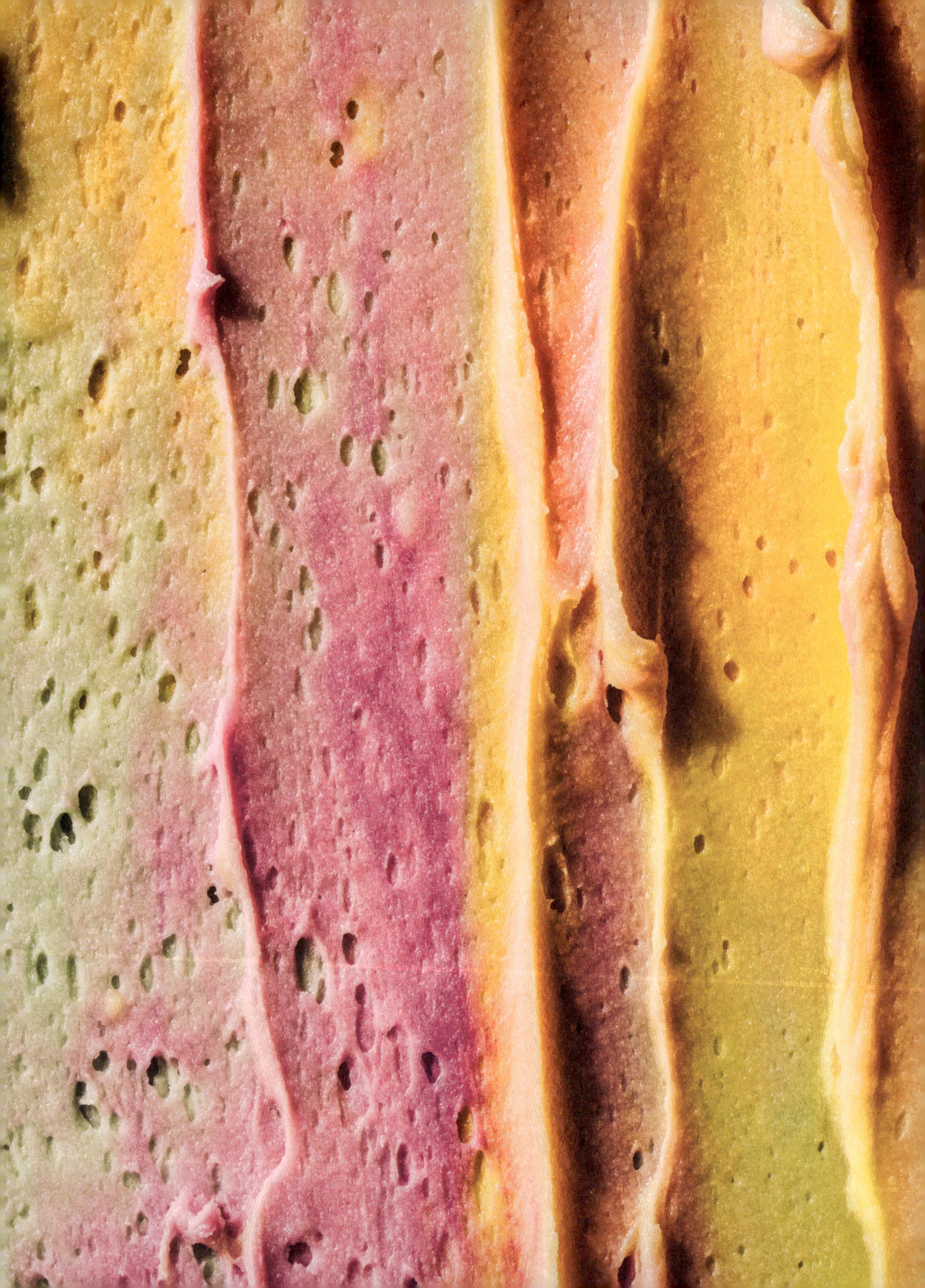

And Then Another Sheep Turned Up

For the Goldmann family. Thank you for letting me be an extra sheep at your seders.—L.G.

For my mum, thank you for the endless supply of support, love and tea!—A.A.

Text copyright © 2015 by Laura Gehl
Illustrations copyright © 2015 by Lerner Publishing Group, Inc.

All rights reserved. International copyright secured. No part of this book may be reproduced, stored in a retrieval system, or transmitted in any form or by any means—electronic, mechanical, photocopying, recording, or otherwise—without the prior written permission of Lerner Publishing Group, Inc., except for the inclusion of brief quotations in an acknowledged review.

KAR-BEN PUBLISHING
A division of Lerner Publishing Group, Inc.
241 First Avenue North
Minneapolis, MN 55401 USA
1-800-4-Karben

Website address: www.karben.com

Main body text set in Chaloops.
Typeface provided by Chank.

Library of Congress Cataloging-in-Publication Data

Gehl, Laura.
    And then another sheep turned up / by Laura Gehl ; illustrated by Amy Adele.
      pages   cm.
    Summary: A family of sheep trying to celebrate a Passover seder are interrupted by the arrival of many additional relatives.
    ISBN 978–1–4677–1188–3 (lib. bdg. : alk. paper)
    ISBN 978–1–4677–1190–6 (eBook)
    [1. Stories in rhyme. 2. Passover—Fiction. 3. Seder—Fiction. 4. Sheep—Fiction.]
    I. Adele, Amy, illustrator. II. Title.
PZ8.3.G273An 2015
[E]—dc23   2014003600

Manufactured in the United States of America
1 – VI – 12/31/14

And Then Another Sheep Turned Up

Laura Gehl

Illustrated by Amy Adele

KAR-BEN
PUBLISHING

Papa Sheep stirred up the pots.

Mama Sheep arranged the chairs.

Hannah Sheep scrubbed off the spots.

Noah Sheep helped sweep the stairs.

"Done!" clapped Mama with delight.
"Everything got clean somehow.
It seems it's just us four tonight,
so we can start our seder now."

And then another sheep turned up!

Grandma hurried through the door,
bringing macaroons and wine.
"Oy! So busy at the store!
Wow, that soup sure smells divine!"

Mama set another place.
Papa found an extra seat.
Hannah squeezed to make more space,
thrilled to have a guest to greet.

And Noah gave a tiny yawn.

"Now for our first cup of wine!"
Papa poured for everyone.
Mama started to recline,
glad that seder had begun.

And then another sheep turned up!

Uncle Sol came in his jeep,
kissed the kids and hugged the rest.
"Can you fit another sheep?
Seder here is always best."

Mama set another place.
Papa found an extra seat.
Hannah squeezed to make more space,
thrilled to have a guest to greet.

And Noah gave a little yawn.

Papa poured more wine for Sol.
Everybody took a sip.
Mama gave karpas to all.
Hannah took a piece to dip.

And then another sheep turned up!

"Wait a minute," Mama cried,
just as Gran began to read.
"I see Grandpa Sheep outside!
Once he's here, we can proceed."

Mama set another place.
Papa found an extra seat.
Hannah squeezed to make more space,
thrilled to have a guest to greet.

And Noah gave a bigger yawn.

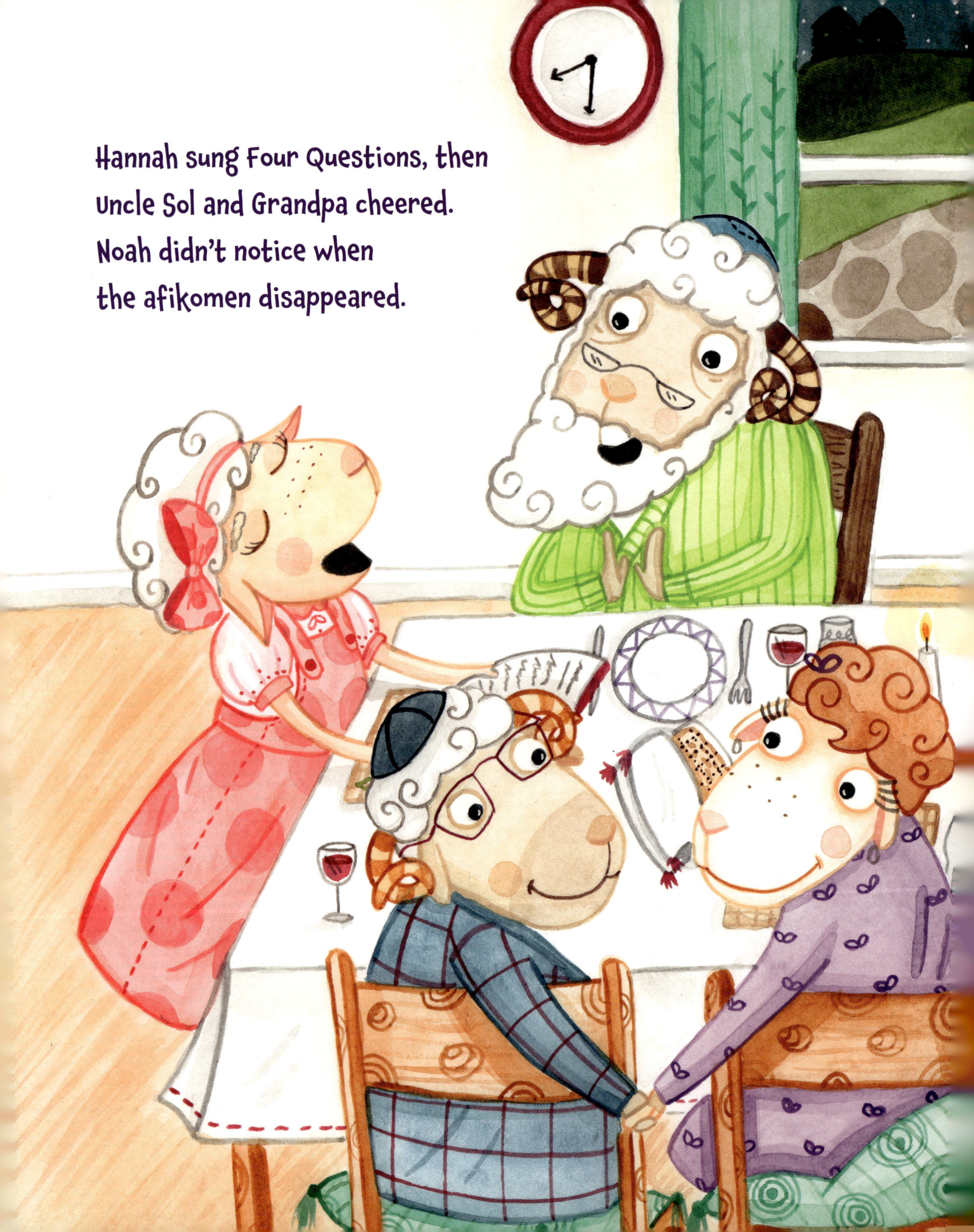

Hannah sung Four Questions, then Uncle Sol and Grandpa cheered. Noah didn't notice when the afikomen disappeared.

And then another sheep turned up!

Danny Sheep came running in.
Put his heavy backpack down.
"Greetings to my lovely kin!
Didn't know I'd be in town."

Mama set another place.
Papa found an extra seat.
Hannah squeezed to make more space,
thrilled to have a guest to greet.

And Noah gave a giant yawn.

"Da-ye-nu" they sang at last.
Shared charoset and maror.
Noah ate his matzah fast.
Hungry still, he asked for more.

And then another sheep turned up!

Sharon Sheep came in at nine,
halfway through the seder meal.

"I'm sure ready to recline.
Getting here was an ordeal."

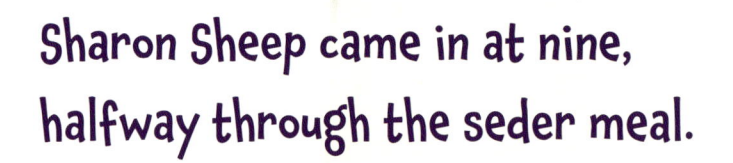

Mama set another place.
Papa found an extra seat.
Hannah squeezed to make more space,
thrilled to have a guest to greet.

And then another sheep turned up!

Aunt Deb came, with gifts in hand:
books and puzzles and a ball.
"Find the afikomen and
get the biggest gift of all."

Mama set another place.
Papa found an extra seat.
Hannah squeezed to make more space, thrilled to have a guest to greet.

And Noah gave one last yawn.

Papa opened up the door.
Mama filled Elijah's cup.
Noah had begun to snore...

...and this time no more sheep turned up!

Noah slept through three more songs.
Grandpa said, "Poor little lamb."
Hannah tried to sing along.
Sleepy-eyed,
she leaned on Gram.

Papa stood up now. "Ahem.
Time to get our kids to bed.
Next year in Jerusalem!
And next year
   ...PLEASE CALL AHEAD!"

About the Author and Illustrator

Laura Gehl enjoys celebrating Passover with her husband, their four children, and any sheep who are able to join them for the seder. Laura's previous books include *One Big Pair of Underwear* and *Hare and Tortoise Race Across Israel.* She lives in Silver Spring, Maryland.

Amy Adele can be found drawing and painting or sewing and stitching, with one eye on the window watching for birds. A graduate of the University College Falmouth with a Masters in Illustration, Amy likes to escape into the imaginative realm of children's book art. She lives in the U.K.